C000225234

THE
NEWCASTLE
MISCELLANY

THE
NEWCASTLE
MISCELLANY

BY MIKE BOLAM

Vision Sports Publishing
2 Coombe Gardens,
London SW20 0QU

www.visionsp.co.uk

Published by Vision Sports Publishing 2008

ISBN 13: 978-1-905326-49-5

Printed and bound in Germany by
GGP Media GmbH, Pössneck

Typeset by Palimpsest Book Production Limited,
Grangemouth, Stirlingshire

A CIP catalogue record for this book is
available from the British Library

Mixed Sources
Product group from well-managed
forests and other controlled sources
www.fsc.org   Cert no. SGS-COC-1940
© 1996 Forest Stewardship Council
FSC

Vision Sports Publishing are
proud that this book is made
from paper certified by the
Forest Stewardship Council

Author's Acknowledgements

I would like to thank Paul Joannou and Alan Candlish for their encouragement and assistance in writing this book, as well as Jim Drewett and Clive Batty at Vision Sports Publishing for helping me produce it.

Credit is also due to my co-writer at NUFC.com, Niall Mackenzie and the readers of that website for their input and continued support over the last decade.

Thanks also to Karen for her invaluable assistance and endless patience in putting up with the author on a daily basis.

To everyone else involved – you know who you are – Biffa says Cheers!

Mike Bolam

Author's note: The term 'competitive match' is used throughout this book as describing Football League, Premiership, FA Cup, League Cup and European games only. Other competitions including Northern League, War Leagues, Anglo-Italian, Anglo-Scottish and Texaco Cups are not included unless stated.

All stats in *The Newcastle Miscellany* are correct up until the start of the 2008/09 season.

Foreword
By Les Ferdinand

I'm delighted to write the introduction to this book, which is full of facts, records and stories about Newcastle. I'm sure that fans of all ages will enjoy reading it.

The two years I spent at Newcastle were probably the most successful part of my career. We were winning most weeks and, in football, if you're winning more games than you're losing it all makes for a much more enjoyable experience. The whole city was involved in the club's success. There was a feelgood factor in Newcastle which made it an amazing place to be for those two years.

From day one, when a load of cheering fans turned up to greet me, the supporters made me feel welcome and that continued right up to the day I left. And it's no different when I go back to Newcastle now. A lot of the fans tell me I'm an adopted Geordie.

I know it's been said before, but Newcastle is a massive club. The support the team generates is just incredible. When I was playing at St James' Park the place was sold out every week with 36,000 season ticket holders. If they'd had the space, the club could have filled the place twice over. I used to bump into people before the match who told me they didn't have a ticket, they just used to come along and stand outside the ground to hear the noise of the crowd. Then, even at the training ground we'd have about 500 fans watching training every day. It's things like that which show why, for me at least, Newcastle supporters are by far the most passionate in the country.

When I signed for the club Kevin Keegan gave me the number nine shirt, worn in the past by some of the club legends profiled in this book like Hughie Gallacher, Jackie Milburn and Malcolm Macdonald. That was a great honour for me, because I knew what the shirt meant, and still means, to the Geordies. I got off to a great start by scoring against Coventry on my debut, and I felt I was off and running. Not as good as Len Shackleton, though, who I now know scored six goals on his Newcastle debut in 1946!

That first season we came very close to winning the Premiership title. Losing out to Manchester United in the end was one of the biggest disappointments of my career. We played some great stuff before Christmas but in the New Year we never quite hit the same heights. We had a bit of a break at one point and we never really got back to playing the way we did at the start of the season.

In the summer of 1996 Alan Shearer joined us from Blackburn. Kevin Keegan told me that Alan would be arriving and I thought it was just what we needed. Then he hit me with the request to give Alan my number nine shirt which, knowing what it means to the Geordie support, I agreed to. The book mentions that there were reports in the press that I approached the Premier League to wear a special '99' shirt, but they weren't true. Kevin Keegan told me I could have any number I wanted but I just went to the kit man and asked him what numbers were available. He said '23' so I said I'd take it, but then the board insisted that I have a number between one and 11. In the end I got the number ten shirt which became available when Lee Clark moved to Sunderland.

Sadly, even with Alan, we again had to settle for second place in 1997 and since then the loyal Newcastle fans have had to endure another decade without a trophy – as the book mentions more than once, you have to go back to 1969 for the last bit of silverware the club won.

Like anyone who has had any association with the club and experienced how passionate the supporters are, I am willing Newcastle to have some success after all those years. The club and the supporters thoroughly deserve it. And after coming so close last time, the return of Kevin Keegan gives the Geordies new hope of winning something at last. Fingers crossed.

Dipping in and out of this book, I've been reminded about a lot of things I already knew about the club and found out loads more I didn't know – like the fact that Newcastle's first foreign players were a pair of brothers from Chile and that wartime striker Albert Stubbins appeared on the cover of The Beatles album *Sgt Pepper*.

I know that Newcastle fans love anything to do with the club and I'm sure that they will get a lot of enjoyment from this cracking little book.

Les Ferdinand

— FROM EASTENDERS TO WEST END BOYS —

Football was first played at St James' Park in October 1880, with a team called Newcastle Rangers occupying the site – although they were to play no part in the creation of the side that went on to be named Newcastle United.

In November 1881, a team named Stanley were founded by the cricket club of the same name, playing on a pitch at Stanley Street, Byker. Eleven months later Stanley changed their name to Newcastle East End and incorporated another recently-founded local team, Rosewood. By 1886 East End were on the move again, this time further out into the Eastern suburbs of Newcastle on Chillingham Road.

Elsewhere in the city, meanwhile, August 1882 had seen the formation of another football club, Newcastle West End, by the cricket club of the same name, playing initially on the Town Moor before relocating near to the Great North Road in Jesmond three years later. Then in May 1886 West End acquired the lease of St James Park, which hadn't been regularly used since Rangers moved out to a site in Byker in 1882.

West End and East End were by now the biggest clubs on Tyneside and, having regularly faced each other in friendlies since their inception and in the Northern League from season 1889/90, became arch rivals. However it was East End who came to dominate both in footballing and financial terms, winning 2–0 and 3–0 at St James' Park in the league and FA Cup respectively in October 1891 and the return game 7–1 at their Heaton Junction ground the following February.

Within three months of that crushing derby defeat West End were declared insolvent. However, rather than lose St James' Park to football, they sportingly offered the lease to their biggest rivals. East End gratefully took them up, kicking off life at St James' Park with a friendly against Celtic in September 1892 watched by 6,000 supporters. Then on December 9th, a public meeting was held seeking agreement on a new name in a bid to increase interest amongst the Tyneside public, with Newcastle United being decided upon.

The rest is history . . . with Newcastle United accepting an invitation to join the Football League (one that East End had rejected the previous season) along with fellow new boys Liverpool, Woolwich Arsenal, Rotherham Town and Middlesbrough Ironopolis in Division Two for the 1893/94 campaign.

— CHAMPIONS! —

Newcastle United: Champions!

The fourth and most recent occasion on which Newcastle United were crowned top-flight champions came on Saturday April 23rd 1927, a 1–1 draw at West Ham United confirming title success with two games still to play.

Only 21 players were used by the Magpies all season, with goalkeeper Willie Wilson, left-back Frank Hudspeth and outside-left Stan Seymour appearing in all 42 games. Top scorer with 36 strikes from 38 appearances was Hughie Gallacher, the talented but temperamental Scottish striker who had controversially succeeded Hudspeth as club captain that season. Seasonal highlights included a 4–0 opening day success over Aston Villa on Tyneside, with Gallacher grabbing all the goals.

United hit top spot for the first time in mid-January after completing the double over Villa. The Magpies' nearest challengers Huddersfield were then beaten 1–0 at St James' Park on Good Friday, 24 hours before Spurs were dispatched 3–2 at the same venue.

Newcastle did take possession of the Football League trophy again in season 1992/93, when Barry Venison was presented with it before a 7–1 home win over Leicester City. By that point, however, the First Division was no longer the top flight of English football – the greater prize being promotion to the Premiership.

Divison One Table, 1926/27:

	P	W	D	L	F	A	Pts
Newcastle United	42	25	6	11	96	58	56
Huddersfield Town	42	17	17	8	76	60	51
Sunderland	42	21	7	14	98	70	49
Bolton Wanderers	42	19	10	13	84	62	48
Burnley	42	19	9	14	91	80	47
West Ham United	42	19	8	15	86	70	46
Leicester City	42	17	12	13	85	70	46
Sheffield United	42	17	10	15	74	86	44
Liverpool	42	18	7	17	69	61	43
Aston Villa	42	18	7	17	81	83	43
The Arsenal	42	17	9	16	77	86	43
Derby County	42	17	7	18	86	73	41
Tottenham Hotspur	42	16	9	17	76	78	41
Cardiff City	42	16	9	17	55	65	41
Manchester United	42	13	14	15	52	64	40
The Wednesday	42	15	9	18	75	92	39
Birmingham	42	17	4	21	64	73	38
Blackburn Rovers	42	15	8	19	77	96	38
Bury	42	12	12	18	68	77	36
Everton	42	12	10	20	64	90	34
Leeds United	42	11	8	23	69	88	30
West Bromwich Albion	42	11	8	23	65	86	30

— THEY CALL US NEWCASTLE UNITED —

"I still love United and follow them, still feel the same delight and agony as everyone else. Once black-and-white, always black-and-white."
Irving Nattrass, Newcastle player and fan

"Newcastle are the one side I stand up for when they score a goal. I supported them as a kid, when me and our Robert used to go every Saturday."
Jack Charlton, Newcastle manager and fan

"They may not have won a trophy for many, many years but still 50,000 Geordies pour into St James' Park every home game. Which other club can command that sort of following?"
Nolberto Solano, Newcastle player and honorary Geordie

"I was worried to death that no-one would turn up. Ten years is a long time. People forget."
A relieved **Jackie Milburn** speaking after 45,000 attended his testimonial match in 1967 – a decade after his retirement

"I just know this fellow can be another Jackie Milburn to the supporters."
Manager **Joe Harvey** introducing his new signing Malcolm Macdonald in 1971

"It was horrible – it ripped my heart out. I didn't want to go, I'd never even thought about going. I was playing for my team, my club."
Tynesider **Steve Watson** following his transfer to Aston Villa

"My career was over when I finished at Newcastle. Emotionally I couldn't play anywhere else."
Glaswegian Geordie **Bobby Mitchell**

"I understand most of what is said to me – unless it's by Alan Shearer. Geordie is a different language to English!"
Laurent Robert's number nine nightmare

"I went to Newcastle, met the Geordies on the Quayside, went out in the pubs and drank their beer."
The Dog on the Tyne was all **David Ginola's**

"He understood the Geordies and gave them what they loved."
Philippe Albert sums up the special gift of Kevin Keegan

— SOME TYNE-WEAR FACTS —

- John Auld became the first player to move from Sunderland to Newcastle, in October 1896.
- December 1906 saw James Raine make the first move in the opposite direction.
- Only three players have scored for both sides in Tyne-Wear derby matches: Ivor Broadis, Bob McKay and 'Pop' Robson.
- The 11 goals netted by Jackie Milburn remains the best scoring return for Newcastle against the Wearsiders.
- Wearsider Kevin Dillon appeared on trial for his hometown club after leaving Newcastle, but wasn't retained.
- Mike Hooper was loaned to Sunderland by Newcastle but failed to make an appearance.
- Albert Stubbins and Jackie Milburn appeared for Sunderland in war-time football.
- Newcastle United players who have refused to sign for Sunderland include: John Anderson (refused to leave Newcastle), Jon Dahl Tomasson (chose Newcastle instead) and David Kelly (chose Newcastle instead but subsequently signed for Sunderland).

— NEWCASTLE LEGENDS: JACKIE MILBURN —

Wor Jackie

Commemorated in books, plays, statues and songs, 'Wor Jackie' enjoyed a lifelong association with Newcastle United and his legend lives on two decades after his death.

Born into a footballing family (which included second cousins Jack and Bobby Charlton), Milburn's reputation was forged in the black and white of Newcastle and, for many football fans, he came to symbolise the club like no other player before or since.

Milburn's Magpies association began in 1943 when, as a 19 year-old, he played two trial matches at St James' Park – scoring twice in the first then blasting home six second-half goals the following weekend. This demonstration of powerful and accurate shooting was a taste of things to come.

His home debut in a war-time match in August 1943 was marked with a goal scored with his first touch, but Milburn had to wait until an end to hostilities and the start of the 1945/46 season to make his competitive bow.

A season before Football League fixtures returned, his debut came in the FA Cup, staged that season over two legs to assist clubs financially. Two goals in a 4–2 win over Barnsley sent a 60,284 crowd away from Gallowgate happy – although a 0–3 second leg reverse at Oakwell ended any Wembley dreams.

Then manager George Martin was to have a profound effect on Milburn's career in 1947, moving him to centre forward from the wing and handing him the number nine shirt. The switch paid instant dividends with a hat-trick away at Bury and a haul of 20 league goals that season as the Magpies returned to Division One.

However, it's for Milburn's FA Cup final exploits that he is best remembered: netting twice against Blackpool in the 1951 final and scoring after 45 seconds against Manchester City in 1955 en route to collecting a third winner's medal.

Many contemporary observers choose the sixth round tie away at Portsmouth in March 1952 as his finest display, a game which featured a hat-trick of memorable strikes.

After having left Tyneside for Belfast club Linfield in 1957, Milburn returned to England three years later at the age of 36, and was greeted with a number of offers.

Amid interest from Stoke City and various Scottish sides came a call from Charlie Mitten – the then Newcastle boss. However, Milburn was denied the chance of a Toon comeback after the Football League refused to sanction a request to repay his player's insurance policy.

Turning down the job of Ashington player-manager, he took a similar position at Yiewsley in Middlesex and briefly, at Carmel College in Wallingford. Milburn then managed Ipswich Town but, after just 18 months in charge, returned to the north-east in 1962 to spend the next two decades reporting on Newcastle United for a Sunday newspaper.

A testimonial game followed in 1967, in front of over 45,000 fans, while 1981 saw him the unwitting subject of the popular TV show *This is Your Life*.

Sadly, lung cancer claimed Jackie Milburn in October 1988. His funeral cortege fittingly slowed on Barrack Road, opposite St James' Park, en route to St Nicholas' Cathedral amid unprecedented numbers of mourners. Milburn's widow Laura later scattered his ashes across the Gallowgate End of the ground before returning to christen the stand that now bears his name.

Jackie Milburn factfile
Born: Ashington, May 11th 1924 Died: October 9th 1988
Newcastle career: 397 apps, 200 goals (1943–57)
Other clubs: Linfield
International: England, 13 caps, 10 goals

— ALL TIME PREMIERSHIP TABLE —

Despite having played one season fewer in the Premiership than ever-presents Everton and Tottenham Hotspur, Newcastle United are statistically the sixth most successful Premiership side in the history of the competition:

Team	P	W	D	L	F	A	Pts
Manchester United	620	394	137	94	1,220	538	1,319
Arsenal	620	332	168	120	1,048	547	1,164
Chelsea	620	310	168	142	977	606	1,098
Liverpool	620	306	157	157	992	607	1,075
Aston Villa	620	230	187	203	782	724	877
Newcastle United	578	240	152	186	844	718	872

— WHO THE **** ARE YOU? —

Current Football League sides that Newcastle have never faced competitively:

Accrington Stanley, Aldershot Town, Barnet, Boston United, Dagenham & Redbridge, Darlington*, Macclesfield Town, Milton Keynes Dons, Rochdale*, Wycombe Wanderers, Yeovil Town.

* Both faced in wartime football

— MIDDLE NAMES —

A selection of uncommon middle names that Newcastle United players have admitted to:

Robert **Sime** Aitken
Robert Francis **Dudgeon** Ancell
Anthony **Eugene** Cunningham
Amdy **Moustapha** Faye
John **Grattan** Hendrie
Frank **Calvert** Houghton
John **Bluey** Park
Alexander **Parrott** Ramsay
Glenn **Victor** Roeder
Kevin **Watson** Scott
William **Salmond** Thomson Penman

— TRUE COLOURS —

114 years of black and white stripes

"It was agreed that the Club's colours should be changed from red shirts and white knickers to black and white shirts (two inch stripe) and dark knickers."
Minutes of Newcastle United board meeting, August 1894

While there is no doubt about when Newcastle began to wear their familiar black and white striped shirts, the origins of that colour scheme remain in some dispute.

The club's inaugural season of league football in 1893/94 saw them appear in both the plain red shirt and white shorts and red and white striped shirts that their forerunners Newcastle East End had worn. Newcastle West End meanwhile had formerly appeared in a red and blue hooped shirt that was used as a basis for the change kit Newcastle United donned in the 1995/96 season.

Various suggestions have been made as to where the black and white colours originate from. One legend has it that the inspiration came from local clergyman, Father Dalmatius Houtman and his black and white uniform, another that there were some Magpies nesting in the ground around the time that the club changed its name. The most credible, however, suggests the black and white colours were copied from the Whitecoat army formed in the Tyneside area during the English Civil War. Favouring the Royalist cause, this army was established by the Cavendish family who were prominent local landowners and dressed their volunteer force in white shirts and dark trousers, boots, belts and hats.

Newcastle's appearance in black and white stripes was pre-dated by Notts County, who adopted that design a decade after being founded in 1880. Those other Magpies are also widely credited with being the inspiration behind Juventus adopting the colour scheme in 1903 after a member of the Italian club returned from England with a set of County strips.

Other Football League teams to have played in a black and white 'home' kit include New Brompton (who later became Gillingham), Rochdale, Grimsby Town and Watford.

— ST JAMES' PARK INTERNATIONALS —

Despite being initially selected as a venue for the 1966 World Cup Finals, wrangles over ground ownership and redevelopment between the club and Newcastle City Council saw the Football Association withdraw their hosting invitation in 1964. Middlesbrough's Ayresome Park was chosen to host three group stage ties instead, which were attended by the lowest crowds of the whole competition.

However, St James' Park has hosted various other senior international fixtures:

Date	Fixture	Competition
March 18th 1901	England 6 Wales 0	Home International
April 6th 1907	England 1 Scotland 1	Home International
November 15th 1933	England 1 Wales 2	Home International
November 9th 1938	England 4 Norway 0	Home International
June 10th 1996	Romania 0 France 1	Euro Championship
June 15th 1996	Bulgaria 1 Romania 0	Euro Championship
June 18th 1996	France 3 Bulgaria 1	Euro Championship
September 5th 2001	England 2 Albania 0	World Cup Qualifier
August 18th 2004	England 3 Ukraine 0	Friendly International
March 30th 2005	England 2 Azerbaijan 0	World Cup Qualifier

The stadium has also been earmarked as one of six UK venues to host the football tournament at the 2012 Olympics.

— CARELESS WHISPERS —

Among a myriad of transfer rumours involving Newcastle, certain non-moves have reached urban myth status:

Jimmy Greaves. Writing in his 2003 autobiography, the former England striker claimed that he turned down an illegal transfer approach from a Newcastle director in 1959. Despite being offered more than double his Chelsea salary, Greaves refused to leave Stamford Bridge – neither he nor his wife Irene fancying a move up north.

Ronnie Glavin. According to the local press, Barnsley's goalscoring midfielder was allegedly on the brink of a move to Tyneside on countless occasions in the late 1970s. He never left Oakwell.

Sócrates. The famed Brazilian midfielder was linked with a move to Tyneside from Corinthians in the early 1980s – the (fictional) justification being that the Doctor of Medicine and Philosophy graduate was coming to study at Newcastle University.

Roberto Baggio. Fans and media men at St James' Park for the press conference announcing the signing of Les Ferdinand spotted a black and white shirt with the name 'Baggio' on the back seat of a car parked outside the ground. The shirt was quickly revealed to be a wind-up perpetrated by director Douglas Hall.

However, it subsequently came to light that a United delegation had recently flown to Italy to speak to Baggio's agent, only to fail to agree financial terms. Within days, the player moved from Juventus to AC Milan.

— THERE'S NO PLACE LIKE HOME . . . PARK —

The longest possible journey between English football league stadia remains the 820-mile round trip between Newcastle and Plymouth.

To date, there have been 33 competitive meetings between the two sides, the Magpies having made 17 pilgrimages to Devon between 1905 and 1991. And on top of the long distance involved, the two most recent two trips to Home Park presented extra problems for the travelling contingent.

December 1990 saw the Division Two fixture scheduled for a noon start on a Sunday – Argyle being reluctant to cancel their lucrative Christmas shopper park and ride scheme based at the stadium car park! A crowd of 7,845 attended.

One year on and another Yuletide fiasco saw travelling Newcastle fans faced with making the journey for a game staged on the Friday evening before Christmas. Only 5,048 fans bothered to show up, including no more than 200 away supporters.

— WMD: WITNESS TO MAGPIE DECEPTION? —

Nowhere has the rise in respectability of football among the chattering classes been more evident than in the political arena, where club affiliations that were once hidden are now worn as a badge of honour. That has inevitably led to some dubious attempts at claiming allegiance – none more so than in the case of one Anthony Charles Lynton Blair. Allegedly.

Speaking in a Radio 5 interview in December 1997, the then-Prime Minister is famously said to have revealed his bogus Newcastle-supporting credentials. In particular, critics and political opponents seized on the fact that he claimed to have sat on the Gallowgate End as a youngster to watch Jackie Milburn play.

Unfortunately for the PM, that part of the ground was all standing until 1994 and 'Wor Jackie' made his final Newcastle appearance in 1957, when young Tony was four years old – and living in Australia.

Routinely trotted out as a prime example of Blair's manufactured personality, it took until 2005 for this popular myth to be tested and then promptly dispelled. An investigation by BBC's *Newsnight* programme uncovered the original tape of the interview and confirmed that it differed from subsequent newspaper reports of it – the latter being the widely-quoted source rather than the former. Absent from the tape are references to sitting or standing at the Gallowgate End or any area of St James' Park, while Blair revealed his Magpies affiliation to have begun 'just after Jackie Milburn'.

It's beyond suggestion though that the former Prime Minister may be implicated in any 'cash for honours' scandal – at least involving his favourite football club. One look in the St James' Park trophy cabinet should be enough to prove that.

— BEFORE WE WERE SO RUDELY INTERRUPTED —

One immediate effect of Britain's formal declaration of war against Germany on September 3rd 1939 was the immediate suspension of competitive football fixtures. That meant that the opening games of the 1939/40 season were expunged from the records, including Newcastle's three games in Division Two:

Date	Result
August 26th 1939	Millwall 3 Newcastle United 0
August 30th 1939	Nottingham Forest 2 Newcastle United 0
September 2nd 1939	Newcastle United 8 Swansea Town 1

Lost to history therefore are the goals scored at St James' Park in an 8–1 win over Swansea Town on the last Saturday before war was declared – a hat-trick from Ray Bowden, two from Tommy Pearson and efforts from David Hamilton, Willie Scott and Billy Cairns.

When the Football League programme resumed after the war, the 1939/40 fixture list was resurrected, with United fairing rather better the second time round:

Date	Result
August 31st 1946	Millwall 1 Newcastle United 4
September 5th 1946	Nottingham Forest 0 Newcastle United 2
September 7th 1946	Newcastle United 1 Swansea Town 1

Appearing in both the opening game of 1939 and 1946 against Millwall at St James' Park were no fewer than five players: Tom Swinburne, Benny Craig, Duggie Wright, Jimmy Woodburn and Tommy Pearson. Of the other six Magpies who played in the 1939 Swansea Town game, five resumed their careers with various clubs after the end of hostilities. Bowden, however, never played competitive football again.

— KNOT FOR THE FAINT-HEARTED —

Gallows humour still thrives at St James' Park

Following a misguided attempt by the club to re-christen it as the South Stand, traditionalists were delighted in 2008 when the southern end of St. James' Park was again referred to as the Gallowgate Stand. That name dates from when the original standing terrace was built on the route from Newcastle's New Gate Gaol to the site of the town's gallows.

The last public execution at the gallows took place in 1844, less than 40 years before football was being played on the same site. On that occasion, a death sentence was served on Mark Sherwood of nearby Blandford Street for the murder of his wife.

Indeed Newcastle was synonymous for its big crowds long before a football was ever kicked at St James' Park. In 1829, more than 20,000 people turned up to witness the hanging of a notorious female murderer.

The exact site of the gallows is believed to have been adjacent to Leazes Terrace, on the site of what is now the East Stand.

— FAIRS CUP GLORY —

Famously, the last major trophy won by Newcastle United was the Fairs Cup of 1969. But exactly how Newcastle ended up in the competition that season is a story in itself.

The Inter Cities Fairs Cup was the precursor to the UEFA Cup, with the original 1955 rules admitting into the competition a single representative team for each city that organised trade fairs. That pretty soon fell by the wayside in favour of a one club per city entry policy.

When Newcastle ended the 1967/68 season in tenth place of Division One, this rule worked spectacularly in their favour. Champions Manchester City were joined in the European Cup by runners-up and holders Manchester United, third-placed Liverpool and fourth-placed Leeds United entering the Fairs Cup. The one-club, one-city rule excluded Everton in fifth spot, but admitted Chelsea in sixth as England's third Fairs Cup side, representing London. Tottenham Hotspur and Arsenal both therefore missed out as a result, despite finishing in seventh and ninth positions respectively.

And when eighth-place finishers West Bromwich Albion beat Everton in the FA Cup Final to take a spot in the European Cup Winners' Cup competition, the fourth and final Fairs Cup place was Newcastle's.

Had the result been reversed and Everton won the FA Cup, the Toffees would have gone into the Cup Winners' Cup and West Brom would have taken the final Fairs Cup place rather than Newcastle. So, indirectly, the man Magpies fans have to thank for their Fairs Cup triumph is West Brom striker Jeff Astle, scorer of the only goal in the 1968 FA Cup Final.

— PREMIERSHIP RECORD —

By the end of the 2007/08 season Newcastle United had played 578 Premiership games, winning 240 of those, drawing 152 and losing 186.

Home:	Played	Won	Drawn	Lost
	289	164	68	57
Away:	Played	Won	Drawn	Lost
	289	76	84	129

In these games the Magpies have scored 844 goals and conceded 718.

— TWIN TOWERS PART I —

One year after the famous 'White Horse Final' of 1923, Newcastle made their first appearance at the new Empire Stadium – with both players and supporters finding it rather to their liking. Here are the club's results at Wembley up to and including Newcastle's last FA Cup win in 1955:

April 27th 1924   FA Cup Final   Won 2–0 against Aston Villa
Newcastle team: William Bradley, Billy Hampson, Frank Hudspeth, Edward Mooney, Charlie Spencer, Willie Gibson, James Low, Willie Cowan, Neil Harris, Tommy McDonald, Stan Seymour
Scorers: Seymour, Harris

April 23rd 1932   FA Cup Final   Won 2–1 against Arsenal
Albert McInroy, Jimmy Nelson, David Fairhurst, Roddie Mackenzie, Dave Davidson, Sammy Weaver, Jimmy Boyd, Jimmy Richardson, Jack Allen, Harry McMenemy, Tommy Lang
Scorer: Allen (2)

April 28th 1951   FA Cup Final   Won 2–0 against Blackpool
Jack Fairbrother, Bobby Cowell, Bobby Corbett, Joe Harvey, Frank Brennan, Charlie Crowe, Tommy Walker, Ernie Taylor, Jackie Milburn, George Robledo, Bobby Mitchell
Scorer: Milburn (2)

April 3rd 1952   FA Cup Final   Won 1–0 against Arsenal
Ronnie Simpson, Bobby Cowell, Alf McMichael, Joe Harvey, Frank Brennan, Ted Robledo, Tommy Walker, Bill Foulkes, Jackie Milburn, George Robledo, Bobby Mitchell
Scorer: G. Robledo

May 22nd 1955   FA Cup Final   Won 3–1 against Manchester City
Ronnie Simpson, Bobby Cowell, Ron Batty, Jimmy Scoular, Bob Stokoe, Tommy Casey, Len White, Jackie Milburn, Vic Keeble, George Hannah, Bobby Mitchell
Scorers: Milburn, Mitchell, Hannah

A local newspaper reporter described the crowd's reaction to Jackie Milburn's second goal in 1951 as follows:

"The Geordies seemed to want to jump right into Heaven. The spectacle was a study of mass delirium, a black and white sketch of mass hysteria in its most nerve-shattering form."

— NEWCASTLE LEGENDS: LEN WHITE —

Yorkshire grit in black and white

Newcastle's failure to appear in a third successive FA Cup Final in 1953 had one silver lining, Len White being signed from Rotherham just days after he had inspired the Millers to a 3–1 fourth round victory at Gallowgate.

The 22-year-old Yorkshireman cost £12,500 and spent the early part of his Newcastle career operating on the right flank, while still working as a miner at Burradon Colliery.

However, White's reputation as one of the best uncapped players of the era was built on his performances for the Magpies at centre forward after the departures of Jackie Milburn and Vic Keeble.

A run of stylish free-scoring displays made White a genuine crowd favourite, although inconsistency elsewhere in the side often meant that his efforts up front were nullified by defensive lapses.

White's sole honour was a 1955 FA Cup Winner's medal – a game in which he delivered the corner for Jackie Milburn to head home against Manchester City in the opening seconds at Wembley. Untimely cup exits at the hands of the likes of Millwall and Scunthorpe United were to follow in subsequent seasons, though, while his haul of 22 goals in 30 league appearances in 1957/58 was only enough to see the club narrowly avoid relegation.

Had White played for a London club, an England call-up would have been likely. As it was though, his appearance for a Football League XI in November 1958 gave a hint of what his country missed. Playing against an Irish League side at Anfield, White scored three goals in eight second-half minutes during a 5–2 victory.

However, like Tony Green a decade later, injury was to overshadow White's career. A challenge by Tottenham's Dave Mackay at White Hart Lane in March 1961 took the gloss off a 2–1 victory against the team who would complete the Double within weeks. Sidelined for six months with ruptured ankle ligaments, by the time White returned to the Magpies line-up they were in Division Two and manager Charlie Mitten was about to be jettisoned, as his side struggled to mount a promotion bid.

It was evident that the injury had robbed White of his pace and in February 1962 he returned to his native Yorkshire, joining Huddersfield as the makeweight in a deal which took Scottish forward Jimmy Kerray to St James' Park.

After being belatedly rewarded for his efforts for the club with a testimonial game in 1989 (held at Whitley Bay after Newcastle United scandalously refused to take part), cancer claimed White in 1994 at the age of 64.

While Jackie Milburn remains synonymous with United's 1950s achievements, Len White is something of a forgotten hero.

Len White factfile
Born: Skellow, March 23rd 1930   Died: June 17th 1994
Newcastle career: 270 apps, 153 goals (1953–62)
Other clubs: Rotherham, Huddersfield, Stockport County

— IT'S A KNOCKOUT —

While no TV coverage of the FA Cup would be complete without footage of 'that' Ronnie Radford goal from 1972, the 'Nightmare on Edgar Street' is by no means the only occasion on which the Magpies have exited from the competition at the hands of lower league opposition.

In the 52 seasons since the resumption of the competition in 1946, United have been humbled by supposedly inferior sides on no fewer than 19 occasions – 11 of those coming in front of disbelieving crowds on Tyneside:

Season Opponent	Score	Feat
1948/49 Bradford Park Ave (h)	0–2	Division 3 beat Division 1
1956/57 Millwall (a)	1–2	Division 3 South beat Division 1
1957/58 Scunthorpe United (h)	1–3	Division 3 North beat Division 1
1960/61 Sheffield United (h)	1–3	Division 2 beat Division 1
1961/62 Peterborough (h)	0–1	Division 3 beat Division 2
1963/64 Bedford Town (h)	1–2	Non-League beat Division 2
1967/68 Carlisle United (h)	0–1	Division 2 beat Division 1
1971/72 Hereford United (a)	1–2	Non-League beat Division 1
1972/73 Luton Town (a)	0–2	Division 2 beat Division 1
1974/75 Walsall (a)	0–1	Division 3 beat Division 1
1977/78 Wrexham (a)	1–4	Division 3 beat Division 1
1979/80 Chester City (h)	0–2	Division 3 beat Division 2
1980/81 Exeter City (a)	0–4	Division 3 beat Division 2
1985/86 Brighton and Hove Albion (h)	0–2	Division 2 beat Division 1
1988/89 Watford (a)	0–1	Division 2 beat Division 1
1991/92 AFC Bournemouth (h)	3–4	Division 3 beat Division 2 (on pens)
1993/94 Luton Town (a)	0–2	Division 1 beat Premier League
2002/03 Wolverhampton Wanderers (a)	2–3	Division 1 beat Premiership
2006/07 Birmingham City (h)	1–5	Championship beat Premiership

— SING IN THE . . . —

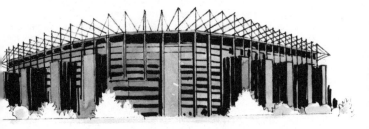

St James' Park

As St James' Park has been altered over the years, so have the names of different parts of the stadium. Here's a bluffer's guide to the Toon's ground:

North

Now known as the 'Sir John Hall Stand', this end of the ground will forever be the 'Leazes End' to diehard black and whiters. Once the home to the most vocal supporters, the covered standing terrace was closed and bulldozed following the home game against Manchester City in March 1978.

In its place came a reduced size uncovered terrace and the retaining walls for a stand that wasn't actually constructed until 1993.

Season 1986/87 saw temporary seating installed, with reconstruction of the West Stand meaning season ticket holders were relocated to an uncovered stand borrowed from a motor racing circuit (hence its unofficial name of the 'Silverstone Stand').

South

Now known again as the Gallowgate Stand after previous club-inspired renamings as the City End and the Newcastle Brown Ale South Stand, this is most commonly referred to as 'The Gallowgate End'. This part of the ground is also known as 'The Scoreboard', after the electronic boards installed there in the 1980s and 1990s and earlier manual efforts. The reconstruction of the stadium saw an all-seater covered stand opened in 1994, with sections linking the stand to the constructions adjoining to the East and West Stands following soon after.

East

Although the East Stand has been in place for over 30 years, this side of the ground is still referred to by some as the 'Popular Side', a reference to the former open terrace that stood here and ran the length of the pitch. Also now gone but still mentioned occasionally are 'The Benches' – seats were installed at the front of this stand following an incident in 1980 when a firebomb was thrown into the travelling West Ham United supporters in the north-east corner. These were removed in the early 1990s when the stand was remodelled and the original executive boxes relocated to the West side of the ground.

West

For decades the only seated accommodation available (with the best seats in the 'Centre Pavilion'), the West Stand was demolished at the end of the 1986/87 season and replaced by a new construction christened 'The Milburn Stand'. Later alterations during the 1990s saw the standing areas that remained in front of the original reconstruction seated, removing the distinct 'Wing Paddocks' (A & E) and 'Centre Paddock' sections.

Corners

The north-east corner of the ground is nicknamed 'Firebomb Corner' – a reference to the previously mentioned events of March 1980. Reconstruction of the West Stand saw the dressing rooms sited in portakabins behind the Leazes End during season 1987/88, with the north-east corner closed to supporters in order to allow the teams to access the field via this section. The south-east corner of the ground is routinely referred to as 'The Corner' or 'The Strawberry Corner' – the latter after the adjacent pub of that name.

— DOUBLE RATIONS —

The once traditional scheduling of League fixtures on both Christmas Day and Boxing Day last saw Newcastle United in action on December 25th and 26th back in 1957.

On Christmas Day Nottingham Forest visited Tyneside and triumphed 4–1 in front of 25,214 spectators. United gained revenge, though, 24 hours later on the banks of the Trent, winning 3–2 at the City Ground watched by a crowd of 32,359.

Some fixtures were scheduled on December 25th in both 1958 and 1959 before the practice was finally discontinued. However, Newcastle didn't have games on Christmas Day in either season.

— LEAGUE OF NATIONS —

By the end of the 2007/08 season, no fewer than 140 players from 37 different countries had represented Newcastle United in their 15 seasons of Premiership football:

Country	Player Total
England	58
France	13
Scotland	8
Republic of Ireland	7
Wales	5
Senegal	4
Northern Ireland	3
Spain	3

Plus double representatives from: Argentina, Australia, Brazil, Czech Republic, Democratic Republic of Congo, Greece, Italy, Netherlands, Nigeria and Portugal. And single representatives from: Belgium, Cameroon, Canada, Chile, Colombia, Croatia, Cyprus, Denmark, Georgia, Germany, Norway, Paraguay, Peru, South Africa, Sweden, Switzerland, Trinidad and Tobago, Turkey and the United States of America. Of those 140 players, 25 came through the ranks from the Newcastle United Academy.

* International affiliation rather than country of birth has been taken as a measure, for example Alan Neilson was born in Germany but played for Wales. Four players have also made Premiership appearances for the club in separate spells – Tommy Wright, Robbie Elliott, Lee Clark and Pavel Srnicek. These players are only counted once in the above totals.

— LET THERE BE LIGHT —

Newcastle United were only the third First Division club to install floodlights. The lights were switched on for a friendly against Celtic in February 1953 . . . and promptly switched-off again during the half-time interval, plunging the entire crowd into darkness.

The lights illuminated the first-ever floodlit FA Cup tie between two league sides, although Newcastle was not one of them. The match in question was a first round replay between Carlisle and Darlington on November 28th 1955.

— NEWCASTLE LEGENDS: SHAY GIVEN —

Shay Given: already a Toon legend

Shay Given celebrated a decade with Newcastle United in May 2007, having been bought from Blackburn for £1.5 million by his former Rovers boss Kenny Dalglish. Dalglish had first spotted the goalkeeper's potential when he was a teenager at Celtic, signing Given for Blackburn in 1994.

Having being loaned to both Swindon Town and Sunderland (who it was rumoured were unable to fund a permanent transfer), Given tussled with Steve Harper for the position of first-choice goalkeeper at St James Park for a number of seasons.

The Irish international took pole position in the 2000/01 campaign, missing just four Premiership fixtures as he established himself in the side after withdrawing a hastily submitted transfer request.

During that season, Given began a run of 140 consecutive Premiership appearances at Leeds in January 2001, making 100 per cent appearance records in the following three seasons. That impressive run was broken in October 2004 when Given remained on Tyneside as his wife gave birth – Steve Harper deputising away at Bolton.

By the end of the 2007/08 season, Given had risen to fourth in Newcastle's all-time appearance table (see *Familiar Faces*, page 36) and with a contract keeping him on Tyneside until 2011, he has a great chance of becoming the first Magpie ever to reach the 500 mark.

An outstanding shot-stopper, Given's importance to Newcastle was recognised by then manager Glenn Roeder when he was appointed captain following the retirement of Alan Shearer in the summer of 2006. Shortly after taking the skipper's armband, however, Given was involved in a sickening collision at West Ham United in September 2006 which left him with abdominal injuries that the surgeon who operated on him likened to those suffered by car crash victims. He returned to action after two months to put in some excellent performances, but ended another season having seen his efforts undermined by the shortcomings of those players in front of him.

Like all goalkeepers, Given has had a few moments he would prefer to forget – none more so than the goal he conceded against Coventry at Highfield Road in November 1997. In an initially innocuous piece of play, Given claimed possession of the ball on the edge of his six-yard box and threw the ball down in front of him in preparation for clearing it downfield. However, as a number of reporters later wryly observed, he was the only Irishman who didn't know where Dublin was – Coventry striker Dion Dublin appearing from behind him and scoring a perfectly legitimate goal by tapping the loose ball into the Newcastle net.

A far better memory for Given was being awarded the captain's armband by Ireland boss Steve Staunton in March 2007, leading his side out at Dublin's Croke Park against Slovakia. That honour came on the occasion of Given's 80th full international cap, which equalled the previous Ireland record for a goalkeeper, held by Packie Bonner.

For consistency, few in the modern game can match Given's record. If, as he must fear, he emulates Alan Shearer's trophy-free stint on Tyneside it would be a poor return indeed for his years of loyal service.

Shay Given factfile
Born: April 20th 1976, Lifford, County Donegal
Newcastle career: 437 apps (1997–)
Other clubs: Celtic, Blackburn Rovers, Swindon Town (loan), Sunderland (loan)
International: Republic of Ireland, 86 caps

— TWIN TOWERS PART II —

Venue of Legends for some, Wembley Stadium has proved to be nothing but an arena of misery for Newcastle supporters since the club's last success there in 1955. As Alan Shearer commented in 2002, 'for Newcastle United, the sooner they knock down this place the better'.

May 4th 1974   FA Cup Final   Lost 0–3 to Liverpool
Newcastle team: Iam McFaul, Frank Clark, Alan Kennedy, Terry McDermott, Pat Howard, Bobby Moncur, Jimmy Smith (Tommy Gibb), Tommy Cassidy, Malcolm Macdonald, John Tudor, Terry Hibbitt.

February 28th 1976   League Cup Final   Lost 1–2 to Manchester City
Mick Mahoney, Irving Nattrass, Alan Kennedy, Stewart Barrowclough, Glen Keely, Pat Howard, Mickey Burns, Tommy Cassidy, Malcolm Macdonald, Alan Gowling, Tommy Craig. Substitute unused: Paul Cannell.
Scorer: Gowling.

August 11th 1996   FA Charity Shield   Lost 0–4 to Manchester United
Pavel Srnicek, Steve Watson, Darren Peacock, Philippe Albert, John Beresford, David Batty, Robert Lee, Peter Beardsley (Tino Asprilla), Alan Shearer, Les Ferdinand, David Ginola (Keith Gillespie). Substitutes unused: Shaka Hislop, Warren Barton, Steve Howey, Lee Clark, Paul Kitson.

May 16th 1998   FA Cup Final   Lost 0–2 to Arsenal
Shay Given, Stuart Pearce (Andreas Andersson), Steve Howey, Nicos Dabizas, Alessandro Pistone, Gary Speed, David Batty, Robert Lee, Alan Shearer, Temuri Ketsbaia (John Barnes), Warren Barton (Steve Watson). Substitutes unused: Shaka Hislop, Philippe Albert.

May 22nd 1999   FA Cup Final   Lost 0–2 to Manchester United
Steve Harper, Andy Griffin, Laurent Charvet, Nicos Dabizas, Didier Domi, Robert Lee, Didi Hamann (Duncan Ferguson), Gary Speed, Alan Shearer, Temuri Ketsbaia (Glass), Nolberto Solano (Silvio Maric). Substitutes unused: Shay Given, Warren Barton, Stephen Glass.

April 9th 2000   FA Cup Semi-final   Lost 1–2 to Chelsea
Shay Given, Warren Barton, Steve Howey, Nicos Dabizas, Aaron Hughes (Temuri Ketsbaia), Robert Lee, Gary Speed, Kieron Dyer, Alan Shearer, Duncan Ferguson (Didier Domi), Nolberto Solano. Substitutes unused: Steve Harper, Alain Goma, Diego Gavilan
Scorer: Lee.

— TRANSFER TRAIL I —

In chronological order, Newcastle United's record purchases have been as follows:

Player	Year	Fee	Paid to
Bobby Templeton	1903	£400	Aston Villa
Andy McCombie	1904	£700	Sunderland
George Wilson	1907	£1,600	Everton
Billy Hibbert	1911	£1,950	Bury
Neil Harris	1920	£3,300	Partick Thistle
Hughie Gallacher	1925	£6,500	Airdrieonians
Jack Hill	1928	£8,100	Burnley
Harry Clifton	1938	£8,500	Chesterfield
Len Shackleton	1946	£13,000	Bradford Park Avenue
George Lowrie	1948	£18,500	Coventry City
Jimmy Scoular	1953	£22,250	Portsmouth
Ivor Allchurch	1958	£28,000	Swansea Town
Barrie Thomas	1962	£45,000	Scunthorpe United
Wyn Davies	1966	£80,000	Bolton Wanderers
Jimmy Smith	1969	£100,000	Aberdeen
Malcolm Macdonald	1971	£180,000	Luton Town
Peter Withe	1978	£200,000	Nottingham Forest
John Trewick	1980	£250,000	West Bromwich Albion
Paul Goddard	1986	£415,000	West Ham United
Mirandinha	1987	£575,000	Palmeiras
John Robertson	1988	£750,000	Heart of Midlothian
Dave Beasant	1988	£850,000	Wimbledon
Andy Thorn	1988	£850,000	Wimbledon
Andy Cole	1993	£1,750,000	Bristol City
Ruel Fox	1995	£2,225,000	Norwich City
Darren Peacock	1995	£2,700,000	Queens Park Rangers
Les Ferdinand	1995	£6,000,000	Queens Park Rangers
Tino Asprilla	1996	£7,500,000	Parma
Alan Shearer	1996	£15,000,000	Blackburn Rovers
Michael Owen	2005	£16,000,000	Real Madrid

— INTERNATIONAL APPEARANCES —

The current holder of the club's international appearance record is Shay Given, who broke the record on April 30th 2003 when playing for the Republic of Ireland against Norway.

A clean sheet that night in a 1–0 win at Lansdowne Road marked the 50th senior cap of the goalkeeper's career and the 41st earned whilst a Newcastle player. In doing so he broke the previous 40-game tally of Northern Ireland's Alf McMichael – a record that had stood for some 43 years.

Since then, Given has extended the record further, reaching 86 caps for Ireland (and therefore 77 as a Magpie) in February 2008. McMichael's tally was also subsequently bettered by Greek defender Nicos Dabizas and Northern Ireland's Aaron Hughes.

Newcastle United's top ten international appearance makers:

Rank	Player	Total	Country
1	Shay Given	77	Republic of Ireland
2	Nicos Dabizas	43	Greece
3	Aaron Hughes	41	Northern Ireland
4	Alf McMichael	40	Northern Ireland
5	Gary Speed	36	Wales
6	Alan Shearer	35	England
7	Kieron Dyer	32	England
8	Nolberto Solano	28	Peru
9=	Peter Beardsley	25	England
9=	David Craig	25	Northern Ireland
10	Dick Keith	23	Northern Ireland

Note: Only caps gained whilst a Newcastle player are included in this list.

— SHOOT-OUT FAILURES —

Before beating Watford on penalties in the League Cup 2006, Newcastle had lost all seven of their previous competitive shoot-outs:

Year	Opponent	Competition
1971	Pecsi Dozsa	Inter-Cities Fairs Cup
1979	Sunderland	League Cup
1992	AFC Bournemouth	FA Cup
1996	Chelsea	FA Cup
1998	Blackburn Rovers	League Cup
2002	Everton	League Cup
2003	Partizan Belgrade	Champions League Qualifier

— NEWCASTLE LEGENDS:
MALCOLM MACDONALD —

Supermac!

One of the finest strikers in Newcastle's illustrious history, Malcolm Macdonald was signed from Luton Town in 1971 for £180,000 by Toon boss Joe Harvey to solve a goalscoring problem.

Arriving at St James' Park in a hired Rolls Royce exuding brashness and confidence, Macdonald had a similar swagger on the pitch. In his five years on Tyneside he scored many memorable goals, beginning with a hat-trick against Liverpool on his home league debut. Fast and powerful, Macdonald possessed an explosive left foot and many of his best strikes – like his rocket shot at home to Leicester City that has gone down in folklore as one of the best ever seen at Gallowgate – gave the opposition keeper absolutely no chance of making a save.

The goals kept on coming, but the writing was on the wall for Macdonald when Harvey was replaced by Gordon Lee, a cautious manager who advocated a strict 'no stars' policy. Relations between club and player soon deteriorated, with an eventual parting of the ways coming in August 1976 when Arsenal shelled out £333,333 to take him to Highbury.

On the field, a parallel can be drawn between Macdonald and his eventual successor in the number nine shirt Alan Shearer. Both were to leave Newcastle without winners' medals or goals in either of their two cup final appearances. However, both enjoyed some happy moments in the semi-finals that led to those Wembley appearances, Macdonald scoring twice against Burnley in 1974 at Hillsborough in front of a fevered Newcastle support.

While Shearer's public image remains spotless and his managerial prowess untested, the same cannot be said for Macdonald. His early career in management at Fulham showed signs of promise before disintegrating in the fall-out from a controversial game with Derby County that blighted hopes of promotion for the Cottagers. Later, in an eight-month spell at Huddersfield, his side was on the wrong end of a confidence-shattering 10–1 league defeat away at Manchester City. After his management career ended, Macdonald experienced a number of setbacks in his business and personal life and for a while was a self-confessed alcoholic.

Happily, he has now recovered and has developed a new career as a talk-in pundit and radio chat show host in the north-east.

Malcolm Macdonald factfile
Born: Fulham, January 7th 1950
Newcastle career: 228 apps, 121 goals (1971–76)
Other clubs: Fulham, Luton Town, Arsenal
International: England, 14 caps, 6 goals

— GOLD STANDARD —

Eighteen players have appeared in World Cup finals while their registration was held by Newcastle United. They are:

Year	Host	Player	Nation
1950	Brazil	Jackie Milburn	England
1950	Brazil	George Robledo	Chile
1954	Switzerland	Ivor Broadis	England
1958	Sweden	Tommy Casey	Northern Ireland
1958	Sweden	Dick Keith	Northern Ireland
1958	Sweden	Alf McMichael	Northern Ireland
1986	Mexico	Peter Beardsley	England
1986	Mexico	David McCreery	Northern Ireland
1986	Mexico	Ian Stewart	Northern Ireland
1990	Italy	Roy Aitken	Scotland
1998	France	David Batty	England
1998	France	Robert Lee	England
1998	France	Alan Shearer	England
2002	Japan/South Korea	Kieron Dyer	England
2002	Japan/South Korea	Diego Gavilan	Paraguay
2002	Japan/South Korea	Shay Given	Republic of Ireland
2006	Germany	Michael Owen	England
2006	Germany	Craig Moore	Australia

In addition, Stephane Guivarc'h officially signed for Newcastle 24 hours after becoming a World Cup winner with France in 1998. The striker made his sixth appearance of the tournament in the final against Brazil, but failed to score in any of them. His lack of form attracted the attention of TV pundits including a certain Ruud Gullit, who was somewhat disparaging. Little did Gullit know though that within a matter of weeks he would be Guivarc'h's manager at St James' Park.

— TRADESMAN'S ENTRANCE —

With the traditional post-career profession of public house landlord having been superseded by media pundit or player's agent, here's a selection of slightly more individual ways in which former Newcastle United players have earned a crust after hanging up their boots:

Player	Profession
Philippe Albert	Market trader (fruit and vegetables)
Martin Burleigh	Painter and decorator
Andy Hunt	Adventure travel host in Belize

Albert Bennett	Joke shop proprietor
Ralph Callachan	Taxi driver
Tommy Casey	Fishmonger
Mick Channon	Racehorse trainer
Tony Cunningham	Solicitor
Bill Curry	Window cleaner
Billy Day	On-course bookmaker
Ed Dixon	Cinema manager
Pat Heard	Illusionist (stage name: Patrick Stewart)
William Hughes	Fisherman
Bill Imrie	Butcher
James Jackson	Blacksmith
Tom Philippson	Lord Mayor (of Wolverhampton)
Eric Ross	Travel agent
Willie Scott	Lollipop man
Scott Sloan	Fireman
George Thompson	Sign writer

— LONDON CALLING —

Saturday 2nd September 1893 saw both Newcastle United and Woolwich Arsenal play their first-ever Football League fixtures, the sides meeting at the Manor Ground in Plumstead, South East London.

However it proved to be a testing debut in the capital for the team from Tyneside who had arrived at Kings Cross by train early on the morning of the game having been unable to afford hotel accommodation.

The teams lined up as follows:

Woolwich Arsenal: Williams, Powell, Jeffrey, Devine, Buist, Howat, Gemmell, Henderson, Shaw, Elliott, Booth.

Newcastle United: Ramsay, Jeffrey, Miller, Crielly, Graham, McKane, Bowman, Crate, Thompson, Sorley, Wallace.

With Newcastle trailing at the interval to a Shaw effort, Arsenal quickly doubled the lead through Elliott. However goals from Tom Crate and Jock Sorley gave Newcastle a point (some contemporary reports crediting Willie Graham as scoring Newcastle's opener).

— SHEAR CLASS —

Alan Shearer is the Premiership's highest ever scorer, closely followed by one Andrew Cole. In fact, four of the Premiership's top scorers have notched a fair few of their tally in the black and white stripes off Newcastle United.

Premiership Top Ten Goalscorers:

Player	Total	For Newcastle
Alan Shearer	260	148
Andrew Cole	188	43
Thierry Henry	174	–
Robbie Fowler	162	–
Les Ferdinand	149	41
Teddy Sheringham	147	–
Michael Owen	136	18
Jimmy Floyd Hasselbaink	127	–
Dwight Yorke	123	–
Ian Wright	113	–

— SHOOT-OUT TRIUMPH —

An instantly forgettable 2006/07 season for Newcastle United was memorable for one achievement – the breaking of a competitive penalty shoot-out hoodoo that had extended over 35 years.

November 7th 2006 saw the Magpies in League Cup fourth round action at Premiership rivals Watford. But after 90 minutes of normal time and an extra half hour left the two sides locked at 2–2, Newcastle faced their eighth competitive penalty shoot-out – having lost the previous seven. With Nolberto Solano stepping up to take the first kick, here's how history was made:

Newcastle:			Watford:		
Solano	scored	1–0	Henderson	scored	5–1
Milner	saved	1–1	Young	missed	1–1
Emre	scored	2–1	Spring	scored	2–2
Duff	scored	3–2	Bangura	scored	3–3
Carr	scored	4–3	Bouazza	scored	4–4
N'Zogbia	scored	5–4	Stewart	saved	5–4

Goalkeeper Steve Harper saved the 12th spot-kick to deny Jordan Stewart, before celebrating with the travelling fans behind him in the Vicarage Road Stand.

— NEWCASTLE LEGENDS: ALAN SHEARER —

Shearer, Shearer!

It is something of a minor tragedy that Alan Shearer ended his career with a single honour, the Premiership winner's medal he collected with Blackburn Rovers.

A one-time schoolboy trialist with Newcastle – contrary to urban myth he only played briefly in goal during his trial – Shearer began his professional career at Southampton before making a big money move to Blackburn in 1992. At Ewood Park his forceful centre forward play and powerful shooting were key factors in the Lancashire side's 1995 title success. However, a year later, after spurning offers from Manchester United, Arsenal and Barcelona, Shearer was persuaded by Kevin Keegan to return to his Geordie roots.

Twenty-five goals in 31 Premiership games earned a second successive runner's up spot for his new club, despite the shock mid-season departure of his teenage hero Keegan (a young Shearer can be seen acting as ball boy in footage of Keegan's testimonial).

His second season at the club began badly when he was seriously injured in a pre-season tournament at Goodison Park in August 1997.

He returned to action to fire the club into successive FA Cup finals in 1998 and 1999, only to end up on the losing side on both occasions.

Despite his goals and clear commitment to the Newcastle cause, both Ruud Gullit and Sir Bobby Robson subsequently attempted to dislodge Shearer from his perch as the uncrowned King of Tyneside – the former by controversially leaving him out of the side against Sunderland, the latter attempting to sell him to Liverpool.

Shearer outlasted both managers, though, and postponed his planned retirement after talks with their successor Graham Souness in 2005. His decision to carry on playing enabled him to set a new Newcastle scoring record. Goal number 200 against Mansfield Town in the FA Cup at St James' Park in January 2006 equalled Jackie Milburn's tally and a month later he claimed the record outright against Portsmouth.

Shearer's goals during this period helped another new manager – caretaker boss Glenn Roeder – to a winning start, amid widespread speculation that Roeder was merely keeping the seat warm for the popular Magpies' skipper.

A revitalised Newcastle rose into the top half of the table in the second half of the 2005/06 season, with a trip to Sunderland giving Shearer more reason to celebrate as he helped his side come from behind by scoring goal number 206.

However, within ten minutes of scoring from the spot, Shearer's playing career was over – caught accidentally in the tackle by Julio Arca and forced off with medial knee ligament damage. The injury meant he missed the remaining three games of the season – although he was able to make a cameo appearance in a farewell testimonial at Gallowgate against Celtic. Shearer appeared for kick-off before leaving the field, returning in the final seconds to sign off by converting a penalty with typical aplomb.

Proceeds from the sell-out game, merchandising and other events eventually totalled £1.64 million – which was donated to various charitable causes.

A regular BBC pundit, Shearer is also now working towards his UEFA 'A' Licence coaching qualification, having enrolled on a course run by the Scottish Football Association.

Medals may have eluded Shearer during his Newcastle career, but the pleasure he provided from his goalscoring exploits remains undiminished. Only he knows though whether he has unfinished business at Gallowgate.

Alan Shearer factfile
Born: Gosforth, August 13th 1970
Newcastle career: 404 apps, 206 goals (1996–2006)
Other clubs: Southampton, Blackburn Rovers
International: England, 63 caps, 30 goals

— TWELFTH NIGHT —

- Albert Bennett holds the distinction of being the first ever Newcastle United substitute, following a change in the rules at the start of the 1965/66 season allowing teams to name a twelfth man (although the sub was only allowed to come onto the pitch to replace an injured player). Consequently, Bennett remained firmly seated on the bench during the Magpies' 2–2 draw with Nottingham Forest at St James' Park on August 21st 1965.
- The honour of being Newcastle's first playing sub went to Ollie Burton on September 4th 1965 when he replaced Trevor Hockey (who had sustained a shin injury) during a 2–0 home victory over Northampton Town. And it was Burton who became the first Newcastle player to net after coming on to the field as a substitute, scoring in a 1–2 defeat to Lincoln City at Sincil Bank in the Football League Cup on September 13th 1967.
- On August 29th 1987 the number of substitutes permissible was raised to two, with the Magpies first using their number 12 and 14 in a 0–1 home loss to Nottingham Forest. On that occasion Kenny Wharton and Paul Goddard gave way to John Anderson and Andy Thomas.
- Three substitutes were permitted for the first time at the start of the 1995/96 season, with then-manager Kevin Keegan making a trio of replacements for the first time in the sixth Premiership game of the season, the visit of Manchester City to Tyneside. In a 3–1 victory for United on September 16th 1995, Warren Barton gave way to Steve Watson, Scott Sellars replaced John Beresford and Ruel Fox was introduced for Peter Beardsley.
- The first-ever substitute to appear back in the 1965/66 season was Keith Peacock of Charlton Athletic. His son Gavin later played for Newcastle United.

— WEAR SO HAPPY —

Saturday April 5th 1980 wasn't a great day for the travelling Newcastle fans among a 41,752 crowd at Roker Park. A Stan Cummins goal settled the 115th Wear-Tyne derby and ultimately helped propel Sunderland to a second place finish in Division Two. However, in 12 trips to Wearside since that defeat up to the start of the 2007/08 season Newcastle have lost none of them:

Season	Score	Newcastle scorer(s)	Crowd
1984/85	0–0		28,246
1989/90	0–0		29,499
1989/90	0–0		26,641
1991/92	1–1	Liam O'Brien	29,224
1992/93	2–1	Liam O'Brien, Gary Owers (own goal)	28,098
1996/97	2–1	Peter Beardsley, Les Ferdinand	22,037
1999/00	2–2	Helder, Didier Domi	42,192
2000/01	1–1	Andy O'Brien	48,277
2001/02	1–0	Nicos Dabizas	48,290
2002/03	1–0	Nolberto Solano (penalty)	45,067
2005/06	4–1	Michael Chopra, Alan Shearer (penalty) Charles N'Zogbia, Albert Luque	40,032
2007/08	1–1	James Milner	47,701

Games up until the 1996/97 season were staged at Roker Park. Since then, the fixture has been played at the Stadium of Light.

— #9 DREAM PART I —

Although the so-called 'Summer of Love' didn't really have much of an impact on Tyneside, Newcastle fans can still claim a (slightly tenuous) link to the record that what was for many the soundtrack of the psychedelic era.

On June 1st 1967 The Beatles released *Sgt Pepper's Lonely Hearts Club Band* on the Parlophone label – an album routinely cited as one of the most innovative and inspirational pieces of popular music ever recorded.

As well as the ground-breaking material though, much attention was also focused on the cover artwork, which consisted of the 'Fab Four' plus a montage of more than 70 iconic personalities that The Beatles themselves had chosen.

These appeared in life-size cardboard cut-out form – a concept originally devised by Paul McCartney, designed by Peter Blake, created by art director Robert Fraser and photographed on March 30th 1967 by Michael Cooper.

Included among the various world leaders, entertainers, philosophers and poets were three sportsmen – boxer Sonny Liston, Olympic swimmer Johnny Weissmuller and former Liverpool centre forward Albert Stubbins (Everton legend William Ralph 'Dixie' Dean was also considered but not included).

Born in Wallsend, Stubbins had moved to Liverpool from Newcastle in 1946, rapidly becoming a Kop favourite and playing for the Anfield club until 1953. His place in the montage has variously been claimed to have been at the urging of both John Lennon and Paul McCartney, the former allegedly because Stubbins was a great favourite of his father Fred Lennon. McCartney also seems to have been a Stubbins fan, later sending him a telegram: "Well done Albert for all those glorious years in football. Long may you bob and weave."

Regardless of whose choice it was, a photo of a grinning Albert in his Liverpool strip can be seen towards the centre of the group – just behind Marlene Dietrich.

In 2003, the International Federation of the Phonographic Industry (IFPI), certified that worldwide sales of *Sgt Pepper's* . . . had exceeded 32 million – that's an awful lot of Alberts . . .

— FAMILIAR FACES —

On January 19th 2008 Shay Given kept a clean sheet in a 0–0 draw with Bolton Wanderers at St. James' Park and moved up another place in the all-time Newcastle United appearances list.

Injury restricted Given to just four more outings that season, but he's still on track to pass fellow goalkeeper Jimmy Lawrence and become the first Newcastle player to break the 500-game barrier.

The top ten competitive appearance makers for the club are:

Rank	Player	Total	Timespan
1	Jimmy Lawrence	496	1904–1922
2	Frank Hudspeth	472	1910–1929
3	Frank Clark	457	1962–1975
4	Shay Given	437	1997–
5	Bill McCracken	432	1904–1923
6	Alf McMichael	431	1949– 1963
7	David Craig	412	1962–1978
8	Bobby Mitchell	408	1949–1961
9	Alan Shearer	404	1996–2006
10	Jackie Milburn	397	1946–1957

— NEWCASTLE LEGENDS: PETER BEARDSLEY —

Time fails to dim the brilliance of Peter Beardsley's finishing

Spotted playing youth football on Tyneside, Peter Beardsley had trials at Gillingham, Cambridge United, Burnley and Newcastle United without earning a professional contract. For a while it seemed the talented but lightweight schemer would have to consider a career outside football.

Fortunately for Beardsley, former Magpies captain Bob Moncur got wind of his abilities and talked the 18-year-old into playing for his Carlisle United reserve side at Newcastle Blue Star in 1979. Beardsley scored that night in a 3–2 win at the Wheatsheaf and quickly agreed terms with the Brunton Park club, where he continued to earn rave reviews.

In 1981 he moved to the North American Soccer League with Vancouver Whitecaps but two years later joined Arthur Cox's Newcastle side after a brief one-game flirtation with Manchester United.

Beardsley helped Newcastle to promotion in his first season with the club but after Cox was replaced by Jack Charlton, he found himself competing for a place up front with burly forwards Tony Cunningham and George Reilly. Under new manager Willie McFaul, Beardsley was back in favour, but he grew increasingly frustrated with a perceived lack of ambition at the club.

In July 1987 he departed for Liverpool in a record £1.9 million deal, and remained on Merseyside for a six-year spell which included two seasons at Everton. It was during this period that Beardsley won the bulk of his 59 England caps, forming a successful forward partnership with Gary Lineker.

In 1993, Kevin Keegan brought Beardsley, now aged 32, back to Tyneside. Using his exceptional close ball skills to supply the prolific Andy Cole when he wasn't scoring sensational goals himself, he was a prime mover in establishing Newcastle United back in the top flight.

After leaving Newcastle for a second time in 1997, he took in stops at Bolton Wanderers, Manchester City, Fulham, Hartlepool and Doncaster Rovers.

A sell-out testimonial game at St James' Park in 1999 saw his boyhood favourites Celtic come to town, the occasion featuring the likes of Kenny Dalglish, Andy Cole and Kevin Keegan back in black and white for one night. None of these stars were surprised to learn that Beardsley, one of the most enthusiastic footballers of his generation, had played for Hartlepool's first team the evening before his big night.

For those who saw this skilful, creative and clever player at his peak certain memories are embedded. Among the most vivid moments are the chip over Brighton goalkeeper Joe Corrigan on the final day of the 1983/84 season, a New Years' Day hat-trick at home to Sunderland in 1985, and from his second spell, superb late winners at White Hart Lane and Selhurst Park. Time fails to dim the brilliance of his finishing.

Since hanging up his boots, Beardsley has worked in a PR capacity at St James' Park and is a popular guest at local charity events.

Peter Beardsley factfile

Born: Longbenton, January 18th 1961
Newcastle career: 324 apps, 119 goals (1983–87 and 1993–97)
Other clubs: Carlisle United, Vancouver Whitecaps, Manchester United, Liverpool, Bolton Wanderers, Manchester City (loan), Fulham, Hartlepool United, Doncaster Rovers, Melbourne Knights
International: England, 59 caps, 9 goals

— SHEARER STATS —

Some number-crunching in honour of Newcastle United's record goalscorer:

Shearer's overall league record:
Alan Shearer career record (Premiership/Div1): 558 games, 283 goals
Alan Shearer career record (all comps): 733 games, 379 goals

By club:

Southampton	140 starts (18 as substitute)	43 goals
Blackburn Rovers	165 starts (6 as substitute)	130 goals
Newcastle United	395 starts (9 as substitute)	206 goals

By season:

Season Club	Games (League)	(all)	Goals (League)	(all)
1987/88 Southampton	5	5	3	3
1988/89 Southampton	10	10	0	0
1989/90 Southampton	26	35	3	5
1990/91 Southampton	36	48	4	14
1991/92 Southampton	41	60	13	21
1992/93 Blackburn Rovers	21	26	16	22
1993/94 Blackburn Rovers	40	48	31	34
1994/95 Blackburn Rovers	42	49	34	37
1995/96 Blackburn Rovers	35	48	31	37
1996/97 Newcastle United	31	40	25	28
1997/98 Newcastle United	17	23	2	7
1998/99 Newcastle United	30	40	14	21
1999/00 Newcastle United	37	50	23	30
2000/01 Newcastle United	19	23	5	7
2001/02 Newcastle United	37	46	23	27
2002/03 Newcastle United	35	48	17	25
2003/04 Newcastle United	37	51	22	28
2004/05 Newcastle United	28	42	7	19
2005/06 Newcastle United	32	41	10	14

Note: Alan Shearer's 63 full England caps and 30 goals are not included in these figures.

— OOPS! —

Toon-related radio and TV commentary foul-ups include:

Rodney Marsh
The former Fulham, Queens Park Rangers, Manchester City and England footballer found himself out of a job in January 2005 after an on-air joke backfired on him.

During the live phone-in programme *You're on Sky Sports*, Marsh commented that: "David Beckham would never move to Newcastle because of all the trouble caused by the Toon Army in Asia."

Coming just weeks after the devastating tsunami tidal wave was estimated to have claimed 300,000 lives, reaction was swift and Marsh's contract was torn up. A Sky Sports spokesman said: "These remarks should never have been made and Sky would like to offer its apologies to those who were offended."

Marsh himself said: "I am hugely disappointed in myself for letting them down. I apologise unreservedly for any offence I caused by my thoughtless and inappropriate comment I made last night. My intention was to make a light-hearted football joke."

Ian Payne, radio reporter
"Tomorrow, the whole of Newcastle versus Manchester United."

Tom Tyrrell, radio reporter
"Newcastle are finally going to end their London bogey. They haven't won there since . . . a long time ago. That would be a ghost . . . no an albatross off their necks."

Jim White, Sky Sports presenter
"Michael Owen to Newcastle is the biggest transfer of the season so far – and it will be until there's a bigger one."

Brian Moore, TV presenter
"Alongside me is Keggy Keegle, sorry Kevin Keegle."

Ian St John, Channel 5 pundit
During an advert break before the Croatia Zagreb versus Newcastle Champions League qualifier in 1997, St John passed the time by picking his nose. Unfortunately for him he failed to realise that the cameras were still rolling – and his nasal explorations were being beamed live on the scoreboard at the Maksimir Stadium.

— THE NAME NOW LEAVING
FROM PLATFORM NINE —

The name of Newcastle United once adorned the sides of a railway locomotive – but only the most keen-eyed would ever have seen it for themselves thanks to some apparent skulduggery on the part of the London and North Eastern Railway.

Often referred to as the 'Footballer Class', the B17 class of locomotives were designed by Sir Herbert Nigel Gresley, with 73 built at various locations between 1928 and 1937; 25 of which were given the names of English football clubs.

No. 2858 rolled out of Darlington Works on May 28th 1936 resplendent in green livery and with a nameplate incorporating a brass football, black and white decoration and the name 'Newcastle United'.

However, when the locomotive appeared at a railway exhibition in Romford just ten days later, it bore nameplates proclaiming it to be 'The Essex Regiment' – a name it carried until it was withdrawn from operating service and scrapped in December 1959.

The reasons for the change of heart were never fully explained, although club rivalries may have played some part in the decision. In the event, the B17 class were never a common sight in the North East due to a lack of power.

It's presumed that the 'Newcastle United' nameplates were scrapped as they have never surfaced, but a replica nameplate was commissioned and presented to the club in 2003 by Magpies fan and railway enthusiast David Tyreman.

— 'THE PIRATE' —

Newcastle chairman between 1964 and 1978, Lord Westwood remains a controversial figure despite passing away in 1991.

Much of the blame for the stagnation of the club in the 1970s and a lack of investment in the team and stadium is laid at his door by commentators of the era. Westwood, who was popularly known as 'The Pirate' due to an eye patch that covered his right eye (the result of a car accident), resigned as chairman in 1978 and left the Board altogether in 1981 – refusing on both occasions to use his own funds to underwrite financial rescue packages.

A one-time president of the Football League, it was said of Westwood that he would swap his patch to cover his good eye when watching Newcastle lose.

— FANZINES —

August 1988 saw the publication of the first issue of *The Mag* – an unofficial fanzine composed and compiled by a small group of Newcastle fans and billing itself as an independent supporters' magazine

Priced at 50p and with a cover including a photograph of a young and trendily attired Paul Gascoigne, *The Mag* certainly wasn't short of targets to snipe at.

Issues covered in this debut copy included the enduring racist chanting at St James' Park and the unwelcome presence of National Front supporters selling their racist publication *Bulldog* outside the ground on matchdays.

Also the subject of grumbling was the continued lack of covered standing accommodation at the stadium, which at the time still had two open ends.

The threat from proposed new coverage of games on satellite TV was also mentioned, while the departure of Peter Beardsley earlier in the year to Liverpool – allegedly to fund the cost of constructing the Milburn Stand – was also discussed.

Fast forward to the end of the 2007/08 season and *The Mag* has enjoyed an uninterrupted run and reached issue number 228, which marks its twentieth anniversary.

A sister publication *True Faith* first appeared at the start of the 1999/00 season, taking a more left-field look at Toon-related events and providing a platform for those writing about football culture. By mid 2008, it had reached issue 66.

Various other unofficial Newcastle United fanzines have come and gone over the years, including:

Black and White
The Geordie Times
The Giant Awakes
Half Mag Half Biscuit
Jim's Bald Heid
The Mighty Quinn
The Number Nine
Oh Wi Ye Naa
Once Upon A Tyne
Talk of the Toon
Talk of the Tyne
Toon Army News

— CHALKED OFF? —

Newcastle United were involved in one of the most controversial incidents in the history of the FA Cup, when they faced Arsenal at Wembley in the 1932 final.

Arsenal took the lead in the 12th minute, but Newcastle equalised seven minutes before half-time with what *The Times* described as 'the most controversial goal in English football history'.

Chasing a ball down the line, Newcastle's Jimmy Richardson stretched to reach the ball and delivered a cross into Jack Allen to score. However, many in the stadium felt the ball had crossed the line before Richardson crossed it.

Allen struck again on 72 minutes to give his side the win and the distinction of being the first side ever to have come from behind to win a Wembley FA Cup final.

However some discontent among supporters and Arsenal officials was evident, with claims that the ball had gone out of play before the first goal strengthened by newspaper reports of the game and photographs which appeared to back up the claims. The incident even knocked Adolf Hitler's victory in the Prussian elections off the front page.

And the conviction that there had been a miscarriage grew the following week when British Movietone News footage of the goal was shown in cinemas that purported to show that the ball was out of play via primitive freeze frame technology.

Invoking the spirit of future Gunners boss Arsene Wenger, Newcastle goalscorer Jack Allen told *The Guardian* newspaper: "From my position I could not see whether it had gone out of play or not."

While Richardson similarly claimed: "I was concentrating so hard on reaching the ball that I couldn't tell you whether it was over the line or not."

Match referee Percy Harper remained adamant, however: "I gave the goal in accordance with the rules and regulations of the Football Association – it was definitely a goal. The ball was definitely in play. I was so certain that the goal was good that I did not even consider it necessary to consult the linesman, and I am still just as certain. I was, of course, well up with the play, and was in a position to see the incident clearly. Whatever the film may appear to show will not make me alter my opinion."

— CELEBRITY FANS PART I —

A selection of celebrity supporters often associated with the club:

Ant and Dec
Geordie-born duo who have been present at games and kit launches etc since the early *Byker Grove* days and were on-field hosts for the Alan Shearer testimonial match in 2006.

Tony Blair
Former Prime Minister and MP for Sedgefield between 1983 and 2007.

Bryan Ferry
Popular singer, both with seventies band Roxy Music and as a solo artist.

Brendan Foster
Former distance runner who won Olympic Bronze and Commonwealth Gold medals before retiring and founding the Great North Run in 1981. Clad in a black and white vest, 'Big Bren' won a 3,000 metres challenge race round the Wembley pitch before the 1974 FA Cup Final between Newcastle and Liverpool. He had told the FA he would run in exchange for ten tickets to the match!

Robson Green
TV actor and St James' Park season ticket holder.

Steve Harmison
The Durham and England fast bowler is a season ticket holder and goes to away games when his cricketing commitments permit. (See *Magpies Cricket Club*, page 70)

Tim Healey
Comic actor who guested as stadium PA announcer before the Oxford United home game in 1992. Unfortunately, his slightly colourful repartee was never to grace the airwaves again.

Brian Johnson
Once the lead singer of Tyneside rock band, Geordie, Johnson's distinctive gravelly tones have been heard fronting mega-grossing heavy metallers AC/DC since 1980. A devoted fan, he played the part of an exiled Toon fan in the film *Goal* and once made an unsuccessful bid to join the Newcastle United board. His former wife Carol is now married to ex-Newcastle striker Malcolm Macdonald.

Mark Knopfler
Supremely talented guitarist and former member of Dire Straits. His instrumental composition 'Going Home' has become synonymous with the club in recent years – often called 'Local Hero' after the film soundtrack it appears on.

Gabby Logan
When known as plain Gabby Yorath (daughter of former Leeds and Wales star Terry), the TV presenter graduated from Durham University into a job on local radio, interviewing players on the touchline at St James' Park. She memorably wrote in *The Times* in April 2007 that:

"St James' Park is up there with the Bernabéu and the Nou Camp for atmosphere and grandeur. I will always love it — I can understand why people have their ashes spread on the pitch and why fans arrive at the ground three hours early. It's possible to appreciate other stadiums, for sure, but you'll only really ever love one."

John McCririck
Horse racing commentator and reality TV contestant.

— FULL SPEED AHEAD —

Gary Speed has made more appearances in the Premiership than any other player, with just under half of those coming in a Newcastle shirt.

Premiership Top Ten Appearance makers:

Player	Total	For Newcastle
Gary Speed	535	213
David James	511	–
Ryan Giggs	492	–
Sol Campbell	449	–
Alan Shearer	441	303
Gareth Southgate	426	–
Teddy Sheringham	418	–
Andy Cole	413	58
Emile Heskey	403	–
Frank Lampard	390	–

— AND HERE'S TO BOBBY MONCUR —

It's a well-worn path to the banks of the Danube, striped goalposts and a funny shaped cup, but Newcastle's Fairs Cup success of 1968/69 remains the last bona fide trophy that the Magpies have won.

Beginning with a resounding home victory on the Magpies' European debut, five two-legged ties brought the club to a home and away final games against Hungarian side Ujpesti Dozsa:

Route to Glory:

Opponent	Score	Newcastle scorer(s)	Crowd
Feyenoord (h)	4–0	Scott, Robson, Gibb, Davies	46,348
Feyenoord (a)	0–2		45,000
Sporting Lisbon (a)	1–1	Scott	9,000
Sporting Lisbon (h)	1–0	Robson	53,747
Real Zaragoza (a)	2–3	Davies, Robson	22,000
Real Zaragoza (h)	2–1	Robson, Gibb	56,055
Vitoria Setubal (h)	5–1	Foggon, Robson, Davies, Robson, Gibb	57,662
Vitoria Setubal (a)	1–3	Davies	34,000
Rangers (a)	0–0		75,580
Rangers (h)	2–0	Scott, Sinclair	59,303
Ujpesti Dozsa (h)	3–0	Moncur 2, Scott	59,234
Ujpesti Dozsa (a)	3–2	Moncur, Arentoft, Foggon	34,000

Final line-ups:

May 29th 1969 St James' Park, Newcastle:
McFaul, Craig, Burton, Moncur, Clark, Gibb, Arentoft, Scott, Davies, Robson, Sinclair (Foggon) Substitutes unused: Hope, Craggs
Goal times: Moncur 63, 71, Scott 84

June 11th 1969 Megyeri Stadium, Budapest:
McFaul, Craig, Burton, Moncur, Clark, Gibb, Arentoft, Scott (Foggon), Davies, Robson, Sinclair. Substitutes unused: Hope, McNamee
Goal times: Moncur 46, Arentoft 53, Foggon 68 (For Ujpesti: Bene 30, Gorocs 43)

Across the 12 ties, Newcastle named 25 players, of whom four were on the field for every minute: Willie McFaul, Tommy Gibb, Wyn Davies and 'Pop' Robson. A further two – Frank Clark and Jimmy Scott – appeared in all 12 ties at some stage. The other 16 players utilised were: Geoff Allen, Benny Arentoft, Albert Bennett, Ollie Burton, John Craggs, David Craig, Keith Dyson, Dave Elliott, Alan Foggon, Ron Guthrie, Arthur Horsfield, Jim Iley, John McNamee, Bobby Moncur,

Jackie Sinclair and Graham Winstanley. Non-appearing goalkeeping substitutes Gordon Marshall, John Hope and Dave Clarke completed the squad.

— DOCTOR FEELGOOD —

When Michael Owen stepped on to the field at Reading's Madejski Stadium on April 30th 2007 after a ten-month absence through injury, Newcastle fans once again had cause to thank a 69-year-old native of Texas who has never seen a live Premiership football match.

The Steadman-Hawkins Clinic in Vail, Colorado, USA has hosted a steady stream of injured sportsmen and women including various golfers, tennis players and Olympic athletes.

A world-renowned Orthopaedics expert, Doctor Richard Steadman has performed over 10,000 operations in his career. However, it is for his work in curing career-threatening knee problems on a trio of Newcastle centre forwards – Alan Shearer, Craig Bellamy and Michael Owen – that Dr Steadman has become something of a hero to Toon fans. In addition, he also carried out a successful knee operation in 2001 on Leeds United striker Michael Bridges, who later signed for Newcastle.

The walls of Steadman's clinic are decorated with replica shirts signed by many of his grateful patients, as well as a signed photograph of Alan Shearer with the dedication: "Just when I was getting frustrated with the pain, you took it away. Many, many thanks."

And as well as the work carried out by Steadman, his colleague Doctor Marc Philippon has also done his bit for the black and white cause. The hip specialist carried out an operation on Newcastle striker Shola Ameobi, who had played in discomfort for over two years before finally breaking down in September 2006.

Ameobi was playing again by April 2007 and also made his first-team comeback alongside Owen in Berkshire that night – watched by Dr Steadman over in the USA on satellite TV.

As Steadman said to Owen as he presented him with a DVD of his operation, "Whatever makes you retire from football, it won't be your knee."

Steadman the Magpie Healer, the complete record:

Player	Injury	Operation	Playing again
Alan Shearer	Right knee	January 2000	August 2001
Craig Bellamy	Right knee	April 2002	September 2002
Craig Bellamy	Left knee	October 2003	January 2004
Michael Owen	Right knee	July 2006	April 2007
Michael Owen	Right knee	September 2006	April 2007

— FOR FORK'S SAKE —

Having ended their four-year winless run in London at the 30th time of asking, Newcastle's players were entitled to feel pleased with themselves on December 19th 2001.

An eventful 3–1 win against Arsenal at Highbury had propelled Newcastle to the top of the Premiership. Unbeknown to them however, a higher power had been at work.

In the following day's *Evening Chronicle* cutlery-bending psychic Uri Geller described how he led the Spoon Army for one night:

"I knew the team would win. I am so happy for everyone who supports them. It was exactly what I said.

"I arrived late and had no ticket. But the moment I got out of the car and touched the Highbury stadium, the Arsenal player Ray Parlour was sent off.

"I started screaming and shouting for Newcastle to win. And soon after the start of the second half I said to my friend that Shearer would score from a penalty. That was half an hour before it happened. But I knew it. I knew the team would win. I am so happy for everyone who supports them. It was exactly what I said.

"While Newcastle were scoring their winning goals I was running round the outside of the ground 11 times to lift the hoodoo.

"I even predicted the 3–1 scoreline after I got to the ground. I sat in the car and listened to the game on the radio. And after Arsenal scored I decided it was time to act.

"There was a lot to do with the number 11. Newcastle had not won in 29 games and two plus nine is 11. Number 11 is very mystical and powerful. So I ran around the ground 11 times. The facts speak for themselves.

"I hope Newcastle will win the league but I have to concentrate and see. Right now I have done what you wanted.

"It is almost a guarantee the team will win when I have a moment to talk to the players in the dressing room, I wasn't able to do that last night but I was physically close to them which is important."

Despite Uri's powers, Newcastle failed to win the Premiership that season, ultimately finishing back in fourth, some 16 points behind champions Arsenal. And things got worse for Geller, with the Exeter City co-chairman seeing his "beloved" Grecians relegated into the Football Conference in 2003 – despite bringing his pal Michael Jackson to visit their St James' Park ground.

— EDSON ENCOUNTER —

The end of the 1971/72 season saw Newcastle embark on an Asian tour, which included visits to Thailand, Hong Kong and Iran.

Providing the opposition in Hong Kong were the Brazilian side Santos, whose most famous player Edson Arantes do Nascimento (aka Pele) was in their line-up.

Newcastle led 2–1 at the interval thanks to a long-range effort from Tony Green and a John Tudor header – Pele at this stage having been virtually anonymous.

However, that all changed in the second half as Pele set to work, scoring a hat-trick in a devastating 15-minute spell that enthralled those fans present and ensured that Newcastle lost 2–4.

John Tudor recalled: "The delicate close-control skills, the amazing acceleration, the powerhouse shooting had the crowd in ecstasy. It was like trying to stop a flash of lightning."

His job done, Pele then left the field – pausing only to shake hands with the stunned Newcastle players.

— DREAM STARTS PART I —

Newcastle United players who scored a hat-trick or better on their competitive debut for the Magpies:

Year	Player	Opponent/venue	
1946	Len Shackleton	Newport County (h)	6 goals
1989	Mick Quinn	Leeds United (h)	4 goals
1926	Bob McKay	West Bromwich Albion (h)	3 goals
1935	Wilf Bott	Bury (h)	3 goals

Shackleton's debut came in an amazing 13–0 success in which his new team-mate Charlie Wayman (who scored four in the game) missed a penalty in the opening moments.

Coming in the days before television coverage and the FA's Dubious Goals Committee, 'Shack' was credited with his sixth and Newcastle's 13th, although Newport's Ken Wookey may have got the final touch. What isn't in doubt, however, is his incredible scoring rate, as he notched his second, third and fourth goals in this game within a 155-second period.

— IS THIS THE WAY TO . . . ? —

Current Football League stadia that Newcastle have never visited competitively:

Accrington Stanley (Fraser Eagle Stadium)*
Barnet (Underhill Stadium)*
Boston United (York Street Stadium)
Brighton and Hove Albion (Withdean Stadium)*
Bristol Rovers (Memorial Stadium)*
Chester City (Saunders Honda Stadium)
Coventry City (Ricoh Arena)*
Darlington (Balfour Webnet Darlington Arena)
Doncaster Rovers (Keepmoat Stadium)*
Hartlepool United (Victoria Park)
Huddersfield Town (Galpharm Stadium)
Hull City (Kingston Communication Stadium)
Macclesfield Town (Moss Rose)*
Millwall (The New Den)*
Milton Keynes Dons (Stadium:mk)*
Northampton Town (Sixfields Stadium)*
Rochdale (Spotland)
Scunthorpe United (Glanford Park)
Swansea City (The Liberty Stadium)*
Torquay United (Plainmoor)
Walsall (Bescot Stadium)
Wycombe Wanderers (Adams Park)*
Yeovil Town (Huish Park)

*Stadia yet to be visited at any level of football eg: friendlies, reserves etc.

— NEWCASTLE'S TOP LEAGUE CUP SCORERS —

Player	Total
Malcolm Macdonald	12
Andy Cole	8
Alan Gowling	7
Alan Shearer	7
Gavin Peacock	5
Peter Beardsley	4
Craig Bellamy	4
Mickey Burns	4
Paul Cannell	4

— UPPERS AND DOWNERS —

Since Newcastle United first took their place in Division Two for the 1893/94 season, the club has enjoyed – and endured – no fewer than nine movements between the top two divisions in England.

Season	Move	Movers
1897/98	Promoted	Burnley, **Newcastle**
	Relegated	None
1933/34	Relegated	**Newcastle**, Sheffield United
	Promoted	Grimsby Town, Preston North End
1947/48	Promoted	Birmingham City, **Newcastle**
	Relegated	Blackburn Rovers, Grimsby Town
1960/61	Relegated	**Newcastle**, Preston North End
	Promoted	Ipswich Town, Sheffield United
1964/65	Promoted	**Newcastle**, Northampton Town
	Relegated	Wolverhampton Wanderers, Birmingham City
1977/78	Relegated	West Ham United, **Newcastle**, Leicester City
	Promoted	Bolton Wanderers, Southampton, Tottenham Hotspur
1983/84	Promoted	Chelsea, Sheffield Wednesday, **Newcastle**
	Relegated	Birmingham City, Notts County, Wolverhampton Wanderers
1988/89	Relegated	Middlesbrough, West Ham United, **Newcastle**
	Promoted	Chelsea, Manchester City, Crystal Palace*
1992/93	Promoted	**Newcastle**, West Ham United, Swindon Town*
	Relegated	Crystal Palace, Middlesbrough, Nottingham Forest

(*promoted via the Play-Offs)

Apart from the 1992/93 promotion, all of the above saw Newcastle move between Football League Divisions One and Two, the exception coming that season, when the Magpies moved from the renamed Division One to the Premier League.

— PACK OF THREE —

Hat-trick pioneers for the club:

First in Division Two: Willie Thompson in a 6–0 home win over Woolwich Arsenal on September 30th 1893.

First in Division One: Jock Peddie in an 8–0 home win over Notts County on October 26th 1901.

First in FA Cup: Bill Appleyard in a 5–1 home win over Grimsby Town on March 7th 1908.

First in Anglo-Italian Cup: Malcolm Macdonald in a 5–1 home win over Crystal Palace on May 21st 1973.

First in League Cup: Malcolm Macdonald in a 6–0 home win over Doncaster Rovers on October 8th 1973.

First in Premiership: Peter Beardsley in a 4–0 home win over Wimbledon on October 30th 1993.

First in UEFA Cup: Robert Lee in a 5–0 away win over Royal Antwerp on September 13th 1994.

First in Champions League: Faustino Asprilla in a 3–2 home win over Barcelona on September 17th 1997.

— WORLD OF SPORT —

Although it has been said that some of the performances served up at St James' Park have borne precious little resemblance to association football, there have been a range of other sports staged at the stadium since United moved in.

Miss Netty Honeyball and her British Ladies Football Club played an exhibition match in 1895, while the first of a number of baseball games were held in June 1918.

At other times, athletics meetings with both track and field events have taken place, along with cycling challenges. The stadium even hosted sheepdog trials in 1944, helping the war effort by raising funds for the adjacent Royal Victoria Infirmary. But perhaps the most famous non-football sports team to visit St James' Park were the Harlem Globetrotters, who made two appearances during the 1950s.

In latter years no additional sporting events have taken place on the field – with plans to relocate the Newcastle Falcons Rugby Union side being jettisoned when the decision to redevelop St James' Park rather than build a new stadium in Leazes Park was taken. However, the club-sponsored Lister Storm GT racing car did make an appearance before one game, painted in the black and white colours that it raced in at Le Mans in 1997.

— GONE FOR A BURTON —

On 15th April 1895 Newcastle played the final game of their second season in Division Two, with a tenth place finish assured. However, their away fixture against Burton Wanderers was to prove memorable for all the wrong reasons, as their Derby Turn ground proved to be venue for United's record defeat.

Trailing 0–4 at half time, the final score was 0–9 in favour of the home side, who avenged their 6–3 defeat on Tyneside earlier that season. For a team who had only managed four clean sheets in their previous 31 league and cup games that season, conceding goals wasn't a major shock to Newcastle and their porous defence.

The rigours of playing two home games in the three days running up to the Wanderers game may be a partial excuse. However, the following season saw all but two of the Newcastle side who appeared in the record defeat shipped out.

Some 38 years later, the Magpies 'celebrated' the anniversary of their record loss by slipping to a mere 1–6 defeat away to Leeds United.

— FAMILIAR FOES —

Since the two sides first met home and away within a few weeks of each other in September 1893 in Division Two, Newcastle United's most frequent competitive opponents have been Arsenal (known as 'Woolwich Arsenal' until 1914).

While St James' Park has remained the home venue for the Magpies throughout, Arsenal have moved twice since hosting Newcastle for the first time at their Manor Ground in Plumstead. A move across the Thames came in 1913, with Newcastle's debut at Highbury in August 1919 marked by a 1–0 away win. November 2006 then saw the Magpies visit the Emirates Stadium for the first time, a 1–1 draw being the outcome.

Newcastle's top ten most played opponents:

Opponent	P	W	D	L	F	A
Arsenal	163	65	36	62	228	228
Manchester City	159	70	37	52	241	215
Liverpool	157	45	38	74	193	267
Everton	154	62	32	60	232	226
Aston Villa	147	63	31	53	231	236
Manchester United	146	39	34	73	216	283
Chelsea	143	47	36	60	179	212
Tottenham Hotspur	139	52	30	57	209	218
Sunderland	139	51	45	43	210	205
Blackburn	133	55	29	49	202	195

— HOME FROM HOME —

Aside from St James' Park, the venue at which Newcastle have earned the most Premiership points is Villa Park. Here's the complete record of how and where the Magpies' have earned their points on the road since promotion in 1993.

Opposition	Frequency	Record	Pts
Aston Villa	15 visits	6 wins, 5 draws, 4 defeats	23
Middlesbrough	12 visits	6 wins, 4 draws, 2 defeats	22
Leeds United	11 visits	6 wins, 3 draws, 2 defeats	21
Tottenham Hotspur	15 visits	6 wins, 1 draw, 8 defeats	19
West Ham United	13 visits	5 wins, 3 draws, 5 defeats	18
Everton	15 visits	4 wins, 3 draws, 8 defeats	15
Sunderland	7 visits	4 wins, 3 draws, 0 defeats	15
Sheffield Wednesday	7 visits	3 wins, 3 draws, 1 defeat	12
Arsenal	15 visits	3 wins, 2 draws, 10 defeats	11
Coventry City	8 visits	3 wins, 2 draws, 3 defeats	11
Blackburn Rovers	13 visits	2 wins, 4 draws, 7 defeats	10
Derby County	7 visits	3 wins, 1 draw, 3 defeats	10
Leicester City	8 visits	2 wins, 4 draws, 2 defeats	10
Bolton Wanderers	9 visits	3 wins, 0 draws, 6 defeats	9
Crystal Palace	3 visits	3 wins, 0 draws, 0 defeats	9
Fulham	7 visits	3 wins, 0 draws, 4 defeats	9
Birmingham City	5 visits	1 win, 4 draws, 0 defeats	7
Charlton Athletic	8 visits	1 win, 4 draws, 3 defeats	7
Ipswich Town	4 visits	2 wins, 1 draw, 1 defeat	7
Manchester City	10 visits	1 win, 4 draws, 5 defeats	7
Nottingham Forest	4 visits	1 win, 3 draws, 0 defeats	6
Queens Park Rangers	3 visits	2 wins, 0 draws, 1 defeat	6
Southampton	12 visits	1 win, 3 draws, 8 defeats	6
Liverpool	15 visits	1 win, 2 draws, 12 defeats	5
Manchester United	15 visits	0 wins, 5 draws, 10 defeats	5
West Bromwich Albion	3 visits	1 win, 2 draws, 0 defeats	5
Chelsea	15 visits	0 wins, 4 draws, 11 defeats	4
Portsmouth	5 visits	0 wins, 4 draws, 1 defeat	4
Wimbledon	7 visits	0 wins, 4 draws, 3 defeats	4
Norwich City	3 visits	1 win, 0 draws, 2 defeats	3
Oldham Athletic	1 visit	1 win, 0 draws, 0 defeats	3
Sheffield United	2 visits	1 win, 0 draws, 1 defeat	3
Watford	2 visits	0 wins, 2 draws, 0 defeats	2
Barnsley	1 visit	0 wins, 1 draw, 0 defeats	1
Bradford City	2 visits	0 wins, 1 draw, 1 defeat	1

Swindon Town	1 visit	0 wins, 1 draw, 0 defeats	1
Wolverhampton Wanderers	1 visit	0 wins, 1 draw, 0 defeats	1
Reading	2 visits	0 wins, 0 draws, 2 defeats	0
Wigan Athletic	3 visits	0 wins, 0 draws, 3 defeats	0
Wigan Athletic	2 visits	0 wins, 0 draws, 2 defeats	0

— BLACK AND WHITE TV —

August 22nd 1964 saw the opening fixtures of the new football season and the debut of a new Saturday evening programme on BBC2, entitled *Match of The Day*. The debut transmission brought the nation highlights of the Division One match at Anfield, where reigning champions Liverpool overcame Arsenal 3–2.

Audience reaction was positive and within months the programme had branched out to cover the occasional lower league fixture. That policy brought fresh-faced young presenter Frank Bough and the cameras to a muddy Brisbane Road on February 20th 1965, to record Leyton Orient's home clash with Second Division leaders Newcastle United. Not for the last time though, Newcastle supporters endured a trial by TV, Joe Elwood netting twice for the Os to cancel out Ron McGarry's penalty.

The BBC then ignored the promoted Magpies in the following season, before covering them once again as they travelled to London in October 1966 – *Match of the Day* having by now graduated to BBC1. Unfortunately, things were little better, Arsenal beating the Toon at Highbury through a Michael Boot effort and a Frank Clark own goal.

A first visit by the cameras to St James' Park came two days before Christmas 1967, Newcastle earning a point in a 1–1 draw with Liverpool. Jimmy Scott scored for the Magpies, Ian St.John netting for the visitors.

Finally, after a televised 0–0 draw at Highbury in February 1968, Newcastle at last tasted victory in front of a nationwide TV audience for the first time on April 12th 1969, as a 'Pop' Robson penalty and Alan Foggon's strike accounted for Manchester United in front of an exuberant Tyneside crowd.

Newcastle's *Match of the Day* debut in colour came in September 1970, when two 'Pop' Robson goals were enough to beat West Ham at Upton Park.

— AWAY FROM THE NUMBERS —

As well as becoming professional footballers, a number of Newcastle United players have shown talent in other branches of sport, including:

Roy Aitken	Basketball
William Aitken	Sprinting
John Anderson	Gaelic Football
John Bailey	Boxing
Jimmy Boyd	Indoor Bowls
Jesse Carver	Weightlifting
David Edgar	Ice Hockey
Tommy Ghee	Water Polo
Chris Guthrie	Fly Fishing
Bobby Moncur	Yachting
Archie Mowatt	Cycling
Ron McGarry	Rugby League
Tommy Pearson	Golf
Jamie Scott	Pole Vaulting
Nigel Walker	Rugby Union
Ron Williams	Crown Green Bowls

— NO CUP OF CHEER —

Milk Cup or Littlewoods, Rumbelows, Coca Cola, Worthington or Carling Cup – call it what you like the 48-year history of the League Cup has been mostly miserable for the Magpies.

Although the competition was first staged in the 1960/61 season, Newcastle actually failed to register a victory until some three years later, a win over Preston North End halting a run of four defeats and two draws.

Of 119 ties played to the start of the 2008/09 season, in the club's complete League Cup history the Magpies have won 51 matches, drawn 19 and lost 49, scoring 183 times and conceding 156 goals (not including penalty shoot-outs).

Newcastle have both scored and conceded seven goals in a League Cup match: enduring a 2–7 reverse at Old Trafford against Manchester United in 1976 and registering a 7–1 success at Meadow Lane against Notts County in 1993.

— THE WIT AND WISDOM OF
SIR BOBBY ROBSON —

"Tickets are selling like cream cakes"

"Rob Lee didn't have a number. Shearer was out of favour. There was
no discipline. Players were going upstairs to eat whenever they wanted,
using mobile phones whenever they wanted, the whole thing needed
an overhaul."
Early days in the Newcastle job

"If we invite any player up to the Quayside to see the girls and then
up to our magnificent stadium, we will be able to persuade any player
to sign."
The attractions of Tyneside

"We can't replace Gary Speed. Where do you get an experienced player
like him with a left foot and a head?"
A quick anatomy lesson

"If you see him stripped, he's like Mike Tyson. But he doesn't bite like Tyson."
Talking about Titus Bramble

"All right, Bellamy came on at Liverpool and did well, but everybody thinks that he's the saviour, he's Jesus Christ. He's not Jesus Christ."
Playing down the cult of Craig

"I handled Bellamy for four years. Graeme Souness couldn't stick four months."
More Craig claims

"We mustn't be despondent. We don't have to play them every week – although we do play them next week as it happens."
Having lost 2–0 to Arsenal, Newcastle prepared to face them in the FA Cup just days later.

"They can't be monks – we don't want them to be monks, we want them to be football players because a monk doesn't play football at this level."
Responding in somewhat bizarre fashion to criticism of player discipline

"When he gets his legs in tandem with his body, we'll make him a player."
On Shola Ameobi

"Tickets are selling like cream cakes."
Before a big match

"We didn't get the rub of the dice."
Mixing his metaphors

"There's a smell of the north-east which drew me back. I've got black and white blood and I'll stick at it because this is the team I love. I've got a big emotional feeling about it."
Smells like Toon Spirit, Bobby

"We are getting criticised for everything at the moment. There are knives going in my back and arrows flying around my head. But I don't think some people have any idea what we have had to do to keep the ship solvent."
Fighting for the Toon Army . . . the navy and the air force

"As for me, I still love it and I need it. I am more than ready for the challenge and I am determined to win at least one more trophy before I gallop off into the sunset."
Refuting retirement talk

"I say I'm almost over it but it will always rankle. I'll never forget what they did."
In unforgiving mood after his dismissal (1)

"I was kept in the dark with contracts and even transfers. Alex Ferguson, Arsène Wenger and Jose Mourinho know exactly what's going on at their clubs. That doesn't seem possible at Newcastle."
In unforgiving mood after his dismissal (2)

"My dad taught me the value of money and not to throw it away. My players have fame, adoration, money, women, fast cars and no mortgage ... in the real world, they'd be lucky to get £20,000 a year, never mind a week."
Telling his players a few home truths

— BLACK AND WHITE RIBBONS ON IT —

Despite failing to win the FA Cup since 1955, Newcastle remain inextricably linked with the world's oldest knockout competition.

Although both East End and West End had participated previously, Newcastle United made their FA Cup bow in January 1893, suffering a 2–3 home defeat at the hands of Middlesbrough.

Since that disappointing debut, the club have gone on to lift the trophy on six occasions, been beaten finalists seven more times and endured four unsuccessful appearances in the semi-finals.

However, the former final venue of Crystal Palace wasn't one that agreed with the Magpies, five visits to Sydenham in South London producing three defeats and two draws.

Final successes:

Season	Score	Opponent	Venue
1909/10	1–1	Barnsley	Crystal Palace, London
1909/10 (replay)	2–0	Barnsley	Goodison Park, Liverpool
1923/24	2–0	Aston Villa	Wembley
1931/32	2–1	Arsenal	Wembley
1950/51	2–0	Blackpool	Wembley
1951/52	1–0	Arsenal	Wembley
1954/55	3–1	Manchester City	Wembley

— NEWCASTLE LEGENDS: HUGHIE GALLACHER —

Hughie of the magic feet

Do you ken Hughie Gallacher the wee Scotch Lad?
The best centre forward Newcastle ever had
Contemporary children's rhyme

Having seen him net both goals for Scotland in an international match against England at Hampden Park in May 1925, Newcastle moved to sign Airdrieonians forward Hughie Gallacher.

However, it took the Magpies six months of protracted negotiations and a £6,500 transfer fee to land the diminutive but prolific 22-year-old goalscorer from Lanarkshire.

Gallacher netted twice on his debut in December 1925 as Newcastle drew 3–3 with Everton at St James' Park (Everton taking a point thanks to three goals from striker Dixie Dean, who Newcastle had attempted to sign before turning their attention to Gallacher).

Before leaving Tyneside in 1930, Gallacher gave the public four and a half goal-filled seasons – notching over 20 goals in each campaign he played in.

Captain of the side during the 1926/27 championship-winning

season, Gallacher's goals failed to bring further success to the club, and he fell foul of Newcastle's board of directors after a number of on-field clashes with both referees and opponents.

There was also the little matter of a colourful off-field lifestyle that saw him mix with supporters in local bars, dance halls and on occasion, Magistrates Courts.

After keeping a declining Newcastle side in the First Division, Gallacher was sold to Chelsea in May 1930 for £10,000 amid an outcry from supporters. A record attendance of almost 69,000 packed St James' to see Gallacher return with the Londoners in September of that year, although United's Jackie Cape deviated from the script by scoring the only goal of the game.

Gallacher was to return to Tyneside in 1938 after having appeared for Derby County, Notts County and Grimsby Town. He played one final season for Gateshead before settling in the town and holding down a variety of jobs, including a stint as a football writer.

And it was in Gateshead that he chose to take his own life, walking out in front of an approaching train in June 1957, having been called to appear in court to answer charges of maltreating his son.

Hughie Gallacher factfile
Born: Bellshill, north Lanarkshire, February 2nd 1903
Died: June 11th 1957
Newcastle career: 174 apps, 143 goals (1925–30)
Other clubs: Queen of the South, Airdrie, Chelsea, Derby County, Notts County, Grimsby Town, Gateshead
International: Scotland, 19 caps, 22 goals

— HOT SHOTS —

Newcastle United's top scorers in all competitive games:

Rank	Player	League	Cup	Total
1.	Alan Shearer	148	58	206
2.	Jackie Milburn	177	23	200
3.	Len White	142	11	153
4.	Hughie Gallacher	133	10	143
5.	Malcolm Macdonald	95	26	121
6.	Peter Beardsley	108	11	119
7.=	Bobby Mitchell	95	18	113
7.=	Tom McDonald	100	13	113
9.	Neil Harris	87	14	101
10.	Bryan 'Pop' Robson	82	15	97

— HUMAN BILLBOARDS —

The Magpies wore shirt advertising for the first time in 1980, with the Newcastle Breweries Blue Star logo appearing on the front of home and away shirts.

However, if match highlights were televised advertising was banned, so the presence of TV cameras at the opening day trip to Hillsborough saw Newcastle wearing unadorned yellow shirts.

The Blue Star debuted in a home draw with Notts County in August 1980, having also been worn at Gallowgate in a friendly against Leeds United earlier that month.

With shirt advertising still frowned upon by the FA, Newcastle were fined £1,000 for wearing strips with the logo in January 1981 against Sheffield Wednesday – even though the FA Cup tie wasn't televised.

Subsequent seasons saw the Blue Star continue to be used, until the brewer's deal expired at the end of the 1985/86 season.

Their replacements were Warrington-based brewer Greenall Whitley, who were looking to extend into the north-east. Shirts appeared emblazoned with 'Greenall's Beers' and a lifting of the TV ban extended the coverage.

The following seasons saw the word 'Beers' dropped from the shirts, before the deal ended after a home draw with Swindon Town in December 1990.

Three days later came the return of Newcastle Breweries and a Blue Star logo on the home kits and black 'McEwan's Lager' lettering on the away shirt. Fans owning now-obsolete Greenalls replica shirts were offered free Blue Star patches to mask the old advertisers!

The next change came in the opening weeks of the 1993/94 season, when home shirts appeared with 'McEwan's Lager' lettering in gold. These gave way to a white on black version of the same design, alternating with the Blue Star – an arrangement continuing into the following season. 1995, though, saw the Blue Star design downsized and relegated to use only on the away kit.

The Newcastle Brown Ale bottle logo replaced it on the home shirts, proving an instant hit and selling in unprecedented quantities. This had an early pre-season airing at Hartlepool in July 1995. That classic logo then survived numerous shirt design changes before a farewell in May 2000 as the brewery sponsorship ended with a home win against Arsenal.

There was one oddity in this era, however. An on-air alcohol advertising ban on French TV led Newcastle to wear shirts advertising holiday park brand 'Centerparcs' for their European tie at Monaco (logo-free shirts had been worn earlier that season in Metz).

Season 2000/01 saw cable TV company NTL's logo appearing on shirts, as part of a deal by which they acquired a stake in the club.

Local building society Northern Rock then began an association with Newcastle that continues up until the present day, shirts first going on sale in May 2003. The Magpies wore the new kit for the first time in the pre-season Asia Cup tournament against Birmingham City in July of that year, with subsequent kit design changes incorporating the 'Northern Rock' legend in varying colours including blue, gold and white.

— TRANSFER TRAIL II —

In chronological order, the record transfer fees received for Newcastle players are:

Player	Year	Fee	Received from
Bobby Templeton	1904	£375	Woolwich Arsenal
Albert Shepherd	1914	£1,500	Bradford City
Hughie Gallacher	1930	£10,000	Chelsea
Albert Stubbins	1946	£12,500	Liverpool
Len Shackleton	1948	£20,050	Sunderland
Ernie Taylor	1951	£25,000	Blackpool
George Eastham	1960	£47,500	Arsenal
Alan Suddick	1966	£63,000	Blackpool
Bryan Robson	1971	£120,000	West Ham United
Terry McDermott	1974	£170,000	Liverpool
Malcolm Macdonald	1976	£333,333	Arsenal
Irving Nattrass	1979	£375,000	Middlesbrough
Peter Withe	1980	£500,000	Aston Villa
Chris Waddle	1985	£590,000	Tottenham Hotspur
Peter Beardsley	1987	£1,900,000	Liverpool
Paul Gascoigne	1988	£2,300,000	Tottenham Hotspur
Andy Cole	1995	£7,000,000	Manchester United
Dietmar Hamann	1999	£7,500,000	Liverpool
Jonathan Woodgate	2004	£13,667,000	Real Madrid

— ALL THE WAY FROM GUAM —

While far from the only former Magpie to manage internationally, Willie McFaul's stint in charge of Guam is undoubtedly the most exotic (although Peter Withe's time with Thailand and Indonesia and John Burridge's Oman posting had their moments).

Having ended his association with Newcastle when removed from the manager's job in 1988, McFaul had returned to his native Northern Ireland and was coaching Ballymena-based side Cullybackey Blues when he was approached by FIFA to help develop the round ball game on Guam, a remote island in the western Pacific Ocean.

When he arrived in 1999, he discovered that the Guam FA (established by an Irish priest in 1975) had a few fundamental problems to overcome. An eight-team football league (including the fantastically-named Crushers) struggled for both fans and players, competing against the counter-attractions of baseball, basketball and American Football that were the staple sports on the military bases located on this US Dependency.

McFaul set about building a team, despite only having seven players at his first training session and losing more than one promising youngster to a college sports scholarship in the USA

A first foray into World Cup qualifying fixtures in November 2000, however, ended with his side making the headlines for the wrong reasons. Hampered by an arduous 48-hour journey to Iran to play in unfamiliar cold and wet conditions, McFaul's side (many of whom had never left Guam before) were thrashed 19–0 by Iran. They improved slightly two days later, going down 16–0 to Tajikistan.

Unbowed but struggling financially, Guam continued to play international football, competing in a qualifying tournament for the East Asian Cup in 2003, which required them to travel to Hong Kong.

Things started badly with an 11–0 loss to the hosts, followed by a 7–0 defeat to Chinese Taipei. However, although his side failed to score, McFaul took some satisfaction from successive 2–0 losses at the hands of Macao and Mongolia.

With the Japanese FA expressing an interest in developing the game on Guam and keen to bring in a coach with J-League experience, McFaul saw out his contract and departed in 2004, returning to a coaching position with the Northern Ireland FA.

— EARLY DOORS —

On Saturday January 18th 2003, Kevin Keegan's Manchester City side visited St James' Park with former Newcastle defenders Steve Howey and Sylvain Distin lining up for the visitors. Just before kick-off Alan Shearer was presented with the Goal of the Month award for a rapier strike against Everton the previous month – and was soon to be hogging the limelight again.

The match got underway with City defending the Leazes End and after kicking off, Howey played the ball back towards his goalkeeper Carlo Nash. Enter Shearer, who raced in and charged down Nash's attempted clearance before passing the ball into the unguarded net. The goal was timed at 10.4 seconds, with no other Newcastle player having touched the ball.

Newcastle went on to win the game 2–0, but Shearer's goal dominated the post-match coverage, being confirmed as the quickest strike of his career and the club's fastest-ever goal in top-flight football.

However, Jackie Milburn's effort in a Second Division game against Cardiff City on November 22nd 1947 is unofficially believed to be the fastest competitive goal for the club. No confirmed measure of the goal time exists, but the goalscorer himself later gave it as six seconds. The Magpies went on to win that match 4-1.

It was quickly established via TV replays that Shearer had just missed out on the record for the fastest ever Premiership goal. That accolade is held by Tottenham defender Ledley King, who netted in a fraction less than 10 seconds in a 3–3 draw against Bradford City at Valley Parade on December 9th 2000.

"I didn't think I had the legs to run half the length of the pitch in 10 seconds. I certainly couldn't have done it late in the game," said Shearer after the game.

— SUPERMAC'S QUICKFIRE GOAL —

Anecdotal evidence gives Malcolm Macdonald the record of scoring the fastest-ever goal in a public match involving the Newcastle first team. That happened at the start of a 7–3 pre-season friendly win over Scottish side St Johnstone on July 29th 1972.

Spotting Saints goalkeeper Derek Robertson still going through his warm-up routine, Macdonald took John Tudor's pass from the kick-off and netted from just inside the St Johnstone half – the goal unofficially timed at four seconds.

— CORNERS OF A FOREIGN FIELD —

Since Newcastle made their away bow in Rotterdam on a Tuesday
night back in September 1969, up until the start of the 2008/09 season
the club have played 60 away ties in various European competitions.
In those games, the Magpies have played in 24 countries against 53
sides in 52 different stadia:

Season/competition	Opponent	Venue
1968/69 Fairs Cup	Feyenoord	De Kuip Stadion, Rotterdam
1968/69 Fairs Cup	Sporting Lisbon	Arvelade Stadium, Lisbon
1968/69 Fairs Cup	Real Zaragoza	Romareda Stadium, Zaragoza
1968/69 Fairs Cup	Vitoria Setubal	Arvelade Stadium, Lisbon
1968/69 Fairs Cup	Glasgow Rangers	Ibrox Park, Glasgow
1968/69 Fairs Cup	Ujpesti Dozsa	Megyeri uti Stadion, Budapest
1969/70 Fairs Cup	Dundee United	Tannadice Park, Dundee
1969/70 Fairs Cup	FC Porto	Estadio das Antas, Porto
1969/70 Fairs Cup	Southampton	The Dell, Southampton
1969/70 Fairs Cup	Anderlecht	Parc Astrid, Brussels
1970/71 Fairs Cup	Inter Milan	Giuseppe Meazza, Milan
1970/71 Fairs Cup	Pecsi Dozsa	Pecsi Vasutas Sport Kor, Pecs
1977/78 UEFA Cup	Bohemians	Dalymount Park, Dublin
1977/78 UEFA Cup	SEC Bastia	Stade Armand Cesari de Furiani
1994/95 UEFA Cup	Royal Antwerp	Bosuil Stadion, Antwerp
1994/95 UEFA Cup	Atletico Bilbao	San Mames, Bilbao
1996/97 UEFA Cup	Halmstads	Orjans vall Stadion, Halmstad
1996/97 UEFA Cup	Ferencvaros	Ulloi uti Stadion, Budapest
1996/97 UEFA Cup	AS Metz	Stade Saint-Symphorien, Metz
1996/97 UEFA Cup	AS Monaco	Stade Louis II, Monaco
1997/98 Champions League	Croatia Zagreb	Maksimir Stadium, Zagreb
1997/98 Champions League	Dynamo Kiev	Olympic Stadium, Kiev
1997/98 Champions League	PSV Eindhoven	Philips Stadium, Eindhoven
1997/98 Champions League	Barcelona	Nou Camp, Barcelona

1998/89 Cup Winner's Cup	Partizan Belgrade	JNA Stadium, Belgrade
1999/00 UEFA Cup	CSKA Sofia	Balgarska Armia, Sofia
1999/00 UEFA Cup	Zurich	Letzigrund, Zurich
1999/00 UEFA Cup	AS Roma	Olympic Stadium, Rome
2001/02 Intertoto Cup	Sporting Lokeren	Daknam Stadium, Lokeren
2001/02 Intertoto Cup	1860 Munich	Olympic Stadium, Munich
2001/02 Intertoto Cup	Troyes	Stade de l'Aube, Troyes
2002/03 Champions League	NK Zeljeznicar	Kosevo Stadium, Sarajevo
2002/03 Champions League	Dynamo Kiev	Olympic Stadium, Kiev
2002/03 Champions League	Juventus	Stadio Delle Alpi, Turin
2002/03 Champions League	Feyenoord	De Kuip Stadion, Rotterdam
2002/03 Champions League	Barcelona	Nou Camp, Barcelona
2002/03 Champions League	Bayer Leverkusen	BayArena, Leverkusen
2002/03 Champions League	Inter Milan	Giuseppe Meazza, Milan
2003/04 Champions League	Partizan Belgrade	JNA Stadium, Belgrade
2003/04 UEFA Cup	NAC Breda	MyCom Stadium, Breda
2003/04 UEFA Cup	FC Basel	St Jakob Park, Basel
2003/04 UEFA Cup	Valerenga IF	Ullevaal Stadium, Oslo
2003/04 UEFA Cup	Real Mallorca	Estadi Son Moix, Palma
2003/04 UEFA Cup	PSV Eindhoven	Phillips Stadium, Eindhoven
2003/04 UEFA Cup	Olympique de Marseille	Stade Velodrome, Marseille
2004/05 UEFA Cup	Hapoel Bnei Sakhnin	Ramat Gan Stadium, Tel Aviv
2004/05 UEFA Cup	Panionios	Nea Smyrni Stadium, Athens
2004/05 UEFA Cup	Sochaux	Stade Auguste Bonal, Sochaux
2004/05 UEFA Cup	Heerenveen	Abe Lenstra Stadium, H'veen

2004/05 UEFA Cup	Olympiakos	Karaiskakis Stadium, Athens
2004/05 UEFA Cup	Sporting Lisbon	Arvelade Stadium, Lisbon
2005/06 Intertoto Cup	FK ZTS Dubnica	Mestsky Stadium, Dubnica
2005/06 Intertoto Cup	Deportivo La Coruna	Riazor Stadium, La Coruna
2006/07 Intertoto Cup	Lillestrom	Arasen Stadium, Oslo
2006/07 UEFA Cup	FK Ventspils	Skonto Stadium, Riga
2006/07 UEFA Cup	Levadia Tallinn	A. Le Coq Arena, Tallinn
2006/07 UEFA Cup	Palermo	Renzo Barbera, Palermo
2006/07 UEFA Cup	Eintracht Frankfurt	Commerzbank Arena, Frankfurt
2006/07 UEFA Cup	Zulte Waregem	Jules Otten Stadium, Ghent
2006/07 UEFA Cup	AZ Alkmaar	DSB Stadium, Alkmaar

— SEMI SUCCESS —

The full list of the club's semi-final triumphs:

Season	Score		Opponent	Venue
1904/05		1–0	Sheffield Wednesday	Hyde Road, Manchester
1905/06		2–0	Arsenal	Victoria Ground, Stoke
1907/08		6–0	Fulham	Anfield, Liverpool
1909/10		2–0	Swindon Town	White Hart Lane, London
1910/11		3–0	Chelsea	St.Andrews', Birmingham
1923/24		2–0	Manchester City	St.Andrews'
1931/32		2–1	Chelsea	Leeds Road, Huddersfield
1950/51		0–0	Wolverhampton Wanderers	Hillsborough, Sheffield
1950/51	(replay)	2–0	Wolverhampton Wanderers	Leeds Road
1951/52		0–0	Blackburn Rovers	Hillsborough
1951/52	(replay)	2–0	Blackburn Rovers	Elland Road, Leeds
1954/55		1–1	York City	Hillsborough
1954/55	(replay)	2–0	York City	Roker Park, Sunderland
1973/74		2–0	Burnley	Hillsborough
1997/98		1–0	Sheffield United	Old Trafford, Manchester
1998/99		2–0	Tottenham Hotspur	Old Trafford, Manchester

— DOUBLE AGENTS —

"This for me is the derby to end all derbies. It can rival Glasgow and is more passionate than Manchester, Liverpool and certainly London. Other derbies have never generated such huge feeling, such elation and deep gloom."

Bobby Moncur (who played on both sides) summing up the mood that envelops the region when Newcastle United and Sunderland face each on the field.

As well as Moncur, other players to have appeared in senior football for both sides are:

William Agnew	Stan Anderson
John Auld	Harry Bedford
Paul Bracewell	Michael Bridges
Ivor Broadis	Alan Brown
Steve Caldwell	Johnny Campbell
Michael Chopra	Jeff Clarke
Lee Clark	John Dowsey
Joe Devine	Robbie Elliott
Dave Elliott	Alan Foggon
Ray Ellison	Tommy Gibb
Howard Gayle	Thomas Grey
Shay Given	Tom Hall
Ron Guthrie	Mick Harford
Steve Hardwick	David Kelly
John Harvey	James Logan
Alan Kennedy	Bob McDermid
Andy McCombie	Bob McKay
Albert McInroy	James Raine
Bobby Moncur	Bobby Robinson
Ray Robinson	Tom Rowlandson
Bryan Robson	Jock Smith
Len Shackleton	Ernie Taylor
Colin Suggett	Thomas Urwin
Bob Thomson	Chris Waddle
Barry Venison	Billy Whitehurst
Nigel Walker	David Young
Dave Willis	Andy Cole

— MCC: MAGPIES CRICKET CLUB —

It's appropriate that a club which can trace their origins back to local cricket sides (see *From Eastenders to West End Boys*, page 1) should have signed a number of players who also showed some prowess with bat and ball.

Here's a Newcastle United XI made up of players who also shone in all white:

Player	On the books of
James Beaumont	Leicestershire
Kevin Brock	Wark (Northumberland League)
Ian Davies	Somerset
Harry Hardinge	Kent
Steve Harper	Easington (Durham Leagues)
Keith Kettleborough	Rotherham Town (Yorkshire League)
John Mitten	Leicestershire, Nottinghamshire, Lancashire
Peter Ramage	Tynemouth (North-East League)
Malcolm Scott	Northamptonshire
Arthur Turner	Hampshire
Sam Weaver	Derbyshire, Somerset

A willing 12th man for this imaginary side would be England pace bowler Steve Harmison, who cured his injury woes under the expert eyes of the Newcastle United medical staff. Magpies season ticket holder Harmison has gone on record as saying he'd willingly have given up cricket had he been given the opportunity to play professional football.

And the man nicknamed 'Toon Harmy' has appeared for the Magpies, lining up in 2005 alongside the likes of Robbie Elliott and Peter Ramage in a training ground friendly against the celebrity XI preparing for the Sky TV *The Match* series.

Barring an unexpected playing contract for Harmison though, the only player to have represented Newcastle United and played test match cricket remains Harry Hardinge – who did so some 13 years after leaving St James' Park.

The batsman widely known as 'Wally' in cricketing circles was selected for England in the Third Test against Australia in July 1921 at Headingley. Hardinge managed a knock of 25 in the first innings but fell after making just five in the second innings. The visiting side won by 219 runs, taking an unassailable 3–0 lead in the five-match series and thus retaining the Ashes.

— AD INFINITUM PART I —

A selection of TV advertisements that have featured former and future Newcastle United players and managers over the years:

Adidas (1996)
At the height of Newcastle's 'entertainers' fame, the iconic black and white home strip with Newcastle Brown Ale logo starred in a series of commercials for the shirt manufacturer. The adverts featured the likes of Kevin Keegan, Peter Beardsley and Les Ferdinand in various situations – including Keegan storming out of his office to remonstrate with Ferdinand, who is practicing his shooting by blazing the ball continually off the wall and disturbing 'the boss'. Prophetically, Keegan was prematurely aged for one shoot – appearing as a wrinkled, grey-haired old man relying on a walking stick. Some unkind media references to this were made when a drawn-looking KK resigned as Newcastle boss the following year . . .

Asda (2006)
Michael Owen joined the list of pocket-tappers in time for the World Cup.

Barclaycard (2001)
Sir Bobby Robson was shown buying rollerskates on his plastic.

Barclays (2004)
Some computer-based trickery in this commercial devised by agency Bartle Bogle Hegarty saw Sir Bobby Robson travelling to a Newcastle home game by bus, only to then encounter himself in a bewildering variety of guises. Bobbys young and old, big and small could be seen – there was even one wearing a dress. Other Premiership managers also featured in the ad, including future Newcastle boss Sam Allardyce, while a miniature Sir Alex Ferguson was screened getting a piggyback at one point. The campaign ended at the time of Robson's dismissal from the Toon hotseat.

Brut (1970s)
Kevin Keegan advertised "the great smell of Brut" aftershave in cahoots with ex-boxer Henry Cooper, who famously urged men to "splash it all over".

BT (1998)
Newcastle boss Kenny Dalglish was filmed at home making a series of phone calls and saying things like "thanks for your support" and "best you've been all season". Asked by his daughter Kelly why he'd changed his habit of not ringing players after games, Kenny replied, "I'm ringing

up the crowd" and, "only another 34,000 to go!" In a fantastically ill-timed airing, the advert was first screened on the weekend that Dalglish's Newcastle side were soundly beaten 4–1 at Leeds.

Carlsberg (2006)
An ad with the strapline, "Probably the best pub team in the world" saw Sir Bobby Robson managing an old England side featuring Jack Charlton, Stuart Pearce, Peter Beardsley and Chris Waddle in a Sunday morning kickabout.

Domino's Pizza (2006)
Owen again, this time in a plot which involved being locked in a cupboard. No wonder he injured himself in Germany.

Lancia Cars (1989)
During Ruud Gullit's time at AC Milan, he starred in this Italian-only advert, in which he leaves training in such a hurry that he drives off across the pitch. The groundsman was not available for comment.

L'Oreal Shampoo (1998)
"Because I'm worth it," emoted David Ginola in his seductive Gallic tones. His contract included a stipulation that he didn't cut his hair short.

Lucozade (1994)
Starred future Magpie John Barnes rambling on about isotonic drinks and hoofing a can in a bin. Michael Owen and Alan Shearer also appeared in ads for the drink.

— ON THE ROAD AGAIN —

By the end of the 2008/09 season, Newcastle will have appeared at 48 different grounds in the Premiership, playing 41 different sides in the process.

Of these 41, they have played eight teams at two different grounds. They are:

Opponent	Stadia
Arsenal	Highbury, Emirates Stadium
Bolton Wanders	Burnden Park, Reebok Stadium
Derby County	Baseball Ground, Pride Park
Fulham	Craven Cottage, Loftus Road
Leicester City	Filbert Street, Walkers Stadium
Manchester City	Maine Road, City of Manchester Stadium
Southampton	The Dell, St. Mary's Stadium
Sunderland	Roker Park, The Stadium of Light

NEWCASTLE
Home and Away Kits
1881-2009

www.historicalkits.co.uk

1881 (East End)

1881 (West End)

1892

1894-97

1897-98

1903-04

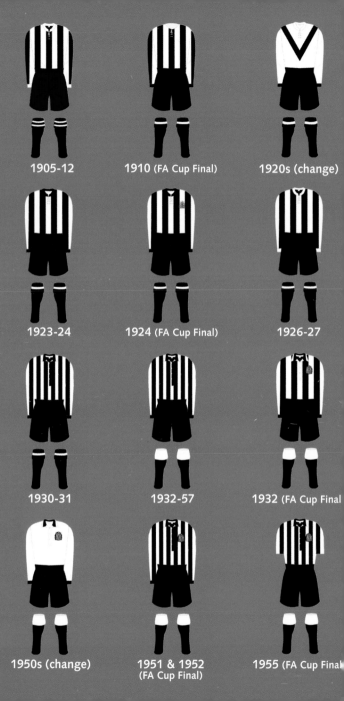

1905-12

1910 (FA Cup Final)

1920s (change)

1923-24

1924 (FA Cup Final)

1926-27

1930-31

1932-57

1932 (FA Cup Final)

1950s (change)

1951 & 1952
(FA Cup Final)

1955 (FA Cup Final)

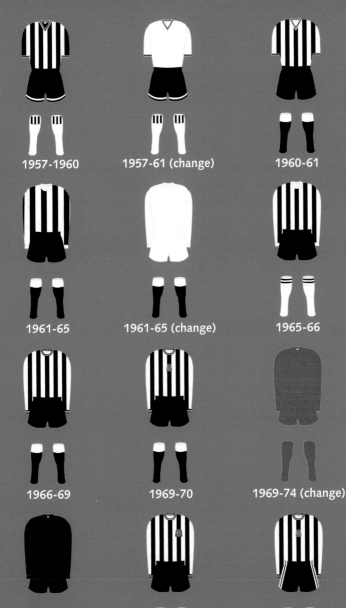

1957-1960

1957-61 (change)

1960-61

1961-65

1961-65 (change)

1965-66

1966-69

1969-70

1969-74 (change)

1969-74 (third)

1970-73

1973-74

1974 (FA Cup Final)

1974-75

1974-75 (change)

1975-76

1975-76 (change)

1976-78

1976-80 (change)

1978-80

1976-80 (third)

1980-83

1982-83 (change)

1983-85

1983-85 (change)

1985-86

1985-86 (change)

1986-87

1986-88 (change)

1987-88

1987-88 (third)

1988-89

1988-90 (change)

1989-90

1990-91

1990-91 (change)

1991-93

1991-93 (change)

1993-95

1993-95 (change)

1993-95 (third)

1995-97

1995-96 (change)

1996-97 (change)

1997-98 (change)

1997-99

1998 (FA Cup Final)

1998-99 (change)

1999 (FA Cup Final)

1999-2000

1999-2000 (change)

2000-01

2000-01 (change)

2001-02 (change)

2001-03

2002-03 (change)

2003-05

2003-04 (change)

2003-04 (third)

2004-05 (change)

2004-05 (third)

2005-07

2005-06 (change)

2005-06 (third)

2006-07 (change)

2006-07 (third)

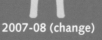

2007-09

2007-08 (change)

2007-08 (third)

2008-09 (change)

2008-09 (third)

— NICKNAMES PART I —

A selection of nicknames from the earlier years of Newcastle United's history:

'Daddler'	Andy Aitken
'Cockles	Bill Appleyard
'Knocker'	Thomas Bartlett
'Ankles'	Albert Bennett
'Rock of Tyneside'	Frank Brennan
'Big Sandy'	Alex Caie
'Hughie'	Joe Ford
'Punky'	Alex Gardner
'The Duke	Doug Graham
'Wally'	Harry Hardinge
'Diddler'	Albert Harris
'Tiger'	Jimmy Hill
'Hurricane Hutch'	Duncan Hutchison
'Camel'	Vic Keeble
'The Laughing Cavalier'	Wilf Low
'Bobby Dazzler'	Bobby Mitchell
'Tucker'	Tom Mordue
'Scots Wullie'	Bill McPhillips
'Peter the Great'	Peter McWilliam
'Clown Prince of Soccer'	Len Shackleton
'Tadger'	Jimmy Stewart
'The Silent Assassin'	Albert Stubbins
'Topper'	Tommy Thompson
'Ginger'	Jack Wilkinson
'Monte'	Johnny Wilkinson

— IT'S WOR CUP . . . SOMETIMES —

Of 357 FA Cup ties played by Newcastle up to the start of the 2008/09 season, United have won 176, drawn 83 and lost 98.

The club's biggest FA Cup victory remains a 9–0 success against Southport in season 1931/32 – this coming after two 1–1 draws in the first two matches of the tie, resulting in this second replay being staged at the neutral venue of Hillsborough, Sheffield.

A 1–7 reverse at Villa Park against Aston Villa in season 1896/97 is Newcastle's heaviest defeat in the competition. Villa went on to complete a League and FA Cup Double.

To date, the Magpies have netted 647 times and conceded 434 goals in the FA Cup (not including penalty shoot-outs).

— NEWCASTLE LEGENDS: TONY GREEN —

Tony Green: Still revered on Tyneside

"It was the saddest day of my life: he was my very best buy. I could watch him play all day and every day." The words of then Newcastle boss Joe Harvey provide some insight into why Tony Green was worshipped by the St James' Park faithful during his brief spell with Newcastle before injury forced his retirement at the age of just 26.

A fantastic combination of speed on the ball, close control and balance had made Green the idol of Bloomfield Road after he joined Blackpool from Albion Rovers in his native Glasgow. Alerted to his promise and goalscoring prowess alongside former Magpie Alan Suddick in the Blackpool midfield, Don Revie tried to sign Green for Leeds United after he had proved his fitness again following a year-long lay-off through injury.

However, Revie found himself out of the loop when the old boy network smoothed the passage of Green's transfer to St James' – Harvey and Blackpool boss Bob Stokoe were former Newcastle team-mates in the 1950s.

For Harvey, Green's arrival on Tyneside in October 1971 relieved the pressure on a side who had slipped to second from bottom in the league. Green took some of the midfield burden from Terry Hibbitt, helping to provide an improvement in the service to striker Malcolm Macdonald and a subsequent climb up the table.

Blackpool, meanwhile, received £90,000 in cash plus striker Keith Dyson, who Stokoe hoped would boost his side's efforts at achieving promotion from Division Two.

Green become an instant terrace hero in his first season at Newcastle and he collected numerous man of the match awards despite the club's unexceptional eleventh place finish and infamous FA Cup exit at Hereford United.

Of his 27 league appearances that season, the victory at Old Trafford one week after the nightmare on Edgar Street remains one of his most celebrated displays. Although Green didn't score that day, his domination of the midfield was lauded in the press and hopes were high that the following season would see the club challenge for major honours once more.

In the event Harvey's side improved their Division One finishing position by three spots, finishing eighth. However, that was to be achieved largely without the contribution of Green. On September 2nd 1972 he was stretchered off the field at Selhurst Park with a knee injury after a tackle by Crystal Palace hardman Mel Blyth.

Green endured three operations before an abortive comeback in a reserve game at Coventry in November 1973 confirmed the inevitable.

Middlesbrough provided the opposition for a testimonial in May 1974 – almost 30,000 supporters turning out despite having seen Newcastle beaten at Wembley less than a week earlier.

Moving back to the Lancashire coast, Green became a school teacher and served on the Pools Panel. His occasional visits to St James' Park still result in a rousing reception from supporters who remember his brief, but wonderful time in Toon.

Tony Green factfile
Born: Glasgow, October 13th 1946
Newcastle career: 38 apps, 3 goals (1971–73)
Other clubs: Albion Rovers, Blackpool
International: Scotland, 6 caps, 0 goals

— NEWCASTLE'S TOP 10 FA CUP SCORERS —

Player	Total
Jackie Milburn	23
Alan Shearer	21
Bobby Mitchell	18
Bill Appleyard	16
Albert Shepherd	16
Neil Harris	14
James Howie	14
Malcolm Macdonald	14
John Rutherford	14
Tom McDonald	13

— FRENCH FOREIGN LEGION —

Aside from Englishmen, Newcastle have relied on more French-born players during their 15 Premiership seasons than from any other nation – no fewer than 13 in all:

Player	Signed	From
David Ginola	July 1995	Paris St Germain
Stephane Guivarc'h	June 1998	Auxerre
Laurent Charvet	July 1998	Cannes
Didier Domi	November 1998	Paris St Germain
Louis Saha	January 1999	Metz (loan)
Alain Goma	June 1999	Paris St Germain
Franck Dumas	July 1999	Monaco
Olivier Bernard	September 2000	Olympique Lyonnais
Laurent Robert	August 2001	Paris St.Germain
Sylvain Distin	September 2001	Paris St.Germain (loan)
Charles N'Zogbia	July 2004	Le Havre
Jean-Alain Boumsong	January 2005	Glasgow Rangers
Antoine Sibierski	August 2006	Manchester City

The Magpies also signed three further French-born players who failed to make a competitive first-team appearance for the club:

Player	Signed	From
David Terrier	January 1998	Unattached
Lionel Perez	June 1998	Sunderland
Olivier Bernard	September 2006	Unattached

Bernard was a free agent when he joined Newcastle for a second time in September 2006, his signing outside the transfer window being permissible after he was released from his playing contract with Glasgow Rangers.

— CAR TOON ARMY —

Driving misadventures involving Newcastle United players include:

September 1990 Five youth team players were injured when their car crashed and rolled over on the A1 in Durham. Driver Michael English and team-mates Phil Mason, Alan Thompson, John Watson and Michael Young were returning after seeing the reserves play at Leeds. Most severely injured was Thompson, who endured two operations on his damaged neck and spent nine months in a brace. He recovered however to enjoy the most successful career of the quintet, culminating in an England cap in 2004.

August 1998 Stuart Pearce walked away almost unscathed from an accident in Nottinghamshire, after his Rover 200 ended up being squashed by a council dustcart. Pearce commented, "I know just how lucky I am to be alive."

May 1999 Driving his Porsche Boxster, Andy Griffin collided with a Metro train at Callerton Parkway. The Metro won. Then-manager Ruud Gullit said: "I don't know how you can drive into a train. I really don't know, but he's okay. We were more concerned about the Porsche!"

February 2000 Another accident involving youth team players, this time on the A189 to the north of Newcastle. Kevin Wealleans plus team-mates Ryan Hogg, Johnny Mann and Paul Dunn all suffered injuries. Driver Wealleans spent time in intensive care.

April 2001 Driving his Mercedes, Nolberto Solano was stopped by police in Gosforth. He was banned and fined for drink-driving.

April 2001 Kieron Dyer was banned and fined after being caught speeding in his Mercedes near Durham. Magistrates heard he was listening to radio coverage of golfer Tiger Woods winning the US Open and he wasn't aware of his speed. Dyer later commented: "What can I say? I'm a huge Tiger Woods fan."

In the same month, Dyer sustained minor injuries after his Mercedes S320 collided with another car outside the club's training ground at Chester-le-Street.

December 2002 Kieron Dyer was fined after being convicted of speeding near Grantham in his BMW. In the same month, Dyer wrote off his Ferrari 360 Modena after it collided with the Swing Bridge over the River Tyne. He was unhurt but his passenger suffered whiplash.

December 2002 Dressed as Captain Hook, Clarence Acuna was returning from the players' fancy dress party when his Mercedes was stopped near Newcastle's Pilgrim Street police station. He was fined and banned for drink-driving.

May 2003 Serial offender Dyer was banned and fined after being caught speeding on the A167 in Durham.

June 2003 Nikos Dabizas smashed his car into traffic lights in Athens hours after playing for Greece. He scrambled free before his vehicle caught fire.

September 2005 Lee Bowyer was banned and fined after being caught speeding on the A1 in Northumberland.

August 2006 Driving his BMW, Titus Bramble hit a wall in the Norfolk village of Newton Flotman.

November 2006 Albert Luque stopped his Porsche Cayenne to check a puncture en route to Newcastle Airport, only for a skip lorry to plough into the back of it. He was unhurt.

— ENGLAND'S DREAMING —

Thirty-four players have appeared in the full England side while being on Newcastle United's books:

Player	Date	Opponent
Matt Kingsley	March 18th 1901	Wales (h)
Jackie Rutherford	April 9th 1904	Scotland (a)
Jack Carr	February 25th 1905	Ireland (h)
Albert Gosnell	February 17th 1906	Ireland (a)
Colin Veitch	February 17th 1906	Ireland (a)
Albert Shepherd	February 11th 1911	Ireland (h)
Jimmy Stewart	April 1st 1911	Scotland (h)
Charlie Spencer	April 12th 1924	Scotland (h)
Frank Hudspeth	October 24th 1925	Northern Ireland (a)
Tom Urwin	March 1st 1926	Wales (h)
Jack Hill	May 9th 1929	France (a)
Samuel Weaver	April 9th 1932	Scotland (h)
Jimmy Richardson	May 13th 1933	Italy (a)
Dave Fairhurst	December 6th 1933	France (h)
Duggie Wright	November 9th 1938	Norway (h)
Jackie Milburn	October 9th 1948	Northern Ireland (a)
Ivor Broadis	April 3rd 1954	Scotland (a)
Malcolm Macdonald	May 20th 1972	Wales (a)
Chris Waddle	March 26th 1985	Republic of Ireland (h)
Peter Beardsley	January 29th 1986	Egypt (a)

Rob Lee	October 12th 1994	Romania (h)
Steve Howey	November 16th 1994	Nigeria (h)
Barry Venison	September 7th 1994	USA (h)
Warren Barton	June 8th 1995	Sweden (h)
Les Ferdinand	December 12th 1995	Portugal (h)
Alan Shearer	September 1st 1996	Moldova (a)
David Batty	September 1st 1996	Moldova (a)
Kieron Dyer	September 4th 1999	Luxembourg (h)
Jermaine Jenas	February 12th 2003	Australia (h)
Jonathan Woodgate	March 31st 2004	Sweden (a)
Nicky Butt	August 18th 2004	Ukraine (h)
Michael Owen	September 7th 2005	Northern Ireland (a)
Scott Parker	October 11th 2006	Croatia (a)
Alan Smith	August 22nd 2007	Germany (h)

Note: the dates and opponents given are the first appearance as a Magpie and therefore not necessarily the player's actual England debut.

Of these players, six marked that first appearance by scoring: Albert Shepherd, Jimmy Stewart, Jackie Milburn, Ivor Broadis, Rob Lee and Alan Shearer.

Meanwhile, Matt Kingsley, Duggie Wright and Nicky Butt all enjoyed the comfort of their England debut as a Newcastle player being staged at St James' Park.

Not included in the list is Paul Gascoigne, who made his England debut while a Tottenham Hotspur player in September 1988 – having moved from Newcastle just two months previously.

— BUY OR SELL ANY SPARES —

The first all-ticket FA Cup final was the 1924 meeting between Newcastle United and Aston Villa – the decision being taken following the chaos of the 'White Horse Final' between Bolton and West Ham 12 months previously when thousands of fans spilled onto the pitch delaying the start.

— NICKNAMES PART II —

Yet more Magpie monikers:

'The Bear'	Roy Aitken
'Prince'	Philippe Albert
'Dick'	David Barton
'Centre Parting'	Warren Barton
'Pedro'	Peter Beardsley
'Lurch'	Dave Beasant
'Bez'	John Beresford
'Bomber'	Ray Blackhall
'Scoop'	John Blackley
'Gnasher'	Lee Clark
'Seamus'	John Cowan
'The Mighty Wyn'	Wyn Davies
'Sir Les'	Les Ferdinand
'Sparrowhawk'	Diego Gavilan
'Sarge'	Paul Goddard
'Boy'	Steve Howey
'Ned'	David Kelly
'Killer'	Brian Kilcline
'Supermac'	Malcolm Macdonald
'Cassius'	Ron McGarry
'Psycho'	Stuart Pearce
'The Mighty Quinn'	Mick Quinn
'Rambo'	George Reilly
'Pop'	Bryan Robson
'Scoot'	Scott Sellars
'Jinky'	Jimmy Smith
'Cannonball'	Colin Taylor
'Bones'	Kenny Wharton

— BOARD GAMES —

Installed at a cost of £66,000 and paid for by Scottish and Newcastle Breweries, St James' Park's first electronic scoreboard made its debut on December 20th 1980 – hardly being tested by a dull 0–0 draw with Bristol City.

The new stadium feature replaced the previous manually operated cricket-type scoreboard, which displayed half-time scores at other grounds alongside a letter corresponding to listings in the match programme.

However, the new technology allowed for all sorts of 'extras', ranging from a fan-friendly time countdown and announcement of the attendance to rather less practical displays of 'winking eyes' and what looked like an assortment of badly-formed dancing Mister Men.

Sited behind the centre section of the uncovered Gallowgate End, an early design defect was noted by those fans who from time to time chose to climb onto it. The game score display relied on the name of the opponents being added for each game in temporary letters. Unfortunately these proved to be less than robust – leading to unfamiliar opponents such as 'elsea' appearing at St James' Park. Some other hitherto unknown teams also appeared on the half-time score lists – including 'Derby City' more than once.

An updated scoreboard was installed in 1988 with assistance from NEI, remaining in place until ground redevelopment reached that end in the close season of 1993.

The dot matrix type display of this scoreboard lent itself to more fanciful output, including some barely recognisable facial portraits of Newcastle players. Strangely, a large number of these belonged to players who barely featured for the club (eg John Robertson), while the Mick Quinn image was surely scanned from a photo of so-called TV entertainer Bob Carolgees.

At other times random messages would flash across the scoreboard with only the vaguest connection to on-pitch events – Jim Smith's side being routinely welcomed with 'the Eagle has landed', while sub-standard loan signing Dave Mitchell's only goal for the club was greeted by 'that's the magic of Mitchell'.

For the punters in the crowd, occasional 'big race' results were displayed – once with disastrous consequences. The 1989 Grand National was staged on Saturday April 8th, which coincided with Newcastle hosting Aston Villa. An on-screen announcement duly confirmed the winning horse as 'Liverpool Bear'. Cue widespread grumbling and the disposing of apparently-worthless betting slips – with nobody seeming to have backed this hitherto unheard-of outsider (a real dark horse?) Unfortunately, it later came to light that a communication breakdown had resulted in the scoreboard operator mishearing the name of the actual winning horse, 'Little Polveir'.

The question of reinstalling a smaller scoreboard has often cropped up in recent years – with the stadium redevelopment ruling out the jumbo efforts seen elsewhere. To date there have been no developments in this area, save for the appearance of electronic countdown clocks at pitchside in July 2007.

— ALL THERE IN BLACK AND WHITE PART I —

A selection of vintage Magpie-related headlines from the written press:

'NORTH TRIUMPHS'
A slightly patronising *Daily Mirror* headline on the Monday following Newcastle United's 2–1 FA Cup Final success over Arsenal in April 1932.

'MILBURN A J.E.T'
The *Sunday Pictorial* created a suitable headline for their reporting of Newcastle United's 2–0 1951 FA Cup Final victory over Blackpool from the initials of the scorer's name.

'IT'S OURS'
Accompanying a report of the cup win, telephoned direct from the Empire Stadium by Stan Bell and published in the *Evening Chronicle*, 1951.

'IT'S OURS AGAIN!'
The obvious accompaniment to news of the 1952 Wembley trophy success. However, the *Evening Chronicle* actually kept this one under wraps until the 3–1 final victory over Manchester City in 1955 (the 1952 headline was "United Bring Home the Cup Again").

'HUGHIE OF THE MAGIC FEET IS DEAD'
The *Newcastle Journal* headline in June 1957, following the discovery of the body of former Magpie legend Hughie Gallacher, who had taken his own life by standing in front of a train.

'HARVEY BRAVES RIP TO EUROPE GLORY'
Confirmation of Newcastle United's Fairs Cup success in 1969 in the *Daily Mirror*.

'SALUTE SUPERMAC'
Tyneside's new hero celebrates his home debut with a hat-trick over Liverpool in August 1971, reports the *Daily Mirror*.

'GORDON WHO?'
The *Newcastle Evening Chronicle* back page headline that greeted new manager Gordon Lee in June 1975. The quote came from United striker Malcolm Macdonald, who was in South Africa when Tyneside journalist John Gibson broke the news to him.

— NOT SO SAFE HANDS —

Outfield players who have gone between the posts for Newcastle in competitive matches include:

Player	Year	Fixture	Comp	Score
John King	1915	Tottenham Hotspur (a)	League	0–0
Bobby Moncur	1970	Manchester United (h)	League	5–1
Chris Waddle	1983	Leeds United (a)	League	1–0
Chris Hedworth	1986	West Ham United (a)	League	1–8
Peter Beardsley	1986	West Ham United (a)	League	1–8
Kevin Brock	1992	Birmingham City (a)	League	3–2

The Hedworth/Beardsley appearances took place in one amazing night at the Boleyn Ground in April 1986. Newcastle had taken to the field with a clearly unfit Martin Thomas between the posts and reserve keeper Dave McKellar sidelined with a hip injury.

After Thomas had further damaged his injured shoulder and conceded four goals, he was replaced by Ian Stewart at the interval with 22-year-old defender Chris Hedworth going in goal on what was only his tenth (and final) appearance for the club.

Hedworth was then also injured whilst challenging Tony Cottee as the West Ham striker scored the fifth goal and also had to be withdrawn, reducing the Magpies to ten men.

Peter Beardsley then took over goalkeeping duties and won the applause of the crowd with some good stops, but ultimately conceded three goals – and left his manager, former Newcastle keeper Willie McFaul calling this the most bizarre game of his career.

West Ham defender Alvin Martin scored a remarkable hat-trick in this game – netting once past each of the three 'keepers. Meanwhile, future Newcastle and West Ham manager Glenn Roeder didn't help the visitors' cause by scoring an own goal.

— IT'S ALL BALLS —

The first time that Newcastle supporters – or at least those with access to a wireless – were able to hear the FA Cup draw 'live' was when the BBC broadcast the third round draw on 16th December 1935.

On that occasion, the Magpies were handed a trip to the Anlaby Road ground of Hull City – a tie that they won 5–1.

It is recorded that the FA Secretary Stanley Rous was requested that day "to ensure that the bag is shaken for a few seconds to produce a distinctive and suitable sound".

— CAN WE PLAY YOU EVERY WEEK? —

Since Premiership football arrived at St James' Park in August 1993, the most welcome (and benevolent) visitors in terms of points gained have been Everton. Here's the complete record of Newcastle's Premiership points earned, and from whom, at St James' Park:

Opposition	Frequency	Record	Points
Everton	15 visits	10 wins, 3 draws, 2 defeats	33
Aston Villa	15 visits	9 wins, 3 draws, 3 defeats	30
Tottenham Hotspur	15 visits	9 wins, 3 draws, 3 defeats	30
Southampton	12 visits	9 wins, 1 draw, 2 defeats	28
Chelsea	15 visits	7 wins, 4 draws, 4 defeats	25
West Ham United	13 visits	7 wins, 4 draws, 2 defeats	25
Middlesbrough	12 visits	6 wins, 5 draws, 1 defeats	23
Coventry City	8 visits	7 wins, 1 draw, 0 defeats	22
Liverpool	15 visits	6 wins, 4 draws, 5 defeats	22
Arsenal	15 visits	5 wins, 6 draws, 4 defeats	21
Bolton Wanderers	9 visits	6 wins, 2 draws, 1 defeat	20
Blackburn Rovers	13 visits	5 wins, 4 draws, 4 defeats	19
Leicester City	8 visits	6 wins, 1 draw, 1 defeat	19
Manchester City	10 visits	6 wins, 1 draw, 3 defeats	19
Leeds United	11 visits	5 wins, 3 draws, 3 defeats	18
Derby County	7 visits	5 wins, 2 draws, 0 defeats	17
Sheffield Wednesday	7 visits	5 wins, 1 draw, 1 defeat	16
Wimbledon	7 visits	5 wins, 1 draw, 1 defeat	16
Charlton Athletic	8 visits	3 wins, 4 draws, 1 defeat	13
Manchester United	15 visits	3 wins, 4 draws, 8 defeats	13
Birmingham City	5 visits	4 wins, 0 draws, 1 defeat	12
Nottingham Forest	4 visits	4 wins, 0 draws, 0 defeats	12
Fulham	7 visits	3 wins, 2 draws, 2 defeats	11
Sunderland	7 visits	3 wins, 2 draws, 2 defeats	11
Portsmouth	5 visits	3 wins, 1 draw, 1 defeat	10
West Bromwich Albion	3 visits	3 wins, 0 draws, 0 defeats	9
Wigan Athletic	3 visits	3 wins, 0 draws, 0 defeats	9
Ipswich Town	4 visits	2 wins, 2 draws, 0 defeats	8
Norwich City	3 visits	2 wins, 1 draw, 0 defeats	7
Queens Park Rangers	3 visits	2 wins, 0 draws, 1 defeat	6
Reading	2 visits	2 wins, 0 draws, 0 defeats	6
Watford	2 visits	2 wins, 0 draws, 0 defeats	6
Crystal Palace	3 visits	1 win, 1 draw, 1 defeat	4
Barnsley	1 visit	1 win, 0 draws, 0 defeats	3
Oldham Athletic	1 visit	1 win, 0 draws, 0 defeats	3

Sheffield United	2 visits	1 win, 0 draws, 1 defeat	3
Swindon Town	1 visit	1 win, 0 draws, 0 defeats	3
Bradford City	2 visits	0 wins, 1 draw, 1 defeat	1
Wolverhampton Wanderers	1 visit	0 wins, 1 draw, 0 defeats	1

— ALL ABOARD THE SKY LARK —

To coincide with their 1,000th live transmission of a Premiership fixture in May 2007, Sky TV asked presenter Richard Keys to compile a top ten of memorable games.

Despite having never won the competition, Newcastle United still figured prominently in the list, featuring in half the games selected:

Southampton 2 Newcastle United 1 (October 24th 1993)
Blue strips for Newcastle, but red faces after two pieces of brilliance from Matthew Le Tissier. More Dell Hell followed, with a touchline fall-out between Kevin Keegan and Lee Clark.

Newcastle United 0 Manchester United 1 (March 4th 1996)
Peter Schmeichel in the Gallowgate goal was battered constantly for 45 minutes but held firm. Eric Cantona scored the vital goal and changed the destiny of the title.

Liverpool 4 Newcastle United 3 (April 3rd 1996)
Routinely trotted out as the best Premiership encounter ever televised – although the corresponding fixture twelve months later with the same scoreline ran it close . . .

Leeds United 0 Newcastle United 1 (April 29th 1996)
The post-match utterances of Kevin Keegan (see *Mind Games*, page 86) make this memorable.

Newcastle United 5 Manchester United 0 (October 20th 1996)
Sheer brilliance. Immortalised in the video release *Howay 5–0*.

— MIND GAMES —

April 29th 1996. Newcastle have just won 1–0 at Elland Road against Leeds United and Kevin Keegan is interviewed live on Sky Sports:

Kevin Keegan: "I think you've got to send Alex Ferguson a tape of this game, haven't you? Isn't that what he asked for?"

Andy Gray (Sky pundit): "Well I'm sure if he was watching it tonight, Kevin, he could have no arguments about the way Leeds went about their job and really tested your team."

Kevin Keegan: "And . . . and . . . we . . . we're playing Notts Forest on Thursday and . . . he objected to that! Now that was fixed up four months ago. We f . . . supposed to play Notts Forest. I mean that sort of stuff, we . . . is it's been . . . we're bet, we're bigger than that."

Richard Keys (Sky Anchorman): "But that's part and parcel of the psychology of the game, Kevin, isn't it?"

Andy Gray: "No, I don't think so."

Kevin Keegan: "No! When you do that, with footballers, like he said about Leeds. And when you do things like that about a man like Stuart Pearce . . . I've kept really quiet, but I'll tell you something, he went down in my estimation when he said that.

"But I'll tell ya – you can tell him now if you're watching it – we're still fighting for this title and he's got to go to Middlesbrough and get something, and I tell you honestly, I will l love it if we beat them . . . love it!"

Richard Keys: "Well, quite plainly the message is, it's a long way from over and you're still in there scrapping and battling and you'll take any of these just as long as you continue to get the results?"

Kevin Keegan: "I think football in this country is so honest and so . . . honestly, when you look sometimes abroad, you've got your doubts. But it really has got to me and I, I, I've not voiced it live, not in front of the press or anywhere – I'm not even going to the Press Conference. But the battle's still on and Man United have not won this yet!"

While the 'love it' segment is routinely used to illustrate Keegan's misplacement of the plot, the full text tells a different story.

Keegan's reference to Pearce stemmed from Newcastle agreeing to participate in the Nottingham Forest defender's testimonial – eight days after the two sides were due to meet in a Premier League fixture.

Alex Ferguson then publicly claimed Forest would go easy on Newcastle because of Pearce's influence and that Leeds would similarly slacken off against Keegan due to their hatred of the Red Devils.

In the event Newcastle's title bid crumbled in a 1–1 draw at Forest, while the one team which lied down and died proved to be former

United star Bryan Robson's Middlesbrough – allowing Manchester United the freedom of the Riverside on the final day of the season, the Red Devils claiming the title after a 3–0 victory on Teesside.

— THE FINAL COUNTDOWN, OR NOT? —

Opinion remains divided over whether the everyday phrase 'back to square one' can be attributed to the first live radio commentaries of sporting events – including one featuring Newcastle United.

The development of portable broadcasting equipment persuaded the BBC to venture into sports events, with a successful experiment to transmit live radio commentary from the England versus Wales rugby union fixture at Twickenham in January 1927. To coincide with this event, the BBC published a diagram of the playing surface divided into eight equal, numbered sections in that week's *Radio Times*. Then as the commentator broadcast news of the play, a second voice solemnly intoned the square number where the action was taking place.

Judged a success, the enterprise decamped to Highbury the following week, where coverage of the Arsenal versus Sheffield United fixture was broadcast, with a similar grid again being published.

Seven days later the BBC broke further new ground by transmitting their first-ever FA Cup tie. The game chosen was the fourth round match between First Division leaders Newcastle United and the renowned amateur side Corinthians – who had only compromised on their principles of non-competitiveness in order to participate in the FA Cup for the first time in 1922.

With the BBC's commentator Captain Henry Blythe Thornhill 'Teddy' Wakelam at the microphone, wireless set owners (with their *Radio Times* grids at the ready) and 56,338 supporters at the Crystal Palace ground in Sydenham heard and saw United end their winless run at this venue with a 3–1 success.

It has long been claimed that the act of the ball moving into the first square on the grid, in other words right back to one end of the pitch, gave rise to the popular phrase 'back to square one'. However, doubt was cast on the tale by the BBC themselves, in an edition of the TV programme *Balderdash and Piffle* in 2006. This questioned the fact that the phrase was in general use before World War II, disputing whether the actual phrase was ever uttered as part of the grid commentary.

— BLACK AND WHITE AND READ ALL OVER —

Saturday December 17th 2005 saw the final curtain fall on a Tyneside sporting institution, when the final edition of the *Pink* rolled off the printing presses at Thomson House.

A dedicated sports newspaper that had been produced by the *Evening Chronicle* for 110 years under various titles, with an (almost) kick-by-kick report of Newcastle's game that afternoon painstakingly rung in from the ground and recorded by copytakers.

Along with results (and later scorers) from the rest of the Football League and that all-important pools information, the whole thing was somehow bundled together, printed and distributed across the region by early evening.

The advent of mobile phone technology and text messaging however ultimately saw sales drop to an unacceptable level. The mortal blow though was the growth of Sky TV – bringing scores instantly into pubs and homes, while also ending the tradition of Saturday afternoon games.

Various attempts to provide alternative content in the *Pink* were made, but ultimately Newcastle's dominance of Sunday live schedules was to provide decisive. Gimmicks like making the publication date Saturday and Sunday just didn't work.

While the coverage of grassroots football, rugby and other minority sports such as speedway attracted some devotees, too few readers were prepared to fork out the increasing cover price on a non-match day, even if Sunderland had lost.

Prior to the 1963/64 season the paper was produced on normal newsprint, but a 3–1 home victory over Derby County on August 24th 1963 was the subject matter of the first 'Sports Edition' to be printed on the distinctive pink paper (although the title didn't change for a number of years).

At least the last-ever edition was able to report on a significant success – that of a 4–2 victory at West Ham for Newcastle, featuring a Michael Owen hat-trick.

The *Pink* name lives on in cyberspace, with post-match reports appearing under that banner on the icnewcastle website.

Some classic *Pink* headlines:

| Aug 1971 | 'Mac Cracks In Super Three' | Newcastle United 3 Liverpool 2 |
| Aug 1982* | 'Kev's Big Day a Hit' | Newcastle United 1 QPR 0 |

Jan 1990	'Cloud Nine'	Newcastle United 5
		Leicester City 4
Feb 1992**	'It's A Kracker'	Newcastle United 3
		Bristol City 0
May 1992	'Safe!'	Leicester City 1
		Newcastle United 2
Apr 1999	'Four-midable'	Derby County 3
		Newcastle United 4
Feb 2000	'Red and Buried'	Newcastle United 3
		Manchester Utd 0
Sep 2002	'Toons of Glory'	Newcastle United 2
		Sunderland 0
Apr 2005+	'Disgrace'	Newcastle United 0
		Aston Villa 3
Dec 2005	'Owe Yes!'	West Ham United 2
		Newcastle United 4

* Kevin Keegan's playing debut for the club.
** Kevin Keegan's managerial debut for the club.
+ Lee Bowyer and Kieron Dyer sent off for fighting with each other.

— TOON TALISMEN —

Newcastle United's top ten Premiership goalscorers:

Player	Total
Alan Shearer	148
Peter Beardsley	47
Andy Cole	43
Les Ferdinand	41
Nolberto Solano	37
Robert Lee	34
Gary Speed	29
Shola Ameobi	27
Craig Bellamy	27
Kieron Dyer	23
Laurent Robert	22

— THE HIGH NUMBERS —

Having missed out on the debut Premiership football season, Newcastle United began their so-far unbroken 15-season stint in the competition allocating squad numbers to players for the first time in preparation for the 1993/94 season.

Saturday August 14th 1993 saw Kevin Keegan's side at home to Tottenham Hotspur and the squad for that game was announced as:

1	Pavel Srnicek	12	Mark Robinson
2	Barry Venison	13	Tommy Wright
3	John Beresford	14	Alex Mathie
4	Paul Bracewell	15	Brian Kilcline
5	Kevin Scott	16	Liam O'Brien
6	Steve Howey	17	Nicky Papavasiliou
7	Robert Lee	18	Kevin Brock
8	Peter Beardsley	19	Steve Watson
9	Andy Cole	20	Alan Neilson
10	Lee Clark	21	Unallocated
11	Scott Sellars	22	Richie Appleby

By the time a fixture with Arsenal ended that first season, that list had seen the following additions and amendments:

5	Ruel Fox	26	Robbie Elliott
13	Unallocated	27	Unallocated
16	Unallocated	28	Unallocated
21	Malcolm Allen	29	Brian Reid
23	Chris Holland	30	Mike Hooper
24	Matty Appleby	31	Mike Jeffrey
25	Unallocated		

Subsequent seasons have seen numerous alterations, the highest number allocated and used competitively to date being the 45 that Hugo Viana donned in 2002.

The most high-profile transfer of a number came in 1996 when Les Ferdinand was persuaded to vacate the number 9 shirt for a certain £15 million signing. It is claimed that Ferdinand was then refused permission by the Premier League to wear the 99 shirt, although in his autobiography the player wrote that he requested 23 in honour of basketball star Michael Jordan. But after the club demanded that he choose a number in the first XI, Ferdinand eventually ended up with 10, Lee Clark being press-ganged into moving to 20.

— TWO-TIME TOONS —

Players who enjoyed two separate spells on the books of Newcastle United include:

Player	First Spell	Second Spell
Peter Beardsley	1983–87	1993–97
John Burridge	1989–91	1993
Lee Clark	1989–97	2005–06
John Craggs	1964–71	1982–83
Bobby Cummings	1954–56	1963–65
Robbie Elliott	1991–97	2001–06
Robert Gibson	1911–12	1919–20
Mick Harford	1980–81	1982
Terry Hibbitt	1971–75	1978–81
George Luke	1950	1959–61
Terry McDermott	1973–74	1982–84
Mark McGhee	1977–79	1989–91
David Mills	1982	1983–84
George Nevin	1925	1928–30
Ken Prior	1952–54	1956–57
Jimmy Richardson	1928–34	1937–38
Nolberto Solano	1998–04	2005–07
Pavel Srnicek	1991–98	2006–07
Tommy Wright	1988–93	1999

The shortest return was undoubtedly that of striker Mick Harford, who rejoined Newcastle on a free transfer from Bristol City after the Ashton Gate side defaulted on their payments, before immediately being sold on to Birmingham City.

A number of other players have subsequently returned to serve at St James' Park in an off-field capacity, including managerial trio Joe Harvey, Kevin Keegan and Glenn Roeder.

Inside-right Charlie Woods can claim the longest gap between stints at Newcastle. Transferred from Newcastle to Bournemouth and Boscombe Athletic in 1962, Woods returned as part of Sir Bobby Robson's backroom team in 2000 – a period of just under 38 years.

— BOER BORE —

Of particular note among Newcastle's many pre- and post-season tours was the 1952 jaunt to Southern Africa, when the FA Cup holders were accompanied by the trophy, thanks to a special licence being granted for it to be taken out of Great Britain.

In total, the tour took 70 days to complete, with the party travelling over 21,000 miles in the process. No fewer than 16 friendly matches were played, with Newcastle scoring 73 goals in the process.

Newcastle travelled with 16 players: Ron Batty, Frank Brennan, Bobby Cowell, Charlie Crowe, Reg Davies, Bill Foulkes, George Hannah, Joe Harvey, Jackie Milburn, Bobby Mitchell, Alf McMichael, Ted Robledo, George Robledo, Ronnie Simpson, Bob Stokoe and Tommy Walker.

Both George Robledo and Jackie Milburn picked up injuries in the early games which restricted their involvement (Milburn played just five times) and forced trainer Norman Smith to play defender Frank Brennan in an unfamiliar forward role.

The best individual scoring performance came in the Border Province fixture, when George Robledo weighed in with seven of the ten goals scored.

When questioned by reporters when the party eventually arrived back in England, captain Joe Harvey was scathing in his criticism of the tour itinerary, saying: "The unending travelling, the hard grounds and the atmospheric conditions were ordeals and I, for one, am glad it's all over. We should have played fewer games and we should have made Johannesburg the base instead of being hawked around South Africa non-stop."

Date	Opposition	Result
17th May	Southern Transvaal	won 3–2
21st May	Natal	won 6–2
24th May	Natal	won 4–0
31st May	Western Province	won 8–0
4th June	Griqualand West	won 3–0
7th June	Northern Transvaal	won 2–1
10th June	Lourenco Marques	won 5–0
14th June	Northern Rhodesia	won 6–1
18th June	Southern Rhodesia	won 4–2
21st June	East Transvaal	won 2–0
25th June	Orange Free State	won 3–0
28th June	South Africa	won 3–0 (in Durban)
2nd July	Border Province	won 10–0
5th July	Eastern Province	won 5–1
12th July	South Africa	lost 3–5 (in Johannesburg)
16th July	Southern Transvaal	won 6–4

— #9 DREAM PART II —

As well as the appearance ex-Toon striker Albert Stubbins on the cover of the *Sgt. Pepper* . . . album by the Beatles (see *#9 Dream Part I*, page 35) a second Magpies/Fab Four-related piece of artwork hit the shelves of the world's record shops during the 1970s.

On October 4th 1974 John Lennon's new album *Walls and Bridges* was released on the Apple/EMI label. While the music isn't remembered as vintage Lennon material despite the presence of guests such as Elton John, the cover artwork captured the work of Lennon the artist. The centrepiece of an intricate fold-out sleeve designed by Roy Kohara is a colour painting entitled 'Football' along with the legend 'John Lennon June 1952 age 11'.

That date and the clear depiction of players wearing the red and white of Arsenal and the black and white of Newcastle United confirm the subject of the painting to be a scene from 1952 FA Cup Final – which the Magpies won 1–0 at Wembley in May of that year.

And while the quality of the drawing is no better than the average 11-year-old would produce, it seems certain that the moment captured is the scoring of the only goal of the game, which came six minutes from full time.

In Lennon's picture, scorer George Robledo is seen tussling with Gunner's defender Lionel Smith in the air, with the ball just about to pass goalkeeper George Swindin en route to the Arsenal net. The whole scene is watched by a fourth player, Newcastle's number nine Jackie Milburn.

However, a November 2005 reissue of *Walls and Bridges* substituted this artwork for a photograph of Lennon taken by Bob Gruen.

— JOSSY'S GIANTS —

Written by TV darts commentator and fanatical Toon fan Sid Waddell, the TV show *Jossy's Giants* recounted the story of Jossy Blair, who after seeing his promising career as a Newcastle United player wrecked by injury, opened a sports shop ('Magpie Sports') and started coaching a junior football team.

Inevitably, the script called for a trip to St James' Park in an episode called 'The Promised Land' and Jossy and co. duly rolled up, to be met by Bobby Charlton and then-Magpies boss Willie McFaul, who guided them round the ground and onto the hallowed turf.

— NEWCASTLE LEGENDS: JOE HARVEY —

Joe Harvey: Honorary Geordie

Had Stan Seymour not been accorded the nickname 'Mister Newcastle', then Joe Harvey would have laid strong claim to it – like Seymour he served the club for many years as both captain and manager. As it is though, Harvey is one of a number of former Magpies deserving of the title of honorary Geordie – settling on Tyneside in preference to his native Yorkshire.

Spotted playing for Bradford City during World War II (when he scored twice against Newcastle), Harvey moved to St James' Park for £4,250 in October 1945.

He made his competitive debut for the club in 1946, in the same FA Cup tie against Barnsley as Jackie Milburn. Appointed captain, Harvey led by example on the field and had no problem making himself heard, having previously served as Company Sergeant-Major in the Royal Artillery.

A mainstay of the Newcastle side at right-half from 1946 to 1953 and a double FA Cup winner, Harvey then moved into the backroom staff before parting company with the club after the 1955 FA Cup Final to begin his managerial career.

He spent two years at Barrow, then moved the short distance to Workington, where he signed striker Ron McGarry, who was to follow Harvey when he returned to Tyneside as Newcastle manager in 1962.

Taking over a recently-relegated side which had flirted with a second relegation, Harvey rebuilt the team with new signings and graduates from the 1962 FA Youth Cup-winning side, eventually achieving promotion back to the First Division at the third attempt in 1964/65.

The summit of his footballing achievements came four years later when Newcastle brought European silverware back to Tyneside in 1969 – the second leg of the Inter-Cities Fairs Cup Final coinciding with Harvey's 51st birthday.

Having enjoyed Wembley success twice with the club on the field, defeat in the 1974 FA Cup Final against Liverpool proved to be a bitter blow and one from which Harvey never fully recovered, leaving his post within a year after some fans turned on him.

He remained on the staff at Gallowgate though, returning in a caretaker manager capacity in 1980 at the age of 62, while the club sought to appoint a replacement after sacking Bill McGarry.

Harvey died in February 1989, aged 70. His funeral, unlike Jackie Milburn's the previous year, was a low-key affair but nonetheless he remains firmly in the affections of generations of Newcastle supporters.

Joe Harvey factfile
Born: Edlington, November 6th 1918
Died: February 24th 1989
Newcastle career: 247 apps, 12 goals
Other clubs: Wolverhampton Wanderers, Bournemouth, Bradford

— THE FOREIGN LEGION —

Players born outside the British Isles to have played first team football for Newcastle:

Player	Year signed	Country of birth
George Robledo	1949	Chile
Ted Robledo	1949	Chile
Arnold Woollard	1952	Bermuda
Preben Arentoft	1969	Denmark
Andy Parkinson	1978	South Africa
Frans Koenen	1980	Netherlands
Tony Cunningham	1985	Jamaica
Mirandinha	1987	Brazil
Bjorn Kristensen	1989	Denmark
Frank Pingel	1989	Denmark
Alan Neilson	1989	Germany
Pavel Srnicek	1990, 2006	Czech Republic
Nicky Papavasiliou	1993	Cyprus
Marc Hottiger	1994	Switzerland
Philippe Albert	1994	Belgium
David Ginola	1995	France
Faustino Asprilla	1996	Colombia
Jimmy Crawford	1997	USA
Alessandro Pistone	1997	Italy
Temuri Ketsbaia	1997	Georgia
Jon Dahl Tomasson	1997	Denmark
John Barnes	1997	Jamaica
Andreas Andersson	1998	Sweden
Nicos Dabizas	1998	Greece
Laurent Charvet	1998	France
Dietmar Hamann	1998	Germany
Nolberto Solano	1998, 2005	Peru
Stephane Guivarc'h	1998	France
George Georgiadis	1998	Greece
Didier Domi	1999	France
Louis Saha	1999	France
Silvio Maric	1999	Croatia
Marcelino	1999	Spain
Alain Goma	1999	France
Franck Dumas	1999	France
John Karelse	1999	Netherlands
Fumaca	1999	Brazil

Helder	1999	Angola
Diego Gavilan	2000	Paraguay
Daniel Cordone	2000	Argentina
Shola Ameobi	2000	Nigeria
Lomana Tresor Lua Lua	2000	DR Congo
Clarence Acuna	2000	Chile
Christian Bassedas	2000	Argentina
Olivier Bernard	2000, 2006	France
Laurent Robert	2001	Reunion Islands
Sylvain Distin	2001	France
Hugo Viana	2002	Portugal
Patrick Kluivert	2004	Netherlands
Charles N'Zogbia	2004	France
Ronny Johnsen	2004	Norway
Celestine Babayaro	2005	Nigeria
Jean-Alain Boumsong	2005	Cameroon
Amdy Faye	2005	Senegal
Emre	2005	Turkey
Albert Luque	2005	Spain
Craig Moore	2005	Australia
Matty Pattison	2006	South Africa
Obafemi Martins	2006	Nigeria
Giuseppe Rossi	2006	Italy
Antoine Sibierski	2006	France
David Edgar	2006	Canada
Oguchi Oneywu	2007	USA
David Rozehnal	2007	Czech Republic
Geremi	2007	Cameroon
Mark Viduka	2007	Australia
Claudio Cacapa	2007	Brazil
Habib Beye	2007	France
Abdoulaye Faye	2007	Senegal
Jose Enrique	2007	Spain
Kazenga LuaLua	2008	DR Congo
Lamine Diatta	2008	Cameroon
Sebastian Bassong	2008	France
Fabricio Coloccini	2008	Argentina
Jonas Gutierrez	2008	Argentina

— CHAIRMEN OF THE BOARD —

The men who have held the power at St James' Park:

Chairman	Appointed
Alex Turnbull	1892
D McPherson	1893
John Cameron	1894
Alex Turnbull	1895
William Nesham	1895
James Telford	1901
John Cameron	1904
Joseph Bell	1908
James Lunn	1909
George T Milne	1911
George G Archibald	1913
John Graham	1915
John P Oliver	1919
David Crawford	1928
James Lunn	1929
George F Rutherford	1941
John W Lee	1949
Robert Rutherford	1951
Stan Seymour	1953
Wilf Taylor	1955
William McKeag	1958
Wallace E Hurford	1959
William Westwood	1964
Robert J Rutherford	1978
Stan Seymour Junior	1981
Gordon McKeag	1988
George Forbes	1990
Sir John Hall	1991
Freddy Shepherd	1996
Sir John Hall	1998
Freddy Shepherd	1998
Chris Mort	2007
Derek Llambias	2008 (job title of Managing Director)

— NEWCASTLE LEGENDS: BOBBY MONCUR —

Bobby Moncur: Desperate to lose the title
'last Newcastle captain to lift a major trophy'

No major cup tie featuring Newcastle would be complete without Bobby Moncur pleading for the current wearer of the armband to unseat him from his position as the last captain to lift a trophy for the club.

Since that balmy night in Budapest in 1969 when Moncur accepted the Fairs Cup from Sir Stanley Rous, no Toon skipper has come close to lifting further silverware.

The son of a policeman (who played centre half for the force), Perth-born Moncur came to the attention of Newcastle in 1960 as a 15-year-old playing for Scotland schoolboys. After summer trials that year with Preston North End, Wolverhampton Wanderers and Manchester United, Moncur turned down them all to sign for Newcastle.

Initially an inside-left, Moncur scored four times against West

Wylam when guesting for the junior side and signed amateur forms before agreeing to put pen to paper as an apprentice for Charlie Mitten's squad in October 1960.

After rising through the junior and reserve sides and captaining the former to FA Youth Cup success in 1962, Moncur signed a full professional contract and made his debut as an 18-year-old away to Luton Town in March 1963. By then he was playing under Joe Harvey and had moved back into defence with some success, covering for injuries in the reserve side earlier that year. However, Moncur was to only feature sporadically for the first team, filling in at various times across the field. Such was his frustration at failing to gain a regular spot in the side that he asked to move on in 1967. Norwich City and Brighton and Hove Albion showed interest, but a move to the Canaries stalled when they were unwilling to meet Newcastle's £25,000 asking price.

After Newcastle's inconsistent start to the 1967/68 season, Moncur won a place in defence and impressed so much that he remained an ever-present, took the captain's armband from Frank Clark and ended the season with his first full Scotland cap. The following season he enhanced his reputation by leading Newcastle to Fairs Cup glory – although few could have predicted that his first three senior goals for the club would all come in the two-legged final against Hungary's Ujpesti Dozsa.

Moncur's final game in a black and white shirt came at Wembley against Liverpool in the 1974 FA Cup Final, before he left St James' Park for a two-year stint at Sunderland. Coaching and management jobs at Carlisle United (where he signed a young Peter Beardsley), Heart of Midlothian, Plymouth Argyle, Whitley Bay and Hartlepool United followed, before he ceased to be actively involved in the game in 1989.

Since then Moncur has been involved in various different recreational activities including managing a squash centre, working at a golf club and skippering ocean-going yachts – both competitively and in the leisure market. He has also continued to watch Newcastle United as an on-air pundit for local radio, despite treatment for colon cancer during the 2007/08 season. Happily, he was given the all-clear in June 2008.

Bobby Moncur factfile
Born: Perth, January 19th 1945
Newcastle career: 361 apps, 10 goals
Other clubs: Sunderland, Carlisle United
International: Scotland, 16 apps, 0 goals

— FULL HOUSE —

Since Newcastle United were promoted to the Premiership, no outfield player has completed an ever-present season of league appearances. However goalkeeper Shay Given has achieved that record on no fewer than four occasions, spending every minute of all 38 games between the posts in seasons 2001/02, 2002/03, 2003/04 and 2005/06.

The last outfield player who started every league game in a season was Lee Clark, with the midfielder wearing the number 10 shirt for all 46 Division One fixtures in 1992/93. Unfortunately, his replacement by substitute Gavin Peacock in the second half of the home game against Notts County denied the Tynesider a perfect record that season.

Midfielder Gary Speed was involved in every Premiership game of both the 1998/99 and 2003/04 seasons, but that record included four substitute run-outs in the former and one in the latter.

Another occupant of the number 10 shirt had a similar record in season 1989/90, striker Mark McGhee starting all 46 Division Two games. For good measure, the Scot was also in the starting XI for the two play-off games and the seven cup ties Newcastle played that season. McGhee's replacement by substitute Paul Sweeney in a home game against Oxford United cost him a full house though.

You have to go back to season 1985/86 for the last example of an outfield player appearing in every minute of every game for the Magpies. That was defender Glenn Roeder, who completed all 42 Division One games and was also on the field for the duration of the club's four cup games that season – one of which included extra-time. Not far behind him that same season was Peter Beardsley, who also made 42 league starts but was substituted once and also missed one of the cup ties.

In terms of the number of games in a season, the record set by Bryan 'Pop' Robson back in 1968/69 remains intact to this day. The striker was an ever-present in every minute of the Magpies' 42 Division One fixtures and also all the club's cup games – this being Newcastle's legendary Fairs Cup-winning season. Beginning the season with a goal in a 1–1 home draw with West Ham in August 1968, 'Pop' was still going strong in Budapest against Ujpesti Dozsa the following June when the trophy was claimed – a total of 59 appearances.

— TEENAGE KICKS PART I —

Since taking their bow in the inaugural season of 1952/53, Newcastle United have captured the FA Youth Cup twice.

Season 1961/62 began with a resounding 14–0 success over Seaton Delaval, before amateur side Corinthians were defeated 3–0 on Tyneside. A 3–1 victory at Roker Park then led to a fourth round tie at Old Trafford against Manchester United – who had won the competition in the first five years it was staged. Goals from future first team players Bobby Moncur and Alan Suddick helped the young Magpies to a 2–1 victory. It's notable that at the time Moncur was playing as a forward, having been unable to force his way into the defence.

A repeat of that scoreline then overcame local side North Shields and set up a two-legged semi-final against Portsmouth. The Magpies travelled to Hampshire by train and during the journey goalkeeper Stan Craig contrived to accidentally smash a carriage window and sit in the broken glass. He was able to play after having three stitches inserted in his backside, but couldn't stop Pompey from taking a one goal lead into the second leg.

A wet evening on Tyneside though saw United concede a further goal to trail by two at the interval. Some hope came from a Les O'Neil effort on 58 minutes, but with Pompey scoring again soon after, a first final appearance was only secured after a supreme effort. Goals from Matty Gowland, Les O'Neil again and a fine chip from George Watkin though won the day and set up a two-legged final against Wolverhampton Wanderers.

Nearly 14,000 fans were at Molineux to see the sides draw 1–1, Clive Chapman equalising for United with a memorable individual goal in which he dribbled past three opponents. The return leg on Tyneside saw 20,588 in attendance at Gallowgate, with the vital goal coming when Bobby Moncur headed home a Les O'Neil corner at the near post.

A week later, Moncur signed his first professional contract with Newcastle United. The club were also billed £10 for the damage to the train window. Eight of the final side went on to feature in the Magpies first team: David Craig, Colin Clish, John Markie, Bobby Moncur, Les O'Neil, Alan Suddick, Dave Turner and George Watkin. The other three players were: Clive Chapman, Stan Craig and Matty Gowland. Alan Wilkinson played in earlier rounds before being injured.

— LEAGUE CUP FINAL ONE-OFF —

Newcastle's sole League Cup final appearance came in February 1976, when Manchester City won 2–1 at Wembley thanks to goals from Peter Barnes and an acrobatic bicycle kick from Geordie Dennis Tueart. Alan Gowling had equalised for Newcastle.

The cup run began with a second round tie against Division Four side Southport that was switched from Haig Avenue to St James' Park in order to earn the Lancashire club extra revenue.

Bristol Rovers of Division Four were then beaten after a draw at Eastville and a replay on Tyneside, before Division One side QPR were overcome at Loftus Road for the second successive season in this competition.

A quarter-final tie with Second Division Notts County followed and despite Newcastle enjoying home advantage, the other Magpies proved to be tricky opponents until goalkeeper Eric McManus fumbled a long Macdonald throw into his own net.

A trip to Wembley was then secured after the team turned round a one-goal deficit from the first leg at White Hart Lane in a memorable home display against Tottenham Hotspur.

Manchester City, meanwhile, had overcome Norwich City, Nottingham Forest, Manchester United and Mansfield Town, and a Tyne-Tees final was avoided when Tony Book's side disposed of Jack Charlton's Middlesbrough at the semi-final stage.

The road to Wembley:

Round	Opponent	Score	Scorers
Second	Southport (h)	6–0	Gowling 4, Cannell 2
Third	Bristol Rovers (a)	1–1	Gowling
Third Replay	Bristol Rovers (h)	2–0	T. Craig (pen), Nattrass
Fourth	Queens Park Rangers (a)	3–1	Macdonald, Burns, Nulty
Fifth	Notts County (h)	1–0	McManus (og)
Semi-final (1)	Tottenham Hotspur (a)	0–1	
Semi-final (2)	Tottenham Hotspur (h)	3–1	Gowling, Keeley, Nulty
Final	Manchester City (n)	1–2	Gowling

— INTERNATIONALISTS —

Newcastle United fielded a starting XI composed entirely of full internationals for the first time in their history when Everton visited St James' Park on February 28th 1998:

Player	Country
Shay Given	Republic of Ireland
Warren Barton	England
Steve Howey	England
Stuart Pearce	England
Philippe Albert	Belgium
David Batty	England
Robert Lee	England
Gary Speed	Wales
Alan Shearer	England
Andreas Andersson	Sweden
Keith Gillespie	Northern Ireland

However, despite putting out this stellar line-up and even bringing on a substitute with full international experience (Georgia's Temuri Ketsbaia), Kenny Dalglish's side were held to a 0–0 draw.

— BACK TO THE FUTURE —

Future Newcastle players and managers who picked up FA Youth Cup honours earlier in their careers, include:

Year	Player	Playing for
1953	Albert Scanlon	Manchester United
1954	Albert Scanlon	Manchester United
1967	Colin Suggett	Sunderland
1970	Graeme Souness	Tottenham Hotspur
1970	Ray Clarke	Tottenham Hotspur
1973	Dave McKellar	Ipswich Town
1977	Kenny Sansom	Crystal Palace
1978	Kenny Sansom	Crystal Palace
1989	Jason Drysdale	Watford
1992	Nicky Butt	Manchester United
1993	Keith Gillespie	Manchester United
1996	Michael Owen	Liverpool
1997	Jonathan Woodgate	Leeds United

— NEUTRAL TERRITORY —

As well as being used as a venue for international matches over the years, St James' Park has hosted various competitive club fixtures not featuring Newcastle United:

Date	Result	Competition
April 18th 1903	Sunderland 2 Middlesbrough 1	Division One
December 23rd 1935	Hartlepool 4 Halifax Town 1	FA Cup replay
February 6th 1952	Gateshead 0 West Bromwich A 2	FA Cup replay
March 13th 1954	Bishop Auckland 5 Brigg Sports 1	FA Amateur Cup
April 19th 1954	Bishop Auckland 2 Crook Town 2	FA Amateur Cup
November 28th 1955	Carlisle United 1 Darlington 3	FA Cup replay
March 17th 1956	Bishop Auckland 5 Kingstonian 1	FA Amateur Cup
March 16th 1957	Bishop Auckland 2 Hayes 0	FA Amateur Cup
March 12th 1960	Crook Town 1 Kingstonian 2	FA Amateur Cup
March 28th 1964	Crook Town 2 Barnet 1	FA Amateur Cup
January 16th 1967	Middlesbrough 4 York City 1	FA Cup replay
March 18th 1972	Blyth Spartans 0 Enfield 0	FA Amateur Cup
February 27th 1978	Blyth Spartans 1 Wrexham 2	FA Cup replay
September 3rd 1994	Gateshead 0 Yeovil Town 3	GM Vauxhall Conference

The Wear-Tees derby of April 1903 was played on Tyneside as a punishment for Sunderland, after their fans had stoned the motor coach carrying players of The Wednesday (later Sheffield Wednesday) on Wearside earlier that month.

The only other occasion when the stadium has been used for a league match not involving Newcastle came in 1994, when cross-Tyne neighbours Gateshead were unable to play at their usual home venue due to an athletics meeting taking place at the International Stadium.

United allowed their fellow Tynesiders use of St James' Park, giving Yeovil fans among the 2,734 crowd their first – and so far only – opportunity to see the Glovers play at Gallowgate.

The appearance of the visitors was fitting, given that Newcastle had provided the opposition four years previously when Yeovil christened their new Huish Park ground.

— CAUGHT IN THE TRIANGLE —

Thanks to some underachievement in the FA Cup in January 1986, fourth round day arrived with Newcastle lacking a fixture. A 0–2 home reverse at the hands of Brighton had ended the Magpies' Wembley dreams for another year, while Brian Clough's Nottingham Forest were similarly underemployed – having lost to Blackburn Rovers in a replay.

A friendly match between the two stages was duly arranged – but in the slightly unexpected and thoroughly exotic venue of Bermuda.

Thanks to a sponsorship deal brokered with a Nottingham-based businessman, the two sides were flown out to the tropical island and faced each other at the Somerset Cricket Club ground in Sandys Parish.

The final score was a resounding 0–3 defeat at the hands of Forest, whose goals came from David Campbell (2) and Ian Bowyer.

Just over a fortnight later the two sides met again, this time in a Division One fixture. On that occasion, two Peter Beardsley goals gave Willie McFaul's side ample revenge at the City Ground – in rather chillier conditions.

That completed a hectic period for Beardsley, who had taken part in the Bermuda game before flying on to Egypt, linking up with the England squad and making his full international debut in Cairo.

— CELEBRITY FANS PART II —

A further selection of celebrity supporters often associated with the club:

Sting
The Wallsend-born former bus conductor, labourer and tax officer, real name Gordon Sumner, who became lead singer of 'The Police' and multi-million album-selling solo star. Doubts do persist, however, over his previous alleged mackem affiliations.

Jimmy Nail
The actor/singer otherwise known as James Michael Aloysius Bradford is reputed to have missed a schoolboy trial with the Magpies because he didn't manage to get out of bed. A trial of a different kind then saw him imprisoned later in life – convicted following an outbreak of violence after a Newcastle away game. His TV appearances have often included references to the club, especially in *Auf Wiedersehen Pet* and *Spender* – a detective series set on Tyneside which used St James' Park as a backdrop for an episode entitled 'The Golden Striker'. Nail is related to Newcastle player (and 1924 FA Cup winner) Edward Mooney.

Sid Waddell
Best known as an enthusiastic TV darts commentator, Sid watched his hero Bobby Mitchell from the terraces as a youngster and later managed to name check Mitch when penning the children's TV series *Jossy's Giants*.

Norman Wisdom
Despite being a childhood Arsenal fan and former director of Brighton and Hove Albion, the veteran actor and comedian has had a black and white allegiance since a meeting with a Geordie squaddie during World War II.

Wisdom has made the journey to Tyneside from his home in the Isle of Man on numerous occasions over the years. He was a guest of honour when England faced Albania at St James' Park in a World Cup Qualifier in September 2001. Some familiar larking about on the field before kick-off delighted the visiting Albanians – for whom Wisdom remains a national hero (he was one of very few foreign actors whose films were broadcast by the state TV station during years of communist rule).

— A QUESTION OF VEXILLOLOGY —

Some flag-related stories:

- Reports of a riot that took place before the scheduled Tyne-Wear derby match of April 1901 mention that the club flag was torn down by rampaging Sunderland fans. Images of St James' Park at that time show a flag flying from the south-west corner of the stadium, but by the 1950s a large Union Jack flag can be seen fluttering from a flag pole at the South East corner.
- The same location also saw the so-called 'ten-minute flag' fly for some years – a large flag with black and white vertical stripes displayed throughout the match until taken down to indicate that the 80th minute had been reached.
- The club's revival in the 1990s then saw Newcastle supporters club together and buy a large flag. This was unfurled for the first time in April 1992 from the East Stand, after victory over Sunderland virtually secured promotion. The horizontally-striped black and white flag read:

NEWCASTLE UNITED
TOON ARMY
CHAMPIONS 1992/93

This flag became a familiar sight at games, being passed back and forward over the heads of fans. It made a belated comeback at Watford's Vicarage Road in the final game of the 2006/07 season.

- An even bigger flag then appeared in the 1993/94 season: another horizontal black and white effort emblazoned with a brewery blue star, two Magpie cartoon figures and the legend:

NEWCASTLE UNITED
HOWAY THE LADS

This was also displayed within St James' Park but later labelled a fire risk and banned.

After being draped from the partially-built Gallowgate Stand when Arsenal were beaten in May 1994, the flag then followed the club into Europe. Numerous appearances on the continent followed, including matches at Antwerp and Metz. However this second flag met its end during the November 1997 trip to Barcelona – failing to make it back from the rain-sodden Nou Camp.

- A third large flag did briefly appear in the 2004/05 season, complete with club badge. This was funded by Newcastle United and unfurled before the FA Cup semi-final tie with Manchester United at Cardiff's Millennium Stadium in April 2005. It also made a brief appearance at St James' Park before a home game.
- Alan Shearer's retirement in May 2006 was marked by a large banner showing him in familiar goalscoring celebration style and titled 'Thanks for Ten Great Years'. This was draped from the back of the Gallowgate Stand in the days leading up to his testimonial against Celtic.
- Another Shearer-related creation made the headlines in April 1998, when a giant replica 'Shearer 9' shirt briefly adorned the 'Angel of the North' sculpture. The mission to clothe Anthony Gormley's statue on the southern approaches to Tyneside was carried out by a group of supporters in the run up to the Wembley FA Cup final involving Newcastle and Arsenal. Fishing lines and catapults were used to hoist the 29 feet by 17 feet replica strip into place early one morning, although it was quickly lowered once the police became aware.

— TRIPLE CROWN —

The last time Newcastle competed in a League game for two points was on May 2nd 1981, when the Toon beat Orient 3–1 at St James' Park to complete an unmemorable eleventh-place finish in Division Two.

The following season three points were up for grabs for the first time when Watford were the opening day visitors to Tyneside. However, Newcastle went down 0–1 to the Hornets and were beaten 0–3 at Loftus Road by Queens Park Rangers the following week. It was only at the third attempt that a three point maximum was recorded, thanks to a 1–0 win over Cambridge United at St James' Park on September 12th 1981. The all-important goal came from midfielder John Trewick.

— NEWCASTLE LEGENDS: JIMMY LAWRENCE —

Jimmy Lawrence: A geat keeper, although the balls
were a lot bigger in those days!

The statistics speak for themselves – record appearance maker, three First Division championship winners' medals, one FA Cup winner's medal and an unbroken 18-year spell on the books at Gallowgate.

Glaswegian keeper Jimmy Lawrence was signed by Newcastle in

July 1904, taking the place of Charlie Watts between the posts in a 2–0 home win over Manchester City in October of that year.

A first championship medal followed that season, but so too did the first of four FA Cup Final defeats – two of which (in 1908 and 1911) came as a direct result of costly individual errors on Lawrence's part.

However, he was to pick up a winner's medal in 1910 against Barnsley – the first of two consecutive seasons when he appeared in FA Cup finals and replays.

Further championship-winning seasons followed in 1906/07 and 1908/09 – the latter being one of three seasons when Lawrence was an ever-present in both league and cup. And during his long Newcastle career, Lawrence boasted the enviable record of having saved four of the five penalty kicks he faced against Sunderland in Tyne-Wear derby fixtures.

Surprisingly for such a consistent performer he was only capped by Scotland once, in a Home International game against England in 1911 at Everton's Goodison Park.

Lawrence played his final game for Newcastle in April 1922 at home to Bradford City, before giving way to his successor Bill Bradley and moving on shortly after to become manager of Division Two side South Shields. A spell in charge of Preston North End followed, before he was persuaded to join German side Karlsruhe.

He enjoyed title success with the club in 1925, before returning to his native Scotland where he served Stranraer as both a director and chairman up until his death in 1934.

Jimmy Lawrence factfile
Born: Glasgow, February 16th 1885   Died: November 1934
Newcastle career: 496 apps (1904–21)
Other clubs: Partick Athletic, Hibernian, Newcastle United, South Shields (manager), Preston North End (manager), Karlsruhe (trainer), Stranraer (director and chairman)
International: Scotland, 1 cap

— SAFE HANDS . . . SOMETIMES —

Since their promotion from the old Division One in 1993, Newcastle have entrusted goalkeeping duties in their 578 Premiership games to just seven players:

Player	Year(s) played	Total	Subs
Shay Given	1997/present	332	0
Pavel Srnicek	1993/1998, 2006/2007	97	2
Shaka Hislop	1995/1998	53	0
Steve Harper	1994/present	65	5
Mike Hooper	1993/1996	23	2
Tommy Wright	1993,1999	5	1
Jon Karelse	1993/2003	3	0

Meanwhile, another six goalkeepers have taken their place on the substitutes' bench for the Magpies in the Premiership without being called into action:

John Burridge	1993
Tony Caig	2003/2006
Fraser Forster	2006/present
Peter Keen	1998/1999
Tim Krul	2006/present
Lionel Perez	1998/2000

Both Perez and Burridge played against Newcastle in the Premiership – for Sunderland and Manchester City respectively. Burridge kept a clean sheet in a 0–0 draw at Maine Road in April 1995 after appearing as a half-time replacement for Tony Coton. And as well as frustrating his former employers, who had released him six months earlier, that game saw him become the oldest player to appear in the Premiership, aged 43 years, four months and 26 days.

— ALL THERE IN BLACK AND WHITE PART II —

A selection of more recent Magpie-related headlines from the written press:

'KING KEVIN'
A suitable *Evening Chronicle* front page headline to accompany a photo of the Newcastle United manager Kevin Keegan wearing a crown, seconds after his side clinched promotion by winning at Grimsby Town in May 1993.

'HOT COLE'

Goal number 39 of the season for Magpies striker Andy Cole equalled the club's scoring record and helped United to a 2–0 victory over Liverpool at Anfield in 1994. *The Mirror* gauged the temperature nicely.

'HOWAY FIVE-0'

Surfing on a wave of mass hysteria on Tyneside, *The Sun* conjured up a classic headline to accompany their report of Newcastle United's 5–0 home success over Manchester United in October 1996.

'HO HO SEVEN'

It may have come three days after Christmas Day 1996, but Newcastle United's 7–1 home win over Tottenham Hotspur still prompted a seasonal effort from the *Sunday Mirror*.

'TEARS OF A TOON'

How *The Sun* reported reaction to the resignation of Kevin Keegan from the manager's job at Newcastle United, in January 1997.

'DREAM TEAM'

An epic night of European football on Tyneside in September 1997 ended with Barcelona on the wrong end of a Tino Asprilla treble.

'CLARKIE IN THE SHIRT'

News reached the *Sunday Sun* in June 1999 that then-Sunderland midfielder Lee Clark had been spotted at Wembley a month previously watching Newcastle United in the FA Cup Final. His attire for part of that day? A T-shirt with the slogan 'sad mackem b*stards'.

'SHEARER THRIVES WITH FIVE'

The *Guardian* documented the return to goalscoring form of striker Alan Shearer in September 1999, as Bobby Robson oversaw his first home game in charge at St James' Park. Final score: Newcastle United 8 Sheffield Wednesday 0 (Shearer 5).

'WOR MIKEY'

How the *Daily Mirror* announced the arrival of Michael Owen to Tyneside in August 2005.

'FINAL'

The *Evening Chronicle* reporting on the career-ending injury suffered by Alan Shearer during Newcastle's 4–1 victory on Wearside in April 2006.

— MEET THE MANAGERS —

Manager	Years in charge
Frank Watt	1895–1930 (secretary)
Andy Cunningham	1930–1935
Tom Mather	1935–1939
Stan Seymour	1939–1947 (honorary)
George Martin	1947–1950
Stan Seymour	1950–1954 (honorary)
Duggie Livingstone	1954–1956
Charlie Mitten	1958–1961
Norman Smith	1961–1962
Joe Harvey	1962–1975
Gordon Lee	1975–1977
Willie McFaul	1977 (caretaker)
Richard Dinnis	1977
Bill McGarry	1977–1980
Joe Harvey	1980 (caretaker)
Arthur Cox	1980–1984
Jack Charlton	1984–1985
Willie McFaul	1985–1988
Colin Suggett	1988 (caretaker)
Jim Smith	1988–1991
Bobby Saxton	1991 (caretaker)
Ossie Ardiles	1991–1992
Kevin Keegan	1992–1997
Terry McDermott*	1997 (caretaker)
Kenny Dalglish	1997–1998
Tommy Craig**	1998 (caretaker)
Ruud Gullit	1998–1999
Steve Clarke	1999 (caretaker)
Sir Bobby Robson	1999–2004
John Carver	2004 (caretaker)
Graeme Souness	2004 –2006
Glenn Roeder	2006–2007
Nigel Pearson***	2007 (caretaker)
Sam Allardyce	2007–2008
Nigel Pearson	2008 (caretaker)
Kevin Keegan	2008–

(*assisted by Arthur Cox)
(**assisted by Alan Irvine)
(***assisted by Lee Clark)

Note: Frank Watt guided the club from its inception, but the side was selected by a committee during this period. Stan Seymour, meanwhile, performed the duties of team manager in two separate periods, although player selection was again officially performed by a committee composed of himself and other club directors.

— THE BATTLE OF SANTIAGO —

"This is Hollywood on Tyne!"
Newcastle Chairman **Freddy Shepherd**

Tyneside in general and Newcastle United were brought to a worldwide cinema audience in 2005 with the release of the film *Goal,* the first of a planned trilogy which charted the rags to riches rise of Mexican-born footballer Santiago Munez.

Work had begun in 2004, with producer Mike Jeffries joining Bobby Robson on the St James' Park pitch to announce the project. However, footage taken that season at the Chelsea home game and Real Mallorca away UEFA Cup tie was scrapped after Mexican actor Diego Luna was replaced in the lead role.

Director Michael Winterbottom also left, replaced by Danny Cannon, who brought his film crew to Tyneside in 2005 with another Mexican-born actor, Kuno Becker, in the role of Munez.

Filming in and around the stadium took place during the home wins over Chelsea and Liverpool in Ferbruary/March 2005 – the latter game then being followed by two days of shooting in front of a 'crowd' composed of local extras.

The high level of co-operation the club gave the film makers was evident when Becker and his on-screen team-mate Gavin Harris (played by Alessandro Nivola) took to the field immediately after the final whistle at a couple of home games, dressed in replica kits.

They then proceeded to join in the authentic celebrations of the real Newcastle team, milking the genuine applause of the crowd – the scenes being captured in close up by hand held cameras.

The whole thing was then stitched together using computer-generated trickery to make empty stands appear full and intersperse real action footage of Newcastle players with specially shot re-enactments featuring the cast. Most notably, this saw Munez apparently score the winning goal in a 3–2 victory over Liverpool – although the free kick driven home at the Leazes end was actually Laurent Robert's rocket.

As Munez made his way from unpromising trialist to first team debutant/goal hero (squad number: 26), various other grounds were used.

Brentford's Griffin Park and the Loftus Road stadium of Queen's Park Rangers were used as venues for reserve games, while footage from Newcastle's victory at Fulham's Craven Cottage in May 2005 was also used.

Alan Shearer was given a brief speaking part, while most of the United first team squad at the time feature. Chairman Freddy Shepherd also pops up at one point.

Former Magpie Rob Lee plays the part of a pundit, alongside Sky commentator Martin Tyler. One of the few obvious ricks in the film, though, sees Lee demonstrate fantastic observational skills, commentating from the Newcastle press box as Munez makes his senior debut for the club – away at Fulham.

Goal had its London premiere on September 15th 2005, with a Tyneside event at 'The Gate' cinema three nights later. It then went on general UK cinema release on September 30th and subsequently worldwide. In the sequel, *Goal 2*, Santiago is sold to Real Madrid. Due to the involvement of the sportswear giant in the movies, Santiago only ever plays for teams who wear kit supplied by adidas.

— THE AGONY OF YOUTH —

Apart from their two successes in the FA Youth Cup, the Magpies have made five more losing appearances in the semi-finals:

Season	Opponent	Score/aggregate
1975/76	Wolverhampton Wanderers	lost 2–4 (1–2, 1–2)
1988/89	Manchester City	lost 1–3 (1–2, 0–1)
1998/99	Coventry City	lost 2–5 (0–4, 2–1)
2005/06	Manchester City	lost 3–4 (2–3, 1–1)
2006/07	Liverpool	lost 3–7 (2–4, 1–3)

— AD INFINITUM PART II —

A further selection of TV advertisements featuring former and future Newcastle United players and managers over the years:

McDonalds (1994)
The then 13-year-old Scott Parker played keepy-uppy in his back garden, only to be called in for his tea — at a burger bar. Paul Gascoigne and Alan Shearer also appeared in ads for the fast food company.

Milk Marketing Board (1988)
A famous ad which featured Ian Rush, with child actor Carl Rice delivering the killer line "Accrington Stanley, who are they?". The first draft of the script mentioned Tottenham Hotspur, but after the thumbs down from White Hart Lane was received, non-league Stanley were substituted.

Nescafé Carte Noire (2001)
Housewives' favourite David Ginola was drafted in to try and punt this posh instant coffee.

Persil (2004)
Michael Owen kept his England top (and image) whiter than white.

Pizza Hut (1996)
England penalty flop duo Chris Waddle and Stuart Pearce indulged in some cringe-worthy puns with new entrant to the spot-kick miss club, Gareth Southgate. Unsurprisingly, a 1998 remake with David Batty never happened. Ruud Gullit later plugged a pizza with corners . . . badly.

Renault (1996)
An ad which featured David Ginola driving his Laguna around Newcastle. A second piece of promotional work for Renault was banned by the club on insurance grounds — the French manufacturer having offered Ginola a spin at the British Touring Car Championships.

Sugar Puffs (1996)
The cereal ad showed Newcastle winning the FA Cup Final and receiving the trophy to the delight of manager Kevin Keegan, thanks to a last-minute header from the Honey Monster. A 20% drop in sales of the breakfast cereal in the North East was reported in the wake of this advert, following a boycott in the Wearside area. A mackem-led complaint was also received by the Advertising Standards Authority,

who were asked to investigate claims there was nothing remotely truthful or honest about Newcastle winning the cup.

Walkers Crisps (1995 onwards)
The High Priest of salty snack food Gary Lineker has at various times appeared alongside a crying Paul Gascoigne, Sir Bobby Robson in the guise of a guardian angel and Michael Owen (Cheese and Owen flavour).

Yellow Pages (1994)
Another outing for Bobby Robson, who was shown consulting with Graham Taylor about what to get new England boss Terry Venables for a present. A cake was the final, not particularly exciting, answer.

Apart from appearing in a number of commercial ads, Kevin Keegan also appeared in a 1976 Public Information Film, joining the likes of Alvin Stardust and Joe Bugner to promote 'The Green Cross Code' children's road safety initiative.

TV advertisers have so far failed to exploit wearside-based situations – although former mackem managers Terry Butcher and Peter Reid both appeared in the Carlsberg pub team commercial (and Reid look-a-likes once advertised PG Tips tea!)

One did slip through the net though, when Southampton boss Lawrie McMenemy (later to manage Sunderland) found himself in the proverbial, after having being convicted of a drink-driving offence. Unfortunately, he was at the time the face of Barbican alcohol-free lager. The campaign was rapidly pulled, meaning that Big Lawrie and his catchphrase, "It's great, man!", sadly disappeared from the nation's TV screens.

— CUP MARATHONS —

Now that FA Cup games are settled after a single replay, extra time or penalties if necessary, it's easy to forget that until comparatively recently, ties were played to a finish – regardless of how many games that required.

The Magpies have required three games to settle a tie on five occasions, while they've twice embarked on four-game marathons. The first of these came in the 1923/24 season, when they were drawn away to lower league Derby County in the second round. A record attendance of 27,873 attended the Baseball Ground for the first game, which ended 2–2 after the Rams recovered from being two goals behind.

The replay took place on a Wednesday afternoon in front of 50,393 fans at St James' Park and again the Magpies took a 2–0 lead only to be pegged back to 2–2 once more – Derby's cause aided by an own goal from Ted Mooney.

With extra time failing to separate the teams, a third game at a neutral ground was required and this was eventually staged at Bolton's Burnden Park after much discussion.

The following Monday afternoon 17,300 fans saw Newcastle grab an equaliser in the dying seconds of extra time for a third consecutive 2–2 draw. Derby were incensed at some alleged favouritism from referee Sam Rothwell, who awarded a dubious penalty and free-kick – both of which United converted.

After further arguments between the sides failed to reach an agreement over the venue for a fourth game, a coin was tossed and Newcastle won the right to stage the tie on Tyneside 48 hours later – with a replacement referee.

A classic encounter at St James' Park saw the Magpies come back from two goals down, a Neil Harris hat-trick providing the platform for an eventual 5–3 win in front of 32,496 spectators.

A rather less incident-packed quartet of matches in season 1988/89 saw Newcastle eventually succumb to lower league Watford in round three.

After a goalless stalemate on Tyneside the teams re-convened at Vicarage Road two nights later, United recovering from conceding an early goal to force a 2–2 draw.

The following Monday it was scoreless against at St James' Park and 48 hours later neither side could break the deadlock back in Hertfordshire.

Finally, a goal came late in extra time with an unprecedented fifth match looking inevitable, a harmless shot being deflected into his own goal by Newcastle's Glenn Roeder (who was to play and manage both sides).

The tie lasted 450 minutes – 30 more than the one with Derby County – and was an unwanted burden as Jim Smith's side struggled unsuccessfully to avoid relegation.

— NEWCASTLE LEGENDS: KEVIN KEEGAN —

Kevin Keegan: Never a dull moment

When Kevin Keegan arrived at St James' Park in August 1982, the effect he had on a club languishing in the wastelands of Division Two was instant. Amid a media frenzy, fans queued across the car park to buy season tickets and suddenly the club was alive again.

England manager Bobby Robson attended his debut, a sell-out crowd of 36,000 delighting in a 1–0 win over Queens Park Rangers thanks to a Keegan goal. Just three months earlier, by comparison, fewer than 11,000 fans had seen Rangers triumph 4–0 at Gallowgate.

However, Keegan's first season wasn't all plain sailing, as he was forced to back his under-fire manager Arthur Cox after a mid-season dip in form. Two defeats in the last ten games put the Magpies on the edge of the promotion race, but in pre-play-off days that wasn't quite enough.

The eve-of-season departure of Imre Varadi was quickly forgotten as Peter Beardsley arrived, and along with Keegan and Chris Waddle went on to score a combined total of 65 league goals in the 1983/84 promotion campaign.

A memorable farewell at home to Brighton and Hove Albion when the trio all netted was followed by a friendly with Liverpool, after which a helicopter landed on the centre circle to spirit Keegan away into retirement.

Slightly less than eight years later he returned however, to rescue a club who had lost the impetus provided by promotion and were again languishing in Division Two.

Once more the uplifting effect was instant, as Keegan brought the same spirit of infectious enthusiasm he had shown as a player to his first stab at a management. Newcastle fans responded in their droves, with a doubling of the previous home attendance to 30,000 for his first game in charge – a 3–0 win over Bristol City.

However, it's sometimes forgotten that the rest of that season was a struggle, with the threat of relegation very real until the final week.

Off-field tensions also saw further intrigue – most notably a Keegan walk-out as his team were playing Swindon Town amid accusations of broken promises by Newcastle's new owners, the Hall family.

That was all forgotten the following season, however, as the team set off at a cracking pace – winning their first eleven league games before succumbing at home to Grimsby Town. Having secured promotion and taken the title, Keegan's side then gave notice of their intention to gatecrash the Premier League with a 7–1 dismantling of Leicester City featuring hat-tricks from Andy Cole and David Kelly.

Keegan dispensed with Kelly though, re-signing Peter Beardsley to spur Cole on to a record-breaking seasonal tally of 41 goals. Cole's goals helped Newcastle to a third-place finish in the Premiership and earned the team the nickname of 'The Entertainers' (coined by Sky after a victory at Oldham Athletic in November 1993).

Sixth and second place finishes in the following two seasons kept the crowds entertained, but a visibly-aged Keegan resigned in January 1997. Various reasons were given for his shock departure, but the demands and restrictions of working for a plc remain the most plausible.

After leaving Newcastle, Keegan had spells in charge of Fulham, England and Manchester City, who he left in 2005. For three years he maintained a low profile until making a sensational return to St. James' Park in January 2008, following the sacking of Sam Allardyce.

Keegan's mere presence at an FA Cup replay with Stoke seemed to galvanize an underperforming team, as the Magpies romped to an emphatic 4–1 victory. It was a different story in the Premiership, though, as Keegan initially seemed helpless to stop an alarming slide down the table, with relegation a distinct possibility. To the relief of the Geordie faithful, however, results picked up and, by the end of the season, King Kev had clearly managed to inject a bit of much-needed confidence and belief into his players. Although Keegan has attempted to play down expectations since his return, the whole of Tyneside will be desperately hoping that the revival in the team's fortunes is a permanent one.

Kevin Keegan factfile
Born: Armthorpe, February 14th 1951
Newcastle career: 85 apps, 49 goals (1982–84)
Other clubs: Scunthorpe United, Liverpool, Hamburg, Southampton
International: England, 63 caps, 21 goals

— EXPERIENCE REQUIRED —

The following players who managed Newcastle at some stage in their career but didn't play for the club participated in the World Cup finals:

Year	Host	Player	Nation
1954	Switzerland	Bill McGarry	England
1958	Sweden	Bobby Robson	England
1962	Chile	Bobby Robson	England (non-playing)
1966	England	Jack Charlton	England
1970	Mexico	Jack Charlton	England
1974	West Germany	Kenny Dalglish	Scotland
1978	Argentina	Osvaldo Ardiles	Argentina
1978	Argentina	Graeme Souness	Scotland
1978	Argentina	Kenny Dalglish	Scotland
1982	Spain	Kenny Dalglish	Scotland
1982	Spain	Osvaldo Ardiles	Argentina
1982	Spain	Graeme Souness	Scotland
1986	Mexico	Graeme Souness	Scotland
1990	Italy	Ruud Gullit	Netherlands

— WALLSEND BOYS' CLUB —

The employees and directors of Swan Hunters Shipyard originally founded Wallsend Boys' Club in 1938 to provide recreational facilities for their apprentices and other local youngsters.

Now Swans have gone but the Boys' Club remains and still plays a key role in the local community, providing a positive influence on young people's lives.

Wallsend graduates who have gone on to join Newcastle United include:

Peter Beardsley
Ian Bogie
Lee Clark
Tony Dinning
Robbie Elliott
Chris Hedworth
Anth Lormor
Neil McDonald
David Robinson
David Roche
Alan Shearer
Eric Steele
Paul Stephenson
Alan Thompson
Steve Watson
John Watson
Jeff Wrightson

Former player Alan Shearer didn't forget his roots and Wallsend were among a large number of organisations to benefit from the proceeds of his 2006 testimonial match and other events, being awarded £15,000.

A certain other United have also indirectly benefited from the Wallsend production line, with Steve Bruce and Michael Carrick finding their way to Premiership-winning success at Old Trafford.

— GONG SHOW —

Newcastle United players and managers who have been recognised with civil or military honours include:

Recipient	Award	Year/event
Sandy Higgins	Military Medal	World War I
Tom Rowlandson	Military Cross	World War I
Donald Bell	Victoria Cross	World War I
Benny Craig	Military Medal	World War II
Ivor Allchurch	MBE	1966
Jack Charlton	OBE	1974
George Eastham	OBE	1975
Kevin Keegan	OBE	1982
Kenny Dalglish	MBE	1984
Bobby Robson	CBE	1990
Peter Beardsley	MBE	1995
Ian Rush	MBE	1996
John Barnes	MBE	1998
Stuart Pearce	MBE	1999
Alan Shearer	OBE	2001
Bobby Robson	Knighthood	2002
Les Ferdinand	MBE	2005

In addition, former Newcastle United Chairman John Hall was knighted in 1991.

Sir Bobby Robson was awarded an honorary degree by Newcastle University in 2003, becoming a Doctor of Civil Law (DCL). The same honour was then bestowed upon Alan Shearer in 2006, this time by Northumbria University.

However, the pair have some distance to go in the free degrees stakes if they're to emulate Jack Charlton. The former Newcastle United boss was honoured by the University of Limerick in 1994, by both Northumbria University and Leeds Metropolitan University in 1995 and most recently by Leeds University in 2004.

— TEENAGE KICKS PART II —

Newcastle United's second successful FA Youth Cup campaign came in the 1984/85 season, beginning with a resounding 6–0 home victory over then holders Everton. Future Magpies star Paul Gascoigne notched two in that game and scored another when Leeds United were beaten 2–0 on Tyneside in the fourth round.

The Fifth Round pitted United against Manchester City and that man Gazza was on target again as a 2–1 success was recorded. Newcastle's name came out of the hat first at the fourth time of asking, with Coventry City promptly dispatched 3–0 – two goals for Gascoigne this time round.

Into the last four and Birmingham City were beaten 2–0 at home, before a resounding 5–2 win at St Andrew's set up a final against Watford.

Just under 7,000 fans were at St James' Park to see a 0–0 stalemate, the young Hornets being captained by future Newcastle striker Malcolm Allen. There were to be no mistakes in the away leg though, Joe Allon and Paul Gascoigne delighting the travelling support in a 7,097 crowd as the team coached by Colin Suggett ran out 4–1 winners.

Seven of the final side went on to feature in the Magpies first team: Joe Allon, Paul Gascoigne, Gary Kelly, Tony Nesbit, Kevin Scott, Brian Tinnion, Jeff Wrightson. An eighth – Paul Stephenson – was on the bench. The other three players were: Stuart Dickinson, Tony Hayton and Stephen Forster.

And a further trio of players featured in ties leading up the final, these being future first team player Ian Bogie, Peter Harbach and Ian McKenzie.

— LEADING BY EXAMPLE —

Newcastle managers have taken to the field on a number of occasions in non-competitive games to show their charges just how it's done. These include:

Charlie Mitten
The former Manchester United and Fulham player celebrated the end of his first season in charge of the Magpies in May 1959 by getting his boots on. United played a three game tour of Southern Ireland, with Mitten scoring once in a 6–3 victory over Drumcondra.

Ossie Ardiles
A midweek friendly at Blyth Spartans in November 1991 gave World Cup winner Ossie the chance to pull his boots on. Ardiles was joined in the Newcastle side by his assistant manager Tony Galvin (ex-Tottenham Hotspur) and also kit man Chris Guthrie (ex- Fulham). And Ossie repeated his performance in January 1992, forming a three-man defence with Galvin and Magpies coach Derek Fazackerley as United took part in a game staged to inaugurate the new floodlights at local league Dunston Federation Brewery.

Kevin Keegan
Putting aside the disappointment of losing the Premiership title just days before, KK pulled on a black and white shirt at the City Ground to take part in Stuart Pearce's testimonial. The final score on an enjoyable evening was 6–5 to Pearce's Forest, with Keegan netting from the penalty spot for the black and whites.

Kevin Keegan and Kenny Dalglish
With Ruud Gullit crying off due to an unspecified illness, his two managerial predecessors both made cameo appearances for Newcastle during Peter Beardsley's testimonial game at St James' Park. For Kenny it was a chance to face his former side Celtic, although both men would have appreciated the original choice of opposition – Liverpool (who were forced to pull out due to league fixture congestion).

Ruud Gullit
Having seen his side beaten in their two previous warm-up games at Dundee United and Livingston, Ruud Gullit's patience ran out when his side trailed 0–2 at half-time away to Reading in July 1999. Withdrawing defender David Beharall from the action, Gullit emerged for the second half to try and organise his failing troops from midfield. A penalty conversion just after the hour from James Coppinger halved the arrears and a late solo effort from Paul Robinson saved the Magpies' blushes, the game ending 2–2.

Gullit then repeated the trick four nights later away at Stoke City, wearing shirt number 16 and replacing Des Hamilton after 38 minutes. He remained on the field for the rest of the evening, although in the final 30 minutes he moved further forward. One attempt at a shot saw the ball fly high and wide of the goal into an unoccupied part of the Britannia Stadium – the game being held up until a replacement ball was found.

— NO PLACE LIKE HOME —

With more and more domestic fixtures taking place in identikit stadia, here is a list of now-defunct grounds that have featured on the club's seasonal itinerary at one time or another since league football resumed in 1946. Many of them have now been replaced by housing estates, supermarkets or just levelled and left – but memories of them remain.

Opponent	Venue	Last visited
Arsenal	Highbury	2005
Bolton Wanderers	Burnden Park	1995
Bradford Park Avenue	Park Avenue	1947
Brighton and Hove Albion	Goldstone Ground	1991
Bristol Rovers	Eastville	1980
Chester City	Sealand Road	1974
Coventry City	Highfield Road	2000
Derby County	The Baseball Ground	1996
Doncaster Rovers	Belle Vue	1947
Huddersfield Town	Leeds Road	1984
Hull City	Boothferry Park	1990
Leicester City	Filbert Street	2002
Manchester City	Maine Road	2002
Middlesbrough	Ayresome Park	1992
Millwall	The Den	1993
Newport County	Somerton Park	1947
Northampton Town	The County Ground	1966
Oxford United	The Manor Ground	1992
Reading	Elm Park	1990
Scunthorpe United	The Old Showground	1974
Southampton	The Dell	2000
Stoke City	The Victoria Ground	1995
Sunderland	Roker Park	1996
Swansea City	Vetch Field	1983
Walsall	Fellows Park	1975
Wigan Athletic	Springfield Park	1954
Wimbledon	Plough Lane	1989

Note: Dates given are of the last competitive first team game Newcastle played at the venue. The Magpies have appeared in friendlies at other grounds which no longer exist but never played competitively there – hence their omission from the list.

— "HELLO NEWCASTLE!" —

Before 1982, the only live musical performances at St James' Park had come from local brass bands entertaining the crowd.

However on June 23rd of that year, a date on the Rolling Stones European Tour marked the debut of the ground as a live popular music venue. Messrs Jagger, Richards, Wood, Wyman and Watts performed on a stage erected across the Leazes End goalmouth with fans in both stands, standing on the matted pitch and spread across the Gallowgate End.

Support act for that gig was American combo, The J Geils Band, while a year later on July 15th 1984, local lads Lindisfarne and Mexican guitarist Carlos Santana opened for Bob Dylan, in town as part of his European Tour.

1985 then saw Bruce Springsteen and The E Street Band perform at the stadium on both 4th and 5th June as part of the 'Born In The USA' tour. Springsteen then moved on to mainland Europe, playing gigs at a number of outdoor venues including football stadia in Rotterdam, Munich and Milan that have all played host to Newcastle in European football fixtures.

A year later and July 9th 1986 saw Queen entertain the crowds, supported by Status Quo. A third act had been due to play, but an accident on the A1 delayed the arrival of the equipment and road crew for the Australian rockers INXS.

After a four-year hiatus, the Rolling Stones returned to the stadium on July 18th 1990, as part of their 'Urban Jungle' tour. Support this time came from US group Dan Reed Network and English rockers The Quireboys – the latter who included Tynesider Spike on lead vocals.

It took another 16 years before live music returned to the venue, when Bryan Adams appeared on June 6th 2006, supported by Beverley Knight. With the stadium having been reconstructed in the intervening years, the stage was constructed to face the North West corner, with fans occupying both seats and a standing area in front of the stage.

June 25th 2007 then saw Rod Stewart in Toon, with support coming from The Pretenders.

Local band Lindisfarne made a return visit to St James' Park on May 7th 1993, playing for the crowd attending the final game of the season, against Leicester City. Promoting their album *Elvis Live on the Moon*, they played from a temporary stage erected on the partly-constructed new Leazes End Stand.

— CAN YOU SPELL THAT PLEASE? —

Some of the more elongated formal names of Newcastle players have included:

Full name	AKA
Faustino Hernan Hinestroza **Asprilla**	Tino
Carlos Daniel Lobo **Cordone**	Daniel
Diego Antonio **Gavilan** Zarate	Diego
Fransiscus Leonardus Albertus **Koenen**	Frans
Elena Sierra **Marcelino**	Martha
Obafemi Akinwunmi **Martins**	Oba
Francisco Ernandi Lima da Silva **Mirandinha**	Mira
Oguchialu Chilioke **Onyewu**	Gooch
Nolberto Albino **Solano** Todco	Nobby
Hugo Miguel Ferreira **Viana**	Hugo

In January 1997, United announced that the Portuguese central defender Raul Oliveira had passed a medical and was set to sign on loan from Farense. However, the deal fell through and Oliveira later appeared briefly for Bradford City, before returning to Portugal. The player's full name was: Raul Miguel Silva da Fonseca Castanheira de Oliveira.

At the opposite end of the scale, the club took goalkeeper An Qi on trial in December 2002 from Chinese club Dalian Shide, but didn't offer him a contract.

— IT'S A FAMILY AFFAIR I —

Brothers who have played for Newcastle United over the years include:

Appleby Teessiders Matty and Richie were at St James' Park together in the early 1990s, but while the elder Matty appeared for the first team in defence, the younger Richie never got the chance to show his midfield skills in a competitive senior game. However, the duo were selected in the same team by Kevin Keegan in Anglo-Italian Cup ties away to Bari and at home to Cesena in 1992.

Caldwell Despite playing together at junior and reserve level, the nearest central defenders Steve and Gary got to partnering each other in the first team came when Sir Bobby Robson brought them both off the bench during a testimonial match at West Bromwich Albion in 2001. After the pair had left

United, they appeared together competitively for the first time at senior level when both were selected for Scotland in a World Cup qualifier away to Moldova in October 2004.

King   Amble-born goalkeeper Ray and his elder striker brother George were both at Gallowgate when World War II ended but never played in the first team together.

Robledo   Chilean pair George and Eduardo ('Ted') were signed from Barnsley in January 1949, United taking the younger left-sided midfielder Ted in order to capture the signature of his striker brother. The brothers appeared together for the first time in a Newcastle shirt on the last day of 1949, away to Aston Villa.

Withe   Merseyside-born duo Peter and Chris were on the books at St James' Park together in the 1970s, but the younger Chris (a defender) only made his first team debut the season after the older Peter (a striker) had left.

The following sets of brothers were on the club's books together, but only the Kennedy brothers both appeared in the football league.

Ameobi	Shola, Tomi and Sami
Elliott	Robbie and John
Hislop	Shaka and Kona
Howie	Jimmy and David
Keating	Bert and Reg
Kennedy	Alan and Keith
Lindsay	Billy and James
Mitten	John and Charles junior
Rutherford	Jackie and Andrew
Smith	'Tot', George and Robert
Wilson	Joe and Glenn

— NEWCASTLE LEGENDS: STAN SEYMOUR —

Stan Seymour: Gave his life to Newcastle United

As captain, manager, director and Vice-President, Seymour served Newcastle United in three spells over a period of almost 70 years.

The man known as 'Mister Newcastle' thanks to his achievements on and off the field was initially discarded by the Magpies as a teenage amateur player before World War I, returning to play local football for Shildon.

After a brief spell at Bradford City, Seymour's career took off after some impressive displays for Greenock Morton, before a move to Newcastle followed in May 1920.

The return on the £2,500 fee was instant as Seymour marked his debut with a goal on the opening day of the season, although his side only managed a 1–1 home draw with West Bromwich Albion.

Four solid seasons in the Newcastle side at outside-left brought successive top ten finishes, culminating in a 2–0 victory in the 1924 FA Cup Final, where Seymour scored the second goal in the dying minutes of the club's Wembley debut.

Seymour's finest campaign, however, came in 1926/27 when he was an ever-present in Newcastle's championship-winning side, scoring 18 goals in the process – the last of which gave his team the 1–1 draw that clinched the title away to West Ham United.

He retired from playing two seasons later, his final appearance coming at Gallowgate against Arsenal in October 1928.

In 1937 Seymour was invited to join the Newcastle board of directors. He accepted, giving up his sideline of reporting on matches for newspapers but retaining ownership of the sports shop he'd established in the city.

After the war years intervened, Seymour set about reconstructing the side which achieved promotion back to the First Division at the second attempt in 1948.

Having handed over nominal control of team affairs to George Martin, Seymour took over again when Martin defected to Aston Villa in 1950, presiding over two Wembley FA Cup Final successes.

A dip in results, however, led to Seymour being persuaded by his fellow directors to try another team manager, Duggie Livingstone arriving in December 1954.

He was to last barely a year though, with Seymour famously over-ruling him before the 1955 FA Cup Final, when the name of Jackie Milburn failed to appear on the first Newcastle teamsheet submitted to the directors.

Seymour remained at St James' Park while Charlie Mitten and Norman Smith were tried in the manager's job. However, his masterstroke proved to be bringing Joe Harvey back to Tyneside in 1962 – the former Magpies captain having been overlooked for the post when Mitten was appointed, moving on to learn his trade at Workington.

With Harvey's departure in 1975, Seymour retired as a director the following year at the age of 83. He passed away two years later, having seen his son join the board – although he didn't live to see Stan Seymour junior emulate his father and become chairman.

George Stanley Seymour factfile
Born: Kelloe, County Durham, May 16th 1893
Died: December 24th 1978
Newcastle career: 1920–29
Other clubs: Shildon Town, Coxhoe, Bradford City, Greenock Morton

— FA CUP HAT-TRICK HEROES —

Seventeen players have scored FA Cup hat-tricks for Newcastle, the last being Paul Kitson against Swansea City back in 1994. The full list is:

Player	Season	Opponent
Bill Appleyard	1907/08	Grimsby Town (h)
George Wilson	1908/09	Clapton Orient (h)
Albert Shepherd	1910/11	Bury (h)
Neil Harris	1923/24	Derby County (h)
Hughie Gallacher	1926/27	Notts County (h)
Tom McDonald	1926/27	Notts County (h)
Jimmy Richardson	1929/30	Clapton Orient (h)
Hughie Gallacher	1929/30	Brighton & Hove Albion (h)
Duncan Hutchison	1930/31	Nottingham Forest (h)
Jimmy Richardson	1931/32	Southport (n)
Charlie Wayman	1946/47	Southampton (h)
Jackie Milburn	1949/50	Oldham Athletic (a)
Jackie Milburn	1951/52	Portsmouth (a)
Len White	1957/58	Plymouth Argyle (a)
Duncan Neale	1960/61	Fulham (h)
Wyn Davies	1966/67	Coventry City (a)
Paul Kitson	1994/95	Swansea City (h)

In addition, Andy Aitken netted four times in an FA Cup qualifying round home tie against local side Willington Athletic in season 1897/98.

— INDIVIDUAL LEAGUE CUP SCORING FEATS —

Player	Season	Opponent	Goals scored
Alan Gowling	1975/76	Southport (h)	4
Malcolm Macdonald	1973/74	Doncaster Rovers (h)	3
Malcolm Macdonald	1974/75	Queens Park Rangers (h)	3
Gavin Peacock	1991/92	Crewe Alexandra (a)	3
Andy Cole	1993/94	Notts County (h)	3
Andy Cole	1993/94	Notts County (a)	3
Craig Bellamy	2001/02	Brentford (h)	3

— TWIN TOWERS PART III —

As well as their various cup final and semi-final outings, a Newcastle side has also appeared at Wembley on another occasion, as part of The Football League Centenary celebrations of 1988.

The Mercantile Credit Football Festival was a two-day knock-out event involving 16 teams, who played each other in limited duration (20 minutes each way) games on a reduced size pitch.

Qualification for the event was based on the number of league points gained during a three month period earlier in the season from Divisions One to Four – eight clubs joining from the First, four from the Second and two each from Divisions Three and Four.

The event took place over a Saturday and Sunday when no league games were scheduled. And in what was already the second game of the day, Newcastle kicked off at 10.50am before a sparsely populated Wembley against Liverpool.

Newcastle fielded a side including the likes of Gary Kelly, Paul Gascoigne, Brian Tinnion, Glenn Roeder, Paul Goddard, Mirandhina, Neil McDonald and Michael O'Neill while John Bailey was an unused substitute. After a 0–0 draw, the tie was settled on penalties – but in a change to the usual practice, these were sudden death from the off. Steve McMahon took the first Liverpool spot kick, only for Kelly to parry it over the crossbar. That meant that Newcastle only had to score to go through and McDonald duly obliged to give the club a rare Wembley victory to savour.

In the second game the Magpies came back down to earth with a bump though, losing 2–0 to Tranmere Rovers of Division Four. The side from Birkenhead netted through John Morrissey and an Ian Muir penalty and Toon misery was complete when the Rovers keeper saved a penalty from Mirandinha.

Tranmere were so up for it that they'd even recorded a tune for their Wembley bow (*We are the Rovers* by Don Woods) and had beaten Division One side Wimbledon in their first game. With many of the 1,000 or so Newcastle followers there having purchased weekend tickets, the Sunday saw them trudge back again for a further day of pointless games not involving their own club.

Nottingham Forest were the eventual winners of the competition, but their manager Brian Clough was so uninterested in proceedings that he declined to attend.

— DREAM STARTS II —

The only Newcastle player to have made his debut as a substitute and scored was Alex Mathie in 1993.

George Dalton netted within six minutes of his debut, at home to Leicester City in 1961. Unfortunately it was an own goal.

Aside from the select few players who scored at least a hat trick on their first competitive appearance for Newcastle, a number of others have also marked their debut in memorable style by bagging two goals:

Year	Player	Opponent/venue
1906	Finlay Speedie	The Wednesday (h)
1907	George Wilson	Liverpool (a)
1925	Hughie Gallacher	Everton (h)
1946	George Stobbart	Coventry City (h)
1946	Jackie Milburn	Barnsley (h)
1958	Arthur Bottom	Everton (a)
1958	Ivor Allchurch	Leicester City (h)
1960	Duncan Neale	Fulham (h)
1998	Duncan Ferguson	Wimbledon (h)

— IT'S A FAMILY AFFAIR II —

The following families have had fathers and sons who have represented Newcastle:

Edgar   Goalkeeper Eddie made one first team appearance in 1976 before emigrating to Canada. His son David (a defender) was born in Kitchener, Ontario but moved to Newcastle and came through the ranks to make his first team debut in December 2006.

Wilson   Defender Joseph and his centre forward son Carl both made a single league appearance for Newcastle's first team – the latter the only one of seven footballing brothers to emulate his father.

Other fathers and sons who have both been on the club's books, include:

Cahill	Tommy and Tommy Junior
Gallacher	Hughie, Hughie junior and Matt
McDermott	Terry, Neale and Greg
McDonald*	James and Neil

Nattrass	Irving and Paul
Niblo	Tom and Alan
Seymour	Stan and Colin
Swinburne	Tom, Alan and Trevor
Wharton	Kenny and Paul
Wrightson	Jeff and Kieran

Note: Second (and third) named didn't play first team football for the club except*, where the father failed but the son succeeded.

— MANX MAGS —

Back in the 1980s when competitive fixtures for Newcastle got no more exotic than trips to Wales, friendly tours provided some variety and a change of scenery for the more intrepid supporter. However, the loyalty of the most diehard Magpie follower was tested when the club opted to participate in the Isle of Man Tournament as part of their pre-season programme in both 1985 and 1986.

Newcastle's first appearance in the tournament coincided with a summer season on the island from singer Tony Christie, while the following year featured cabaret delights in the shape of Les Dennis, Max Boyce and Rod Hull and Emu!

1985:

Venue	Fixture/result	Newcastle scorer(s)
Douglas	Leicester City 3 Newcastle 2	Peter Beardsley, George Reilly
Ramsey	Blackburn Rovers 2 Newcastle 1	Paul Gascoigne
Castletown	Wigan Athletic 1 Newcastle 4	Neil McDonald 2, Glenn Roeder, Peter Beardsley

1986:

Venue	Fixture/result	Newcastle scorer(s)
Douglas	Blackburn Rovers 2 Newcastle 2	Paul Gascoigne, Neil McDonald
Castletown	Portsmouth 2 Newcastle 2	Neil McDonald, Joe Allon
Castletown	Isle of Man XI 1 Newcastle 5	Ian Stewart, Peter Beardsley Joe Allon 2, Paul Ferris

— BIG DAY OUT IN THE NORTH —

A selection of crucial final fixtures at St James' Park over the years – crucial for the opposition that is:

April 1903 Requiring a victory on Tyneside to retain the First Division title, Sunderland blew their big chance by losing 1–0 to Newcastle. The Wearsiders' defeat meant they finished third behind title winners The Wednesday and runners-up Aston Villa.

May 1926 Having lost the FA Cup final on the previous Saturday, Manchester City arrived at Gallowgate needing to avoid defeat in order to secure their First Division status. Sadly for them, the game finished in a 3–2 victory for Newcastle with City missing a penalty.

April 1949 A resounding 5–0 away success by Portsmouth confirmed the status of the south coast team as Division One champions, Jack Froggatt leading the way with a hat-trick.

April 1962 The start of the Don Revie era of success came at St James' Park as Leeds United won 3–0 to banish any fear of relegation to Division Three (although other results meant they were safe regardless of the score). The visitors led at the interval thanks to an own goal, with second half efforts from Billy McAdams and Albert Johanneson securing victory. Just three years later Leeds were runners-up in Division One.

May 1968 Manchester City were pressed all the way by the home side before triumphing 4–3 to lift the First Division title, thanks to goals from Neil Young (2), Mike Summerbee and Francis Lee.

May 1979 The penultimate home game of the season saw the gate increase by some 19,000 to over 28,000 as Malcolm Allison brought his Brighton and Hove Albion side to Tyneside. Having been at St James' Park the previous Wednesday to watch Newcastle beat Bristol Rovers 3–0, The Seagulls raced into a similar lead before the interval after Brian Horton, Peter Ward and Gerry Ryan all netted.

And although Alan Shoulder reduced the arrears after the break, Brighton were never in danger of losing the points that confirmed their promotion to Division One for the first time in their history, behind title winners Crystal Palace.

— PREMIERSHIP DISMISSALS —

Prior to the start of the 2007/08 season, 45 players had been dismissed while appearing for Newcastle United in their 578 Premiership fixtures. Four of those decisions were subsequently rescinded. The full list is:

Year	Player	Fixture/venue	Result
1993	Pavel Srnicek	Coventry City (a)	lost 1–2
1994	Pavel Srnicek	Leicester City (a)	won 3–1
1994	Philippe Albert	Liverpool (h)	drew 1–1
1995	Robert Lee	Everton (a)	lost 0–2
1995	Pavel Srnicek	Tottenham Hotspur (h)	drew 3–3
1995	John Beresford	Everton (h)	won 1–0
1996	David Batty	Chelsea (a)	drew 1–1
1997	Keith Gillespie	Arsenal (a)	won 1–0
1997	David Batty	Aston Villa (h)	won 1–0
1997	David Batty	Derby County (a)	lost 0–1
1998	David Batty	Blackburn Rovers (a)	lost 0–1
1998	Nicos Dabizas	Arsenal (a)	lost 0–3
1998	Stuart Pearce	West Ham United (h)	lost 0–3
1998	Didi Hamann	Liverpool (a)	lost 2–4
1999	Nicos Dabizas	Charlton Athletic (a)	drew 2–2
1999	Alan Shearer	Aston Villa (h)	lost 0–1
1999	Nicos Dabizas	Manchester United (a)	lost 1–5
1999	Warren Barton	Coventry City (a)	lost 1–4
2000	Warren Barton	Derby County (h)	won 3–2
2001	Nolberto Solano	Tottenham Hotspur (a)	lost 2–4
2001	Kieron Dyer	Tottenham Hotspur (a)	lost 2–4
2001	Nolberto Solano	Ipswich Town (a)	lost 0–1
2001	Gary Speed*	Aston Villa (h)	won 3–0
2001	Alan Shearer*	Charlton Athletic (a)	drew 1–1
2001	Craig Bellamy*	Arsenal (a)	won 3–1
2002	Nicos Dabizas	Blackburn Rovers (a)	lost 2–5
2003	Laurent Robert	Arsenal (h)	drew 1–1
2003	Andy Griffin	Fulham (a)	lost 1–2
2003	Laurent Robert	Everton (a)	drew 2–2
2003	Andy O'Brien	Chelsea (a)	lost 0–5
2004	Andy O'Brien	Aston Villa (a)	drew 0–0
2004	Lee Bowyer	Liverpool (a)	lost 1–3
2005	Lee Bowyer	Aston Villa (h)	lost 0–3
2005	Kieron Dyer	Aston Villa (h)	lost 0–3
2005	Steven Taylor	Aston Villa (h)	lost 0–3
2005	Shola Ameobi	Everton (a)	lost 0–2

2005	Jermaine Jenas*	Arsenal (a)	lost 0–2
2005	Scott Parker	Fulham (a)	drew 1–1
2005	Steven Taylor	Blackburn Rovers (a)	won 3–0
2005	Lee Bowyer	Liverpool (a)	lost 0–2
2006	Celestine Babayaro	Aston Villa (a)	won 2–1
2006	Jean-Alain Boumsong	Liverpool (h)	lost 1–3
2006	Stephen Carr	Chelsea (h)	won 1–0
2006	Titus Bramble	Everton (h)	drew 1–1
2008	Alan Smith	Manchester United (a)	lost 0–6

* Subsequently rescinded

Saturday April 2nd 2005 remains Newcastle's blackest day in the Premiership, with Bowyer and Dyer dismissed for fighting with each other in the 82nd minute of the game. That reduced the Magpies to eight men, Steven Taylor having been red carded nine minutes previously by referee Barry Knight for deliberate handball.

In addition, there has been one instance of a Newcastle player being red carded while not on the field of play. This came in October 2005 at St James' Park when a case of mistaken identity saw Scott Parker wrongly yellow carded. When the error was realised post-match, the booking was transferred to the guilty party, Stephen Carr, who had already been booked in the game and was subsequently banned.

— SINGLETOONS —

The following 60 players made one league start for Newcastle United but never featured in any other competitive game for the club.

Name	Year	Name	Year
J W Barr	1893	M. Keir	1893
John Patten	1893	Alex Ramsay	1893
Isaac Ryder	1893	William Simm	1893
Haynes	1895	Thomas Blyth	1897
John Allen	1898	Archie Mowatt	1898
George Mole	1900	Daniel Pattinson	1902
Ord Richardson	1902	Bob Benson	1903
Hugh Bolton	1905	Tom Rowlandson	1905
R.E. Rutherford	1906	George Hedley	1907
Ben Nicholson	1907	Noel Brown	1908
Bob Blanthorne	1908	William Hughes	1908
Alex McCulloch	1908	Jack Thomas	1912

Jack Alderson	1913	Thomas Grey	1914
Tom Cairns	1915	John Soulsby	1915
Alex Rainnie	1920	John Thain	1921
John Archibald	1922	Allan Taylor	1925
Billy Halliday	1927	Stan Barber	1928
Robert Bradley	1928	Joe Wilson	1929
Ike Keen	1930	James Robinson	1931
Joe Ford	1932	Tom McBain	1932
David Smith	1936	John Shiel	1937
George Bradley	1938	Dominic Kelly	1939
Ron Anderson	1947	Albert Clark	1948
Andy Graver	1950	Alex Gaskell	1953
Bill Redhead	1956	Chris Harker	1958
Carl Wilson	1958	Grant Malcolm	1959
George Watkin	1962	Les O'Neil	1963
John Hope	1969	Keith Kennedy	1972
Tony Bell	1974	Rob McKinnon	1985*
Paul Moran	1991*		

(*substituted during the game)

In addition, five players made their only Newcastle appearance as substitutes in league games:

Martin Gorry	1977
Keith Mulgrove	1978
Kevin Pugh	1981
John Watson	1991
James Coppinger	2000

Another five players made their only appearance for the club in the League Cup:

Billy Wilson	1961
Derek Craig	1971
Phil Leaver	1980
Justin Fashanu	1991 (as sub)
Steve Guppy	1994 (as sub)

Two more players made their sole outing to date in the UEFA Cup:

Lewis Guy	2004 (as sub)
Tim Krul	2006

And finally, the FA Cup saw one debutant who never appeared again:

Eddie Edgar	1976

Perhaps the most luckless trio of 'singletoons' are Thomas Blyth, George Mole and Daniel Pattinson – who all marked their only game for the club by scoring a goal.

James Coppinger's Premiership experience consisted of 11 minutes at home to Chelsea, while fellow striker Lewis Guy played for exactly the same duration at home to Sporting Lisbon in the UEFA Cup. The pair subsequently played together when both moved on to Doncaster Rovers.

— CLOSE BUT . . . —

Players who were selected as first team substitutes for Newcastle United but failed to make a competitive senior appearance include:

Player	Season(s) selected
Terry Melling	1965/66
Terry Johnson	1968/69
Dave Clarke	1968/69
Billy Coulson	1971/72
Brian Reid	1993/94
Jason Drysdale	1994/95
Paul Barrett	1996/97
Stuart Elliott	1996/97, 1997/98
David Terrier	1997/98
Ralf Keidel	1997/98
Brian Pinas	1997/98
Lionel Perez	1998/99, 1999/00
Peter Keen	1998/99
Gary Caldwell	1999/00, 2000/01
Stuart Green	1999/00, 2001/02
Tony Caig	2002/03, 2003/04, 2004/05
Bradley Orr	2003/04
Kris Gate	2005/06
James Troisi	2006/07
Fraser Forster	2006/07
James Troisi	2007/08
Ben Tozer	2007/08

— ATLANTIC CROSSING —

A number of Newcastle players or managers have given service to 'soccer' clubs in The United States of America, since the round ball game was popularised in the 1880s:

Player	Club	Year joined
Celestine Babayaro	LA Galaxy	2008
Jerry Best	Providence Clamdiggers	1924
Jerry Best	New Bedford Whalers	1926
Jerry Best	Fall River Marksmen	1929
Jerry Best	Pawtucket Rangers	1929
Viv Busby	Tulsa Roughnecks	1980
Tony Caig	Houston Dynamo	2007
Paul Cannell	Washington Diplomats	1978
Paul Cannell	Memphis Rogues	1979
Paul Cannell	Detroit Express	1981
Franz Carr	Pittsburgh Riverhounds	2000
Paul Dalglish	Houston Dynamo	2006
Ian Davies	Detroit Express	1978
George Eastham	Cleveland Stokers	1967
Eddie Edgar	New York Cosmos	1979
Justin Fashanu	Los Angeles Heat	1988
Alan Foggon	Rochester Lancers	1976
Alan Foggon	Hartford BiCentennials	1976
Howard Gayle	Dallas Sidekicks	1986
Ruud Gullit	LA Galaxy (manager)	2007
Steve Guppy	DC United	2005
Steve Hardwick	Detroit Express	1978
Bryan Harvey	New York Americans	1962
Gordon Hindson	Hartford Bicentennials	1976
Shaka Hislop	Baltimore Blast	1992
Shaka Hislop	FC Dallas	2006
Trevor Hockey	San Diego Jaws	1976
Trevor Hockey	Las Vegas Quicksilvers	1977
Trevor Hockey	San Jose Earthquakes	1977
Pat Howard	Portland Timbers	1978
Steve Howey	New England Revolution	2004
Rocky Hudson	Fort Lauderdale Strikers	1978
Rocky Hudson	Minnesota Strikers	1986
Mike Mahoney	Chicago Sting	1978
Mike Mahoney	California Surf	1979
Mike Mahoney	Los Angeles Lazers	1982

Mick Martin	Vancouver Whitecaps	1984
Kenny Mitchell	Tulsa Roughnecks	1978
David McCreery	Tulsa Roughnecks	1981
John McGuigan	New York Americans	1962
Michael O'Neill	Portland Timbers	2001
Graham Oates	Detroit Express	1978
Graham Oates	California Surf	1981
Andy Parkinson	Philadelphia Fury	1980
Andy Parkinson	Team America	1983
Andy Parkinson	New York Cosmos	1984
Andy Parkinson	Fort Lauderdale Strikers	1988
Willie Penman	Seattle Sounders	1974
Keith Robson	Team Hawaii	1977
Eric Ross	Detroit Cougars	1967
Liam Tuohy	Boston Rovers	1967
Nigel Walker	San Diego Sockers	1982
Peter Withe	Portland Timbers	1975

In addition, a smaller number of Magpies have found themselves playing the game in Canada over the years:

Player	Club	Year joined
Peter Beardsley	Vancouver Whitecaps	1981
Martin Brittain	Toronto FC	2007
Alex Caie	Westmount	circa 1914
Alex Caie	Sons of Scotland	circa 1914
Tony Caig	Vancouver Whitecaps	2006
Paul Cannell	Calgary Boomers	1980
John Carver	Toronto FC (manager)	2008
Tommy Casey	Inter Roma	1963
Alex Cropley	Toronto Blizzard	1981
Eddie Edgar	London City	1980
Justin Fashanu	Edmonton Brickmen	1988
Rocky Hudson	Edmonton Brickmen	1987
Peter Kelly	London City	1981
Andy Parkinson	Montreal Manic	1981
Laurent Robert	Toronto FC	2008
Craig Robson	Vancouver Whitecaps	2003
Colin Suggett	Vancouver Canadians	1967
Andy Walker	Toronto Blizzard	1983
Kenny Wharton	Winnipeg Furies	1990
Darren Huckerby	Vancouver Whitecaps	2008

Both Graeme Souness (Montreal Olympique as a player) and Sir Bobby Robson (Vancouver Royals as manager) had spells in Canada.

— ONLY THE LOANEES —

Players who have moved from other clubs for temporary stints in a Newcastle shirt include:

Player	Loaned from	Year
Viv Busby	Luton Town	1971
Alex Cropley	Aston Villa	1980
Alan Brown	Sunderland	1981
David Mills	West Bromwich Albion	1982
Howard Gayle	Liverpool	1982
Martin Thomas	Bristol Rovers	1983
Ian Baird	Southampton	1984
Dave McKellar	Hibernian	1986
Darren Bradshaw	York City	1989
Tommy Gaynor	Nottingham Forest	1990
Dave Mitchell	Chelsea	1991
Paul Moran	Tottenham Hotspur	1991
Andy Walker	Celtic	1991
Gavin Maguire	Portsmouth	1991
Paul Bodin	Crystal Palace	1991
Terry Wilson	Nottingham Forest	1992
Brian Kilcline	Oldham Athletic	1992
Brian Reid	Glasgow Rangers	1994
Tommy Wright	Manchester City	1999
Helder	Deportivo La Coruna	1999
Wayne Quinn	Sheffield United	2001
Sylvain Distin	Paris St.Germain	2001
Michael Bridges	Leeds United	2004
Giuseppe Rossi	Manchester United	2006
Oguchi Onyewu	Standard Liege	2007

Of these players, Mills, Thomas, Bradshaw, Kilcline and Quinn were ultimately signed by Newcastle on permanent contracts. Attempts were made to sign both Brown and Distin – the former returning to Wearside after allegedly failing a medical amid rumours the Magpies lacked the funds to fund the deal.

Distin, on the other hand, opted not to prolong his stay at Gallowgate despite offers to do so and a £4m transfer fee having been agreed with his club. He moved on to newly-promoted Manchester City, with Newcastle lodging a formal complaint of 'tapping up' allegations. Even since then, Distin has been the target for vocal abuse from Newcastle supporters when he has played for City against his former club.

One player who was never in danger of being offered a contract was Paul Moran, who made one ill-starred appearance at home to Wolverhampton Wanderers and was soon on his way back to White Hart Lane.

— BRIEF ENCOUNTERS I —

A selection of some of the more exotic players who spent time on trial with Newcastle United but never appeared for the club competitively:

Player	Country of Birth
Bernard Allou	Ivory Coast
Teoman Arika	Turkey
Paulo Baier	Brazil
Jean-Hugues Ateba Bilayi	Cameroon
Jorge Bohme	Germany
Dries Boussatta	Morocco
Pierre Boya	Cameroon
Erol Bulut	Germany
Francesco Coco	Italy
Costas Costa	Cyprus
George Christouplos	Australia
Garra Dembele	Mali
John Doyle	USA
Jan Eriksson	Sweden
Carlos Sierra Fumero	Spain
Wael Gomaa	Egypt
Sergei Gurenko	Belarus
Ove Hansen	Denmark
Esteban Herrera	Argentina
Martin Hidalgo	Peru
Leo Houtsanan	Finland
Thomas Huschbeck	Germany
Sami Hyppia	Finland
Rodney Jack	Jamaica
Sun Jihai	China

— CLUB TRIPS —

Newcastle United have regularly embarked upon pre and post-season tours to an array of overseas destinations, where they've played numerous friendly matches:

Year	Destination
1904	Denmark
1905	Bohemia
1906	Bohemia
1907	Germany
1909	Denmark
1911	Germany/Switzerland
1913	Denmark
1921	Spain/France
1922	Norway/Sweden/Denmark
1924	Spain
1927	Holland
1929	Austria/Czechoslovakia/Hungary
1932	France/Germany
1946	Norway/Sweden
1949	USA/Canada
1952	Southern Africa
1955	West Germany
1956	Spain/West Germany
1958	Spain/Romania
1959	Southern Ireland
1959	Spain (Mallorca)*
1960	West Germany/Yugoslavia/Spain
1965	Denmark/West Germany
1970	USA/Canada
1972	Thailand/Hong Kong/Iran
1976	Norway
1977	Malta
1977	Holland*
1978	Sweden*
1980	Sweden*
1982	Portugal (Madeira)*
1983	Malaysia/Thailand/Japan
1983	West Germany/Greece*
1985	New Zealand/Fiji
1988	Sweden*
1989	Sweden*
1990	Hungary (Budapest)*

1991	Sweden*
1994	Finland*
1996	Thailand/Singapore/Japan*
1999	Holland*
2000	Trinidad/Tobago
2000	USA*
2002	Holland*
2003	Malaysia*
2004	Thailand/Hong Kong*
2008	Spain*

*Pre-season trip

— BRIEF ENCOUNTERS II —

A further selection of overseas players who spent time on trial with Newcastle United but never made a competitive appearance for the club:

Player	Country of Birth
Hamed Kavianpour	Iran
Joonas Kolka	Finland
Yoann Lachor	France
Dennis Lawrence	Trinidad
Erwin Lemmens	Belgium
Dragan Lukic	Yugoslavia
Ernest Mtawali	Malawi
Markus Munch	Germany
Nicki Bille Nielsen	Denmark
Victor Nogueira	Portugal
Massimo Oddo	Italy
Isaac Okoronkwo	Nigeria
Pietro Parente	Italy
Pablo Paz	Argentina
Bruno Pereira	Portugal
Bachirou Salou	Togo
Christian Schwegler	Switzerland
Diaby Sekana	Ivory Coast
Tariq	Libya
Shalom Tikva	Israel
Diego Tur	Denmark
Frank Wiblishauser	Germany
Ray Xuerub	Malta
Marc Ziegler	Germany
Chris Zoricich	New Zealand

— WEMBLEY MISCELLANY —

A few random facts related to the Toon's numerous Twin Towers trips:

Year	Guest of honour	Referee
1924	HRH The Duke of York	W.E. Russell
1932	King George V	Percy Harper
1951	King George VI	William Ling
1952	Winston Churchill (Prime Minister)	Arthur Ellis
1955	Queen Elizabeth II	Reg Leafe
1974	HRH Princess Anne	Gordon Kew
1976*	Duke of Norfolk	Jack Taylor
1996**	James Ross (Littlewoods Chairman)	Paul Durkin
1998	Duke and Duchess of Kent	Paul Durkin
1999	HRH Prince of Wales	Peter Jones

Note: All the above were FA Cup finals, except for *League Cup Final and **Charity Shield.

Organised community singing first became a fixture at Wembley Finals in 1927, when a TP Radcliff aka 'The Man in White' appeared on a podium to conduct the crowds. Appearing on the first songsheet was 'Abide with Me'. By the time Newcastle made their trio of successful Wembley appearances in the 1950s, the baton has been passed on to Arthur Caiger.

Incidentally, Arthur Ellis, the referee of the 1952 final went on to be better known to many as 'Uncle Arthur', resident judge of the hit TV programme *It's A Knockout!*.

In 1974, when Newcastle played Liverpool at Wembley, TV personality and *Generation Game* host Bruce Forsyth attempted to lead the singing.

— NEWCASTLE UNITED'S
LEAGUE RECORD 1893–2007 —

SEASON	(DIV)	Home						Away							
		P	W	D	L	F	A	W	D	L	F	A	Pts	Pos	
1893/94	2	28	12	1	1	44	10	3	5	6	22	29	36	4th	
1894/95	2	30	11	1	3	51	28	1	2	12	21	56	27	10th	
1895/96	2	30	14	0	1	57	14	2	2	11	16	36	34	5th	
1896/97	2	30	13	1	1	42	13	4	0	11	14	39	35	5th	
1897/98	2	30	14	0	1	43	10	7	3	5	21	22	45	2nd	
														(Promoted)	
1898/99	1	34	9	3	5	33	18	2	5	10	16	30	30	13th	
1899/00	1	34	10	5	2	34	15	3	5	9	19	28	36	5th	
1900/01	1	34	10	5	2	27	13	4	5	8	15	24	38	6th	
1901/02	1	34	11	3	3	41	14	3	6	8	7	20	37	3rd	
1902/03	1	34	12	1	4	31	11	2	3	12	10	40	32	14th	
1903/04	1	34	12	3	2	31	13	6	3	8	27	32	42	4th	
1904/05	1	34	14	1	2	41	12	9	1	7	31	21	48	1st	
														(Champions)	
1905/06	1	38	12	4	3	49	23	6	3	10	25	25	43	4th	
1906/07	1	38	18	1	0	51	12	4	6	9	23	34	51	1st	
														(Champions)	
1907/08	1	38	11	4	4	41	24	4	8	7	24	30	42	4th	
1908/09	1	38	14	1	4	32	20	10	4	5	33	21	53	1st	
														(Champions)	
1909/10	1	38	11	3	5	33	22	8	4	7	37	34	45	4th	
1910/11	1	38	8	7	4	37	18	7	3	9	24	25	40	8th	
1911/12	1	38	10	4	5	37	25	8	4	7	27	25	44	3rd	
1912/13	1	38	8	5	6	30	23	5	3	11	17	24	34	14th	
1913/14	1	38	9	6	4	27	18	4	5	10	12	30	37	11th	
1914/15	1	38	8	4	7	29	23	3	6	10	17	25	32	15th	
1915/19					FIRST WORLD WAR										
1919/20	1	42	11	5	5	31	13	6	4	11	13	26	43	8th	
1920/21	1	42	14	3	4	43	18	6	7	8	23	27	50	5th	
1921/22	1	42	11	5	5	36	19	7	5	9	23	26	46	7th	
1922/23	1	42	13	6	2	31	11	5	6	10	14	26	48	4th	
1923/24	1	42	13	5	3	40	21	4	5	12	20	33	42	9th	
1924/25	1	42	11	6	4	43	18	5	10	6	18	24	48	6th	
1925/26	1	42	13	3	5	59	33	3	7	11	25	42	42	10th	
1926/27	1	42	19	1	1	64	20	6	5	10	32	38	56	1st	
														(Champions)	
1927/28	1	42	9	7	5	49	41	6	6	9	30	40	43	9th	

1928/29	1	42	15	2	4	48	29	4	4	13	22	43	44	10th
1929/30	1	42	13	4	4	52	32	2	3	16	19	60	37	19th
1930/31	1	42	9	2	10	41	45	6	4	11	37	42	36	17th
1931/32	1	42	13	5	3	52	31	5	1	15	28	56	42	11th
1932/33	1	42	15	2	4	44	24	7	3	11	27	39	49	5th
1933/34	1	42	6	11	4	42	29	4	3	14	26	48	34	21st
														(Relegated)
1934/35	2	42	14	2	5	55	25	8	2	11	34	43	48	6th
1935/36	2	42	13	5	3	56	27	7	1	13	32	52	46	8th
1936/37	2	42	11	3	7	45	23	11	2	8	35	33	49	4th
1937/38	2	42	12	4	5	38	18	2	4	15	13	40	36	19th
1938/39	2	42	13	3	5	44	21	5	7	9	17	27	46	9th
1939/46					SECOND WORLD WAR									
1946/47	2	42	11	4	6	60	32	8	6	7	35	30	48	5th
1947/48	2	42	18	1	2	46	13	6	7	8	26	28	56	2nd
														(Promoted)
1948/49	1	42	12	5	4	35	29	8	7	6	35	27	52	4th
1949/50	1	42	14	4	3	49	23	5	8	8	28	32	50	5th
1950/51	1	42	10	6	5	36	22	8	7	6	26	31	49	4th
1951/52	1	42	12	4	5	62	28	6	5	10	36	45	45	8th
1952/53	1	42	9	5	7	34	33	5	4	12	25	37	37	16th
1953/54	1	42	9	2	10	43	40	5	8	8	29	37	38	15th
1954/55	1	42	12	5	4	53	27	5	4	12	36	50	43	8th
1955/56	1	42	12	4	5	49	24	5	3	13	36	46	41	11th
1956/57	1	42	10	5	6	43	31	4	3	14	24	56	36	17th
1957/58	1	42	6	4	11	38	42	6	4	11	35	39	32	19th
1958/59	1	42	11	3	7	40	29	6	4	11	40	51	41	11th
1959/60	1	42	10	5	6	42	32	8	3	10	40	46	44	8th
1960/61	1	42	7	7	7	51	49	4	3	14	35	60	32	21st
														(Relegated)
1961/62	2	42	10	5	6	40	27	5	4	12	24	31	39	11th
1962/63	2	42	11	8	2	48	23	7	3	11	31	36	47	7th
1963/64	2	42	14	2	5	49	26	6	3	12	25	43	45	8th
1964/65	2	42	16	4	1	50	16	8	5	8	31	29	57	1st
														(Promoted)
1965/66	1	42	10	5	6	26	20	4	4	13	24	43	37	15th
1966/67	1	42	9	5	7	24	27	3	4	14	15	54	33	20th
1967/68	1	42	12	7	2	38	20	1	8	12	16	47	41	10th
1968/69	1	42	12	7	2	40	20	3	7	11	21	35	44	9th
1969/70	1	42	14	2	5	42	16	3	11	7	15	19	47	7th
1970/71	1	42	9	9	3	27	16	5	4	12	17	30	41	12th
1971/72	1	42	10	6	5	30	18	5	5	11	19	34	41	11th

Season	Div	P	W	D	L	F	A	W	D	L	F	A	Pts	Pos
1972/73	1	42	12	6	3	35	19	4	7	10	25	32	45	9th
1973/74	1	42	9	6	6	28	21	4	6	11	21	27	38	15th
1974/75	1	42	12	4	5	39	23	3	5	13	20	49	39	15th
1975/76	1	42	11	4	6	51	26	4	5	12	20	36	39	15th
1976/77	1	42	14	6	1	40	15	4	7	10	24	34	49	5th
1977/78	1	42	4	6	11	26	37	2	4	15	16	41	22	21st (Relegated)
1978/79	2	42	13	3	5	35	24	4	5	12	16	31	42	8th
1979/80	2	42	13	6	2	35	19	2	8	11	18	30	44	9th
1980/81	2	42	11	7	3	22	13	3	7	11	8	32	42	11th
1981/82	2	42	14	4	3	30	14	4	4	13	22	36	62	9th
1982/83	2	42	13	6	2	43	21	5	7	9	32	32	67	5th
1983/84	2	42	16	2	3	51	18	8	6	7	34	35	80	3rd (Promoted)
1984/85	1	42	11	4	6	33	26	2	9	10	22	44	52	14th
1985/86	1	42	12	5	4	46	31	5	7	9	21	41	63	11th
1986/87	1	42	10	4	07	33	29	2	7	12	14	36	47	17th
1987/88	1	40	9	6	5	32	23	5	8	7	23	30	56	8th
1988/89	1	38	3	6	10	19	28	4	4	11	13	35	31	20th (Relegated)
1989/90	2	46	17	4	2	51	26	5	10	8	29	29	80	3rd
1990/91	2	46	8	10	5	24	22	6	7	10	25	34	59	11th
1991/92	2	46	9	8	6	38	30	4	5	14	28	54	52	20th
1992/93	(1)	46	16	6	1	58	15	13	3	7	34	23	96	1st (Promoted)
1993/94	Pr	42	14	4	3	51	14	9	4	8	31	27	77	3rd
1994/95	Pr	42	14	6	1	46	20	6	6	9	21	27	72	6th
1995/96	Pr	38	17	1	1	38	9	7	5	7	28	28	78	2nd
1996/97	Pr	38	13	3	3	54	20	6	8	5	19	20	68	2nd
1997/98	Pr	38	8	5	6	22	20	3	6	10	13	24	44	13th
1998/99	Pr	38	7	6	6	26	25	4	7	8	22	29	46	13th
1999/00	Pr	38	10	5	4	42	20	4	5	10	21	34	52	11th
2000/01	Pr	38	10	4	5	26	17	4	5	10	18	33	51	11th
2001/02	Pr	38	12	3	4	40	23	9	5	5	34	29	71	4th
2002/03	Pr	38	15	2	2	36	17	6	4	9	27	31	69	3rd
2003/04	Pr	38	11	5	3	33	14	2	12	5	19	26	56	5th
2004/05	Pr	38	7	7	5	25	25	3	7	9	22	32	44	14th
2005/06	Pr	38	11	5	3	28	15	6	2	11	19	27	58	7th
2006/07	Pr	38	7	7	5	23	20	4	3	12	15	27	43	13th
2007/08	Pr	38	8	5	6	25	26	3	5	11	29	39	43	12th

The Windswept Isle

a novella

Terri Brisbin

Across a Windswept Isle

Book Cover Design: © Carrie Divine of Seductive Designs
Photo copyright © Period Images
Photo copyright: © Veneratio
(Matthew Gibson)/Depositphotos.com

Print Formatting: Nina Pierce
Seaside Publications

Dedication

To the wonderful authors who contributed stories to the *Forbidden Highlands* anthology – Kathryn LeVeque, Eliza Knight, Amy Jarecki, Collette Cameron, Emma Prince, Victoria Vane and Violetta Rand – thanks for allowing me to be part of this project and for your help and support!

Prologue

Aros Castle, Isle of Mull
September, In the Year of Our Lord 1490

Death stalked a slow path through the village and keep of the Clan MacLean on the Isle of Mull. It took the young and the old, the weak and the strong, and the rich and the poor. It cared not if a life had been well- or ill-lived. It took and took until, satiated, it left as silently as it had arrived. Clan MacLean mourned the deaths of so many of its own.

Lachlan MacLean surveyed the number of graves before him with a bit of shock and sadness. His mother and brother lay beneath a newly-strewn covering of dirt at his feet. His father, devastated in a way Lachlan had never seen, stared off into the misty hills that led away from their village. Lachlan swore that Dougal MacLean aged a score of years in just this last fortnight.

Villagers, kith and kin drifted away after the priest finished his blessing. Lachlan turned to go. The rough hold stopped

1

him.

"Her father comes on the morrow. We will discuss the matter when he does." His father nodded across the graves to tall, lithe Wynda MacLeod, his late brother's betrothed.

He'd completely forgotten about the young woman in the hurried arrangements for the many burials. Now, Lachlan noted that her calm, blue eyes stared over at the keep, unfocused as though in deep contemplation. When her eyes shifted and met his, the lack of grief in hers surprised him.

"The matter?" The older man now clenched his arm harder and shook him. "Father, I canna …"

"Ye will do yer duty now that ye are my heir."

With those words, his father released him and strode to the keep, not glancing back at his living son, or the dead one, again. Lachlan understood the message and the warning in his father's words. Everything had changed on the death of his brother.

He must get word to Ailis before she heard it from someone else.

Ailis MacKinnon believed they would marry. He had pledged his heart and honor to her. They had plans and had promised their lives to each other. They hoped that their fathers would eventually agree as a way to keep the peace, though neither would like the idea of linking their families. The MacKinnons were a thorn in the side of the MacLeans of Mull and had been for generations, so he and Ailis had made certain that few knew the true extent of their relationship.

If his father wished to broker a marriage between his second son, and now heir, and The MacLeod's daughter, Lachlan would be expected to disavow his promises to Ailis. If word got out that he'd broken faith with her, the tenuous peace between their families would shatter and make their clans enemies.

But none of that was the worst thing about this. The worst was that he would be forced to marry another and break Ailis' heart.

Lachlan went into the keep and climbed the stone steps into the tower to his own chamber. He found some parchment and wrote the message that would bring her to their trysting place. He'd just handed it to a boy to take to her when Artair stepped in front of him.

"Do ye think that is a good idea?" he asked, looking in the direction the servant had gone. Artair knew how they communicated secretly … and where they met.

"She must hear it from me."

"So, 'tis a deal already done?" Artair asked.

"The MacLeod comes on the morrow to make the arrangements. Father has decided that I will take my brother's place and marry the MacLeod lass."

"Wynda." So much anger infused the one word. Lachlan looked closely at his closest friend.

"Have ye knowledge of the woman that I dinna have?" At his friend's silence, he narrowed his gaze and asked again. "Is there aught I should ken, Artair?"

"She had no liking for yer brother," he muttered.

"It matters not, the betrothal was made and she agreed. As will this next one."

"Aye, it matters not," Artair repeated. "Ye are the heir now."

Lachlan couldn't understand why his friend's words, nay the tone of his words, bothered him. Something swirled in the back of his thoughts, glimpses of gestures and looks exchanged between his friend and his brother's betrothed. The truth struck him. He gasped at the recognition of it.

"I would never betray ye, Lachlan. 'Tis done as of this moment."

Artair held out his hand, offering his word and solemn vow that he wouldn't betray his trust and consort with the woman Lachlan would marry. Lachlan paused before accepting his friend's hand. Artair was a man of his word. Artair was one of few men Lachlan would trust and had trusted with his life and safety.

"I ken," he said, clasping the man's forearm with his hand. After a few seconds, he released his hold and stepped back.

"When will ye see *her*?" Artair asked as they walked out of the keep and into the yard. Not many knew of the extent of his involvement with Ailis. They kept it quiet because of the tenuous situation between their families.

"In the morn. Once The MacLeod is sighted, word will spread." Lachlan nodded to the stables. "I have matters to arrange."

As he walked away, Artair spoke his name. Lachlan turned and saw a strange expression on his friend's face.

"She is not as she appears, Lachlan. She never was."

Did his friend speak of Wynda or of Ailis? Did he know something more after all? Before he could ask for an explanation, Artair walked away.

The rest of the day passed in silence, his family still reeling from the deaths around them. Supper was a somber meal. Those living in the keep had little patience for idle or joyful chatter that night. Rest wouldn't come to him, so he rose long before dawn to be on his way.

He reached the cottage just as the sun broke the eastern horizon. There was no sign of Ailis, so he walked inside to wait. Smiling at the memories of this place and of her, Lachlan tugged open the wooden shutters to watch for her approach. When the sound of footsteps behind him interrupted his thoughts, he turned, thinking he'd missed her arrival.

"Lachlan," she said softly as he turned.

That was the last thing he would remember.

One

Dun Ara Castle, Isle of Mull
Eight months later

Ailis MacKinnon sat at the table on the dais, waiting for her father's words. From his ruddy face and the way he kept starting and stopping, he was angry. Davina threw furtive glances in her direction, as though asking for her help. Ailis snorted. Davina, her stepmother and former closest friend would rot in Hell before Ailis helped her.

"Ye're being willful, girl," her father shouted. "Ye will accept this man!"

Silence reigned over the entire hall as all gathered there waited for the next argument between the chieftain and his daughter. Ailis knew it. Her father prepared for it. Even Davina saw it coming. It was Davina's voice that gave her father pause.

"Husband," she said, rising and walking to his side. "Mayhap we should discuss this in the solar?" Davina placed her hand on Ailis' father's arm. He took a breath, clearly considering his wife's plea. For a moment, Ailis thought he might accept Davina's suggestion but he shook off her hand and stomped his foot.

"Nay, Wife," he said, "'tis too late for a private word on this matter."

Davina startled at the sharpness of his tone and stepped back. Ailis watched as he grabbed Davina's hand and tugged her closer to him. Tears burned in Ailis' eyes as she watched, yet again, as her father softened for … *her*.

Ailis wanted to run. She wanted to leave the table, leave the keep and even her father's lands. Everything in her life had fallen apart. There was no way to put the pieces back together. Her friend was happy. Her father was happy. She was desolate and no one seemed to notice or care.

"Ailis! Come here now!"

She'd not realized she'd turned away until his call turned her back towards him. Lord Duncan MacNeil stood at her father's side watching the drama unfold. As she walked around the table towards them, she saw neither anger nor any emotion on the old man's face. If he was insulted by her refusal, she cared not. Pushing her hair over her shoulders, she stopped before her father and curtsied.

She nodded at Lord Duncan, out of respect, truly. The poor man had no idea of what he'd agreed to in bringing his suit to her father. He likely believed his offer was a kind one for a noble born woman with such … deformities as she did. That thought made her tug the leather gloves higher onto her arms before she faced her father.

"Lord Duncan is of good standing with his chieftain and his king. A marriage like this will benefit ye. Ye will accept his offer of marriage."

Ailis felt the eyes of those gathered moving from one to another as they watched this disagreement continue. A glance past her father revealed Davina's concern. Ailis looked away from her.

"I fear I canna."

The simple statement sent everyone into chaos. Shouts and whispers filled the air around them until her father waved his hand and everyone quieted.

"Ye seem to think this is a request, Daughter. Mistake not my resolve that ye will marry Lord Duncan."

Ailis felt a small trickle of sweat run down her face and another on her back. Defying her father wasn't an easy task, nor one she did lightly. But the thought of taking this man to husband when she had already promised herself to another was too hard, even if that man was now dead. Facing her father's bluster wasn't something she wished to do, even knowing he had promised her mother as she lay dying that he would never force their daughter to marry.

"Father," she began, lowering her head and her voice. "I canna and willna marry this man."

He reached out for her hands and realized his error before touching her. Instead, he lifted her chin with his finger to bring their gazes to meet.

"Ye must marry, Ailis. Ye will marry Lord Duncan."

"Nay."

Instead of the reaction she expected of her father, that of any irate man when faced with a recalcitrant and defiant daughter, the one she witnessed startled her. His gaze narrowed, he glanced from her to the man involved before huffing out a loud breath and walking to the table. Even Davina was surprised. She met Ailis' eyes and shrugged.

Her father grabbed a goblet and filled it from the pitcher sitting there. He drank it down and filled it again. Turning to face them, he swallowed the contents in several mouthfuls and slammed the cup on the table. She jumped, Davina jumped and the rest gasped.

"Ye willna marry Lord Duncan then?" She shook her head. "Fine." He walked to her and stared at her, his gaze softening for so short a time she thought she'd not seen it happen. "I have labored under a promise, sworn as all of ye ken, to my late, sainted wife not to force our daughter to marry against her will. A man of honor, I have upheld that promise."

"Father—" she began. Mayhap she had pushed him too far? Glancing at Lord Duncan, she wondered if she should relent.

"But even my beloved dead wife wouldna expect this behavior in her daughter."

Ailis gasped in shock and pain. Tears escaped before she could stop them. Her mother had passed before she had lost Lachlan. Her mother couldn't have known how this would be for her. Or how hard it would be to watch her friend betray her and marry her father, fresh from her mother's death. Now, 'twas clear that her father's regard for her mother and the vow made was at an end.

"My late wife would understand there has to be an end to this and a way to give ye into the care of a husband." She heard Davina's whispered pleas and saw her father brush her words off.

"I will give ye a choice, Ailis," her father said. "Consent to marry Lord Duncan now or ye will marry the man who next enters my keep."

She couldn't help herself. She looked to doors of the keep across the chamber. Closed because of the storm raging outside, 'twas almost as though everyone witnessing this expected the doors to crash open and a man to enter as if told beforehand to do so.

After that did not happen, she turned back to face her father. Certain that, if given time, she'd find a way to change his mind on this declaration, Ailis decided to agree with his demand. Aye, there would be time to allow her stepmother to soothe his temper as she seemed to in times like this one.

"I will marry the next man through the door, Father."

'Twas her father's turn to be surprised and his expression

showed him so. Davina whispered out a warning, but Ailis would listen not. Ailis spoke her words louder so all could hear.

"I will accept the next man through the door."

Would her father call her bluff or accept it? He stared for a long moment before nodding. Chances were that any man entering was someone in their clan and married already. Content that she would have more time to chip away at her father's demands, she glanced at Lord Duncan.

God bless him, the man appeared relieved at this development. Ailis didn't doubt that the man, nigh on sixty years of age, was silently thanking the Almighty for saving him. When her father took Davina's hand and led her back to table, Lord Duncan followed. Ailis returned to her seat and held up her cup to be filled by the servant. She'd barely settled on the wooden chair when one of the doors blew open with a bang. Ailis jumped to her feet and wondered if the fates had called her to task for her bold bluff.

A form appeared there; tall, swaddled in layers of soaking plaid. She squinted across the smoky chamber, trying to determine who it was. Her father rose and called out.

"Come ye inside!" he said to the stranger. "Come ye forward into the light and the warmth of my hall."

Her stomach roiled as the person walked slowly into the chamber. The gasps rippled as those closest got a better view of this man. All she could see was the plaid that covered his body and head. With the shadows thrown by the hearth and the lanterns around the hall, she could see little but his shape.

What had she done?

The world around her faded. She stared as the man approached. He could tear that world apart, she knew that much. When he reached the bottom of the steps, her father walked to the edge and called out.

"Tell me the name of the man who will call my daughter wife!"

"My lord?" the man said in a hoarse voice.

"My lord!" Davina called out as she rushed to Ailis' side and pulled her close.

"Father!" she whispered as shadows as dark as the man before them rose up to claim her.

Two

Had this man, this laird, just offered his daughter to him?

Surprised by the chieftain's welcome, he'd made his way slowly through the arranged tables to the front of the hall, dripping every step along the path. He studied everything around him as he moved and somehow he knew that this hall, though impressive, was not as big as …

His? Someone's … A place he'd seen before.

Though those present had been quick to lower their gazes from his, he'd examined their faces, looking, always looking, for one that would be familiar to him. His sleep was haunted with faces, so surely he would see one of them sooner or later?

The mask, fashioned by the monks who'd cared for his injuries, chafed the skin of his neck and the upper half of his face. No matter what fabric they used, 'twas always the same. The healer suggested leather, but the expense was something the poor monks could not afford. So, he trained himself not to scratch against the itch or it worsened. Tugging his hood down closer to his brow, he reached the steps that led to the high

11

table and watched as the nobleman positioned himself there.

Before he could ask a question, the young woman, dressed in a gown the color of spring, wilted just like a flower too long in the sun. Her long, flowing blonde hair, free of anything but a circlet, swirled around her body like a cloud as the woman fainted.

He was up the steps, around the table and at her side before any of the others reacted to her condition. He slid his arm under her and eased her onto the chair. The other young woman aided him and, by the time the one he'd assisted was settled there, her eyes began to flutter open.

Eyes the color of the emeralds in his ... father's? ... mother's? ... Eyes so deep and green that he could lose himself in them gazed back at him. Now 'twas his turn to be surprised.

It was her.

The one.

The woman who came to him in the dark of night and the light of day. He could always see her, but never once did she speak to him. He would reach out and call out to her, but she would fade even as daylight did at evening's arrival.

Now, she was here. Alive. Real. Breathing.

"Who are ye?" she asked, giving a voice to all the imaginings he'd had these last months.

"I ..." He released her and moved back. He glanced from her to the woman at her side and then to the chieftain standing across from them. "I ken not."

"I dinna understand," she said. "What are ye called?"

"Come now, tell us yer name," the nobleman said as he beckoned him over. "Are ye kith or kin?"

"My lord, I ken not. The monks who cared for me didna recognize me when they found me."

"Found ye?"

"Husband, let us take this to a private place," the other young woman said, arriving at the laird's side. She was the mighty man's wife ... second or third from the looks of her youthfulness.

The one who filled his dreams just stared wordlessly as he searched his memories for something to tell them. To tell her. He wanted to scream out in frustration and pain.

The weeks and weeks of searching for a place or a person who would be able to tell him his story wore heavily on him. The last hours spent walking in the wind-blown rain had sapped his strength. No one knew him. No one was missing from among them. And he'd not recognized anyone he'd met along the way.

Until now. Until this place and this woman.

From the way her face paled and those eyes filled with fear and something else, some great sadness, she didn't know him. The laird nodded at his wife. He motioned to two servants who led the way for him out of this great hall and up a stairway to the next floor.

He stepped aside as the nobleman led his wife and daughter into the room. Allowing the women to sit, the laird motioned to his servants to bring cups and stoke the fire. When the flames flared, he found himself stepping back, even from the welcomed warmth of it.

"Who are ye and why are ye at my keep in this storm in the dark of night?" The laird drank deeply from his cup. "A few minutes more and my gates would have closed until morn."

"The monks told me they found me unconscious and gravely injured some months ago," he began explaining what he knew. "They expected me to die." At the slight sound of distress, his gaze moved to the woman of his dreams.

"The mask?"

"The scars." The laird nodded. "I beg yer pardon, my lord, but I dinna ken who ye are. I have been traveling for days ..."

"Were ye with the monks of Iona?" the laird's wife asked.

"Nay, my lady," he said. His throat labored to speak aloud after months of mostly silence. "A small community some days from here to the south."

"I am MacKinnon and this is my wife, Lady Davina." Then the man nodded at his daughter, the one he'd offered in marriage. "That is my eldest, Lady Ailis MacKinnon."

Ailis MacKinnon.

Now, the beauty had a name. He let it roll through his thoughts, not struggling to find a connection, for that most often led to failure. Instead, as Brother Gavin had instructed him, he let it simply be there. Staring at her and repeating it again within himself, he waited on a revelation. 'Twas simply a feeling when it finally happened. Joy. Joy and contentment. He closed his eyes and waited for more.

"Father," she said. He opened his eyes and watched her speak. "I canna marry this … stranger."

"If he will have ye, aye, ye will."

The laird's pronouncement shocked him. What in the name of the Almighty had he walked into?

"But, Father, we ken not his name or anything about him. Ye canna mean to give me to him." Her voice was edged in fear and desperation. It sliced through him. He didn't want her fearful. He didn't want her to worry.

"What is yer name?" The MacKinnon asked again.

"When I couldna remember, the monks called me 'Iain', after their favorite of the blessed Apostles."

The MacKinnon walked closer to him, examining him frankly and openly, from his boots to the plaid that covered the hood on his head. They were of a similar size and build it seemed.

"Ye have the look of a warrior about ye. Have ye fought before?"

"Aye." He did not remember when or why, but he knew, his body knew, he was a warrior. Even now, he shifted on his feet and slightly turned as the laird moved around him.

A warrior must be always in readiness for the fight when it came.

14

At first, Iain thought the laird spoke the words. Then he realized they were a memory, spoken by another. An older man. The man who trained him. The shadows wouldn't part enough for him to see the man, so he brought his attention back to the laird.

"Are ye sworn to any man?" the laird asked.

"Aye." Iain shook his head. "I dinna ken who, but I think I must be."

"Are ye married then?"

"Nay."

He glanced over at Ailis and watched as any remaining color drained from her lovely face. Those eyes widened in anticipation of the next words from her father.

"Before yer arrival, my disobedient daughter swore to marry the next man who entered our hall if I allowed her to refuse Lord Duncan."

"The older man at the table?" he asked, his gaze still captured by hers. The slightest of nods gave her answer before her father confirmed it.

"Aye. Lord Duncan agreed to marry her after she refused others. I allowed her to refuse due to promises made in a moment of weakness. I realize now 'twas a grievous error on my part in dealing with her."

"Father," Ailis whispered. "I pray ye ..."

"My lord husband," his ladywife began.

"Nay, Ailis. Nay, Davina, my love," the laird said.

If Iain had not been watching her so closely he would have missed the pain that shone in her eyes when her father spoke so to his wife. Only then did Iain realize that these two women were close in age.

"I stand by our agreement, Daughter. Ye promised to marry him and, if he will have ye, ye will."

The MacKinnon meant it. He would give his daughter to Iain, if he but said the word. A complete and utter stranger, not only to them but to himself, who had nothing to offer in return. Had the whole world gone mad? Or was this one of those waking dreams he'd suffered for weeks after the monks had found him?

It took but one more glance at her to know that there was some connection between them. How else could he explain her presence in his dreams? Now that he'd heard her voice, he could hear the words she spoke to him every night since the first one he could remember.

"All the days of our lives," she whispered.

She stood before him, naked. Her hair formed a golden, shimmering curtain around her. Her pert nipples, seen as they parted the locks of hair, grew into tight rosettes, begging for his mouth. She moved and her hair moved with her, sliding across her rosy breasts and over the curves of her hips. The darker triangle of hair at the place above her thighs, beckoned to be touched. He reached out his hand and she waited with eyes closed for his caress.

"Iain?" The MacKinnon asked.

All the days of our lives.

Iain blinked to clear his thoughts of the erotic vision he'd remembered, or dreamt, and knew what his answer must be.

"Aye."

Three

Ailis sat, silent with shock, as her father and this man bargained and bartered for her. How had this come to be? She feared she understood the truth but didn't wish to accept it.

Davina flitted around, sometimes standing by her side and other times hovering over her father as he spoke to 'Iain'. Ailis wanted to both shout at her to stop moving and hug her tightly as they used to do before … before all of this.

Should she refuse? Should she run away? Davina spoke just as Ailis was about to lose control and do something rash.

"Finnan, ye must listen to me." In a voice and tone that Ailis had never heard before, her stepmother spoke again, "Finnan, ye must stop this and listen to me."

Ailis had never heard Davina press herself forth in such a manner. Not in public. Unless this was their manner in private? She shook herself rather than contemplate that.

Her father faced Davina. One glance at her used-to-be-friend's face and his gaze softened. He guided her into the alcove near the doorway to listen to her. Ailis could not look away from them. Since their marriage, he had changed. Though he had respected her mother, and loved her in his own way, Finnan MacKinnon never accepted her counsel the way he had Davina's. He had never listened to Ailis either.

A sound from the man drew her attention. She watched him stretch his neck one direction and then the other. He reached inside his hood and tugged on the mask. A sigh not unlike the one she made when she removed her gloves at night echoed to her. The skin on her hands and arms itched then as though reminded of their discomfort.

What had happened to him? What did the mask and hood cover? Shouldn't she know before they were man and wife? As though he'd felt her regard, he met her gaze and she thought his eyes might be blue. Mayhap like Lachlan's were? The ever-present pain reared inside her and she looked away.

"Ailis," Davina said. "Yer father wishes to give ye some time to acquaint yerself with this man before the marriage is held."

Ailis stood quickly and nodded. "Several months?"

A strange grating sound drew her gaze to the man in question. If she didn't know otherwise, she thought he might have just laughed. Why was his voice so rough?

"Nay," Davina continued to speak for Ailis' father. "Three days." At her loud gasp, Davina waved her off. "If, after three days, ye have some specific objection, yer father will consider it." Davina glanced at her husband and back to Ailis. "If there is no true objection, the marriage vows will be spoken on the fourth morning."

Torn between thanking Davina for her intervention and screaming like a *ban-sidhe*, Ailis sat down in the chair nearest the fire and tried to concentrate on finding a way out of this predicament. The scraping of wood across the floor brought her from her reverie. Glancing up, she realized that only the stranger remained.

"So, my lady, tell me honestly why yer father does this?"

Iain asked as he slid a chair across the chamber and placed it next to hers. "Is he kenned for fits of madness?"

She couldn't help herself. She laughed at his candidness before taking a mouthful of ale from her cup.

"He is the most sober and methodical man I've ever seen," she replied. "But none of us have been the same since my mother died last year."

"Grief can change a person, I think," he said. "Has his own pain made him wish this upon ye?"

"Why does it matter, sir?" she asked harshly. "Ye walk in here and find yerself marrying a noblewoman. A wealthy one at that. I would think a man like ye would thank the Almighty for such a change in fortune." She jumped to her feet and strode away.

Grief can change a person, he'd said.

She put the cup down and realized she had nowhere to go. Ailis realized the truth in his words. Grief for her mother's passing had colored her feelings for the way her father had remarried so quickly. 'Twas expected for a man of his position and age to continue to seek sons, but marrying her closest friend was a step too far.

And the worst blow of them all ... Lachlan's death.

Her conscience bothered her in a most disturbing way. This man, who had suffered grievous harm, didn't deserve to be the target of her ire. He'd played no part in the events of this last year and shouldn't be burdened by her rudeness.

"Sir," she said without turning to face him. "I beg yer forgiveness for my rude behavior." She let out a breath and turned. He stood before her, his height and breadth now apparent to her. She had to lean her head back to see his face, much like ... Ailis pushed the pain down once more and tried to make amends. "Ye played no part in what brought me and my father and his wife to this place."

"May I ask again, what did?"

His voice was softer when he whispered, the hoarseness

almost gone and she could understand his words clearly. Though he had dropped the plaid down onto his shoulders, the hood still covered his hair and the mask his face. Ailis should be afraid of this man who would lay claim to her in four days. Yet, she was not.

Mayhap the truth would make him reconsider this madness? Mayhap if he knew how vicious and mean she could be to those she cared about, he would refuse this devil's bargain or be willing to be paid off to walk away?

"I pushed him into this fit of madness, as ye called it. I did it," she said while gazing at the ties on his tunic. "I drove him to marry Davina and force me out of my home."

It took a few uncomfortable moments for her look up to see his reaction. With his head tilted down and the hood low over his brow, it was difficult to see his eyes. For some reason, it felt better not to be able to see the certain censure in this stranger's gaze.

After several moments, he canted his head as though studying her even more closely. Still wordless, she heard his breathing grow shallow until he leaned down and kissed her.

Everything around her, even her wits, faded as he pressed his mouth to hers. Whatever she'd expected to feel was not what she did. The rough material covering most of his face did not stop his mouth from touching hers, even as it rubbed against her cheek. The lips that touched hers were strong and smooth and undamaged. Worse, or better, she did not mind the kiss.

That made her pull free and step away. She scrambled back so quickly that she stumbled and fell. Before she touched the floor, his hands encircled her waist and he lifted her up. Held there, her back to his front, Ailis could not help but compare him to the last, and only, man who had kissed her and touched her body.

Lachlan.

Pain pierced her heart as it always did at the thought of him and Ailis shrugged off this man's hold. This time, she took two measured steps back from him. He'd not spoken a word, not about her accepting the blame for this debacle or the kiss he'd pressed on her.

"I fear I should beg yer pardon for that," he whispered. "But, I canna." His hand moved towards that mask again, but he dropped it to his side before he touched it. "Will ye explain how ye are to blame for this … situation in which we find ourselves?"

Any words she might have spoken wouldn't come out. The kiss sent her thoughts and memories flailing. He nodded then.

"This is happening quickly and ye have no reason to trust me." She could almost hear a smile in his voice. "I dinna remember much about myself, but I willna harm ye." He reached out, crossing the distance between them, and caressed her cheek with the back of his gloved hand.

Whatever she'd planned to ask or say was halted when the door to the chamber swung open and her father stood there.

"A chamber is readied for ye," The MacKinnon announced.

Ailis jumped back as though burned by his glove. That was Iain's first thought but he realized she was reacting to her father's arrival. He was too familiar with the reaction most people had to his appearance. His hood and mask caused fear in many. The reaction would be much worse if they saw him without it.

"Have ye eaten supper?" Ailis asked him. Her gaze fell to his mouth. From the blush that rose into her pale cheeks, he suspected she was thinking on that kiss. Thoughts of that kiss led to more of the vision he'd seen of her naked before him.

"Nay, I havena," he finally remembered to say.

"Come, I will take you to the kitchen for …" she began.

"Nay."

From the way they both startled, Iain realized his tone had been too forceful. "Yer pardon," he said, nodding to each one. "I find it better to eat alone." From the way their eyes darted from his gloves to his hood and then to his mask, they were trying to figure out his injuries. "Just so."

"Here now," Lord MacKinnon said. "The maid will take ye to yer chamber and send for food."

"My thanks for yer hospitality, my lord."

He had not included being gifted with the man's daughter, but the thought made Iain want to laugh. His throat tightened, making laughter impossible.

The lady stepped away and watched him leave to follow the servant. She averted those lovely blue eyes as he walked to the doorway.

"My lady." He waited for her to raise her gaze to him. When she did not, he nodded and moved on to the corridor, behind the girl waiting next to the laird.

The young servant glanced nervously over her shoulder as he walked behind her. By the time they reached the stairway, her pace quickened and he couldn't keep up. The day had been long, he was hungry and he ached. He turned into the stairwell and found her several steps up waiting for him. Soon, they stood before a chamber. She lifted the latch to open it.

"Yer name, girl?"

"Agneis, my ... sir," she said with a curtsy.

"My thanks, Agneis," he said as he entered the chamber. "Will the food take long?"

"Nay, sir, I will fetch it quickly." She curtsied before darting away.

Iain glanced around and saw a small but clean bedchamber. A fire burned in the hearth, bringing warmth to the room. He left the door ajar so the servant bringing food could enter. Iain tugged the wet plaid from his shoulders and tossed it over one of the chairs near the fire so it would dry. Feeling exhaustion overtaking him, Iain slumped into another chair to wait for food.

If not for his stomach rumbling, he'd have fallen onto the bed and given in to the growing fatigue. Lord MacKinnon's servants were quick. Only minutes later, he heard heavy footsteps climbing the stairs. A burly lad carried a tray laden with bowls, plates and a large pitcher.

Iain stood while the lad placed the tray on the table. Fragrant aromas surrounded him and his stomach answered. The lad laughed and lowered his head in a polite nod before leaving.

Not long after the stew, bread, cheese and a fair amount of the strong ale filled his stomach, Iain felt himself drifting to sleep. Without enough strength to walk the four or five paces across to the bed, he tugged the mask free of his head and laid it on the table. Leaning his head on his arms, he fell asleep.

Iain didn't know how much later, but he woke with the knowledge that someone else was in the chamber. The soft scent of a woman revealed the intruder's gender and he guessed it was Ailis. If she'd wanted him to know she was there, she would have knocked so she must want to catch him unaware. Now that his hood rested on his neck, the candle's light on the table would reveal his appearance if she walked to his side. Was that her intent?

He blew at the candle softly and watched as the flame wavered and then went out. A soft gasp told him she knew she'd been caught. Iain waited for her to pull the door closed before he moved. The soft glow of the fire gave him enough light to see. He dropped the bar next to the door into its brackets and listened. Soft footsteps padded away and he let out the breath he'd been holding.

Truly alone and secure, he tugged the hooded tunic over his head. He sighed with relief at its removal. The gloves came next, but they were harder to take off. The skin on his forearms remained sensitive. Once the gloves were in place, it felt more comfortable. He'd been unable to undress for almost a sennight. The air around him hurt and soothed at the same time.

Sliding his breeches down after pulling his boots off, his legs felt the same, both torment and respite. The thin shirt was the last piece of fabric off. Iain stood naked, waiting for the inevitable wave of sensation. He hissed through clenched teeth as his body recovered from the shock of exposure to the cooling bedchamber.

He quickly mixed cold water from the jug with some water heating near the fire and washed as much as he could. Then he cleaned his shirt, placing it over a chair to dry. He needed to stretch or his skin would tighten while he slept.

Checking the bar, he moved as close to the fire as he could before the terror overtook him. Burned, the monks said. His back, legs, arms and hands. Part of his face and the back of his neck. All marked with fire's touch.

He clasped his hands and leaned over, reaching down to touch the floor. Then, up towards the ceiling. Iain moved as Brother Isiah had shown him. Similar to how he'd trained …

Another shard of memory caught his attention. He had trained as a warrior, wielding sword and staff in battles against…

And that quickly, the opening in the haze of his mind closed, leaving him with another frustrating glimmer of his past.

Barely making it through the entire series of stretching motions he did before sleeping, Iain crawled into the clean bed and sank into its comfortable layers. The ropes beneath him groaned as loudly as he did.

He'd arrived here a stranger, hoping for a meal and shelter from the storm. He ended this day, betrothed to the laird's daughter, to be married within days unless she could find a true objection to him. Would she? Was his damaged body enough to form an impediment?

The reaction of certain parts of him at the memory of her

naked before him proved there would be no impairment of that kind.

The strange events of the day plagued him. His thoughts blended with phantom bits of sounds and images, all moving around in his thoughts. His restless mind sought truths and proofs for hours before he found sleep.

Four

"Ye must be angry."

Ailis didn't turn at the familiar voice. She continued watching the man who would be her husband. From the windy edge of the battlements, she could see him as he walked around the keep and the outbuildings of Dun Ara Castle. He didn't pause too long in any place, but kept walking, covering every square foot within the walls. Since just past dawn, nigh on two hours by her measure, he walked.

"Ye are angry," Davina said, from a much closer spot than where she'd first spoken.

Ailis closed her eyes for a moment, trying to regain control before speaking. She couldn't help but shrug free of Davina's hand when her former closest friend placed it on Ailis' shoulder in what she thought must be an offer of sympathy.

"I think most reasonable women would be upset and angered, nay stunned, at this, Davina. My father gives me away to a total stranger." She turned and crossed her arms over her chest. "A man who could be an enemy or ally and who has no claim or right to a chieftain's daughter."

When Davina opened her mouth to reply, Ailis shook her head. "And why does he do this? Simply to teach his willful daughter a lesson? To prove he can shame and humiliate her and force her obedience before their clan?"

Refusing to stop now that she'd begun, Ailis shrugged.

"For those reasons and one more; to rid himself of his only daughter now that he has a new wife and a son to inherit all."

Davina had supplanted Ailis and Ailis' mother in the keep and in her father's heart. That was the root of all of this. Ailis refused to accept her former friend's new place in their family shortly after Ailis' mother had died. Then Lachlan's death only months later left her inconsolable and alone, with no one to share that grief. Recently, the birth of her half-brother Kennan had driven the divide even deeper. Her father's satisfaction at finally having a son overrode any attempt to please his daughter.

A moment passed. Ailis realized that Davina had not disagreed with her. Ailis leaned into the winds across the battlements, trying to let them carry away or dry the tears she couldn't stop.

"If ye hadna made yer refusals so public, he wouldna have gone to such drastic actions."

Though her voice was soft, the accusation was harsh and painful. Once, this woman would have defended her and been her counsel when facing the choice of a husband or the loss of her beloved. Once, Davina would have been at her side rather than at her father's. But the marriage offer Davina accepted made everything different and difficult between them.

Ailis couldn't deny her own behavior had brought this result. No words came to her. No rebuttal. Her inability to say anything would have become obvious had not a servant approached just then.

"My lady. The babe is ready," the girl said, bobbing respectfully before them. Kennan was hungry.

Davina nodded at the girl and turned to follow. Part of Ailis was glad to see her go. But another part wanted to beg her forgiveness and exult in her happiness. Just before Davina entered the stairway back into the keep, she stopped.

"He doesna abandon ye, Lis." Davina walked back closer. "He loves ye and worries over yer happiness. Ye have been so caught up in yer misery, ye havena noticed. Even now, he sends men out to check this man's story."

Shocked by this news, Ailis shook her head. Her father was not as calloused as he appeared to be?

"Come up with a real objection or accept Lord Duncan, who yet stands willing to wed ye." A baby's wail echoed up the stairs and Davina brought both arms across her chest in a telling gesture. "Think on my words, Lis, and on yer part in this," Davina said as she walked away.

Ailis stood in the silence that was disturbed only by the sounds of the winds and the seabirds overhead looking for food. She didn't want to think on what Davina said. Turning back to look over the battlements, she couldn't see Iain.

When her stomach rumbled loudly, Ailis knew it was past the time when everyone would eat. Did Iain know that? No one had approached him in all the time he walked below. And he'd gone no closer than several paces from anyone. So, she thought not.

He'd looked worn and exhausted when he'd taken leave and gone to the chamber assigned to him. She'd snuck inside because she wanted to find out more about him and the mask he wore. If her gloves covered damaged arms and hands, what did his cover? And what did that piece of cloth that draped over his face and neck hide? Did he sleep in it? She'd found him asleep, sprawled across the table with the bowls and cup pushed aside.

One candle lit the dark shadows of the chamber but 'twas not enough to see what she wanted to see. The mask lay at his hand and the hood was pushed back, exposing the back of his head. Whether black or brown, she couldn't tell, but his hair grew in ragged patches across his head. The sides appeared long but the back looked almost sheared off. Her hand reached out and only the slight exhalation and extinguishing of the candle warned her that he'd roused.

"Lady?" As though her thoughts had conjured him up, Iain stood before her now. "They wait at the table below for ye," he said, holding out his arm to her. With the other, he held the hood to keep it in place when the winds would pull it sideways.

She accepted his arm. To refuse would be rude. She had no reason to treat this man, this puppet, this bluff of her father's, in such a manner. When they stepped within, he adjusted the hood, tugging it forward so it created a shadow over the mask.

Ailis noticed that their hands were not dissimilar. Both encased in gloves, she felt the ripples of his skin under the thin, worn layer of leather. She knew that his hid the same that hers did, scars from damage. Had his been some injury in a battle? He'd said he was a warrior, so 'twas possible.

The servants and others who lived and worked in the keep parted as they passed. Ailis heard the whispered questions and saw the pity in their gazes. Lowering her eyes to watch the flagstones of the floor as they walked, she wondered if their pity was for her, the lord's daughter they knew, or for this stranger being given her in marriage?

Caught up in her thoughts, she didn't realize he'd slowed until he laid his other gloved hand on hers. He drew her into a small alcove just before the entrance to the hall.

"Ye came to my chamber last night." He released her hand and lifted her chin. "Why?"

Was this a test of some sort? To see if she had the courage to face him and admit the truth? He wouldn't find her wanting in this regard.

"Curiosity, I fear." When all she heard was a slight huff, she continued. "I wanted to see yer face, uncovered, before we wed. To see the man ye truly are." She shrugged a bit. "'Tis the truth."

"Ye wouldna like what ye see, my lady. And that is my truth." He slid his leather-covered hand to hers and traced a path with a finger down her glove. "I suspect yer gloves hide much the same from view."

She blinked but didn't look away first. He did, stepping back and waiting for her to move to his side. Instead, Ailis grabbed hold of his sleeve and pulled him back.

"Ye walked in a stranger and accepted this offer. Why? Do ye not fear entangling yerself in matters that could offer ye more danger than benefit?"

She tried to ask the question without making it an accusation. She'd done that already and insulted him. But Ailis wanted, needed, to know the truth. Most men would be highly guarded of such an offer and not trust it to be in good faith. A man without memory was at a greater disadvantage than most. His eyes met hers as he slid his hands to her shoulders.

Did he mean to kiss her? Again? Here, where they'd be witnessed? Her body remembered the last one and readied for another.

"I had to, my lady. When I saw it was ye in the middle of it, I had to accept."

"But why?" Though his hood covered the top of his face in shadows, she could feel his hot stare on her mouth as she waited for his reply.

"So I could do this."

He followed those few words with that dreaded, feared, anticipated and desired kiss after all. His mouth momentarily touched hers gently and then he took possession of it completely. Strong and powerful, the kiss claimed and confused her in the same moment. Then he tilted his head, dipping his tongue into her mouth. Her body understood and she pressed closer, her hips and breasts against his hard body.

Hot, masculine and possessive it was. She opened wider to give him purchase and was swept into the heat and desire that swirled as his tongue did. Heat pooled in her body, in that place deep within, touched only by Lach …

Ailis pulled free and stared at this man.

Why did this kiss remind her of Lachlan? Would she forever be owned by a man now dead? Would her body not react as he'd taught it to? How long would it take before the pain of every memory eased into something softer, something she could bear? She brushed her hand over her mouth, feeling the way her lips swelled even through the layer of leather. His breathing showed he was affected as well. She wanted to lean back in to taste him as he'd done her.

"I had to accept … ye." His words came out on a breathy sigh.

Anger, her companion for so long, flared quickly at his assumption that she was his for the taking. No matter who she eventually had to marry, her heart and soul would never be part of that bargain.

"Ye willna find what ye think, sir, if ye pursue this to the end," she warned. "This is a devil's bargain and there will be no virgin bride in your marriage bed." Though she'd admitted that to none but Davina, she spoke it now to this man. Meant only as a warning, mayhap a challenge, she knew she'd failed when his chin set, making the lines of his jaw more prominent. His shadowed eyes took on a glassy look for a second and then cleared.

"Though I can say little of my past, I can say ye will not find a virgin husband there either, my lady."

He'd turned her blatant admission into a reminder of the unknowns that stood between them. She turned away, but he held her there with his fingers encircling one wrist. His grasp did not hurt, yet she comprehended that she was being held there.

"Is that why yer father bargains ye away in such a manner?

31

Is this a punishment for yer shame?"

"Nay! My father kens not about this." Pulling against his hold, she whispered, "I didna tell him such a thing."

"And is there proof wrapped in swaddling out there as a result of yer … experience?"

She wanted to slap him for such words. But the image of holding Lachlan's child filled her thoughts and took her breath and words away.

Oh, that she had been blessed to bear such a *result* of their love. At least she would have had a part of him with her now. Ailis could do naught but answer his question with a shake of her head before ducking around him and entering the hall.

Those waiting watched in silence as she walked to the table where her father and Davina sat. Could they see the grief that threatened to overwhelm her? Had the stranger? Or had he been insulted to learn the truth which, if she admitted the truth, had been her aim?

Ailis continued on, pulling the tattered edges of her control back into place, as she made her way to her seat. Acknowledging her father and Davina, she sat. This meal was less formal, so the tables were all on the lower floor. No one sat up on the dais. Iain had caught up with her and he took the seat offered to him by the steward at her side.

Wallowing in pain and loss, Ailis couldn't bring herself to chatter about the weather or the condition of the sheep or any other inane topics Davina brought up as she tried to engender polite discourse at the meal. Finally, her stepmother gave up her attempts to bring Ailis into the discussion and spoke across her to Iain.

The servants brought trays of breads, cheeses and other plain foods and held them out to each one there. Before Ailis could make the pretense of wanting to eat, Iain selected several pieces off each tray and placed them on her plate.

If it had been Lord Duncan, a man raised as a noble, 'twould have felt right. But this man, who remembered not his own life or past, acted with the manners expected of one. Ailis tried not to stare as he continued the polite manners expected at a laird's table.

Who was he?

Five

Though she spoke to him during the meal, 'twas only the formalities expected at the table. *Aye. Nay. My thanks.* By rote, she accepted his offer of food and drink as the servants circled them, holding out trays and pitchers.

He served her as a man of noble birth would have known to do. Stunned by what that revealed to him, phantom memories swirled through his thoughts and teased him to remember.

A table filled with people.

A powerful man at its center.

A hall filled with men and women, food and ale.

He tried to grab hold of them and peer into their murky depths to find … himself there, but they faded as the morning fog did when the sun appeared. Glancing around this table and this hall, Iain found no one who he'd seen in that vision. The only thing he discovered was that he didn't belong here.

If that were true, then why had the lady at his side been in his dreams? Why had he seen Ailis there, her face contorted with fear or ethereal with love or glowing in passion? When his damaged body wished to give up its tenuous hold on life over the last months, she had been the only constant thing other than the pain.

The lad working in the stables this morn had let it slip that she'd changed after her mother passed and then again some months ago when she'd suffered some accident. The lad confided that accident was the reason she wore the leather gloves now. Like a madwoman she'd been, he'd offered with a shrug.

Iain pushed the small portion of food he'd placed on his plate around, preferring not to eat with others present. The left side of his face had sustained the worst of the damage and shifting the mask to eat could reveal some of it. Though, he realized, kissing Ailis had not caused it to move at all. With his mouth on hers, he could feel the warmth of her cheek through the fabric.

He tried to converse with Lady Davina, but found his attention drawn back to the woman sitting at his side. In the corridor, he thought she meant to slap him for his rude question about a bastard bairn. Instead, a stricken expression filled her eyes and he knew more than just the answer to his query. He knew that she had loved and lost a man. The loss in her eyes tore into him. He wanted to beg for pardon for his ill-advised, terrible words. Especially those about a bairn.

Just thinking on it made him feel ill. He lifted his cup and drank most of the ale down, hoping it would settle him and his stomach. Turning to the vigilant servants behind the table, he used that movement to lean closer to her so no one else would hear his words.

"I pray yer pardon, my lady," he whispered as he held the cup out to the servant. "My words were ill-advised at best and my accusation was something I regret. I didna mean to cause ye pain."

Her body stiffened as she heard his words of apology and

35

then gave him the slightest nod of acceptance. The lady wouldn't meet his gaze and he didn't blame her. Still, she seemed a bit more at ease as the meal progressed.

Iain glanced at those gathered for this meal and saw the older man The MacKinnon was trying to betroth to his daughter. At ease, it seemed, at one of the other tables giving no sign of leaving ... or giving up his claim on the lady. The chieftain's plan became clear to him. Iain was simply his way of forcing his daughter to accept his choice of husband.

A wise and canny move on the man's part, when Iain thought on it. Bring in a completely unacceptable choice and she would have to *choose* the one he wanted her to pick. Something his own father would have appreciated and done. Iain blinked as the image of an older man grew stronger and clearer in his mind. His father?

"Are ye well?" Her voice broke into his confusion. She touched his arm gently but lifted her hand as soon as he stared at it. "Ye stilled. I feared ye had stopped breathing."

Iain drew in a ragged breath and nodded at her. "Aye, I am well, my lady. Just a momentary lapse of attention while thinking on something."

"Did ye eat earlier?" she asked, leaning closer. "Ye dinna seem hungry and I ken ye prefer to take your meals alone."

Iain stared at her face, searching her green eyes and placid expression for ... something. "I didna."

With a nod of her head, she called a servant and whispered some instructions to the girl. Once the girl had scampered off to the kitchens, Ailis turned back to him and smiled. Indeed, he could lose his breath at the sight of it.

She intrigued him. She certainly dazzled him. She confused him. But, the main feeling that filled him when he looked at her was a deep sense of connection. Of something lost and now found. And a need to protect her. He wanted to ask if she knew him, but could not reveal the worst of himself to her in order to find out. For, if he had been attacked and left for dead, being unknown was his best defense until he found his own identity and the one, or those, responsible for his condition.

"Food will be waiting in yer chamber," she said.

Iain marveled at the easy way she'd handled his quandary. And at the way she'd noticed it was a thing to be solved. "My thanks, lady."

She was a woman used to handling the running of a keep such as this one. A woman like her would have been raised to do so from her childhood on, but she would be expected to run her husband's household and not her father's. Glancing at both women seated there, Iain thought he could guess at the reason for the discord between father and daughter: Lady Davina.

Ailis became prickly and irritated by everything the lady, her stepmother, suggested. Every encounter between them that he'd witnessed was the same. Iain sensed no ill will from the laird's wife. Yet, The MacKinnon's daughter responded as though her words were insults or unreasonable orders. Studying them, Iain realized they must be the same age.

Had Ailis taken a disliking to her new stepmother because of her age? Or because this young woman supplanted her own place within her father's house? That seemed the most likely explanation. And now, the young woman ruled the household and her husband. Ailis disapproved heartily from the appearance of it all. Was it simple jealousy at the heart of her behavior?

But, there was another thing he must be missing, for Ailis wasn't mean-spirited. If she were, she would have no care for his eating or starving. And, though she'd struck at him with words, he could see the regret in her eyes when she had.

Nay, Ailis was not a vicious, unfeeling person. As the chieftain rose, holding out his hand to his wife, Ailis' expression betrayed the truth of the matter to him. From the briefest flash in her gaze, he recognized what she felt so intensely.

Pain. Loss. Betrayal.

As she rose, he did. With a nod at him, she walked off in the opposite direction her father had taken. Standing there, Iain knew he would have no place here once this confrontation between father and daughter settled. When the three days ended, Ailis MacKinnon would wed the stalwart Sir Duncan as The MacKinnon had arranged.

Iain nodded to no one in particular and walked where his feet took him. But his thoughts turned over as he tried to understand why this chieftain's daughter should concern him at all. Oh, aye, he'd been drawn into their battle of wills. But something inside tugged at him to help her.

Especially since he should have left, with thanks to the chieftain for his overly magnanimous marriage offer, Iain remained. His purpose here, and at every other town, village and keep where he'd stopped over these weeks, was to find out his own truth. So, why did he want to put that aside and help this woman?

The dreams. It always came back to the dreams of her.

Had his pain-addled mind conjured her up to give him something to concentrate on during the tormented months? Had he truly seen Lady Ailis or just a pale-haired temptress?

Iain heard a shout and looked around. Without paying heed, he'd walked to the yard where the MacKinnon men trained. Watching them challenge each other with weapons, his own hands itched as though missing the feel of something strong and metallic.

"Come there!" a voice called out to him. "Come."

An impossibly-large older man, garbed only in trews and covered in sweat, motioned to him. He'd been directing the training, ordering men about and assessing their movements, strengths and weaknesses while Iain had watched earlier. Before he could accept or reject the call, the man strode closer and tossed a sword, hilt-first, at him. Iain caught it without difficulty and adjusted his gloved grip around the hilt.

"Ye look like ye might need some work."

Iain looked down at the weapon in his grasp and recognized the feel of it. Climbing over the fence, he waited as the man studied him, in a prelude to an attack Iain understood would come. Moving with a speed that belied his size, the man raised his sword and swung at Iain as he crossed the few paces between them.

Iain's body reacted on its own, clearly experienced in this. From his ability to hold this huge warrior at bay, he was clearly skilled at it. Though his muscles protested from their too-long period of inactivity, his movements became smoother, more defined, stronger as they fought.

He stopped thinking and planning his next action and let his body remember what to do. Sometime later, his opponent finally knocked the sword from his grasp, ending their fight.

"Ye fight well with the sword, man." As he picked up the blade from the dirt, the man nodded. "Verra well, indeed."

"It has been a long time," Iain explained.

"Well, ye havena lost any of yer skills." The man held out his hand. "I am Breac, commander of The MacKinnon's warriors."

"I am called Iain," he said, accepting the man's strong grasp around his forearm and returning it. "And ye are his brother as well?"

"I am." The man looked as startled by Iain's declaration as he felt. He released his hold and stepped back. "Not many ken that and fewer speak of it. How do ye come by such?"

Iain could not explain the knowledge that filled his thoughts. This man was the chieftain's natural half-brother though he was acknowledged as *cousin*. A bastard born from the old laird's loins sired on a servant girl. A fact known by very few. More importantly, he was considered a worthy contender for the high seat if not for his illegitimacy.

"I dinna ken," he said, shaking his head.

If Breac felt threatened by Iain's knowledge, it didn't

show. The large man shrugged and, with a quick warning about keeping that to himself, Breac strode off, calling out orders. Iain walked to the fence to climb out, but Breac called him once more.

"Ye should come back and work with us. Yer sword arm is weak," he said. Others who'd watched them fight called out other opinions, both rude and helpful, about Iain's weak sword... arm and he laughed.

"I will." His stomach grumbled, reminding Iain he had not eaten all morning.

He rolled his shoulders as he found his way to the kitchen, stretching to loosen the muscles that were not used to such work. It had felt good though. The sword felt as if it belonged in his grasp. The gloves did not slow him down, but his hand ached for the feel of the hilt against its palm. Mayhap he would remove them the next time?

Iain sought out a servant and asked for a bucket of heated water. Sweat poured down him now, making the layers he wore unpleasant and sticky. He needed to find a way to wash and not just quickly from a bucket. The man he asked promised to bring it to his chamber, so Iain went there to wait.

He dropped the bar to block the door once the water arrived. He took his time, removing every piece of clothing. The hood and mask hadn't impeded his ability to swing a sword. But he found the heat they held in would tire him quickly in a real fight. The mask would also impede his vision in a true battle.

After he'd washed, and while allowing his garments dry a bit, he walked around the chamber and ate the food that was waiting, as promised, for him. He considered the choices that faced him now and how he could best reclaim his own identity and life, wherever that might be.

Now that he comprehended the chieftain's plan to bait his daughter with him as an unworthy choice to push her where he wanted her to be, Iain thought about leaving. There was truly nothing to keep him here. He owed no allegiance to this lord or this place. Aye, he'd sworn his oath to someone, but here they knew him not.

He could bide his time this day and slip out just before the gates locked for the night or just after they opened in the morn. That was when many slipped in or out with little notice, returning to their houses in the village or coming to their work in the keep. One more man would gain little notice.

By this time on the morrow, he could be well away from here and the spectacle between The MacKinnon and his headstrong daughter. And back to his task of finding his own life. He finished the bread and cheese, content that he'd chosen his path.

The soft knock at the door brought him to a halt.

"Iain?" Her voice, clear and strong, called out his name.

As quickly as he'd made the decision to leave, this woman changed it. There was some reason he could not walk away from here, from her. She was somehow connected to his past and his present. He must find that link.

"Lady," he said, approaching the door. He grabbed up his trews and hooded tunic and tugged them on as he walked.

"Would ye like to see the village?" she asked. "The day is fair and I thought … Well," she said. "I thought ye might like to see more than just the keep."

He pulled the hood down to cover his face and lifted the bar, careful not to face the opening door. Though, if he were honest with himself, he wanted to stare at her and never look away. "I would like that, my lady." He shifted back. "I will join ye in the hall shortly."

The lady walked away and he allowed himself to watch her as she did. When she'd turned down the stairway, he closed his door and got dressed. Iain rushed and arrived downstairs before the lady had time to reach the other end of the hall. When she turned at someone's call, Iain felt as though he was in his dreams again.

*It was the first one of the many different times when he saw
her in his dreams. Whether 'twas in this hall or another, it
mattered not. Someone called her name and she turned and
saw him. Her eyes brightened as she saw him and the green of
them deepened in arousal and in love. She nodded with the
slightest bowing of her head. Then she winked. A secret. Their
secret. And he'd kept it, knowing she was his.*

All the days of our lives.

The strangeness of the moment faded and the lady stood
waiting for him with a question in her gaze. 'Twas more than
likely the same question he was thinking.

Who was he?

But that begged a further one. If he knew her, did she him?

With that next step toward her, Iain decided to stay and
discover the truth, no matter the cost. And he had no doubt
there would be a cost.

To him. To her. To them.

Six

The sun held its control over the day. As they walked through the yard and out the gates, Ailis couldn't help but peek over at him. She'd seen him only in the shadows of the dark corridors, corners and chambers in the keep. Now, she would finally see him.

She tugged the sleeves of her gown down as low as she could, still mindful of the appearance of her hands without the gloves to cover the worst of it. 'Twas an offering of a sort to him and she wondered how long it would take him to notice. As they walked along the road to the village, he didn't speak at all. But she could feel his gaze on her when he looked out on the village.

"'Twas dark when I arrived," he rasped. "I didna see the extent of the village." His voice always began rough then it seemed to ease the more he spoke.

"Ye did not seek refuge with any of them?" she asked, pointing at the cottages and buildings along the road.

"Nay, I could see only the keep when the lightning flashed.

I just kept walking to it."

"Think of what could have happened if ye had sought the comfort of the miller's cottage." She pointed to it. "Or anywhere else."

"Aye, just think of the possibilities, my lady."

He tilted his head up and she could see his eyes clearly … and the merriment in them. He teased her. The laugh that escaped her felt good. A sense of humor was not a bad thing in a man. He chuckled and held out his hand for her.

Taking a deep breath, she placed her ungloved hands in his. The slight hitch in his breath told her he'd noticed.

"But, my lady," he began. "I wonder if ye would feel better or worse for kenning that the pigsticker walked behind me to the keep."

They laughed together and it eased some of Ailis' fears. He found humor in this strange and tense situation, which spoke about his nature. Even if he didn't know himself.

Some of the villagers called out greetings to her and she stopped to speak to several of the women along the road. Beitris' husband had been injured recently and was not faring well. Old Elizabeth's granddaughter had recovered from the fever that still tried to gain a foothold. Ailis promised beef broth from the keep's kitchen for the child and promised the healer would visit Beitris' husband on the morrow.

Iain remained on the road when she stopped, but she felt him there, watching and listening to her every word. Soon, he accepted every small gift she received and tucked them under his arm to carry them. A loaf of bread. A ribbon. None were costly but each was precious to her.

For no matter had happened in her life, these people accepted her. When her mother died, it was here among them that she found true solace. When she lost … when Lachlan died, the women held comforted her and treated her burns. She fought off the sad thoughts and continued to make her way along the row of cottages.

By the time they reached the end of the road, all sorts of trinkets and treats that the villagers had presented to their lady filled with his arms. They were not heavy and so no burden to him, but they spoke of the regard and esteem in which these people held their lady. And from the way she spoke to each one, making inquiries, offering aid or supplies, she knew those who lived on the largess and condescension of their chieftain by name. Coming to his side, she took one look at his collection and laughed.

"I dinna think to bring a sack or basket for such things."

"They are no trouble, my lady," he said. Seeing the joy in her face as she greeted her people lightened his own spirit. "Are there more to see to?"

"Nay, no one to visit, but I had hoped to take ye to the sea." She glanced down the road as it curved toward the sea.

"We could ask yer father's men to take this back to the keep."

The widening of her eyes spoke of her ignorance of those who followed their every move. Ah, so her father had a care for her, whether he did it to protect her or to spy on Iain mattered not. The MacKinnon would play both of them against each other if it suited his aims. Iain must remember that.

"Where?" she asked, hands on hips, as she turned to face the path they'd walked.

"There, my lady," he said, pointing back two cottages. "And there." The guards followed them, one on each side of the road, inching their way along as Ailis had walked at Iain's side.

"Have they been following us all along?" Her pale brow furrowed and he almost reached out to touch and smooth it.

"Aye."

He'd noticed them in the hall first and then as they walked

from the keep. It made sense on her father's part and confirmed what Iain suspected. The chieftain had no intention of allowing his daughter to marry some unknown stranger who'd appeared on his doorstep.

"Ronald!" she called out. Though the man looked like he wanted to disappear, he nodded and came to them. "I pray ye, take these things back to my chamber."

"But, my lady," Ronald said, glancing between the lady and his assignment. "I must stay …"

"I see Robbie over there," she said, pointing at the second guard. "He can follow along until ye return."

When faced with the lady's orders, the man did the only thing left to him. He gathered up everything that Iain held and walked away, nodding to Robbie as he walked past him. With that settled, she stepped back to Iain's side and waited until he raised his arm for her.

She directed him toward the path to the sea. The air grew saltier and the winds picked up as they climbed a small rise and stood at the top looking out at the water.

"The harbor is to the west of the castle," she said, pointing past the stone walls. "This part is mostly unapproachable by sea due to the sea stacks and rock formations all along this coast."

That made Dun Ara Castle safe from most invasions using the sea. Guard the small harbor, he could see, and the only approach was by land.

Iain looked farther across the sea knowing that Coll lay closest to them, with Barra and Rum and Skye some distance across the sea. His father's people were on those islands.

"Ye did it again." Iain turned to find her studying him as he studied the sea. "Ye make a sound, like a slight inhalation, and stop moving." She stepped to him, standing between him and the sea. "Is that when a memory returns to ye?"

He nodded, unable to speak as he struggled to find and keep the bit of knowledge he'd just gained.

"What did ye remember? Just then?" she asked, her body close enough to feel her heat. She placed her hand, her ungloved hand, on his chest, making it hard to breathe.

"Something about my father's kin. Here," he nodded at the lands to the south of where they stood now. "And out there, too." He gazed over her head and across the sea to the islands in the distance.

"What other memories have returned?" she asked quietly, lifting her head, staring into the openings in the fabric where his eyes lay. Could she see his eyes? See him there within?

"Ye. Ye are there, too."

He admitted it against his will. He wanted her to know that she somehow lived in his thoughts. In that moment, all he wanted to do was touch her. Feel her skin on his. Mayhap that would make him remember why she was such a presence during his recovery.

All it would take was for him to tug his own glove off, as she had hers, and touch her. Reaching behind his back, he grasped the tips of one glove and pulled it off.

Iain lifted his hand as the skin tingled at the feeling of the air on it. She gasped at his touch, as he slid his fingers over her hand on his chest and wrapped them around hers.

Other than the good brothers touching him in their care of his wounds, he had neither sought nor desired the touch of another until now. And, even as he felt the uneven ridges of flesh on the top of her hand, he knew she could see the same on his.

Something shifted in him. A hope that she wouldn't shy away from him or his touch. A prayer that she understood the step he took and his appreciation of the one she had. An awareness of how right it was to hold her. To be close to her. To touch her. To kiss ...

His mouth was on hers before the thought finished. She opened to him. He dipped his tongue deeply inside her mouth, searching and tasting. His body reacted to the touch of her

47

tongue against his, hardening and readying. She slid her hand off his chest and she entwined their fingers, keeping their hands touching.

The kiss intensified and he wanted more. To touch more and taste more. To have more. He noticed when she slid her hand along his arm to rest on his shoulder. Iain used his other hand to claim her, pulling her tight against him.

She fit. Her mouth fit his.

Her body against his felt right. She moaned. He found her staring into his eyes as their mouths possessed each other. In that moment, Iain knew that she must be his. She was his. He tugged his other hand free and placed both around her head, sliding into her hair so he could take her mouth as he wanted to take her body.

They had done this before, of that he was certain. They had kissed and touched and possessed one another. But when? Then her hands sought purchase and touched his back and he pulled back.

"Did I do something wrong?" she asked in a whisper, her voice filled with passion and wanting. She released her grasp on him, reaching up to cover his hands as they gripped her head.

So why couldn't he remember her? What would make his mind not want to remember her? He searched every inch of her face, willing himself to remember who she was to him, but nothing. Had she something to do with what happened to him?

"Nay. 'Tis a wonder to me how ye feel. How ye fit to me."

He wasn't ready to explain the memories of her or describe the intensity and pleasure of them. Mayhap 'twas as the good brother who treated injuries said after all? That the woman in his dreams was not real, but a manifestation of his memories. But that was before he'd walked into Dun Ara and seen her.

Iain had just spoken her very thoughts back to her.

The last thing she needed to be doing was falling under this stranger's enticement. As she faced her father's ire and

Davina's disapproval, Ailis needed a clear head and a plan to thwart her father. This man clearly muddled those for her. She'd held out this long, avoiding any man's attentions or intentions, and wasn't ready to behave as though all was well.

Ailis glanced up at Iain and noticed the way her lips felt swollen from his kisses. How she'd pressed against him during those kisses, losing herself to the passion as she did with … Lachlan.

She narrowed her gaze and studied what she could see of him and his form. Something in him was calling up her own memories of the man she'd loved, to whom she'd pledged her love, heart and body. But what was it?

He shifted, taking a step away, as her father's guard called out to them. Would the men report back to her father that she had flung herself into this stranger's arms? She heard the slow, deep breathing as he held out his hand, his bare hand, to her. Ailis placed her palm in his hand, feeling the uneven skin under her touch.

They walked in silence back toward the village, leaving the sea and the memories and that kiss behind. Ailis couldn't help herself. She thought of Lachlan's kisses and the way their hands would touch, fingers entwined. And the way he would kiss her until they were breathless and panting in want and need.

He slowed his pace to keep their strides matched, his longer legs covering the same distance much faster than she could. With each matched step, comfort filled her. It felt right at his side. Which was mad and not something that should be.

It should be Lachlan at her side.

It should be Lachlan she married.

But, she thought with a glance up at this masked stranger, if she didn't come up with a plan to circumvent her father's will, this was the man she would marry in just a few days.

Could she betray Lachlan's memory in that way? Could she betray their love?

Seven

If her father thought that spending time with this man would make her more amenable to accepting Sir Duncan, he'd misjudged her badly. And if Davina thought her counsel would be welcomed, she had as well.

The woman who had been her closest friend breathed betrayal into every conversation with Ailis' father. No matter that she'd managed to forestall a decision by imploring her father for a reprieve. No matter that Davina carried out the tasks that Ailis' mother had and did it well. Or that she'd provided Finnan MacKinnon with the one thing he'd always sought and had never achieved, a son.

None of that mattered to Ailis as she sat through meals over the next days with her family, her father's chosen husband and the stranger who'd walked unsuspectingly into their battle of wills. What interested her most right now was how effortlessly the stranger fit at the table and at her side.

They'd spent hours together each day since his arrival and she looked forward to their next encounter. A wry sense of humor revealed itself when they went to the stables to choose a horse for him to ride. His strength was clear in the way he fought during a few more training bouts in the yard. His kindness was shown when they visited the village and he was made to wait while she saw to the needs of those in her care.

His manners at table were no different from Sir Duncan's and his ease at speaking to the chieftain or his servant hinted of experience. He also seemed well-educated, for he'd offered his opinion on several topics and her father accepted them easily.

He fought well, too.

Ailis had hidden behind the corner of the stables and watched as her father and three of his best warriors challenged Iain to fight. Thought not as strong as they were, Iain held them off well. She could tell when his clothing impeded his movements, but he took nothing off to make it easier for himself.

Oh, how she wanted to see beneath those garments and the mask he wore to the true man beneath! As though he understood her thoughts, he lifted his head and met her gaze.

"Curiosity again, my lady?" Could he read her thoughts? "I saw ye watching today. Did ye see what ye wished to?"

"Nay." Why deny it? Everyone in the keep and village wondered about the man beneath the layers.

He laughed and she noticed his voice was smoother now than when he'd first arrived. Almost as if he'd not used it before and now it was warming up because he talked more. It remained hoarse and not more than a whisper, at that. But he didn't struggle to get the words out as he had before.

"If ye would like to speak honestly, I would as well," he said. He leaned in closer so only she would hear his words. "There are matters to settle between us before this situation escalates further."

His words, which could have an ominous tone, thrilled her instead. Over these last days, they had spoken on many

51

matters and Ailis always felt as though he considered her words in a way no one here ever did. Only Lachlan had.

"There now. Ye have that look in yer eyes," he said. "What were ye thinking just then?"

Ailis swallowed down the tears and grief and shrugged at his question. "A memory, sir."

"So that is what my face," he began, "What my eyes look like when I remember something?"

She would have run away, uncomfortable at the thought of discussing Lachlan with this stranger, but he reached out and took her hand. Guiding it under the table, he entwined their fingers and squeezed her hand.

"Who was he?"

His question, stated softly and plainly, threatened to shatter her very being. Other than Davina, no one here knew about Lachlan or their love. The only word that ever arrived was that one of The MacLean's sons had died in a fire. Since their clans were not in good standing with each other, barely a moment was wasted on that news. Her own injury in that fire had been hidden and blamed on something completely separate from that. Only she and Davina knew that truth as well. When he squeezed her hand, she decided to speak the name of the man she would never stop loving.

"His name was Lachlan. He died last year."

In the few moments after her disclosure, Ailis waited for his reaction. Her previous words about the loss of her virtue, spoken in anger that first night, must be on his mind now. When she could no longer bear the heavy silence between them, she glanced at his face.

His gaze was empty. He stared over her head and didn't seem to know she was there. He was remembering something!

"Does the name mean something to ye, Iain?" she whispered, tugging on their joined hands to gain his attention. "Do ye remember that name?"

Was he a MacLean? Had Lachlan been his kin? Mayhap

52

there was some family resemblance that caused her to think of her lost love when he spoke … or when he kissed her? Another suspicion tickled her memory, but she pushed it away for its absurdity. Lachlan was dead, she was certain. She squeezed his hand harder and called his name once more.

"Iain? Did ye ken Lachlan MacLean?"

He blinked. She could see his eyes moving within the mask's openings. His hand shook in her hold and she held her breath awaiting his disclosure.

"I thought for a moment that I did," he admitted, his voice hoarse again. "But, like the other memories that have haunted my dreams and my mind, it flitted away."

"But that doesna mean ye didna ken him." He shook his head and released her hand.

"Alas, my lady," he said, regret filling his voice. "I have no memory of anyone by that name. Or any MacLeans."

Davina had chosen that moment to eavesdrop. Ailis heard her gasp at the name of their enemies.

"Ailis, I pray ye leave that subject," she warned.

Ailis took in a breath and let it out before saying a word. Even that did not help curb the anger she felt.

"And I pray ye to stop interfering."

Iain stopped any further exchanges when he stood between them. He asked her father's leave to go before stepping back.

"I would speak to ye," her father said, rising as well. "Come now."

Though the words were spoken in an easy manner, they were an order and Iain nodded. She glanced over and saw Breac and another of his men rise, too. Strange that. Fear flooded her and she worried that her father had some ominous fate planned for Iain. She reached out and took his hand, pulling him back to her.

"Have a care, Iain," she whispered. "If ye still wish to talk," she said and then paused. At his nod, she continued, "I will await ye in yer chamber."

Watching as the four men made their way out of the hall, Ailis was surprised when Davina slid across and sat in the chair at her side. Their usual practice was to go their own way once the meal was done.

"Is it wise to speak of the MacLeans with this stranger, Ailis?" Davina asked. "With tensions so high and the recent conflict so fresh?"

The MacKinnons and the MacLeans, and the MacLeods for that matter, all claimed different and changing portions of the Isle of Mull. Lands and cattle, moved from owner to owner every year, it seemed. The MacKinnons had lost their lands to the south and had been pushed to almost the very northern edge of Mull in the most recent feuding. And, the alliances with the king shifted at a furious pace, one clan or another in his good graces or outlawed as they met or refused his demands.

"Iain but asked a question, Davina. I answered him."

"But ye swore never to speak *his* name," she said in a softer voice and tone. "Yet ye told this stranger. Was that wise?"

"I promised him honesty and so I answered his question."

"Honesty?" Davina leaned back against the chair. "Why would ye promise him such a thing? Ye dinna ken him. Ye dinna owe him."

"He walked in seeking the hospitality of our hall, a refuge from the storm, and found himself in the middle of … a clan war of sorts. He will leave with a full stomach and a few nights' rest and some coin if my father is feeling generous. But not the bride he has been promised. The least he deserves from me is honesty, Davina."

Davina smiled now. Ailis recognized that smug, satisfied smile from their years as friends. It signified a task gone well or a prank enjoyed.

"So ye will marry Sir Duncan then?" Davina asked.

"I wish to marry no one," Ailis admitted aloud. "I have no heart in me for a husband."

Davina reached over and covered Ailis' hand. She leaned forward and pressed against Ailis the way they used to when sharing secrets or plotting some mischief.

"Lachlan is gone, Lis," Davina whispered. "Ye must go on with yer life." The tears burned in her eyes. "Ye have lost so much in such a short time, but ye canna live in the past forever."

This was the first time that Davina had advised her on any matter since she'd married Ailis' father. The longing for such comradery shook Ailis to her bones. Ailis missed Davina almost as much as she missed Lachlan and her mother.

"I ken ye dinna understand why I accepted the offer of marriage to yer father, but 'twas not done to hurt ye or tarnish the memory of Lady Elisabet. I had so few choices to make a good marriage, Lis. Yer father—"

"Was a good match?" she asked. The bitterness couldn't be held in after all. It burned in her gut like the fire that consumed Lachlan had. Hot. Strong. Corrosive.

"Aye, a better match than a lowly MacNab cousin could have or should have hoped for. Ye ken that. Ye kenned my circumstances." Davina shrugged. "More than that, Lis, he makes me happy."

"He is old enough—" she began.

"To be my father? Aye, he is that. I grieve for yer losses, Lis, but I refuse to beg forgiveness for seeking and finding my own happiness."

Davina didn't wait on her response. Truly, what could she say? As she watched in silence, Davina rose and stepped away from the table. Before she left, she leaned back down to Ailis.

"And, no matter what ye might think, I never once broke a confidence of yers. I havena told yer father anything about our time as friends." She left the table, followed by a servant and the steward.

The other servants, who had clearly understood the private nature of the conversation between the lady of the keep and the chieftain's daughter, now returned to clean up the dishes, plates and cups from the table. As she walked to Iain's chamber, her thoughts turned back to Davina's words. She could admit to herself that she had feared the exact thing that Davina denied, that she'd revealed private knowledge to Ailis' father in the intimacy of their marriage.

If Ailis had been in her right mind and not driven nearly mad with grief, she wouldn't have begrudged her friend's happiness, no matter where she'd found it. Davina was a distant cousin to Ailis' mother with few prospects. She had hoped to find a place in Ailis' household on her marriage and never dreamed of anything higher than that.

She sighed as she approached the bedchamber at the end of the corridor. No sounds came from within, so she knew Iain was still with her father. With a warning knock before she lifted the latch, she spoke his name and opened the door. As she entered, she left the door ajar so he would be aware of her presence when he arrived.

The room was as she'd directed. A fire tended in the hearth, food on the table and jugs of ale and water waiting for him. She walked to the small chest along one wall and found two tunics and trews folded neatly on top of it. Ailis touched the unused garments.

'Twas almost as if he didn't want to take anything offered him. As if he didn't belong.

It amazed Iain how cold the chambers in a stone keep could be. If not for the well-set fire in the chieftain's hearth, Iain would have been chilled. Standing naked, except for his boots, before The MacKinnon was not what he had planned to do, but the man would brook no refusal. Breac and the other man stood nearby in case he thought to naysay their laird, though their gazes were directed elsewhere throughout this inspection.

"Does it yet pain ye?" The MacKinnon asked as he nodded his permission for Iain to dress.

Iain shook his head as he turned his back and tugged the trews up, tying the laces at his waist. The hooded tunic followed, but he left the hood gathered at his neck as he placed the fabric mask over his face and tied it behind his head. When he eased the hood into place, Iain felt more secure. Facing the others as he slid on the gloves, he looked for their reaction to his disfigurement and was surprised by the lack of it.

"I'd sent men to the brothers to confirm yer story," The MacKinnon said as he offered Iain an empty cup.

The older man reached up on a shelf and took down a precious glass bottle. Opening it himself, the laird poured a good amount of the golden liquid into Iain's cup before pouring some for himself. Breac and the other two were dismissed with another nod before the powerful man directed him to sit.

Iain waited for him to take a drink of the *uisge beatha* first and then sipped from his cup. This was a powerful brew and he waited as it moved over his tongue and down his throat. 'Twas a smooth, deep, intense and rich flavor of a skillfully-distilled spirit. He paused before drinking more and looked at the chieftain.

"Did ye find what ye were seeking?" he asked. Iain had questioned the brothers for days trying to find out more about himself.

"Gold has a way of loosening men's tongues," The MacKinnon began. "Much like this does."

He held up his cup of *uisge beatha* between them and drank more of it. Did the man think Iain held back some secret that spirits would free? If only it was that simple. Iain took a deep swallow and waited for the rest of The MacKinnon's disclosures. The warmth of the golden liquid spread from his stomach to his limbs, removing any lingering discomfort. But it didn't ease the sense of warning in his blood.

The chieftain's gaze revealed not a glimmer of recognition. No sign that the man saw anything in his features, those that had not been burned, that were familiar to him. Iain let out a breath and waited for what the chieftain would say, now that Iain understood his identity was yet unknown.

"They told me exactly what ye had said. Injured and left for dead. Ye spent the last several months in their care." The laird drank another mouthful and then nodded at Iain. "They said that ye are lucky, blessed, to be alive at all. That ye should have died ten times over but ye are a stubborn one and wouldna give in." Another deep draw on his cup. "They pray that 'tis not vengeance that drives ye so."

"Someone tried to kill me."

He'd thought on it in the long hours filled with pain and torment. Someone wanted him dead. Did they know they hadn't succeeded? Were they watching him as he sought out his past? Or had they thought themselves safe?

"Aye. From the look of ye, they almost succeeded. That ye stand before me speaks to yer strength and courage. Admirable traits in a man."

Iain could hear the hesitation and the coming word.

But …

"Ye will be on yer way on the morrow."

Iain smiled as the chieftain confirmed what he'd suspected. The man would never let this stranger marry his daughter. His instincts had been proven correct. No man as powerful and intelligent as this one would let some stranger walk in and take his daughter in marriage.

"I was a convenient weapon to force her to yer will."

He stated the words without rancor. 'Twas what his own father would have done. Though he didn't know who his father was, he knew to his marrow that he was as canny and strong as the man who stared at him over cups of *uisge beatha*.

"Just so," the man said, finishing his spirits and rising to his feet. "I dinna wish ill of ye," he said. Iain drank the last drops from his cup and placed it on the table. "But my daughter will marry Duncan MacNeil."

Iain almost asked if his daughter understood that, but he held the words behind his teeth. He walked across the chamber to the door and would have left without another word exchanged, if the laird hadn't called out.

"She may not wish to, but she kens her place and her duty." The man paused as though waiting for the conviction of his own words to make him believe them. "When ye sort things out or if ye canna, I could find ye a place if ye have need of one."

He understood that by the time that happened, Ailis would be safely married and sent off across the sea to Barra, one of the MacNeils' lands.

"I will think on yer offer, my lord," he said before lifting the latch.

"Iain? One more thing." The man crossed the chamber and stood in front of him. "The brothers said that ye were found elsewhere before they brought ye to their community."

"I was?" He'd not been told that before. "Did they say where? When?"

"Only that two of their number were traveling back from Iona and found ye closer to the coast in the south. Once they thought ye might survive, they took ye to the settlement and cared for ye there."

When he met the laird's gaze, the gleam told Iain that The MacKinnon knew or suspected more than he was saying. The coast to the south of Mull belonged to the MacLeans, from just below Tobermory, around past Craignure and towards Iona, the Holy Isle.

The MacLeans were enemies of the MacKinnons.

The man's green eyes, the same as his daughter had, narrowed ever so slightly. Iain might have missed it if he hadn't been looking at just that moment.

"See yerself gone by the noon meal. Breac will see to ye if ye dawdle."

Iain walked out, passing Breac in the corridor as he waited on his brother's orders. The chieftain had things in hand, but Iain wondered if Ailis understood her father's plan.

But right now, all Iain could think about was the woman waiting in his chamber and getting to her.

Eight

Finnan MacKinnon watched the young man leave and poured himself another half-cup of the potent spirit before sitting down. He'd seen many things in his life, many injuries in battle and accidents, but nothing compared to the damage wrought on this man.

Like he'd survived Hell's fires on earth was how his men said the brothers had described his condition when they'd found him. Burned over half of his body, the back of his head and the side of his face and neck. From his own inspection just now, Finnan couldn't imagine the amount of pain and suffering the man had endured to survive.

Yet, he had. Not only had he survived but he was recovering and regaining his strength. The training bout with him, Breac and the others demonstrated that this man made it this far back into living by sheer force of will. He drank another mouthful and thought on the other information his men had brought back.

Finnan had asked him if he lived for revenge. 'Twas a

powerful emotion, nay a need, and one that could give purpose and focus when everything seemed hopeless. And this man had lived in the constant torment of his injuries for months. So only something as powerful as vengeance could drive him back from the edge of death.

Or …

The brothers had also told his men something else. That this man's dreaming and waking hours were filled with visions of a woman. He'd spoken to her in his delirium, called out to her for help and declared his love for her countless times. He screamed for her in the worst of his pain so much that the brothers feared he'd damaged his already-burned throat and voice.

He'd never spoken and said he didn't know her name or her identity. Iain, as they called him, could describe every single feature of the woman, some of it shocking in its intimacy and, yet, couldn't recall her name.

Long, flowing, blonde hair that reached below her hips.

Deep, emerald-green eyes surrounded by long lashes.

Full lips, creamy skin and a lithe figure.

In other words, Finnan's own daughter, Ailis.

He tossed back the rest of the *uisge beatha* and was tempted to fill his cup again. That report had forced his hand. He took the distasteful action of making the man undress before him.

He needed to discover if he recognized this man. Had he some connection to their clan? Finnan needed to know what the injuries did to him. He needed to know … if this man knew his Ailis.

But what bothered Finnan most were the bits of other details he was now remembering that might be linked to this man.

Though Ailis might not believe it, he had and still grieved the loss of Elisabet. The last year since her passing had been a jumble of loss and grief and life moving on. If it wasn't something critical to his rule of Clan MacKinnon, Finnan would admit that he paid little heed in the confusion of the times.

His precipitous marriage to Davina had seemed harsh and unfeeling to his daughter, but he'd had his reasons for doing so. Good reasons, too, in his mind, for the lass' father had a much different fate in mind for her. The only way Finnan could stop it was by offering marriage. That it had brought the intelligent, kind and passionate woman into his bed and his heart and given him a son were results he wouldn't argue about. Best of all, she was safe ... and she was his.

He'd watched as Ailis sank into the clutches of grief and almost madness after her own injuries that left her marred. Now, considering the timing of this man's injuries and his daughter's, Finnan wondered if they were linked. Had there been a fire in a place where they'd both been?

Something struck him, a memory of word coming from the MacLeans in the south. A son. Lost in a fire. When had it happened? Could Ailis have been involved?

Could this man truly be a MacLean? Could he be the MacLean son his family believed had perished in that fire? It would explain the man's skills with the sword, ease on horseback and other small details that had shown in his behavior.

Since his daughter had not a civil word for him, Finnan knew there was only one person he could ask such things. One person who would know if his daughter had been injured with the MacLean son. *Involved* with the MacLean son.

And she would return to this chamber after seeing to their son's needs in a short while.

Davina knew more about Ailis than anyone, living or dead. She'd been closer to his daughter than even Elisabet had been. Though he had poked and prodded, his wife had never spoken of his daughter except in general terms. She'd offered her opinion and advice, made suggestions about how to deal with

Ailis, but had never revealed anything of their time spent as friends.

It had frustrated him. It angered him sometimes when trying to manage her. But Davina wouldn't speak against her friend no matter what he asked of her.

Would she speak now? Would she tell him the truth of Ailis and any involvement with this man?

Remembering the day of Ailis' injury, Finnan realized there had been no actual explanation of the burns. Just a lot of crying and tears and calling the healer from the village. Once she'd been seen to and as she healed, Finnan had brushed the incident aside. He paid heed more to his then-pregnant wife than his stubborn, strong-willed daughter who refused his wishes at every turn.

And now?

The possibilities of the truth shocked him as he connected seemingly unrelated events.

Well, no matter what his wife would tell him or not, on the morrow, whether a MacLean or from some other clan, Iain would be on the road away from Dun Ara. When Iain was gone, Finnan would think on whether he should send word to The MacLean to speak to the man. After all, if Kennan had been in a situation such as this, he would sell his soul for word of his survival. Enemies or not, The MacLean deserved that consideration.

Since, by the end of the day, Ailis would be married to Duncan and his responsibility to bear, 'twould do no harm.

Iain pushed the door open and found Ailis sitting on the bed. He stepped inside. With a glance at the guard that now dogged his steps, he closed the door. She jumped up as though embarrassed to be found sitting there.

"That took longer than I expected," she said, walking

towards him. "What did he say?"

"His men returned from speaking with the brothers. He wanted me to ken what they told him." He could see the interest in her lovely eyes as he spoke. She wanted to know and knew her father wouldn't speak to her of it.

"And?" she blurted out as she wrung her hands together. He had offered to speak candidly with her and he would.

"It mattered not, for yer father has no intention of allowing me to marry ye, lady."

From her reaction, or lack of one, it had surprised her as little as it had him. She nodded and it made her hair ripple over her shoulders and down her back. He'd only just noticed that it was loose … as in his dreams.

"So it surprises ye not?"

She shook her head, a slight sadness in her green gaze. "I ken his ways," she admitted. "I had hoped …"

Iain watched her as she smiled, but it was not like the smiles he'd seen these last days. Instead, it was one filled with the wistfulness and wanting of a woman who would never be permitted to marry as she chose. Surely not a man without a memory, without kith or kin.

"He has ordered me gone by midday on the morrow."

Her gasp echoed across the chamber. He stood by the door, believing the distance between them would keep him from doing anything foolish before he departed Dun Ara. Like taking her in his arms and kissing her breathless until she melted in his embrace. And peeling off her garments and finding out if he did, indeed, know every inch of her body as he thought. He would finally know if her place in his dreams was just the machinations of a disturbed mind or something else.

He would discover if she had a birthmark on the inside of her right thigh or if he'd only dreamt it. And if she had a weakness to being tickled in the curve of her buttocks that made her sigh and laugh. He would kiss her there and lick a path between her … He shook at the intensity of the wanting that flooded him.

So lost in his lustful thoughts was he that he never heard her approach. She stood inches away from him. He fought the urge to grab her, take her and mark her in some way as his.

"I have felt both a comfort and a desire in yer embrace that I never thought to feel again, Iain," she whispered.

The tip of her tongue darted out to moisten her pink lips. His control frayed with every second that passed and with every movement she made toward him.

"Ye shouldna speak of such things, lady," he warned. Iain tried to step back and found the wood of the door in his way. "I leave in the morn and …"

"Aye, ye leave on the morrow and I face marrying a man I dinna wish to marry."

"Lady –"

"Ailis." She took the final step between them and he felt her soft curves against his body. "I pray ye, say my name."

Iain understood the dangers of letting her name free on his tongue. Desire filled her eyes and flushed her cheeks. Her breathing grew shallow and quick. His body reacted to the signs of her arousal.

"Ailis."

He reached out, slid his gloved hands into her hair and pulled her face to his. For once, he hated the mask and hood that usually gave him comfort and security. He wanted to touch her skin to skin, but he couldn't bear to see the disgust in her gaze if she saw the disfigurement her father had just witnessed.

"Iain," she said on a sigh.

He ached for her touch, her kiss and her love. Since he could never lay claim to that, he would take her desire and passion instead and give her pleasure in return. He searched her eyes for any sign of hesitation before taking her mouth. Now he would kiss her breathless.

And he did, plunging his tongue in to taste and feel hers. She opened to him, even leaned into his embrace, and he delved deeply into the heat he found there. He heard the moan she made as he suckled on her tongue. He stilled when he felt her hands, her bare hands, cover his gloved ones.

Ailis slid her hands down, over his wrists and into the sleeves of his tunic until she reached the edges of the leather. He released his hold and allowed her to remove the gloves, knowing what she would behold there. Would it stop her? Iain held his breath for her reaction.

His right hand and arm bore some damage, but the left was worse by far. The brothers had surmised that he'd landed on his right side, protecting that part of his body from the fire that had burned him so badly. His left hand and arm had few places on them where the skin was intact and not melted in ridges, either while it burned or when it healed.

Her soft caresses on his skin caused a series of bursts to move along his arms. Not painful, exactly. But not the pleasure such a touch should elicit. *That* he'd felt there ... before. If she was repulsed by the feeling of it, neither her gaze nor her continued caress revealed it.

Iain leaned in and kissed her again, as she gently slid her hands over his arms. He caught her sighs and tugged her closer so their bodies pressed against each other. Against her quiet protest, he moved his arm free of her grasp and reached up to loosen her hair. He wanted to see the curtain of silky tresses hanging around her. Only the silky tresses, if he had his way.

As though she'd heard is thoughts, Ailis began to loosen the ties of her gown and the shift that lay beneath it. 'Twas what he wanted, but he wouldn't take her standing up fully dressed like a whore. She was a lady who deserved better treatment. She deserved pleasure and love.

"Ailis," he whispered as he moved her one very small step back from him. "Ye should go." Every fiber of his body and soul and heart waited on her next words.

"Do ye want me to leave, Iain?"

"Nay, Ailis. I want ye to stay. But I think mayhap the best thing for ye would be to leave me now."

He could hear his breathing, shallow and quick. He listened to hers match his in the few seconds that seemed an eternity of waiting. Iain closed his eyes behind the damned mask and steeled himself for the inevitable disappointment that must come from such a lady.

"I want to stay, Iain. For this night. To discover what truly lies between us."

His eyes opened to witness a smile that must have been like the one that Eve gave Adam to tempt him to sin. And, damn his soul and his desire for her, he would fall into that temptation. Iain spent only one moment finding and dropping the bar to secure the door before he turned back to her.

"Get on the bed," he said in a voice thick with desire and need. His hands itched now as they had as they'd healed but, this time, it was for her. "And take off yer gown."

Nine

Ailis stared at Iain as he dropped the bar and faced her.

Was he going to do this? Would they …? How would they…?

Her body shuddered at his gruff command, but she quickly moved to his bed. Facing him, she reached for the edge of her gown and tugged it over her head. His breathing grew labored and he clenched and released his fists with every movement she made.

It emboldened her. It heated her blood and made her breasts swell. It … aroused her. She'd not felt anything like this in so long, as though she were alive again. Tears filled her eyes and she blinked them away. It would never be Lachlan again and she must accept that. In that moment, Ailis found herself wanting the touch of this man. The one before her, not the one she had mourned for so long.

With no more delay, she reached down and took off the shift and climbed on his bed. Leaning against the pillows strewn along the headboard, Ailis waited to see how he would do this. He didn't move for a while. He stood there, staring through that mask of his, watching her settle on top of the bedcovers. Her body readied itself for what she knew was coming.

Then, without a word, he circled the chamber, dousing the fire in the hearth, closing the shutters on the window and extinguishing the candles that threw light around the room. The last one sat on the table next to the bed and she held her breath as he walked to it. He wet his fingers and squeezed out the flame, but as it flickered, she swore she felt that touch on her nipples.

Now, the chamber was in darkness with only a sliver of light creeping in under the bottom of the door. It wasn't enough to allow her to see him clearly. Then, the unmistakable sounds of him moving away and undressing followed. More desire flowed through her body as she imagined each layer of his garments coming off.

She'd felt his muscular build under her hands when they kissed and now she would feel it against her skin as they … made love. Did the damage she'd felt on his arms extend everywhere? Had he been burned, as she had, to mar his skin in that way? The sounds of his footsteps approaching the bed gave her pause and she stilled, waiting for him to join her. When he didn't, she slid from the bed and reached out to him.

Her hands met a hard chest. Muscles, defined and strong, quivered under her fingers. Ailis skimmed over his chest and up to his shoulders, noticing that one side, his left side, had more damage than the other. He didn't stop her exploration, but Ailis thought he would at any moment. Instead, he gathered her hair in his hands and tossed it over her shoulders. It tickled as it fell over her back and hips, the length of it reaching her thighs.

"I have wanted to touch yer hair for a long time," he whispered, sliding his hands around her shoulders and pulling her body to his.

70

She gasped at the contact. His skin was hot and his prick was hard against her belly. And, unmarred, it seemed. Then he lifted her chin and took her mouth in a kiss that was both gentle and possessive. Ailis opened to him, feeling the strength of his male flesh as he pressed against her. When she reached out to hold him closer, he startled.

"Lady ..."

"Ailis," she repeated. "Does it pain ye? If I touch ye there, will it bring ye pain?"

"Nay. I think not." He didn't move away or push her hands down, which she took as a good sign.

"Then, may I?" she asked.

Not truly intending to allow him to naysay her, she didn't wait for his permission. With a light touch, she eased her hands around his back and caressed him there. Wide patches of thickened flesh covered him. Unlike other injuries she'd seen, these were not raised as ridges, but the skin had melted and reformed roughly.

The pain he'd endured must have been tenfold more than hers. She leaned her face to his chest and kissed him there before letting her hands glide over his body, down and up, across and over, trying to please him with her touch. Trying to erase some of the memories of pain and replace them with pleasure. That he remained under her touch brought a smile to her.

He stood there unmoving, breathing in shallow gasps and allowing her to have her way, until he did not. One moment, they stood, her breasts on his chest, her belly against his erect manhood. The next, he lifted her from her feet and carried her to the bed. Then, she was on her back covered by him. The only shock was how good it felt. Her body, aroused and waiting, accepted his and he settled between her thighs before kissing her. And he kissed her again and again. She tried to slide her fingers into his hair to hold him closer, but he stopped her.

"Nay, la … Ailis. Not there," he said, leaning away.

"Does it pain ye?" she asked. She felt him shake his head. "Then allow me my way in this, Iain. If I canna see ye, I would ken yer body and face through my hands."

This night would never happen again. He would never happen again. As much as she'd fought the inevitable, Ailis understood what her path must be and it would not include Iain. Hers would be a life of duty and vows. So she would take and savor every moment, every caress and sigh that this night, and this man, offered and remember it across the years.

Without waiting, she reached up and touched his face. Beginning at his jaw, she slid her hands up, feeling every inch of him. Once again, the left side was damaged more than the right. Using the tip of her fingers, she outlined the angles of his cheeks and caressed his forehead. His mouth had been affected the least which is why his kisses never revealed much to her, other than stealing her wits and making her want more.

His face, on one side, bore the brunt of the injury. Sliding her hands to his shoulders she drew him down to kiss her. He relaxed into her, his body easing down and pressing her into the surface of the bedding. His hair fell forward, tickling her face. When she moved her hands into it, Ailis felt the rest of his head and the damage wrought there. She couldn't help it. She shifted from under him until they lay side by side.

"Yer skin feels like mine … worse though." Ailis paused before asking the question she truly wanted to ask. "Was it a fire?" she asked, smoothing his hair away from his face and wishing she could see him.

"I dinna remember, but, aye, the brothers said 'twas that." His quiet admission gave them another thing in common.

"Ye remember it not? None of it?"

"Only the aftermath," he said, reaching across the tiny space between them to rest his hand on her hip. "Most of the first months are lost to me."

"Yer back is the worst then?"

The topic had not quenched the desire in each of them, for his flesh remained hard. He eased her leg up over his waist and opened her to his touch. Almost a challenge to her, continue talking or ... pleasure? When he slid her leg along his, she knew the answer. His leg was just as bad. Then he caught her knee and brought it back to his waist. With his large hand around her thigh, he slid his fingers closer to the place between her legs and swirled them on her skin.

She could not breathe. Or speak. Or do anything but feel the wonderful sensations that raced into the very center of her. When she shifted her hips to bring his hand to that heated flesh, he chuckled in that throaty, hoarse voice.

"Ah, so now ye are ready?" he asked. "No more questions?"

"None that I can think on," she admitted.

He pressed her shoulder and rolled their bodies. Ailis found herself on her back once more. But he remained at her side and she understood why. He could touch her now.

He did touch her.

Everywhere. Her breasts. Her neck. Her legs. The sensitive place behind her knees. The curls that both hid and led to the part of her that ached and throbbed for him.

Her body was a mess of need and want. He teased her until she panted and was ready to beg him to finish this torment. His hand pushed between her legs and welcomed his touch. She moaned when he reached the throbbing flesh and rubbed it. Faster, harder and deeper, his fingers worked some enchantment on her until she fell apart. Something she had not felt in so long coiled within her, tighter and tighter, until it broke free and she cried out in the pleasure of it.

Iain didn't wait for the wave of release to ebb before he entered her. He shifted onto his knees, moved between her legs and placed himself at the sensitive entry to her woman's core.

One thrust and she was his.

She clutched at his shoulders as he eased her knees up to his hips. He canted his and then plunged deeper. Her body took every inch of his flesh and swelled around his cock. He leaned his head down into the pool of her hair next to her neck and kissed and suckled her there as he moved deeper with every thrust.

She gasped every time and began to move in rhythm with him. His body's need to take hers overwhelmed whatever control he thought he had and he became relentless. Something lay just outside his grasp. Some truth, some realization, teased him even as he plundered the tightness of her channel. Her sighs, the way she moved and the way her hands clutched at his arse spurred him on until he could feel his own release growing closer.

"Iain!" she cried out as she climaxed a second time.

Tiny spasms surrounded his male flesh as she arched against him. His cock hardened, lengthened and thickened within her and his sac clenched until his seed pushed forth. He barely withdrew in time and even that was a near thing. He wanted to fill her with his seed even as he pushed beneath her and allowed its release under her buttocks.

He lay on her, sweat making their skin slick. The heather and honey scent of her hair surrounded him and he didn't want to let her go.

Not now. Not ever.

He must have fallen asleep, satiated and replete. One minute he was in the pitch dark of a bedchamber and the next, he lay on a plaid spread out in a sundrenched field.

"For you, my love," he said, holding out a bunch of just-picked wildflowers.

Sitting up, he looked down on her naked body, covered only by the length of her hair. He began to place the blossoms on her, several across her breasts, another few over the lush blonde curls at the junction of her thighs. Then he knelt over her and decorated her hair with the rest.

74

She laughed and pushed him back, climbing on him, spreading her legs over his hips and seating herself on his erect flesh. As she took him deep within her body, he arched his hips and thrust deeper. When she leaned forward, her hair fell in waves over him, the scent of the flowers mixing with those of honey and heather around him.

"All the days of our lives," she whispered as he poured his seed into her. "All the days of our lives."

Iain jolted awake, knowing he'd been dreaming. The feel of Ailis' soft body next to his soothed him. But the dreams felt even more real now that they had joined in passion. The feel of his flesh in hers, the scent of her hair and the taste of her skin felt more like memories than phantom visions of a disturbed mind.

No matter these visions or dreams. No matter how much he wanted to keep the woman who had given him a respite from the storm surrounding him and given him of herself. None of that mattered for, on the morrow, he would leave and she would live the life she was destined to live.

She mumbled, clearly words of love, though he couldn't make out the individual words. Though he would like to have seen her face when she'd reached satisfaction, he couldn't chance it. This was the way it had to be. He'd arrived a stranger and had been given a special gift by this lady.

She nestled closer to him, turning on her side and drawing him behind her. It took little time for his body, long-deprived of this kind of intimacy, to respond to her soft curves and enticing shape. When she eased her bottom back against his now-erect prick and whispered his name, he couldn't resist the warm invitation.

This time, their joining was slow and gentle, more sighs than moans, more caresses than thrusts. But the release they both found shattered him. And the soft words about her lost love and his lost life that they exchanged in the darkest hours of the night both surprised and soothed him.

The bitter, angry young woman he'd discovered just days ago seemed more at peace now. 'Twas as if she had taken a step out of her personal darkness and was ready to move into living once more, even as he would move on and try to discover his past.

His resolve to leave before the dawn weakened until the last moment when the sun began to rise. Iain eased away from Ailis and found his garments on the chair where he'd placed them. It took little time to covered himself and place the mask into position over his face.

Dawn's light was pushing its way through the opening between the shutters when he carefully covered Ailis and walked to the door. After slowly lifting the bar and opening the door a scant inch or two, he turned back to take one last look at her. One to last him the rest of his days.

The light from the torch on the wall illuminated her for a moment before he pulled the door closed. Tugging his hood closer to his face, Iain turned down the corridor and led the guard away from the bedchamber where the chieftain's daughter yet slumbered.

He broke his fast in silence in the hall with the others who began their tasks and duties at sunrise. Once finished, he was surprised when he was given a sack of food and a skin of ale for his journey by one of the servants. The laird's orders, the girl said. She told him to seek out the stable master before leaving Dun Ara, again at The MacKinnon's order.

Another surprise awaited him there, for the chieftain gave him a horse to use on the rest of his journey. Iain laughed as he realized the reason behind these gestures. Finnan MacKinnon was rewarding him for his cooperation and his use in bringing the laird's daughter to heel. Though he would like to stand on some principles and refuse, he knew only the wealthy or the foolish would reject such gifts.

By the time the sun broke through the morning's fog and rose above the mountains to the south and east, Iain was on his way out of the gates of Dun Ara. He would never know what caught his eye, but as he approached the end of the cluster of cottages and buildings that made up the village, he saw a woman making her way along the road.

Dressed as every other goodwife here and carrying the usual basket in hand, Iain couldn't figure out why he watched her. At least not until a long, blonde curl fell out from her kerchief over her shoulder. She handed off the basket and accepted the help of the blacksmith to climb upon a horse hidden behind his smithy. Iain wondered why Ailis MacKinnon was hiding her identity.

And why she was sneaking out of Dun Ara?

Ten

Though she had not been to the cottage in many months, she could find the way with her eyes closed. Even the horse beneath her seemed to remember it, for it had carried her many times. The blacksmith let her borrow his horse when she had the need of it and never asked why. Other than Lachlan, his friend and Davina, no one knew where they met.

This morn, as she crossed the miles south towards the coast, she ached. Her body ached in places she'd forgotten could feel such a thing. Her head throbbed from so little sleep these last days. And her heart hurt for what she must do now.

This stranger, this man called Iain, had been some kind of catalyst for her since his arrival. She'd been mired in pain and grief. Her whole life had spun down around that. Ailis knew she shouldn't treat her father and friend as she had, but it seemed out of her control. For all his real or imagined similarities to Lachlan, something about Iain had given her true comfort, providing a chance to break with the grief and the past. She could move forward, to be the woman she was meant to be. The woman Lachlan would have expected of her, a woman of honor, a woman who didn't waste love when it came to her.

And now she was ready for the next step.

After more than an hour of riding, she turned down a path. It led to the place that held both happiness and complete sorrow for her. The cottage hadn't been much, just a place where drovers would shelter as they took their herd to the south for the winter. Over the years, it had been built up from a simple shelter to more of a cabin with a real roof and walls and a door. Ailis tugged the reins and slid off the horse's back.

Now, only a blackened area of destruction and death with some strewn remnants of the wood that had not been burned to ashes sat where the cottage used to be. It had been a fast fire. She saw the first flicker of it and then the whole cottage was engulfed in flames before she could reach it … reach him.

She'd tried to get to the door, to get to him, but her sleeves had caught fire and the pain had driven her back. What must he have suffered within this place when it became Hell on earth?

Ailis didn't try to stop the tears. She walked around the perimeter of the clearing and sat on a large rock under the trees.

"I have come to beg yer forgiveness, Lachlan," she said aloud. "If it werena for me, ye would be alive now."

There. The truth of what lay at the bottom of her soul. If not for her, Lachlan would be alive this very day. That truth and her own guilt in his death had kept her from being able to let it go and live the life she had. Mayhap if she confessed to him, to his eternal soul as the priests taught, she could begin to live once more.

Oh, she would never, could never, forget him or their love. But if she accepted her part in bringing him here to his death, could she forgive herself someday?

"I admit it to ye and confess my guilt, Lachlan. If I hadna

pressed the matter, if I hadna lied about my father's knowledge about us, ye would be alive today."

She let the words out and the wind carried them away. Ailis had thought it time to announce their intentions to their families. Lachlan thought it best to wait until the matter of his brother's marriage and the rising conflicts between their clans had been settled. Then, when word came of his brother's and mother's deaths, she'd sent word for him to come. She'd lied in her note to him that her father knew.

"I beg yer forgiveness, Lachlan. For lying to ye. For bringing ye here when it was not safe. For … all of it."

Ailis closed her eyes and waited. She was not certain that she expected a reply or a sign he'd heard her words. Truly, just speaking them had lightened her soul. There was more within her, but the only thing she could do was go on without him. She must move on from the stubborn daughter she had been to a more mature woman who thought on the cost of her actions before she acted.

She wiped the tears away from her eyes and took a breath before standing. Walking towards the horse, Ailis understood she'd never return here. Lachlan was gone and nothing could bring him back. She managed to mount using the rock. As she rode down the path, she turned back for one last look. And one last moment of regret.

If only …

The storm clouds gathered ahead of her as she made her way back to Dun Ara. She still had to speak to Davina before this was all settled. Then it would be done.

He was Lachlan MacLean.

Not Iain the Unknown.

Lachlan MacLean, the second son of Dougal MacLean, chieftain here on Mull.

He knew it now. He knew it even if his memory hadn't returned. He *was* Lachlan MacLean and he had died on this spot almost nine months ago.

He was the man Ailis claimed to have loved and lost.

He was the same man she had just confessed to having a part in his death.

Lachlan walked from the shadows of the forest that surrounded the burnt cottage and pulled his hood back. Removing the mask, he let the cool breeze soothe his skin. He glanced around this clearing, studying the landscape and recognizing it.

It would take him almost two hours of hard riding to get here from … Aros Castle down the coast. He stared off in that direction trying to will more memories to come. Only the simplest ones did. Nothing that would explain her confession or her role in killing him.

Or how he'd survived the inferno that had destroyed the cottage. He walked to the edge of the ashes and moved some of them with his foot, hoping it would make something happen within his mind. Surely, facing the place where he'd nearly died would elicit some strong reaction?

Something, a trick of the light mayhap, caught his gaze. He made his way through the ashes and lumps of wood to the very center. He waited to relive the fire that destroyed this place and him, but it didn't happen. No flash of memory. No feelings.

Then his foot snagged on something under the ashes.

Lachlan knelt and pushed aside the layers of wood, ash and dirt that had been matted down by rain since the fire and found what had tripped him. An unburned panel of wood. Cleaning the debris from it, he discovered the entrance to a root cellar dug into the ground. He pulled on the edge and it came free, sending him careening off balance. He regained his stance and stared into a hole of darkness.

If he could get to the cellar, he thought he might survive.

When he regained consciousness, he lay on the floor of the blazing cottage. The flames crept up all the walls. The rough sod roof would do nothing to stop them. The door was blocked and he could not push his way out.

Somehow, he managed to find the opening in the smoke that burned his eyes and throat. Pieces of wood dropped like flaming ingots on him as he tugged open the wooden panel, jumping into the space. But the smoke followed and filled the cellar around him. Coughing and gasping, he waited as long as he could before trying one last escape. Hoping that the less-than-sturdy cottage walls were gone now, he pushed up, intending to rush through the remaining flames.

He felt the ungodly heat around him as he climbed out, trying to avoid the worst of it. The flimsy walls still burned but Lachlan saw a path to the window. He crouched low, trying to see his way when an ominous crack sounded above him. With no more warning than that, the roof came down on him, trapping him there.

He screamed …

Lachlan's throat convulsed against the terror and the scream that would not come now. He fell to his knees as his stomach heaved and he vomited up the meager meal he'd eaten.

He remembered nothing before waking there and nothing after the roof caved in on him. Somehow, though in God's Holy Name he could not figure how, he'd survived and made it out. The brothers hadn't given him a specific location where he'd been found, but Lachlan knew it had to be close to here.

As he stood, he realized something else. He didn't know himself when he'd woken up amidst the fire. His identity was gone from him already, taken by … Reaching up, he felt the back of his head. A deep gash had been there. The brothers said his skull had been damaged by a blow. They suspected that had been the cause of his memory loss.

He'd been struck from behind before the fire began.

Whoever set the fire, did it knowing he was inside and unconscious. Knowing he would perish.

Lachlan felt the change in the winds. The threatening storms were closer. A surreal sense of control filled him as the information he'd discovered took hold. The memories began to return. He had kith and kin. He had a place he belonged.

He had someone who'd wanted him dead.

Ailis' words of confession echoed in his head now.

I admit it to ye and confess my guilt, Lachlan, she'd said. *I beg yer forgiveness, Lachlan. For lying to ye. For bringing ye here when it was not safe. For ... all of it.*

It made no sense. Whenever she'd mentioned or thought on him, he'd seen only grief and loss. Considering her words now, had he misinterpreted her expression?

He kicked the dirt and headed back into the forest where he'd left his horse. Mounting, he headed north, back to Dun Ara, back to Ailis.

Lachlan would discover the truth before he let her go. If he let her go ... For now that he knew who he was and that the visions of her, of them, were memories and not the imaginings of a pain-crippled mind, Lachlan wouldn't give her up easily, if at all. He didn't doubt the rest of his life would return to him.

Virtue. Mine. Honor.

The words of the MacLean motto seemed appropriate as he rode to take back what, who, was his.

Eleven

"May I come in, Davina?" Ailis asked when the maid opened the door to her stepmother's chamber.

Davina nodded and she entered. She waited as Davina instructed the maid about the bairn and watched the girl leave. Her courage nearly buckled in the face of Davina's welcome.

"Ye are always welcome here, Lis," she said. "Always." Davina motioned to a chair and waited for her to sit. "Would ye like something to drink?"

"Nay," she replied. "I would just like to talk with ye."

She'd gotten back to the keep just as her father sent word that she was to join them for the evening meal. Suspecting that her betrothal would be both broken and remade then, Ailis needed to speak to Davina first. She couldn't leave here with a new husband without reestablishing peace between them. Davina sat abruptly as though expecting the worst. Clutching her hands, she watched Ailis and waited.

"Since Lachlan's death, nay, since my mother's, I have behaved terribly towards ye. Ye are correct. Ye have the right to seek yer own happiness and I have no right to begrudge ye that."

Daring a glance, she saw the color drain from Davina's face. But when her friend reached out and took Ailis' hand, Ailis kept speaking. The words, the guilt, the fear poured out as if they had been waiting.

"It was easier to be hateful than accept the changes in my life. And easier to spurn yer attempts to make peace than consider yer needs. I was desperately unhappy, mired in my grief and couldna stop to think about anyone else."

"What has brought this on, Lis?" Davina asked.

"Iain," she replied. "And Lachlan."

The soft sound of distress made her meet Davina's gaze. She was ghostly pale now.

"Davina? Are ye well?" Ailis stood and fetched a cup from the table. Filling it with ale, she held it while Davina drank deeply.

"I am better now," Davina said. "Iain made ye speak to me?"

"His arrival here made me question many things. The way he reacted to me and the position he found himself made me realize how terrible I have been," she admitted. Ailis realized there was more to it than that. "'Twas time, Davina. 'Twas simply time for me to move on and let him go."

It didn't hurt as much when she spoke the words as she thought it would. Mayhap saying it to Lachlan had eased the way of it.

"Of Lachlan?" Davina questioned. "Or Iain?"

"Iain and I understood how it would be. Father wouldna allow a marriage between us. He was using Iain to pressure me to my duty. I," she said, letting out a sigh, "I am ready to do that."

"Did anything happen between ye and Iain?"

"Davina, I dinna think that is important." As soon as the words left her mouth, she knew it was the wrong thing to say.

"Ye were attracted to him?" Davina's previous distress was gone. She seemed to have regained her color and her interest.

"I found many things about him that …"

Dare she admit the truth? A shared truth could bridge the distance between them.

"He reminded me of Lachlan in many ways, Davina. His mannerisms. The words he used. The way he stood." Ailis paused as she remembered the last time she'd seen Lachlan. They had made love in that cottage. He laughed as she said something outrageous as she rode away. She never dreamt it would be the last time for them. "Iain made me think and forced me to consider how I have been treating ye."

"Did Iain show ye his face? The injuries he sustained?"

"Nay," Ailis said shaking her head. "I asked him to, but he wouldna." She believed her friend's words about not sharing her secrets with Ailis' father. It gave her courage to admit another truth. "I felt the damage."

Davina looked as if she'd swallowed her tongue. She'd sucked in so deep a breath that it left her gasping. Ailis ran to her side and smacked her on the back, trying to help her breathe. When Davina waved her off, Ailis waited for the stern admonition to begin.

"Why? Why did ye do such a thing?" Davina asked softly. Ailis didn't expect that.

"I've been lonely, Davina. Without Mother, without Lachlan, without ye, I had no one. Iain made me feel something other than grief and pain for the first time in a long time. I needed him. I ken that it's sinful and wrong. But, Davina, I owe him so much for what he gave me."

"And Lachlan?"

And now the hard part. Admitting her part in his death.

"I lied to him, Davina. I drew him to his death."

"What?" Davina asked, rising and walking to her side. "What do ye mean?"

86

"I told him that Father kenned of our relationship and we needed to talk. Now, thinking back on it, I wonder if he did not."

"Ye think yer father had some involvement in the fire?" Davina grabbed her hand. "Why would ye think that?"

"I think Father kenned about us meeting. He said some things at the time about my time spent away from the village, about being seen in the south. I think he had someone following me and kenned the truth."

"Ye think yer father would burn a man to death?"

Davina's whisper was furious. But then, she was the man's wife. Ailis had seen the ruthless part of him before. He was first the chieftain of the clan. She'd thought on this the entire ride home today.

There were surely others who wouldn't want Lachlan and Ailis to be together, in addition to her father. Lachlan's father wouldn't be happy, but he would never cause his son's death. Nay, the most likely one behind it was Finnan MacKinnon.

"He wouldna want me married to his enemy's son. He wouldna allow me the choice …"

"If he had Lachlan killed, why would he …" Davina clamped her lips closed before she finished. "If yer father wanted him dead, then why …"

Davina shook her head several times before letting out a shriek and stamping her feet. Ailis couldn't ever remember seeing this kind of display and loss of control in her friend.

A terrible feeling crept over Ailis. Her stomach gripped at the tension growing within.

She closed her eyes and many images raced through her thoughts. Lachlan laughing and taking hold of her shoulders. Then the image changed and Iain was in his place. Lachlan murmuring as he touched her and brought her to completion. Then it was Iain's touch last night.

Lachlan. Iain.

Iain.

Oh, God in Heaven, Iain *was* Lachlan!

"How?" she screamed at Davina. "How could he have survived? I saw it burn, Davina. I saw it burn!"

Ailis held out her hands, sliding back her sleeves to reveal the burns she'd suffered. They were only superficial compared to what he'd suffered. Large areas of his skin had melted and reformed. She'd felt them. His back and legs. His head and neck. His face and jaw. And he'd survived?

Aye, he had lived through it.

"He is alive?" She grabbed Davina and shook her. "How long have ye kenned? Does Father know?"

Then the worst thought struck her. Did Iain know who he was? Had he known when they had …? Had he known when he'd left?

"Did he ken that he was … is Lachlan MacLean?"

"Nay, I dinna think so," Davina said, easing out of Ailis' grasp. "Yer father suspected his identity and spoke with me. He asked many questions about ye and the possibility. Lis, I dinna tell him about ye."

Lachlan was alive. Alive and gone from here without knowing the truth.

"I must go. I must find him and tell him. Where could he have gone?"

Now it was Davina's turn to grab hold of her and bring her to a stop.

"Look at me, Lis!" she said, while shaking her. "Think a moment. If yer father planned that fire, why would he allow him to live even now with the knowledge he has? If Finnan had no part, as I believe, how safe will Lachlan be if he reveals himself? Ailis, he only remains safe if that person believes him dead."

Ailis wanted to challenge her words, but they made sense. No matter that Lachlan was alive! How could she not find him? How could she let him go?

"He has no memory of who he is, Lis. He doesna ken his

Terri Brisbin

allies from his enemies. Or his kith and kin. If he looked on ye, kissed ye and *loved* ye, and dinna remember ye, what chance will he have if he faces the person responsible for his condition without kenning them?"

Lachlan told her that he'd seen her in his dreams or memories, but he had never remembered her or that they were together. He'd walked out of her life without knowing the truth. But what would happen if she told him about himself? Or about them? If he didn't remember, would he still love her?

Would the promises they'd made still bind them if he didn't remember making them?

"Ye are betrothed to another man now."

Ailis turned to face her stepmother. Surely, if Lachlan lived, she couldn't marry another man. Her father wouldn't force her to this, would he? One glance at Davina's expression gave her the truth. He would.

Worse, if she confirmed his identity, her father could have him killed and no one would miss the stranger. He would rid himself of an enemy in one move.

"I need to find him. If he truly doesna remember me, I will let him go and not tell him."

She rushed to the door but stopped with her hand on the latch. Ailis had heard the selfishness in her words. After what he'd suffered and lost, how could she think only of her pain and loss in this situation? If he didn't remember her, it didn't add to the burden he carried. It only hurt her.

Leaning her head against the door, she wanted to scream at the unfairness. He lived and yet she must live without him? Could she do that? Could she live without him if it gave him a chance to be safe?

She must. For him. For what they had. Even a few days ago, that wouldn't have been her answer. But now, she knew he meant more to her than her own happiness.

"I will treasure every moment I spent with him," she whispered against the wood. "Especially these last days."

89

Turning, she brushed away the tears. "For all the days of my life."

She had spoken those words to him many times. When they vowed to be together and promised their love to each other, they'd promised it for all the days of their lives.

If his memory returned, he would need to find the person responsible. If it returned, she would be married and gone. For even if her father relented on Sir Duncan, there would be another man and she would eventually have to marry and leave here.

All the days of my life.

The words spoken in love and hope now described the emptiness ahead of her life without him.

But he would live. And be safe.

All the days of his life.

Twelve

A hint of excitement spread through the hall as the evening meal began. There was a frivolity that Ailis did not feel. Sir Duncan was pleasant and engaged her in conversation even though she wanted to curl up in the corner and sob out her anguish. When she felt that urge, Davina would reach out and offer a comfort that Ailis had missed for months.

Her father was generous in his praise now that she had capitulated and accepted her fate and his choice of husband. She realized that the feeling spreading through the people was not excitement as much as relief. The battle between father and daughter, between chieftain and kin, was over. Their chieftain was happy. Drink flowed and food was served until everyone was satisfied.

If she was devastated over the knowledge she carried in her heart, no one seemed to notice. Or rather, no one commented on her demeanor or lack of mirth at the prospect of marrying the wealthy and well-connected Sir Duncan.

Then, from the back of the hall, words began buzzing about

like a swarm of bees. The noise moved forward with a sense of alarm and danger. Men jumped to their feet, women whispered and fear grew. Ailis could see it but didn't know the cause. A small group of her father's warriors strode quickly toward the dais. Breac drew her father away from the table to speak to only him.

"Davina? What is the cause of this?" she asked. But her friend's gaze was centered on Ailis' father and Davina looked both worried and guilty. "Davina?"

Turning her attention to her father, Ailis was able to hear only bits of his exchange with Breac. What she heard shocked her to her core.

Dozens ready to attack. An army at their gates. Surrounded but for the sea.

But the last words took her breath away.

The MacLean demands the prisoner.

Ailis stood. She'd have gone to her father's side had Davina not grabbed her and pulled her back. Searching her friend's face, she read the truth.

Lachlan was not only alive, he was here. Now.

A prisoner of her father's.

"Father!" she called out. She pulled free of Davina's hold and ran to him. "He is no danger to ye, to us. Set him free and …" Ailis knew she must handle this quickly and the price she must pay. "I willna delay in marrying Sir Duncan."

Her father's gaze narrowed. He looked from her to Davina to Sir Duncan and back.

"He doesna remember himself," she said in a quiet voice so few heard her. "He doesna remember … me."

By now, Davina reached her side. Although her father threw dark glances at his wife, her friend didn't flinch. Had Davina some part in this?

"Finnan," Davina said. "I pray ye, just let him go."

With a nod to Breac, the order was given. The commander and his men rushed off towards the stairway that led below to the prisoners' cells. Ailis took a step in that direction with the intent to follow them, but her father stopped her.

"Remain where ye are, Daughter." His words and tone made everyone stop. She met his stare until the sounds of footsteps approached from where the men had gone. "Stay!"

Even in his angriest moments, he'd never spoken to her thus and everyone witnessing this scene knew it. She didn't move as Breac and the others entered, dragging Lachlan between them. When he turned his head, she started again.

"Stay," he ordered through clenched teeth.

Ailis couldn't look. She couldn't watch him being dragged away from her, now that she knew the truth. It took every bit of strength and control to remain where she stood. She turned her head so she didn't see him.

The footsteps moved steadily away from the front of the hall towards the doorway in the back. Then the sounds of a struggle erupted. Yelling and chaos spread forward.

"Ye lied to me, Ailis!" Though hoarse and rough, she could hear Lachlan in every word. "Ye lied!"

Then he was standing before her as he had just days ago, tall and strong and a threat more now than before. He fought Breac and the others as they tried to grab hold of him and take him away. He didn't behave like a man being taken to freedom and returned to his life. His accusation echoed and every MacKinnon heard it.

"Tell me the truth now, Ailis," he said as he struggled.

Davina stood at her father's side and touched his arm, a message spoken louder than any words could. A simple nod brought action and Breac and the men stepped away.

"What truth do ye wish me to say, *Iain*?" she asked, wiping her damp hands down her gown to ease her nervousness. She'd given her father her word. If she spoke wrongly, it could cost Lachlan so much. "That I loved a man but cost him his life?" She lifted her head and met his gaze. *How had she not known him or recognized the eyes staring out at her through*

93

the scrap of fabric? "I called a man to me and he came … and he died."

Gasps rose from those listening. As she watched, he shook his head.

"Did ye set the fire, Ailis?" He came closer and she lost the ability to breathe. "Did ye block the door so I couldna escape?" Oh, dear God in Heaven, he was remembering details of it! "Did ye knock me unconscious so there was no chance I would survive?"

"Nay," she whispered.

He'd spoken of things no one could know unless he had been there. He lifted his bare hand to touch her face and she knew she wouldn't be able to let him go if he did. She must step back and not allow it to happen.

"Ye lied to me, Ailis." His words sounded like an endearment rather than an accusation.

He did the most surprising thing. He tugged a few tendrils of her hair free from the braid she wore and let them tumble over her breasts. When he met her gaze, she was certain he remembered it all.

As he'd spoken the words about what happened to him, Lachlan remembered her. He remembered everything about her. Everything they'd done and said and planned and hoped flooded back into his mind. And he knew that she played no part in what had happened in that cottage on that terrible day.

That she felt guilty just eased his pain and warmed his heart and soul. That she was going to buy his freedom with her own bondage told him even more. No matter what happened next, he wanted her at his side. If she would be there …

"Ye promised me, Ailis. All the days of our lives, ye said," he whispered. "I would be yer wedded husband and ye—"

"I would be yer wedded wife," she finished the words.

"All the days of our lives."

Those were words he'd heard countless times in his head during the worst moments of his life. They reminded him of some of the best times. Time spent with Ailis in his arms. Time spent making her his. Time spent loving her until she screamed in pleasure.

She was his and he wouldn't give her up. Lachlan leaned in to kiss her to remind her of his love. The doors to the hall crashed open and a large group of warriors wearing the colors of the MacLeans poured in. Without thought, he grabbed her and placed her behind him.

"I want my son, MacKinnon!" Dougal MacLean yelled as he and those with him ran between the tables to the front. "Ye willna keep me from my son!"

Lachlan wondered what his father would say when he saw the extent of his injuries. The older man slowed as he reached the steps to the dais. He motioned for the others to remain there. He noticed Artair and nodded to him and his other kin. What they thought, he couldn't guess. But Lachlan understood that he would have to show himself and pray they saw him in the mangled flesh beneath the hood and mask.

Dougal strode past The MacKinnon who'd not said another word and stopped before Sir Duncan. The two had been old friends. They had fostered with Duncan's uncle on Barra as boys.

"Duncan, why are ye here?" his father said, offering his hand in greeting.

"I came to marry The MacKinnon's daughter. But now have the pleasure of wishing her and yer son happy."

"What?" Lachlan said at the same time his father did. Ailis pushed around him.

"Ye both declared yerselves married before." He paused and nodded at those in the room, "before witnesses. The old way, but a marriage respected still."

Lachlan didn't know whether to laugh or shout at the man's declaration. He and Ailis had used the words many times to pledge their love but never in front of others. Until just now.

"How do I ken ye are Lachlan?" his father asked. "I would look on ye myself." His father had never thought being the doubting apostle was a bad part of the church's teachings. He would want to see with his own eyes before believing the impossible was possible.

But that would mean Ailis would see him, too. And she was truly the only one who mattered to him. Would she find him repulsive or would she react the way her father had? Not many women had seen the injuries The MacKinnon had in his life and his experience, so Lachlan doubted she could be unmoved about his appearance.

"Lachlan," she whispered, touching his hand. He'd taken off his gloves so he felt her warmth. "Do ye wish to do this here?"

"They matter not to me, Ailis," he said. "I only care about what ye think when ye see me as I am."

She released him then and he nodded at his father.

He didn't draw out the process. They need only see his face and, hopefully, they would recognize him through the damage. Hopefully, she could still see him there.

A burst of cool air rushed over his head when he tugged the hood off. The hair on the right side and some of the front of his head remained almost untouched while the back and the left side had burned. The head wound added to the injury and so the back near his neck was nearly bald. He heard the soft inhalation from Ailis as he reached for the back of the mask and untied it. Lifting it off, he heard gasps from those close enough to see his face. Lachlan stood in silence and waited for Ailis' reaction.

"I would have kenned ye, Lachlan. If I hadna thought ye dead. If I'd seen yer face," she said, reaching up to cup the cheek that had sustained the worst of it. The tears slid down her cheeks and he wanted to kiss them away. "I see ye there."

He kissed her. Without the mask and hood to cover him, he felt the softness of her face against his. There was no hesitation in her kiss. When he dared to open his eyes during that kiss, he found her watching him back.

"How?" his father asked in a voice thick with emotion. "How did ye survive?"

With Ailis at his side, Lachlan explained what he remembered about the fire, waking within it, the cellar and his near death. He had no memories from the time the roof fell on him until many, many days later after the brothers had found him. Only when he stopped did he notice the silence around him. Glancing up, he saw the expression of disbelief on his father's rough features. And he noticed that his father now looked much older than the last time Lachlan had seen him.

Before he could say another word, The MacLean strode across the few paces separating them and took hold of Lachlan. Dragging him in, his father hugged him and didn't let go.

"Thank the Almighty," he whispered over and over so low that only Lachlan could hear his words. "My son. My son."

Lachlan felt tears burning his eyes and throat at the expression of love and loss in his father's gaze. That day, all those months ago, the man had lost two sons and his wife and he'd suffered for it.

His father released him and studied Ailis. Clearing his throat, he called out to her father.

"So, MacKinnon, will ye approve their marriage or do I call for the attack?"

From the nervous laughter through the hall, Lachlan knew that no one could tell if his father's threat was serious or not. They all waited on their chieftain to say aye or nay.

"They spoke the words before witnesses, MacLean. They have a year to declare them before a priest."

"Then give me some ale so I can raise a cup to my son and his wife!"

Lachlan took advantage of the confusion to wave Artair up to meet Ailis. Though Artair had accompanied him to the clearing a few times and had seen Ailis in the distance, they'd never been introduced. Lachlan had questions for his cousin. Taking her hand and kissing it, he wrapped his arm around her shoulders to keep her close. 'Twould be some time before he let her out of his sight.

"Ailis, this is my cousin, Artair," he said, nodding to his cousin. "Artair, Lady Ailis MacKinnon."

After a few minutes of a polite exchange, Artair signaled that he would speak privately with Lachlan. When Davina called Ailis to her side, he had the chance.

"Did Wynda accompany ye here or is she back at Aros?" he asked. A strange expression filled Artair's gaze and his cousin looked away before replying.

"Nay, Lachlan," he said. "Lachlan, Wynda …"

In that moment, he was back in the cottage waiting for Ailis to arrive. Watching out the window, he heard the steps behind him and wondered how she could have gotten in without him seeing her approach.

"Lachlan."

He recognized her voice and began to turn. He caught a glimpse out of the corner of his eye before she struck him.

Wynda.

"Wynda?" Lachlan stared at Artair. "Why would she do such a thing? Where is she?" he whispered, searching the crowd for the woman who had done that to him.

Looking back at his cousin, he saw the same strange expression that he'd seen those months ago when they both understood it would be Lachlan's duty to marry The MacLeod's daughter.

"She wasna right in the head, Lachlan," Artair said, his voice filled with pity. "Something wasna right." His cousin let out a breath. "She kenned about the two of ye and yer meeting place. When she was told that she wouldna be free and that her betrothal would now be to ye, she went a little mad, I think."

"Artair, where is she now?"

"She told me what she'd done when we got to the cottage and found it burned to ashes. She confessed it to me," he paused and shook his head. "Before she walked off the battlements of Aros into the sea." Lachlan crossed himself at the thought of her unshriven soul, condemned for eternity.

"Artair, I am sorry. For ye, for her," he said. He had never considered the woman's wishes or Artair's words of warning that day.

"I think yer bride wants ye, Lachlan. Ye are truly a lucky man."

As Lachlan watched Ailis make her way back to him, he agreed with Artair, he was a very lucky man. He would spend the rest of his life with the woman he loved. She stared at him as he held out his hand.

"When did ye remember, Lachlan?" she asked, walking into his arms.

"I heard ye speak at the cottage and something came back to me. I kenned I was Lachlan but didna have the memories yet."

"Ye were there?" She leaned back and looked at him.

"Aye. I saw ye sneaking out and followed ye. I heard yer confession but it confused me."

"And then? The rest of the memories?"

"I'd heard ye speak some of them in my dreams. In my pain and in my head. But when I saw yer hair and it fell over ye, I remembered the last time we'd met at the cottage. The hours spent in yer arms. And all ye wore was yer hair."

His body reacted as he knew it would. Better still, he could see the way her eyes darkened in arousal. And he felt the way she pressed against him, her soft curves against his hardness.

"All the days of our lives," she whispered.

"Aye, my love," he said as he kissed her. "All the days … and all the nights, too."

Epilogue

Four Months Later ...

"This is just how I saw ye in my dreams, my love." Lachlan shifted one of the flowers to lay on the swell of Ailis' naked breast. "Covered in blossoms and yer hair and nothing else."

They'd taken advantage of one of the last days of summer weather and ridden off into the hills above Aros. Then, he spoke of the visions of her that had helped him survive the worst of his pain and suffering. Now, it was time to make more pleasurable memories.

He slid the back of his hand over the tight nipples of her lovely breasts and was rewarded by a sigh. Tracing over her ribs, he reached the slight swell of her belly and laid his hand there.

A bairn. *His* bairn grew within her body. A miracle for certain.

"And nothing else?" she asked in a breathy voice.

"Well ..." He outlined the curves of her hips and laughed.

"I covered ye, my love."

He must have been too slow for her needs for she covered his hand with hers and guided it lower still. She pressed his fingers between her legs and he smiled. Impatient as ever. Lachlan laid his head on her belly and did as she wanted him to do. Watching as her legs moved restlessly and her hips canted up to meet his strokes, he kissed a path down to that sensitive flesh that readied for his cock.

"Lachlan!" she moaned. "Have mercy!"

His flesh urged him not for mercy but for satisfaction, so he climbed between her legs, lifted them over his shoulders and tasted her arousal. Sweet. Salty. Ailis. His tongue laved the folds and the tiny bud until her moans became screams and he felt her climax against his mouth. Letting her body ease, he lifted his mouth from her and noticed the small mark on her thigh.

He'd not remembered himself or even her identity, but that mark had been clear in his visions of her. He pressed his lips to it before beginning his attentions to her other places once more. This time, he kissed around her waist to her arse, turning her onto her belly as he did. With an arm beneath her, he lifted her to her knees, allowing his cock to slide between her legs. Then, with one arm encircling her belly and the other covering her breasts, he thrust into her tight, wet channel.

Ailis angled her hips to allow him in deeper and he went there, filling her. With powerful thrusts, he moved in and out, over and over, until her woman's flesh tightened around his cock and he felt his seed spilling. He held her so closely, barely breathing, while feeling her reaching her own satisfaction.

With a care, he eased them down to the blanket and to their sides. He kept her close, remaining within her until they dozed.

Together.

Lachlan heard her whispering and leaned closer to hear her

words.

"I canna believe I didna ken it was ye," she said, turning her head to him. He kissed her gently and smiled. "I should have recognized yer touch. Yer mouth. Yer body on mine."

They'd discussed it many times and understood that Ailis never saw *him* because she never expected a dead man to rise.

"I canna believe I found my way back to ye," he admitted. Dark months had tried his resolve to survive and only the visions of her guided him through the struggles and pain.

"But ye did," she said, staring at his mouth.

"Aye, I did."

As he kissed her, the randy fellow still within her roused.

"All the days of our lives," she promised, pressing her hips back against him, accepting him, allowing him … loving him.

Lachlan slid his hand around her body, cupping her belly and the promise she carried there. This time, their joining was slow and quiet, as though they had accepted the truth of their lives, for there was no need to rush any longer.

They would have all the days of their lives together.

About the Author

When not living the glamorous life of a USA TODAY bestselling romance author, **Terri Brisbin** spends her time being as a wife, mom/mom-in-law, grandmom and a dental hygienist in the southern NJ suburbs.

A three-time RWA RITA® finalist and award-winning author, Terri has sold more than 2.5 million copies of her historical and paranormal romance novels, novellas and short stories in more than 20 languages in 25 countries around the world since 1998. She's been published by Berkley/Jove, Harlequin, Kensington Books, NAL/Signet (and soon SMP Swerve) and indie published and has more romances scheduled release through 2020!

Connect with Terri:
Facebook: TerriBrisbin
Facebook Author Page: TerriBrisbinAuthor
Twitter: @Terri_Brisbin

TerriBrisbin.com

Other Books by

Terri Brisbin

THE DUMONT STORIES:
The Dumont Bride
The Norman's Bride
The Countess Bride ****
"Love at First Step", THE CHRISTMAS VISIT
The King's Mistress ****
"The Claiming of Lady Joanna", THE BETROTHAL

THE MacLERIE STORIES:
Taming the Highlander
Surrender to the Highlander
Possessed by the Highlander ♥
"Taming The Highlander Rogue" ebook
The Highlander's Stolen Touch
At The Highlander's Mercy
"The Forbidden Highlander" in HIGHLANDERS
The Highlander's Dangerous Temptation ♦
Yield to The Highlander

Related stories (same clan 500 years later)
The Earl's Secret
"Blame It On The Mistletoe" in ONE CANDLELIT CHRISTMAS

STAND-ALONE STORIES:
The Queen's Man (re-release)
The Duchess's Next Husband
The Maid of Lorne
"Kidnapping the Laird" ebook & in MAMMOTH BOOK OF
SCOTTISH ROMANCES
"What The Duchess Wants" ebook & in ROYAL WEDDINGS
THROUGH THE AGES
"Upon A Misty Skye" in ONCE UPON A HAUNTED CASTLE ♦

THE KNIGHTS of BRITTANY STORIES:
"*A Night for Her Pleasure*" ebook & in PLEASURABLY
UNDONE
The Conqueror's Lady
The Mercenary's Bride
His Enemy's Daughter

THE STORM STORIES:
A Storm of Passion
"A Storm of Love" in UNDONE
A Storm of Pleasure
Mistress of the Storm

THE MacKENDIMEN STORIES:
A Love Through Time (re-release)
Once Forbidden (re-release)
A Matter of Time (re-release)

NOVELS OF THE STONE CIRCLES STORIES:
Rising Fire ♥
Raging Sea
Blazing Earth

A HIGHLAND FEUDING STORIES:
Stolen by the Highlander
The Highlander's Runaway Bride
Kidnapped by the Highland Rogue

Coming soon –
"A Traitor's Heart" in BRANDYWINE BRIDES
Claiming His Highland Bride
"Upon A Highland Moor" in FORBIDDEN HIGHLANDS
anthology

**** RWA RITA® Finalist!! ♥ *NJRW Golden Leaf Winner!!* ♦
USA TODAY Bestseller!!

CHARLO

ON THE
money

TAKE CONTROL OF
YOUR FINANCES
TO BUILD A
LIFE YOU
LOVE

A STUDIO PRESS BOOK

First published in the UK in 2022 by Studio Press Books,
an imprint of Bonnier Books UK,
4th Floor, Victoria House, Bloomsbury Square, London WC1B 4DA
Owned by Bonnier Books,
Sveavägen 56, Stockholm, Sweden
www.bonnierbooks.co.uk

ISBN 978-1-80078-140-5

Edited by Ellie Rose
Designed by Rob Ward and Wendy Bartlet
Production by Emma Kidd

A CIP catalogue for this book is available from the British Library
Printed and bound in the United Kingdom

CHARLOTTE BURNS

ON THE
money

TAKE CONTROL OF
YOUR FINANCES
TO BUILD A
LIFE YOU
LOVE

I can't believe I've written a book! I want to say a massive thank you to Bronni Hughes and Sam McFaul. Without your help, there would be no chance I could have managed it.

Caroline Laws, Teresa Fritz and Andrew Johnson; thank you for being brilliantly smart and generous with your time.

And to my family; Mum, Dad, Francesca, Phil, Oliver and Rosie, I can't thank you enough for all the times you looked after baby Matilda while I typed away in the evenings and at weekends.

Harry, my wonderful partner; thank you for the endless supply of love and support.

CONTENTS

1 GET ON THE ROAD TO FINANCIAL FREEDOM

Congratulations on one of the best investments you've made so far – buying this book!
Who needs Bitcoin?!

Is that statement too braggy? Well, I might be a bit biased but you're not going to regret it when you're living the life you want with total financial freedom. This book is my way of helping you get there.

Choosing to read this book tells me that you're smart enough to understand that when it comes to finances, you have to be proactive. Most people float through life without intention, hitting one unexpected financial problem after another. Often, and usually through no fault of their own, there's a lack of knowledge and zero strategy.

Let me throw some stats at you from research conducted by the Money and Pensions Service in 2021. I think they're pretty shocking.

In the UK:

- *11.5 million people have less than £100 in savings.*
- *9 million people have to borrow money to pay for food.*
- *22 million people say they don't have the knowledge to plan for their retirement.*

Big yikes, guys.

WHO AM I TO HELP YOU?

I've been a consumer writer and editor for over 10 years and am utterly obsessed with helping people to be better with their money because I know what it's like to have nothing and get back on my (financial) feet.

I graduated from university with a Law degree in 2008 as the financial crash happened. It was shit. People were losing their jobs, homes, life savings and, unbelievably, no one wanted to hire a plucky graduate with a talent for downing £1 pints of Snakebite.

I moved to London right after graduating because I felt it was my best chance of getting a job and spent a good few years on benefits, before finding a role, being made redundant (twice) and then finding myself on benefits again. This all caused a decline in my mental health and after losing my job and flat, and sofa surfing for far too long, I was ready to give up until I spotted a job advert that changed my life.

You see, while having no money – I'm talking sobbing and causing a scene at the bank because I went over my overdraft and the fine would eat massively into my benefits levels of no money – I became obsessed with finding ways to save money. It gave me back some of the control I had lost.

I'd find free tickets to the cinema, or print out coupons and wait until the item was discounted so I could buy it for free, or as close to free as possible. I became a pro and was seriously good at bargain hunting.

The job advert was for a deals hunter at Martin Lewis' Money Saving Expert. At the job interview, they asked me why they should hire me as I had no journalism experience. In my head I did an impassioned Erin Brockovich-esque speech on how I had no relevant qualifications but there was no one who knew how to save on everyday stuff like me and they wouldn't meet anyone who cared as much as I do. It was probably cringeworthy, but it worked.

I worked there a few years before leaving to become editor at a leading student money website, then I went freelance and set up my blog, LottyEarns, two-time winner of Financial Blog of the Year at the Headlinemoney Awards (the Oscars of the financial industry!). I also started writing for national newspapers and magazines.

I'm currently the senior digital editor at the Money Advice Service, which is my dream job. I get to spend a lot of time figuring out what financial problems people really have, work out how they can be fixed and then come up with new and exciting ways to package up that information so it reaches the people who need it.

WHY MIGHT WE BE A BIT RUBBISH WITH OUR FINANCES

The truth is, we probably have very similar money values and habits to our parents, whether we realise it or not. They got theirs from their parents, who got it from their parents and so on. It's a cycle and as with any family cycle, there can be really healthy aspects alongside pieces you want to break. Figuring out where the problems are and then improving them is key.

On top of this, there is little to no financial education taught in schools. Sure, they teach you how to do Pythagoras theorem (still no clue what it is) that the majority of us will never use in the real world, but not what taxes are and how they work, which we all need.

Where I grew up, it's completely normal to have £1,000's worth of debt, live in a rented home and live pay cheque to pay cheque. And no one is breaking a sweat over this at all.

I work for a company that aims to help people with money management skills, sort problem debt and encourage people to make good pension decisions. We don't target people who are well off (though there is a lot of relevant information for them) and don't massively focus on people with hardly any cash but are doing well, because believe me, people who are seriously skint know exactly what money they have, where their next penny is coming from and what they need to spend it on.

We spend a big chunk of our time trying to reach people who don't know they need help, which is a lot of people. So many people own expensive items, take yearly holidays, buy fancy cars on finance and so on. From the outside looking in, they seem comfortable, but the reality is that a lot of it is paid for on credit – they have no savings and the smallest thing could send them into a debt spiral.

And now we've had a pandemic to contend with. The world is a tougher place now with uncertain employment, an increased cost of living and rising debt. People who didn't have to worry about money a couple of years ago are now paying for their supermarket shop on a credit card.

Getting on the housing ladder has become close to impossible for many, so it's easier if they just don't think about it. The same can be said when it comes to retirement plans.

I NEED YOU TO STOP COMPARING YOURSELF WITH OTHER PEOPLE

I've worked directly with hundreds of people who are struggling with money and if you're picturing some Oliver Twist-esque urchin or someone from *The Jeremy Kyle Show*, that's not always the case. It's often the people who wear nice clothes, have good jobs, a good education and are smart who are up shit creek.

Don't believe what you see! You might have friends who have a nice car and a big house and wonder how on earth they can afford their lifestyle. But the likelihood is they're up to their eyeballs in debt, have no savings and no retirement plan. And that's nothing to be jealous about.

So I need you to stop comparing yourselves with the people around you or on social media.

- I don't care if someone earns more than you, it doesn't mean they are, or will be, better off than you.

- I don't care if someone can go on fancy holidays and buy nice things, it's often debt.

- I don't care if someone has bought a house when you can't afford to. There are lots of bad mortgage deals out there and more often than not, money from family comes into play here.

Follow your own path and have trust in the financial strategies you are going to create. Being financially secure is a million times better than giving the illusion you are. Because here's the truth: you can't enjoy the things you buy if you can't afford them. Not really. There will always be some guilt and anxiety associated with them. Get them the right way.

BREAK THE BAD HABITS

Throughout this book, I'm going to help you break any bad money habits you may have inherited and educate you about money management and planning. I'm going to tell you the truth and challenge some preconceptions.

I've been in this industry a very long time and have learned from the best. I'm not going to tell you to ask the universe for cash, invest in risky schemes or give you empty promises of becoming a millionaire.

I'm not one to sugarcoat things so let me be clear: the things I will ask you to do aren't always fun, and they aren't always (or ever) sexy but they are realistic and do-able, no matter where you are on your financial journey. You don't need a six-figure salary to have financial freedom but you do need to commit to making some changes.

If there's one thing I can promise, it's that if you do the things I suggest, you will be better with money and, therefore, you will have more of it. So buckle up!

MONEY MYTH BUSTING

Before we get stuck in, here are some common misconceptions about money that I want you to shake off:

- If you're rubbish with money, you'll always be rubbish with money.
- You can't gain control of your finances.
- A high income automatically makes you more wealthy.
- You can only save if you earn lots of money.
- It's too late to start saving.

- It's normal to have a lot of debt.
- Only rich people can invest.
- Other people are doing better financially than you.
- Pensions aren't safe or are a waste of time.
- You need to have a job you love.

ACTIVITY

After each chapter, I'm going to set an activity based on what you've learned to help you in a practical way.

Before you go any further, I want you to visualise what you want to achieve by reading this book. The more specific your goals are, the better. For example, 'I want to buy a house' is a very general goal so it will be hard to mark your progress and keep focused. Something like 'I want to save £20,000 towards a deposit in three years' is better – it's specific and has a time frame attached so you can easily measure your progress.

When things get hard, having a clear goal to anchor you is really important. Keeping your goal in mind helps you to stay motivated and reminds you why you're doing what you're doing.

Visualisation techniques are used by the most successful people to help them reach their goals. Your brain is constantly using visualisation in the process of simulating future experiences. This happens naturally and you probably aren't aware of it (unless you have anxiety like me and a brain that likes to imagine every potential disastrous future situation!). Using this knowledge, you can hack the process and visualise the goals and steps you need to take to be successful. It will help you to direct the process, rather than be passive. It's going to improve your motivation and increase your belief in your ability to reach your financial goals.

Breaking goals down into smaller, more achievable tasks means you are much more likely to stick with it. It doesn't matter how you do it but remind yourself daily of your goal. Try some of the techniques below and see what works for you.

Shut your eyes and picture your dream scenario vividly – imagine opening your own front door for the first time, or going on your ultimate holiday.

Collate images of the things you want and put them where you can see them every day. You could cut them out of magazines and make a collage, or save images as your phone home screen.

If you're someone who likes to see and track data, put your financial goals in a spreadsheet and update it regularly to watch as you get closer to achieving your goal.

Once you have a goal in mind, think about the chain of events that needs to happen and use the techniques in this book to get you there.

Remember, small steps over time = big changes.

2 YOU'VE GOT TO MAKE A BUDGET

This is where it all starts. Budgeting means that you will always have enough money for things you need and the things that are important to you.

The term has got a bad rap, which is a shame, as people think if you budget, you won't be able to have or do something. But it's the opposite – I promise.

You can spend years trying to save and balance the books. Something that takes effort and headspace – and will get you absolutely nowhere if you don't have a proper plan in place. Trust me – I half-heartedly saved for about eight years before I got it together. When I did, I achieved my saving goals relatively quickly.

If you're like most people, you probably aren't keeping to a budget right now. I'm going to convince you to change your ways and you're going to thank me for it.

TIME TO BE HONEST

Let's be real for a second. A budget only works if you are honest about both your income and expenses.

It's really easy to avoid facing facts or lie to yourself about what's coming in and what's going out.

If you're going to be collaborating with someone else to reach your financial goals, this might mean you need to have tough, non-judgemental conversations with someone else and plan how you want to move forward together.

This bit might be painful, but once it's all out in the open, you can begin to make proper changes and plan for the future.

Keep your eyes on the prize! It's hard to do anything without a clear endgame. So spend some time working out exactly what you want and how much it's going to cost you.

SET SOME GOALS

What's your dream? Is it to become a millionaire? Go on incredible holidays? Save up for a deposit on a house? Stay on top of your bills every month? Or get rid of some debt?

It's pretty basic but I remember my first boss having a Mulberry bag and I was obsessed with it. I was working and earning money (hardly any!) but decided I was going to budget to buy one of my own. That way, even though I was someone without a lot of money, I could buy my dream bag and enjoy it completely guilt free.

Because, let's be real here: spending money you know you can't afford only feels good for a little while. If you budget for something it feels great because you get the thing you wanted, plus a dose of pride for doing it without hurting your wallet.

I'm going to bet that you're haemorrhaging money in unexpected places. There will be surprises. As you use cash less and less and use debit or credit cards more and more, it's pretty much impossible to keep track of what you're spending on a daily basis. Also, contactless is the devil! It makes it so easy to spend small amounts without thinking about it because you don't even have the physical act of entering a PIN to remind you. It's far too easy to quietly slip into your overdraft or use your credit card and risk losing control of the situation.

Oh, and don't get me started on Buy Now Pay Later schemes (BNPL). I can't stand them! I'll talk more about why they are the worst thing you can do in chapter six but for now I'll just say, if you want something, budget for it.

When talking about budgeting I have to mention a couple of points about debt. Budgeting is a great way to stop you getting into debt, and the only way you're going to get out of it.

When you can see exactly what money is coming in and where it's going, it's much more difficult to slide into debt. And if you can see when you're heading towards a problem, you'll know what steps you need to take to stop it. You can't deal with a problem you don't know about.

If you're worried about debt, get free and impartial advice. It doesn't matter how small or huge the debt is, charities such as StepChange and Citizens Advice can help you.

I used Citizens Advice myself when I was stressed about debt and they were able to stop interest accruing on my bank loan, which was a huge help. See chapter seven for more on debt management.

CITIZENS ADVICE

Visit the website to find services in your local area, make an appointment or speak to a debt adviser online: www.citizensadvice.org.uk

Contact an adviser through their national phone service:
Adviceline (England): 0800 144 8848
Advicelink (Wales): 0800 702 2020
Advice Helpline (Scotland): 0800 028 1456
Advice NI (Northern Ireland): 0800 915 4604

WHAT YOU NEED TO GET STARTED

Hopefully I've done enough to convince you that a budget is essential, so let's get started.

1   **Gather Your Financial Information**
We're talking bank statements, bills, payslips and so on. The last three months are a good place to start. If you're freelance or self-employed with irregular pay, choose your lowest paid month and base your budget on that so you don't get caught out. If you don't have this paperwork to hand, don't worry – an estimate will be enough for now.

2   **Calculate Your Income**
If you are employed and have a regular income, this will be easy. On your payslip, look for your take-home pay (sometimes called 'net pay'). This is your salary once income tax, student loan repayments, National Insurance, pension contributions and so on have been deducted. This is the amount that will actually go into your bank account and is the money you've got to save or spend.

If you have a side hustle (see chapter eight for more on this), include your average earnings in your budget, too. And don't forget about income from any benefits.

3 Create a List of Monthly Expenses

Go through your bank statements and write down how you spend your money. It's helpful to split your outgoings into categories so you can see exactly how your money is split between necessities and extras.

If you're self-employed you should set aside money every month to pay your tax bill at the end of the financial year, so make sure you factor this into your expenses.

Let's look at an example of monthly expenses:

BILLS

Rent	Water	Council Tax
Gas & Electric	Broadband & TV	Mobile Phone

PAYMENTS

Car Insurance	Credit Card

ENTERTAINMENT

Pub	Eating Out	Gym
Cinema	Netflix	Festivals

SHOPPING

Clothes	Gaming	Supermarket

4 ***Fixed vs Variable Expenses***

Now you have a list of your expenses, note whether they are variable or fixed. 'Fixed' means you pay the same amount every month. Typical fixed expenses are mortgage or rent payments, phone bills and so on. Set up Direct Debit payments for these expenses so you don't miss a payment and run the risk of a late payment charge.

'Variable' means the amount you spend will vary month to month. Typical variable expenses are money you spend on eating out, new clothes and so on.

5 ***Do Some Maths***

Add up your total income and total expenses and see what the difference is. If you're spending more money than you are bringing in, take a look at your variable expenses and see what you can cut down or out altogether.

Cutting costs doesn't mean you have to stop having any fun. You just need to find ways to do what you love for less – see chapter 10 for more on this.

6 ***Monitor and Adjust Your Budget***

A budget shouldn't be set and then never referred to again. Your budget will need to adapt and change as your goals or circumstances change.

Want to go on holiday? Add a savings goal to your budget and cut down in another expense to make up the difference.

THE 50/30/20 SYSTEM

My favourite way to budget is the 50/30/20 system. It's really simple and you can play around with the percentages to see what works for you.

50 percent of your income goes on needs
This is everything you have to spend money on such as rent or mortgage payments, bills, food and transport.

30 percent of your income goes on wants
This is the fun stuff! It can include holidays, eating out, going to the cinema, shopping and so on.

20 percent of your income goes on saving or debt
You should always prioritise debt before savings, see chapter seven. For more on how and where you can save, skip to chapter four.

If your monthly net income is £1,500 you might spend:

£750 on needs
£450 on wants
£300 on saving or debt

Everyone's situation is different so this system can be adjusted to suit you. If you live in an expensive city, for example, you might have to allocate a bigger percentage to 'needs' and cut back on 'wants'. If you live with your parents and pay little or no rent, whack up the 'saving' percentage.

It's tempting to cut back on the 'saving or debt' percentage rather than 'wants' but it's always good to prioritise paying off debt or saving to avoid problems later down the line. This category also includes your pension contributions, which, as I'll go into in chapter five, are important for the future.

When you first start budgeting, try changing up your percentages every few months until you find what works best for you.

TOOLS TO MAKE LIFE EASIER

Now you have a budget in place, there are lots of tools out there that do some of the hard work for you. They vary from the simple, where you enter expenses to discover where you spend the most, to the complex, which include a complete interrogation of your finances and saving recommendations.

A Note on Financial Tools

Any tool that helps you to switch providers will be making money, even if there is no cost to you. You should be switching regularly (I'll go into this in chapter 11) but don't assume they are offering the best deal for you, always do your own research.

Below are the most popular tools and apps that have a good reputation and security protection. Most use open banking, which means you give them access to your bank statements – so if you decide to go your own way and use different apps, make sure they are trusted and secure.

FREE TOOLS

Emma (app)

Emma uses open banking to combine information from all of your bank and savings accounts, credit cards and investments. You can track your spending by category, manage bills and subscriptions, set monthly budgets and money goals, automatically categorise transactions, find and cancel transactions, and get weekly spending reports. And that's just the start of it, it has all the bells and whistles.

Be aware that this app has a paid-for version called 'Emma Pro', which offers tools such as calculating your net worth (why?!) and exporting your data. You might be nudged to upgrade from time to time.

MoneyHelper (online tool)

If you're not looking for anything too complicated, keep it simple with the MoneyHelper tool. This has been created by the Money and Pensions Service, which is sponsored by the government. It puts you in control of your household spending and analyses your accounts to help you take control of your money.

Money Dashboard (app and online tool)

Money Dashboard also uses open banking to connect all of your financial interests in one place. Unlike other tools, it doesn't let you move money between accounts but it will help you keep track of your money. Money Dashboard also comes with a decent community area where people can ask questions. This is useful if you have a technical query.

PAID TOOLS

You Need A Budget (YNAB)

Some of the best personal finance experts I know use this and swear by it. You have to pay for it but there's usually a free trial so you can test it out and see if it works for you.

At the time of writing, the monthly plan costs $14.99 a month, which you can cancel any time, and the annual plan is $98.99. YNAB says that, on average, new users of its app save $600 in their first two months. Of course, YNAB wants you to sign up so take that figure with a pinch of salt.

Along with everything you can expect from a budgeting app, YNAB also offers over 100 live money workshops every week and personal one-to-one support online. You can also connect with other users of the app so you can budget together. This is especially useful if you and a partner are trying to save for common goals.

YNAB is currently the only paid-for tool I'd recommend as many free tools are brilliant and do enough for most people.

It's worth seeing what budgeting tools your bank offers too, though they might be limited compared to other apps on the market.

ACTIVITY

This is a no-brainer! Use the information in this chapter to set up your own budget. Be ruthless and honest with yourself about your spending to make it worthwhile.

Once you have set up a basic budget, leave it for a day and come back to it with fresh eyes. Look over it again and see if you're still happy with how you've split your expenses, savings goals and so on.

3 BANK ACCOUNT BASICS

Let's talk banking. You probably have a number of bank accounts but do you know how they differ? Do you understand the terminology and are you maximising your earning potential?

I'm going to take you through everything you could possibly want to know about current and savings accounts. You might think it's pretty simple, but there are lots of options out there and picking the right accounts for you is important. Getting it wrong can mean you're not making as much money as you could be.

You might be looking at your accounts thinking, 'What's the problem? These seem to do the job.' But I'm here to show you how to maximise your money!

KEY TERMINOLOGY

Before we get into different types of bank accounts, let's go through some key terminology. Banks often make things harder than they need to be – they're actually pretty simple when they're explained properly.

Account number
This is your bank account's unique number.

AER
Stands for Annual Equivalent Rate. It's a type of interest rate on savings and shows you how much interest you can earn on your account. This is not to be confused with **APR** or 'gross interest rate'.

APR
Stands for Annual Percentage Rate. It is the official rate, expressed as a percentage, which helps you understand the cost of your borrowing.

ATM (Automated Teller Machine)
a.k.a. cash machine (does anyone in the UK call it an ATM?). You can withdraw cash, pay in cheques and notes, pay bills and get a bank statement. You can also stand in line forever wondering what on earth the person in front of you could possibly be doing because it takes 30 seconds to get out a tenner. ATMs are generally free, but there are ones that charge a fee.

Available balance
Your available balance is the money you have to spend. This includes

any pending payments and excludes any cheques that haven't cleared yet. Some banks will include your overdraft limit in your available balance and some won't. Check with your bank to avoid any confusion – and overspend!

BACS payment
Stands for Bankers Automated Clearing System, which is a system for sending money electronically between banks. It's mainly used for **Direct Debits** and direct credits from organisations. It's typically used for making regular payments, such as salaries, pensions, state benefits and tax credits.

Balance
Your current account balance is the amount of money you are either in credit or overdrawn.

Bank statement
A summary of financial transactions that occurred at a specific place and time. It will show you **deposits** and **withdrawals** (and that you spend too much on takeaways).

BIC
This stands for Bank Identifier Code and is the number that identifies your bank. You'll need this if you want to send or receive money outside the UK.

Cheque
A cheque is a written order, addressed to a bank, instructing them to pay an amount of money to the person or organisation named on the cheque. They are hardly used any more but you never know, you might get one from your granny or find Jeff Brazier turn up at

your door because you've won the Postcode Lottery. Government organisations still tend to use cheques, such as HMRC or the DVLA.

Compound interest
This is interest on money saved, plus interest on any interest already added. It's a little complicated to understand, but I'll go into why this is so brilliant later in the book (it's how you'll earn free money from the bank).

Contactless payment
Most cards allow you to pay by touching it on a card machine. You can also use contactless payment through your phone, if you've set this feature up.

Credit
Credit in your bank account is money you have available, whereas credit on a **credit card** is money you owe. It's the same term, so it can be confusing.

Credit card
A card that is issued by a lender (a bank or building society) that allows you to buy items on credit. It is used in the same way as a **debit card**, but a credit card uses the bank's cash and they will bill you later. You pay back the amount you borrowed either in full or in monthly repayments. If you don't repay in full, you'll also have to pay interest. A credit card will have a **credit limit**.

Credit limit
This is the amount of money you are allowed to borrow. It's not a target, but the maximum you can spend. Lenders decide how much to loan you based on your **credit score**.

Credit score
Your credit score measures your reliability at paying back debt. Banks and lenders will check your score before deciding whether to accept you as a customer. Be aware that if you apply for too much credit in a short period of time, it will negatively impact your credit score, which will affect a lender's decision.

Creditor
A person or company to whom you owe money.

Current account
This is a type of bank account that helps you manage your everyday money and expenses. Payments like your wages, benefits and tax credits will go into it, and you can withdraw cash and transfer money out.

Debit
When your account is in debit, it's overdrawn. Your account is 'debited' when money is withdrawn from it.

Debit card
You can use a debit card to make cash withdrawals from **ATMs** as well as pay for items in person, online or over the phone. The money is automatically taken from your **current account** when you spend it, so you must have enough money in your account or agreed **overdraft** to cover the transaction (or you're going to get the awkward 'Sorry your card has been declined' moment).

Debtor
A person or company who owes you money.

Default
This means that someone has failed to do something that they had agreed to do. For example, if you don't pay a bill on time you have 'defaulted' on the payment.

Deposit
Money paid into your account – as in 'making a deposit'.

Direct Debit
A payment from your bank account to another account on a specific date, recurring date, or dates set by yourself and the recipient. Unlike a **standing order**, the amount paid by a Direct Debit can be changed by the recipient, but they have to give you notice of this.

EAR
Stands for Equivalent Annual Rate. This is the rate you would pay on your overdraft if interest was charged annually on the amount you owe. EAR doesn't take into account any fees.

Equity
This is the value of something (such as a house) less money owing on it.

Fiscal
This word is used to describe the finances controlled by the government. You'll hear it a lot around the Budget when the government decides how it's going to spend the country's money over the financial year. A fiscal policy might be the price of booze going up as the tax on alcohol rises.

Fixed interest rate
This is an interest rate that does not change during the life of the loan (or savings account).

Foreign exchange rate
The exchange rate is the value of one currency compared to another. It's why you feel like a millionaire when travelling to Thailand, as you get around 45 Thai baht for 1 GBP.

FSCS
Stands for the Financial Services Compensation Scheme. It's a government-backed scheme that protects you from losing money (up to £85,000) if authorised financial services go bust.

Guarantee
A guarantee is sometimes needed before a bank will lend money to a customer. Another person, called the guarantor, signs a contract with the bank stating they'll cover the debt if the **debtor** fails to pay. The guarantor is often a family member, which can cause a lot of heartache if the situation goes wrong.

IBAN
This stands for International Bank Account Number. It identifies accounts held at any bank in any country. You should be able to find your IBAN on your bank statement.

Income tax
Income tax is calculated according to how much income you earn under various categories. It's used to fund public services, such as the NHS, police, welfare system, libraries, culture, housing and education.

Inflation
This is the name for general price increases. Each year the price of everyday stuff goes up. It's why a house cost £6,000 in the 70s and now is unaffordable for a lot of young people. Your wages should go up every year to match inflation, so you have the same living standard. If they don't, you are effectively losing money.

Inheritance
This is a financial term to describe the assets passed down to individuals after someone dies. This often includes things such as property, cash, stocks/shares, jewellery and antiques but it could be anything valuable.

Inheritance tax
This is the tax charged on the monetary value of everything acquired by either gift or inheritance (including property).

ISA
ISA stands for Individual Savings Account. These are savings accounts that are available to all UK residents over 18 (or 16 for a cash ISA). You don't have to pay tax on money your ISA earns, unlike with regular savings accounts, so it's a legitimate tax loophole. Junior ISAs are available for under 18s. In the 2021/22 tax year, your ISA allowance is £20,000.

Joint account
This is a bank account held by more than one person.

Limited company
A limited company is a form of business that is legally separate from its owners and managers. In the UK it must be incorporated

at Companies House. It must make all its returns public. This means that if the company is sued (even if it only consists of one person), the company is liable, not the person or people within it, so nobody's personal assets are on the line. An alternative way to structure a business is by being a **sole trader**.

Mortgage

A mortgage uses a property as security for a debt, most often used to purchase the property. If you can't make your mortgage payments, the result may be that the bank or building society takes your home off you. The amount you can borrow is based on your salary, the deposit you have and the value of the property.

National Insurance (NI)

This is a tax on your earnings that helps pay for and gives you entitlement to some state benefits, which include a State Pension, statutory sick pay and maternity leave. NI is automatically deducted from your monthly pay by your employer, or if you're self-employed, you'll need to pay contributions through your self-assessment tax return.

Net interest

This is interest that has had **income tax** taken off it.

Overdraft (arranged)

Most current accounts allow you to apply for an arranged overdraft. This means you and the bank or building society agree in advance that you may want to borrow money when there is no money left in your current account. The arranged overdraft limit, which is the maximum amount you can borrow, is based on your credit rating and how much you can afford. There's usually a cost for using an arranged overdraft (but it's a lot cheaper than going into an unarranged one) and this comes in the form of interest or sometimes fees.

Overdraft (unarranged)
If you go over your overdraft, it becomes 'unarranged' and the cost of it will sting, so keep an eye on it if you're getting close.

Pay (Net and Gross)
Your gross salary will usually appear as the highest number on your payslip. It's the number that your employer pays you based on your agreed upon salary. Your net salary is what you take home after your contributions (such as a pension) and taxes are deducted from your gross salary.

Payee
The person or company you're paying.

Payer
The person who makes a payment.

Pending transactions
Payments or deposits you've made that haven't yet come out of your bank balance. When checking your **balance**, it's important to consider pending payments as it can look like you have more money in your account than you do.

Personal allowance
Everyone gets a **tax allowance** on their earnings, meaning there is an amount of income you do not have to pay income tax on. This amount depends on personal circumstances but is currently £12,570 for most people earning less than £100,000.

Recurring transactions

This is an agreed payment where a business can take money from your debit or credit card when needed.

Savings accounts

These accounts pay you interest on the money you keep in them.

Security

This is something of value (a property, for example), which is pledged to a bank by the person wanting to take out a loan. If you fail to make the payments, the bank will take the security and sell it to repay the debt out of the proceeds of the sale. You can get loans where you don't need security – these are called unsecured debts. **Credit card** debt is usually unsecured.

Sole trader

This is someone who runs their own business as an individual, often referred to as self-employed or freelance. They don't have business partners and they do not trade through a company.

Sort code

This is the six-digit number (often on your debit card) that identifies your bank branch.

Stamp Duty

This is a tax on the transfer of documents for certain types of transaction. The biggie is when buying a property.

Standing order

A regular payment you make from your bank account. It's different from a **Direct Debit** as the amount paid by a standing order is fixed, and you're the only one who can change the amount. Standing orders are often used to pay rent.

State Pension scheme
The government pays a basic State Pension to everyone who has paid the minimum **National Insurance** contributions when they reach the State Pension age. It's nice to have, but really not enough to live on so you're likely to want to supplement this with other money, such as a private pension, savings and/or property.

Statement
Your bank statement shows all the transactions that have taken place over a set period. It also shows any interest and fees that have been added to or deducted from your account. These can be physical but most people now view them online.

Statutory Sick Pay
Employers must pay this to employees who are off work because they are unwell, currently for up to 28 weeks. The government sets the rates.

Stock exchange
A stock exchange (or stock market) is a market for stocks and shares. Organisations can raise capital by selling securities through a stock exchange.

Stockbroker
A stockbroker buys and sells stocks and shares for clients on the **stock exchange**. They could be a firm or an individual and will charge a fee to do this.

Tax allowance
Taxpayers are given tax allowances to reduce the amount of tax they must pay. The allowances are taken off their income before the tax is worked out.

Tax avoidance
This is something you might hear about in the news. It is a legal way to reduce the amount of tax you need to pay. There are levels to this, of course: you can open an **ISA** to avoid tax on savings, or you can go full millionaire and get yourself a bank account in Monaco.

Tax evasion
Don't do this one – it's illegal. This is hiding how much you earn (like being paid cash in hand), so you don't have to pay any tax.

Transfer
This is when you send money between your own accounts, for example, from a current account to a savings account.

VAT
Value Added Tax. Most traders in the UK are registered for VAT. This means that they must charge customers VAT (20 percent on all purchases) on any goods and services they supply that are not VAT exempt. This money then goes to the government. You won't notice this day to day unless you're at a shop like Costco, which doesn't add VAT until you're at the till so you get a nasty surprise when your rotisserie chicken is 20 percent more than you thought it was.

Will
This really isn't just for the oldies out there, it's a legal document that people use to bequeath (leave a gift of) money and property

when they die. If you have anything valuable, or you're in a relationship or have children, it's definitely something you should consider getting.

Withdrawal
Taking money out of your account.

CURRENT ACCOUNTS

When people talk about bank accounts, they probably mean current accounts. It's a type of bank account to help you manage your everyday money and expenses.

A current account is the centre of your financial world. It will be your hardest-working bank account, so you need to make sure you understand what it can do and what it's not good at (spoiler alert... keeping large amounts of money in there – move it where you'll earn interest!).

It's where you'll receive all your money – wages, pension income, benefits or credits. It's also where money comes out – rent, bills, Direct Debits, money to family and friends and so on.

To open a current account, you have to be a UK resident, have a UK address and be aged 18 or over. You can have as many current accounts as you like and there are different types you can apply for, see more later in the chapter. If you're under 18, a children's bank account might be best for you.

When you open a current account, you are usually assigned an eight-digit account number, a six-digit sort code and a debit card, which means you can access your money. In the old days, you'd get a cheque book automatically, but now you have to ask your bank to send you one.

You can deal with your finances in a branch (though good luck with that as they keep closing them down), over the phone or via video banking. Most current accounts can also be accessed through the bank's app or online banking website, so you can usually do your day-to-day banking from a smartphone or computer. A lot of new banks, such as Starling or Monzo, are completely online based.

All banks or building societies will ask for proof of your identity and address before you can open a bank account. This can be a bit difficult if your name isn't on bills and it can take time to get paperwork sorted out. It's always worth having something in your name, such as a phone bill, for this purpose. If your current account comes with an overdraft facility (most do), then the bank will also check your credit score before it accepts your application.

Not many people know this, but if you're someone who is in a women's shelter and has no way to get ID and the paperwork needed, some banks will accommodate you and get you set up with a bank account.

Just because you have a current account with a bank, doesn't mean you have to do all your banking with them. You might find them trying to sell you other products or accounts. Be aware it doesn't always seem like selling and they often present it as 'advice'. As always, do a bit of research to make sure you're getting a good deal and are not being talked into financial products you don't need or don't suit your circumstances.

Because banks want you to join, they may offer you incentives like opening bonuses, free cinema tickets, insurance, cashback and so on when you sign up. These benefits are worth taking into account but shouldn't be the only reason you choose a bank.

If you don't have the capability to deal with your finances, the bank can allow a trusted person to bank on your behalf. There are a few ways to do this, which can be useful if you get ill or are unable to deal with your finances. Contact your bank and see what they offer. If you go down this route, make sure it is someone you really trust as it can open you up to financial abuse.

ARE CURRENT ACCOUNTS FREE?

Sort of... They are generally free but there are some fees you might see on your current account statement.

Unplanned overdraft interest
You are charged interest if you go into any unplanned overdraft – it's an expensive way to 'borrow' money.

Charges for refused Direct Debits and standing orders
If there's not enough money in your account to cover this, you might get charged up to £25. You should get a text from your bank or building society first, giving you time to put money in your account before being charged.

Foreign transaction fees
There are sometimes fees for using your account and debit cards abroad.

Admin charges
You may get charged for bank references, banker's drafts or duplicate statements.

Overdraft fees
Overdrafts can be one of the most useful features of a current account. They can be a cheap and easy way to get short-term credit if you have the right interest rate. That said, as they are a form of debt, they are always subject to your current financial circumstances and credit history.

Unplanned overdrafts (when you go over your overdraft limit or spend more than is in your account) are incredibly expensive and can cost you more than a typical rate for a personal loan. Not that long ago, you'd get an automatic £30 charge at some banks for going over your overdraft. Banks would really take advantage of the poorest people with extortionate charges. However, these days, current accounts now have a Monthly Maximum Charge (MMC) in place. This is the maximum amount you have to pay each month in fees, charges and interest.

It's really easy to think of an overdraft as 'your money'. I lived in my overdraft for about six years – I was never out of 'debt' but didn't think of it like that. In my head, it was only a problem when I went OVER my overdraft. If your overdraft interest is 0 percent, there are worse forms of debt, but it's important to think of it as debt. I can't tell you how good it felt to leave my overdraft behind.

JOINT ACCOUNTS

I've got quite controversial opinions on joint accounts and plenty of people disagree with me. But here's my opinion: there's no way I'd ever get a joint account. I believe you have to look out for yourself when it comes to your finances – be hardheaded and take emotions out of it. Opening a joint account links you to someone financially, which makes it easy for that person to bring you down or take advantage of you.

I think any financial expert worth their salt would tell you to never get a joint account with flatmates. Missed payments, unarranged overdrafts and bad credit will all impact your financial health negatively. There are safer, and more sensible, ways to sort out bills.

I've been with my boyfriend for over 15 years. We have a baby and I trust him with my life – but we still don't have a joint account. I don't see the point. You can do all the things you need to do without one. I understand why you may want one if one of you earns much more than the other – but apart from that, why risk it?

I think we can be a bit sentimental at times. I know we all think our partners are brilliant, but over 50 percent of marriages end in divorce and many more relationships go wrong. I used to write for newspapers and would talk to people who had lovely relationships but woke up one day with their partner gone, all the money emptied out of their account and in a load of debt. They didn't see it coming. Protect yourself.

That being said, there are plenty of other financial experts who think differently and would say that the pros of a joint account are:

- It simplifies your joint finances, for example rent or mortgage payments, bills and so on.
- It makes it easier to track spending.

Of course, it's up to you. I think if you could do without one then you shouldn't bother but if not, make sure you really trust whoever you're setting up a joint account with.

TYPES OF CURRENT ACCOUNTS

Standard Current Account
This is the most common type. They do everything I've already outlined and are typically free. A credit check may be required to open one.

Basic Bank Account
These are free, limited accounts for those who are not able to have a standard current account. For example, you may struggle to open a standard current account if you've recently been made bankrupt. These accounts are somewhere you can receive wages or benefits and pay bills. You wouldn't be able to get an overdraft. Usually, you can't simply apply for one of these but have to be recommended by your bank after applying for a standard current account.

Packaged Account
Also known as a premium account. This type of current account comes with some swanky perks in return for a monthly fee. Perks may be a better interest rate, car breakdown cover, mobile insurance cover, retail discounts and so on. Packaged accounts typically range from £2 to £20 a month.

Student Account

These are for students, obvs. They tend to come with an exciting, yet dangerous, interest-free overdraft (it's all good until you graduate and you now owe a load of money – with interest!). They'll often offer things such as rail cards or gift cards to entice you to sign up.

Children's Account

Designed to introduce children and teenagers to everyday banking. They're a lot like basic bank accounts with limited functions.

HOW TO PICK A CURRENT ACCOUNT

If there's one thing to remember when it comes to current accounts, it's that you should switch if it's not working for you. Your needs will change, and loyalty doesn't pay.

It's super easy to switch current accounts these days, as UK banks offer a seven-day current account switch guarantee, so switching bank accounts should be simple.

Things to consider when choosing a current account:

- Are you a student or are you going to be?
- Are you always in your overdraft? If so, you'll want to make sure the interest charged on it is 0 percent.
- Are you always in credit? If so, you want one that pays interest.
- Do you have a really bad credit rating? You might want or need a basic account.
- Do you want a joint account?
- Do you want specific rewards, such as opening bonuses or cashback perks?

- How important is customer service to you?
- How does the bank or building society treat customers with mental health issues?
- Do you travel a lot? Some accounts have travel benefits such as travel insurance.

Once you know what is important to you, research and compare current accounts from different banks. Websites such as Money Saving Expert and Which? offer clear and simple comparisons.

SAVINGS ACCOUNTS

Savings accounts are very different from current accounts. Your current account is supposed to be busy. You're probably dealing with it every day. Money is going in, and money is going out. With a savings account, the ideal is for you to leave your money in there for as long as possible. This will let it build up and earn interest.

Opening a savings account, and committing to regularly putting money in it, is a great way to start building up a savings pot that could be used for all sorts of good things.

Savings accounts normally have higher interest rates than current accounts, but, generally, you can't access your money as easily. You won't be able to use a debit card or cheque book and you might have to let your bank know in advance if you want to take money out of the account. Apart from earning interest, putting money in a savings account can help you avoid the temptation to spend it.

You don't have to have your savings account with the same bank as your current account but it can make it easier to have everything in one place. It's not the best reason to pick a savings account but it's a good option if you want to keep things as simple as possible.

Your money is safe, too (assuming I don't have super-rich people like Jeff Bezos reading who have more than £85,000 stashed away). The government decided to guarantee personal deposits in UK banks through the FSCS (Financial Services Compensation Scheme). This ensures that customers will receive up to £85,000 of their deposit from any banking group that goes bust.

Almost anyone can open a savings account, as long as you are a UK resident. Some accounts require a minimum opening deposit while others may involve a minimum monthly contribution.

Personal Savings Allowance
Here's a good thing you might not know – you have a savings allowance that lets you earn a certain amount of interest on your savings before you need to pay any tax:

- If you're a basic-rate taxpayer, you can earn at least £1,000 worth of interest before paying tax.
- If you're a higher-rate taxpayer, you can earn £500 worth of interest before paying tax.
- If you're an additional-rate taxpayer you do not qualify for personal savings allowance.
- Any interest you earn above your personal savings allowance will have tax deducted.

Some savings accounts mean you can get around paying tax. They are called ISAs. I love them. You should get one and love it, too.

TYPES OF SAVING ACCOUNTS

Different savings accounts have different rules about paying money in and taking money out. Picking the wrong one could cause trouble. If the point of your savings account is to provide an emergency fund, you don't want one that locks away your money for years and charges you a fortune to get access to your cash.

The more you save, and the longer you save for, the more important it is to pick the right account. Different types of accounts offer different ways to access your money, as well as different benefits.

Cash ISA
A cash ISA means all interest you earn is tax-free so you can get more for your money. This interest will be paid monthly or annually, depending on the account.

Everyone has an ISA allowance, set by the government, which is the most you can save in an ISA each tax year (which starts and ends in April). For 2021/22, the allowance is £20,000. Once you hit this limit, you will have to use another type of savings account in order to save more money. Some non-ISA savings accounts let you save up to £5 million every year but don't have the same tax benefits.

You can have a cash ISA along with another savings account, but you can only have one cash ISA. It's not an either/or situation but the general rule of thumb is to max out the amount you can put in your ISA before moving on to another savings account. It's important to

01997c48-bdf2-7ca9-bba3-2a2e7099b9a7

note that if you plan on moving accounts, get the new provider to switch it over rather than taking the money out yourself to move it, because done incorrectly, your money could lose its tax-free status and you'll end up with a bill.

It won't cost you anything to move your money to a new account with the vast majority of cash ISAs, but there are some exceptions with fixed-rate cash ISAs where you might lose interest accrued if you move the money earlier than you agreed to.

Stocks and Shares ISA

With a cash ISA, you get a fixed rate of interest in return for depositing your money at that bank or building society. A stocks and shares ISA gives you all the tax benefits of a standard cash ISA, but a stocks and shares ISA doesn't pay a fixed interest rate.

With this type of ISA, you invest money (up to £20,000 per tax year) on the stock market, such as the FTSE 100. As markets rise or fall, so does the value of your investments. This means you can get back less than you put in it, but your money also has the potential to grow further than in a cash ISA. Read chapter nine for more information on investing.

Lifetime ISA (LISA)

If you want to buy your own home, you should seriously consider a Lifetime ISA (LISA). It is designed to help those saving for a first home and retirement.

Here's why it's really good: the government will pay you an annual bonus of 25 percent (capped at £1,000 per year) on any contributions you make. That's free money. A lot of it, too. So if you put in £4,000 across the tax year, you will receive £1,000 for free.

Money can be withdrawn tax-free at any time to buy your first home worth up to £450,000. You can also take out the money, tax-free, once you're over 60, for any reason you like.

However, if you want to spend the money on anything other than your first property and you're under the age of 60, you'll be hit with a 25 percent penalty when you withdraw your cash. That's a lot of money to lose.

You are currently able to put £20,000 into ISAs each tax year. It doesn't matter what type, or how many you have, you can split that cash between them however you like. For more information on the LISA, check out chapter 14.

Easy or Instant Access Accounts
These accounts allow you to pay in and take out money whenever you need to. The downside to these accounts is that you'll get a lower interest rate. They are nice and simple though, so are a good starting point if you're not confident when it comes to saving, or you need easy access to your money.

Regular Deposit Account
A regular deposit account rewards you for paying money in every month. You'll get bonus interest for every month that you pay in a certain amount. With some accounts, you'll lose this bonus if you take money out.

These deals are often time-limited, which means that after a year you go back to a lower interest rate.

It's a really bad idea to set one of these up if putting in the amount needed every month is going to be a struggle. Leave yourself lots of wiggle room. If you're not sure you can save the same every month, consider sticking with an easy-access account which will give you more flexibility.

Fixed-term Bonds

With a fixed-term bond, you put money in an account for a fixed length of time at a fixed interest rate, which means you know exactly how much you'll end up with at the end of that specified time. You'll need to lock away your money for a set amount of time – usually one to three years. The interest rate is usually better the longer you lock your money away for. However, you'll have to pay a fee if you want to take your money out early.

This is a particularly good option if you have a long-term savings goal in mind and won't need access to your money.

Notice Account

These accounts ask you to let the bank know in advance (get it – you give 'notice') if you want to take money out.

Normally, you'll get more interest the longer the required notice – so an account that asks for 30 days' notice will give you a better rate than one that asks for seven days. If you want to get your money out without giving notice, you'll have to pay a fee.

Limited Withdrawal Account

A limited withdrawal account lets you make a certain number of withdrawals each month. If you make more than this you'll have to pay a fee.

HOW TO CHOOSE A SAVINGS ACCOUNT

This will of course depend on what's going on in your life, how much you can afford to save and if you need easy access to money. It's important to keep an eye on your savings – know what your interest rate is and switch accounts if a better deal is on offer, as long as moving won't incur any fees.

When it comes to banking, you aren't rewarded for your loyalty and new customers normally get the best deals, so it's worth switching. Figure out what's important to you and consider:

- **Convenience**
  How easily do you need to access your money?
- **Savings goals**
  Can you trust yourself to not dip into your savings?
- **Potential earnings**
  Do you want to make as much money through your savings as possible?
- **Deposits**
  Can you afford to add regular payments or will they be more ad hoc?

As with your current account, once you've decided on your preferred method of saving, use comparison tools on trusted websites to find the best deal. Offers change regularly so keep an eye out for new deals.

ACTIVITY

Now that you know your options when it comes to current and savings accounts, I've got two challenges for you.

Take 10 minutes to see what your current account is offering. Is it pretty basic? Check if other banks are offering incentives to switch (some offer over £100), then make the switch. After all, who doesn't like free money?

If you don't have a savings account, open one up and set up a Direct Debit so money goes in every month. I don't care if it's only £1. Research shows that the key to saving successfully is small amounts put away consistently. Check out the budgeting tips in chapter two to see how much you could put away.

4 SAVING

Budgeting and saving go hand in hand, so if you want financial freedom, you're going to have to master a budget as well as plan and execute saving goals.

Here's the truth about saving (and there are stats and studies to back this up!): small amounts put away consistently are the best way to save.

A couple of quid every single week, something you can afford and sustain for years, is better than throwing in big amounts now and then. That said, if you do come into some cash from a birthday or Christmas, dropping it into your savings account is not going to be a bad thing.

So here's what you need to know about saving, because unless you hit it big with a lottery win or come up with the new Facebook, saving is the only way to get what you want without getting into debt.

YOU NEED A PLAN

It's far too easy to say you're saving but not actually achieve anything. For about eight years I was 'saving for a deposit', which meant I would put a few quid away now and then, but when I was skint would dip into it and end up at square one. It was half-arsed and the goal was too big. If I was honest with myself, I didn't really believe I was ever going to save enough money to put a deposit down on a flat, but it felt good to tell myself I was trying.

Eventually, I wanted my own home enough to make a proper change. It wasn't until I sat down with my boyfriend, crunched some numbers, worked out how much was actually affordable to put away every month, with an end date, that we got somewhere.

So what do you want? Is it a holiday? A wedding? A deposit for a home? Comparison website Compare the Market has some averages that show how much you need to put away. Of course, you can tweak so the numbers work for you.

LET'S SAVE FOR A HOLIDAY

- Median UK annual salary in April 2021 = **£31,772**
- Monthly salary, after tax and deductions = **£2,000**
- The average holiday cost = **£670**
- If saving for one year, this would mean saving **£55.83** each month, or slightly less than **3 percent** of a monthly salary.

If we're following the 50/30/20 system from chapter two and saving the optimum 20 percent of your salary, this would mean saving **£400** each month, and it would take less than two months to save for your holiday.

HOW MUCH SHOULD YOU BE SAVING?

Kate Moss famously said that nothing tastes as good as being thin feels (she's clearly never had a Toblerone) and I'm here to say that nothing feels better than being debt free with a load of cash in the bank. That feeling doesn't disappear, unlike a shopping high.

So how much should you be putting away? As covered in chapter two, 20 percent of your income each month is a brilliant target, which is based on the 50/30/20 budgeting rule. With this method you spend 50 percent of your income on essentials, have 30 percent of your income for fun and save the remaining 20 percent.

You will need to be flexible when it comes to these figures as the world is changing and food, energy and petrol prices are all going up. Make the system work for you by working with what you have.

When I first started saving, that 20 percent included my pension contributions. When I started earning more, I put 10 percent of my wage into my private pension and then saved 20 percent elsewhere. Then when I paid off my student loan, I had an extra 9 percent which I was used to not having, so I decided to invest it.

Do whatever works for you and don't get too hung up on this rule – 20 percent is ideal to start with but it's just not do-able for a lot of people.

The key is putting away whatever you can afford every month, consistently – whatever that percentage is.

Saving Priorities

As much as buying a new car or a holiday feels like a saving priority, it likely isn't. There are things you need to achieve first. It's not fun, but these rules are there to protect you.

Pay Off Debt or Save?

My general rule is to pay off debt before you start saving and here's why. Debt is typically very expensive and saving interest rates (what you can earn from your savings) won't be as high, so interest rates on your debt payments will quickly overtake your savings.

For example, interest made on a savings account might be around 1 percent while interest costs for you on an overdraft could be 5 percent. A payday loan could be as high as 30 percent! You're swimming against the tide here.

LET'S CRUNCH SOME NUMBERS

- You owe £1,000 on a store card with **30 percent** interest.
- You have a savings account with **2 percent** interest.
- If you were to pay £250 a month for four months, you'd pay off the £1,000 debt but you'd also pay **£58.53** interest.
- If you were to save £250 a month for four months, you'd earn just **£1.67** interest on your savings.

This example shows why it makes no sense to save until you've paid off your expensive debt.

While meeting all minimum payments, pay off your highest interest debt first, then move on to the next highest. Once your debt is all paid off, you can focus on a saving goal. This is the cheapest and quickest way to do this.

That said, and breaking my rule slightly, it is a good idea to have some emergency money put away before paying off all your debt. But it really is for emergencies only, and buying a new outfit doesn't count!

Emergency Fund

In 2019 the charity Shelter reported that 40 percent of renters in the UK are one missed pay cheque from potential homelessness. Just **ONE** missed pay cheque – could this be you if you lost your job or became too sick to work?

Most people are overconfident when it comes to their financial security. They think that Universal Credit, the Jobcentre, debt and homelessness are for other people, not them.

If your car was written off tomorrow and you had to buy a new one straight away, could you find £2,000? What if your boiler broke? Emergencies happen and even if they aren't big enough to make you lose your home, it's really easy to get into a debt spiral.

We live in a time where we have to create our own safety nets, so you must make sure you could survive for enough time to get your life back together if the shit hits the fan. The general rule of thumb when putting together an emergency fund is about three to six months of wages.

It should cover your rent or mortgage, food and bills. You should know from your budget what your essential costs are so make sure your fund will cover them for at least three months. Put this money away in an easy-access savings account and forget about it until you really need it. Once you've saved your emergency fund, you can then start another savings account.

If you already have money saved that you can immediately set aside into a dedicated emergency fund, that's a great start.

Fuck-off Fund

This is for those of you in relationships or living in a situation where you rely financially, whether fully or partially, on others.

A fuck-off fund (or a freedom fund) is a secret amount of money you put away so that you can quickly leave the situation you are in while you find help or start somewhere new. This amount might be a couple of hundred quid so you can afford travel and a hotel for a few nights, or a few months' rent.

A few years ago, during a health check, a nurse wanted me to get some routine STI (sexually transmitted infection) tests done. I told her there was no need as I was in a loving, committed relationship. She told me that I was to NEVER entrust my health to someone else – it's my responsibility to make sure I'm safe and I'd be naive to assume that I couldn't be let down by the people I love.

That has always stuck with me. And it's exactly the same when it comes to your finances. Just because everything is rosy now, doesn't mean it will be in the future. Consider putting some money aside in a bank account that only you can access, just in case you need it.

THE EASY WAY TO DO IT (THE GAME CHANGER)

The easiest way to save is to do it without noticing. I managed to save £2,700 in a year with something called microsaving or automatic saving. I used the app Chip (which has a paid-for element) but there are lots of other apps out there, notably Cleo and Plum. Some banks, such as Starling Bank and Monzo, offer the service, too.

These apps help you save by rounding up transactions or squirrelling away small amounts of money. The point is, you don't notice the money leaving your account as the amounts are so small.

The best microsaving apps analyse what you earn and your spending habits, then, based on that information, withdraw small amounts of money several days per week. We're talking around one to five pounds per week.

However, most apps charge a fee each month, which will be more than the interest income. It will also be keeping your money in an account with a pretty weak interest saving rate. So make sure to move that saved money every now and then and decide whether the amount you're saving is worth the fee.

ACTIVITY

This is an easy one.

- Come up with a saving goal(s), for example a holiday, a new car or a deposit
- Figure out exactly how much it's going to cost
- Calculate how much you can afford to put away every month and how long it will take (see chapter two for budgeting tips)
- Automate the saving – set up a weekly or monthly internal transfer or a Direct Debit into a savings account to ensure regular saving without having to think about it.

5 WHY PENSIONS ARE FREE MONEY

Buckle up, everyone, we're in for a wild ride with a whole chapter on pensions. Don't skip this bit because you're assuming it's going to be dry – I'm going to prove to you that pensions are exciting stuff. Okay, exciting might be a bit much, but I do love free money, and that's what they are.

Get your pension planning right and you're hopefully (fingers crossed) going to be spending the last 20+ years of your life living it up. It's a long time to not be enjoying yourself. I don't know about you but I plan to spend my retirement in the Caribbean, eyeing up bartenders who serve me strawberry daiquiris. Not shivering in a cold house, cutting out coupons for discounted beans. I have loftier ambitions!

YOU'RE GOING TO LIVE LONGER THAN YOU THINK

How long do you think you'll live? I bet you reckon you'll kick the bucket somewhere in your eighties.

When do you hope to retire? Currently, the date you can claim your State Pension depends on your date of birth and sex. As it stands, most of us will be 68 before we can get it. But the odds are, the age we can claim will go up a few times before we get our hands on the State Pension.

Compare this with your personal pension, which you can technically take out at 55 years old – though this might not be a good idea considering how long you could live.

So, if you think you're likely to die in your eighties, you're probably estimating you'll need about 15–20 years' worth of money.

You've probably never had to think about it before but have you seen the price of living in a nursing home? The average cost is currently £888 per week. Your eyes are not deceiving you, you read correctly – 888 British pounds PER WEEK!

This is why you see old people living on cruise ships. It's literally cheaper for them to float around the Caribbean in five-star luxury than live in a very basic nursing home.

When you're thinking about how many years you need to cover yourself for, you have to be realistic about how potentially expensive it's going to be.

Right, so if your assumption is that you only ('only' – LOL) need to cover yourself for 15–20 years, you need a completely different strategy if you live, let's say, into your 90s or even 100s. Don't forget that you need to take into account inflation, too – your money has to grow with inflation, or above it, in an ideal world.

At the time of writing, the Office of National Statistics (ONS) says that the most common age to die for a man is 86.7 years and for a woman it's 89.3 years. It also says, and this is terrifying to me, that one in three of today's babies will live to see their 100th birthday.

Which? spoke to thousands of retirees in a survey to see how much they spend every year. They worked out that as a retired individual, to have an 'essentials' lifestyle you need £12,500 each year, to have a 'comfortable' lifestyle you'll need £19,000 and you'll need to aim for £31,000 a year for a 'luxurious' retirement.

I hear this all the time: 'I don't want to pay into a pension because what if I die before I can spend the money? It's money down the drain.' Well, as you've probably realised, it's pretty easy to burn through money in your retirement and it's better to have it and not need it.

There is no more miserable way to spend the last years of your life than cold, hungry and poor. Especially when you are likely used to a better standard of living from when you were working. And even if you die before being able to spend some of it, the remaining money will go to the people you love.

SO WHAT CAN YOU DO ABOUT IT?

Short of finding a billionaire to marry or winning the Euromillions, you've got three options:

- Save more
- Work longer
- Expect less.

Expect Less

I'm not a fan of this for obvious reasons. You don't have to have a miserable retirement – there's always time to improve your prospects.

Work Longer

Urgh, I don't know about you, but I'm already sick of working. I really want to be able to stop working in my 60s, but the truth is a lot of us will be working in some way past retirement to supplement our pension income.

When it comes to working into your 70s and 80s, it really depends on the work you do. I would imagine it would be pretty miserable continuing with manual labour into your 70s – my back is in constant agony from carrying a baby around and I'm only in my 30s.

It's worth bearing in mind that continuing to learn and developing new skills, especially ones that aren't physically demanding, such as selling homemade items, affiliate marketing, tutoring, content creation and so on, could be worth a lot to you in your retirement if you need or want supplemental income.

Save More

This is the big one and the key here is to start saving for your retirement as soon as possible. In a nutshell:

- Pick the right pension for you
- Pick the right amount to put in it
- Watch compound interest do its thing.

Have I scared you enough yet? Good. Let's get into it.

IS A PENSION REALLY THE BEST WAY TO SAVE MONEY FOR RETIREMENT?

So many people understand that they need to invest money for their retirement, and are willing to, but write off the idea of a pension as being too boring.

With TikTok 'money gurus' (*cough* unqualified bullshit merchants *cough*) encouraging you to throw your money into cryptocurrency and dodgy investment opportunities for big wins, it does feel like you might be missing out by sticking your money into something your granny has.

I find that if I even mention the word *pension* on Twitter or Instagram, all the crypto bros and bots come out of the woodwork to tell me how

I'll never be rich putting my money into a pension.

And yeah, I can't guarantee I'll be rich if I do (it is investing at the end of the day, your money could go up or down) but I can guarantee I'll be absolutely skint if I don't.

Get-rich-quick schemes don't work and you shouldn't take wild risks in unregulated schemes when it comes to your retirement. Like I said, 20/30/40+ years is a long time to be cold and hungry.

SO, WHAT IS A PENSION?

Let's say this up front: when you are paying into a pension, you are 'investing'. It's literally stocks and shares. And as with all investing, your money is at risk. The value of your investments can go up as well as down and you may get back less than you invest. If you are unsure if a pension is right for you, please seek independent financial advice from someone qualified to give it.

A pension is a tax-efficient way to put money aside for later in life. This may sound like a load of words that don't mean very much, but a pension is a tax loophole. And we like a loophole around here.

There are three types of pension:

- Government pension (also known as a State Pension)
- A workplace pension
- A personal pension.

If you've paid National Insurance through employment for 10 or more qualifying years (being on Universal Credit, statutory sickness, maternity leave and so on count as employment), you'll get some State Pension. But don't make the mistake of thinking it will be enough to survive on when you retire.

Most people will then top up their State Pension with a work-based pension. Since 2012 employers have been gradually required to automatically sign their employees up to a pension. This is called automatic enrolment (there's more information on this later). You can choose to opt out of it (please don't), or put more money away every month (please do).

Those contributions are then invested by the pension provider, typically in stocks and shares. You can let them choose where your money is invested or you can choose yourself. You can also choose how much risk you are happy for them to take with your money. With my pension, I let them choose which stocks and shares to invest in because I figure they know more than me. Risk-wise, the younger you are, the easier it is to rebound from a knock if your options lose value, so the decision whether to choose low, medium or high risk can be age dependent. Remember, the income you will get from your pension isn't guaranteed. It depends on how well the investments do – the value can go up as well as down.

You can pay into as many pensions as you want, however, there are limits to how much you can contribute to your pensions each tax year, as well as over your lifetime. It's common over the course of your career to acquire a new pension with every new workplace. It might be a good idea to consolidate them all into one pot because you won't believe how many people forget about them.

Let's go into a bit more detail about each kind of pension (remember, you can have all three if you like) and why they are good.

TYPES OF PENSION

State Pension

The State Pension is a pension you'll receive from the government once you reach the state retirement age, as long as you have your 10 years' worth of qualifying National Insurance contributions, as discussed. You'll get this income for the rest of your life and, with a system called a triple lock, the government promises to increase your State Pension in line with inflation, earnings or 2.5 percent every April – whichever is higher.

A lot of people think that because they will be entitled to a State Pension, they're sorted. They couldn't be more wrong. Most people would agree that it's nowhere near enough money to have a decent lifestyle – it's bare-bones stuff.

The State Pension is currently £179.60 per week (2021), but the actual amount depends on your National Insurance record. You'll need 35 qualifying payment years to get the full State Pension.

There's also a myth that there won't be a State Pension when you retire. Every year you pay National Insurance (NI), you are building up that State Pension and anything you 'earn' while you are paying NI can't be taken away. So, it's money in the bank even if future governments might change.

Workplace Pension

If you are employed, then the employer is legally obliged to have set up a pension scheme for you. It also has to automatically enrol all its eligible employees. You'll be automatically enrolled if:

- You work full time or part time.
- You work in the UK.
- You are at least 22 years old, but under State Pension age.
- You earn more than £10,000 a year for the tax year 2021/22.

If you earn less than £10,000 but above £6,240 (for the tax year 2021/22), your employer doesn't have to automatically enrol you into a scheme, but if you ask to join one, they can't legally refuse and will have to make contributions for you.

Here's the best bit about a workplace pension: your employer has to contribute to it. You can look at that like a pay rise.

When your employer sets up the pension scheme they decide whether you, and the company, pay contributions on your full wage or on what's called your 'qualifying earnings'. The current banding for qualifying earnings is £6,240 to £50,270.

There are two types of workplace pension schemes: a defined contribution pension scheme (DC scheme) and a defined benefit pension scheme (DB scheme).

Most people will have a DC pension where you and your employer pay in a percentage of your salary. You may be in a job where your employer will only put in the minimum contribution (currently 3 percent) but it doesn't stop you putting in more. I've personally always aimed for 10 percent, but you do you. If your employer is putting in the minimum 3 percent and you choose to put in 5 percent, you will have 8 percent in total contributions.

Some employers will match your contributions up to a certain amount. For example, if you choose to put in 8 percent, your company will also contribute 8 percent. If you can afford it, get the maximum contribution out of your employer. Again, and I'll probably say this a hundred times in this chapter, this is free money.

Now if you're really lucky (or work in some public sector jobs), you might have a DB pension, also known as a final salary pension scheme. Employers don't hand these out very much any more.

The benefit of a DB pension is you get a specified amount as income when you reach retirement age. Both you and your employer still make contributions but your pension is calculated by multiplying your length of service by your final salary, which is divided by a fraction such as 1/60th or 1/80th.

You don't have to stay with the same employer offering the DB scheme until the day of your retirement. If you were to leave your job, the fund still belongs to you. You can leave it in the current scheme for as long as you like, or you can transfer it if rules allow. But, and it's a big one, you should always get independent financial advice before touching a DB scheme and shouldn't rely on your ex-employer to suggest the best option.

When I move on from my current role, the pension plan offered is going to be one of the biggest determining factors for where I go (assuming the salary is right). I'm going to do my best to get my hands on a pension where my employer at least matches what I pay in, but ideally pays in more. And if I were to go back in time, I'd be looking for a well-paid job with a DB pension, as with a DC pension, you only get what you've put in.

When you retire, you can take up to 25 percent of the money built up in your pension as a tax-free lump sum. You'll then have six months to start taking out the remaining 75 percent, which you'll usually pay tax on.

The options you have for taking the rest of your pension pot include:

- Taking all or some of it as cash
- Buying a product that gives you a guaranteed income for life (sometimes known as an annuity)
- Investing it to get a regular, adjustable income (sometimes known as 'flexi-access' drawdown).

This is a massive decision and there is no one right answer that works for everyone – it all depends on your circumstances. Make the wrong choice though, and you may find that you lose a large chunk of your savings to tax and/or don't have enough to cover your retirement. Always speak to an independent pension expert before making a decision.

Personal Pension

A personal pension, also known as a private pension, is one you can set up yourself.

It's not an alternative to your workplace pension if you are employed because you will lose that free money I've talked about (that is, the employer's contribution). Since automatic enrolment began, for most people in full-time employment, a personal pension is only a good idea if you are not eligible for a workplace pension.

If you open a personal pension, you have to pick your provider and how much you're going to contribute.

There are two types of personal pensions:

Stakeholder Pension
A stakeholder pension allows you to make low minimum contributions (as low as £16 a month and you'll still get tax relief to boost your savings) and is aimed at people who want to save for their retirement, but don't have a huge amount to put in their pension pot each month. You can stop and start payments, and transfer out at no cost.

Self-invested Personal Pension (SIPP)
This is for anyone who wants to manage their own investments and have a bigger range of asset types to invest in (though it would be wise to get a financial adviser involved). Some schemes offer a wider and more sophisticated range of investment options than a stakeholder pension. Once you've opened a SIPP, you can make one-off, monthly or yearly payments into your pension. You're in full control of your pension pot so you'll need to be confident in your ability, as well as be willing to do your research.

Personal pensions are particularly useful for the self-employed as you won't have a workplace pension.

SELF-EMPLOYMENT

If you're self-employed and don't fancy living off your State Pension, you're going to have to sort out a pension on your own.

According to *The Times*, four out of five self-employed people don't have a pension plan, leaving them without the financial security they'll need in later life. Yikes!

Let me just highlight those tax benefits again — as a self-employed person, you're entitled to all of the same tax reliefs on pension contributions as employed people.

You get a tax top-up when you contribute to your retirement pot at the rate of 20, 40 or 45 percent, depending on your tax bracket. So, if you're a basic-rate taxpayer who puts £800 into your pension, the government will top it up by 20 percent, automatically turning it into £1,000.

Do I need to shout it from the rooftops? That's a massive pay rise. You'd be mad to not take advantage of that.

If you're self-employed and thinking about opening a personal pension, I would really recommend investing in an independent financial adviser as your future literally depends on making a good decision here.

ACTIVITY

Now you have all the facts, use a pension tool (such as the one available on MoneyHelper) to work out how much you will have when you retire if you continue paying in at your current level. Think about whether that will be enough to live on and if you can afford to start upping your contributions.

If you don't have a pension, research what kind of pension would work best for you, how much you can afford to put in and get it set up ASAP.

6 WE NEED TO TALK ABOUT BUY NOW PAY LATER SCHEMES

This might be a controversial one, because so many people love Buy Now Pay Later (BNPL) schemes and they've become very normalised over the last few years, but I wanted to talk about why I hate them and think they can be dangerous.

A QUICK RANT

Okay, full disclosure: I really hate BNPL. You might not have heard of the term before but you've definitely heard of the companies that offer it, such as Klarna, Clearpay and Laybuy. There are more out there, but those are the biggies.

The scheme does exactly what it says on the tin – you can buy something now but pay for it at a later date. Some give you 30 days to pay, while others allow you up to 12 months. What could go wrong?

These days, most shopping websites offer BNPL as a payment option, mainly because stats from BNPL companies themselves brag that it makes people more likely to click 'buy', and when they do, basket sizes are bigger.

But I hear you cry, 'Lotty, what's your problem? Most of them charge 0 percent interest, so it's free.' Well, let me tell you something, they aren't offering these products out of the goodness of their hearts – there's money to be made out of misery.

I'll break down my issue into two points:

- Anyone can take out these products without understanding the consequences.
- The often predatory and unethical behaviour of the company offering the product.

Point One: Unintended Consequences
You would not believe the amount of people who have come to me with debt problems because they have got into trouble through BNPL, buying a £25 pair of shoes they could have afforded to pay for outright in the first place.

When a bank, for example, decides whether to lend someone money, it will carry out an affordability check to make sure that the borrower can pay the money back. This isn't necessarily because they want the money back (they do, but it's not completely the reason they do it), it's because they are forced by a regulatory body called the Financial Conduct Authority (FCA) to ensure that they are looking out for the customer, making sure they aren't borrowing more than they could reasonably afford to pay back. After all, a lender could make far more money out of someone paying an extortionate amount of interest and fines on missed payments than if they just simply paid the money back on time.

With BNPL, it's common for people not to realise they've taken out a financial product because the application process is different from other credit accounts. This can lead people to assume they're harmless. Even if you can afford to make the payments, they are too easy to enter into and are a slippery slope into spending more money than you can afford.

If you miss a payment or fail to pay back what you owe when the time comes, it can be noted on your credit report. A missed payment knocks at least 100 points off your credit score, which could potentially hang around for six years. This lowering of your credit score means you might find it hard to get credit in the future, such as applying for a credit card or a mortgage.

The website Compare the Market conducted research and found that one in 11 people (9 percent) have missed a BNPL payment so the number of people being negatively affected is not insignificant.

Some BNPL companies will allow you to spread the cost of your loan over a longer period but then charge a high rate of interest, such as 39.9 percent APR.

Point Two: Unethical Behaviour

Getting into debt is generally not considered a cool or fashionable thing to do. In fact, lots of people are pretty judgemental about it. But weirdly, when it comes to BNPL, people don't seem to mind.

BNPL marketing teams are savvy and have been able to normalise choosing to shop using next month's money. They use social media to aggressively target young people and those who are likely living pay cheque to pay cheque. It's Instagram-worthy finance.

BNPL companies will partner with influencers on Instagram to sell BNPL – even Lady Gaga was encouraging people to use Klarna! To me, this is madness. When they first launched in the UK, Klarna even sent jellybeans to customers to encourage engagement.

Last year when I was getting coffee, I saw a woman who had a bag with Klarna written all over it in the queue. That's incredible. Can you imagine someone with a payday loan company plastered all over their clothing?

And sure, Klarna and other BNPL brands have marketed themselves as cool and modern but one of their tactics is to target students after their loans come in and encourage them to 'Shop like a queen', sending messages to young people saying 'Don't wait until payday!' So nah, not cool. In fact, the industry has behaved so badly, the FCA who 'police' the finance industry is creating new rules to protect people.

BNPL is expanding its reach into (in my opinion) even more unethical waters, too. Right now, it's mainly fashion retail that uses BNPL but we've already seen the launch of the first BNPL supermarket in the UK. This means you can spread the cost of your baked beans and tea bags. I hate this.

With more and more people living in poverty needing to choose between eating and heating, you know there will be people who use

BNPL to pay for dinner even though there's no chance of paying it back. Then bam, you're in a debt cycle.

WHY YOU SHOULDN'T USE BNPL

Look, because of the industry I work in, I see where this goes wrong every day so I'm not expecting everyone to see the worst-case scenario of using BNPL like I do.

That said, if you're serious about getting yourself into a strong financial position, buying something you can't afford and paying for it later doesn't fit into the plan at all.

Because people often open a new BNPL account to pay for something small, it's easy to forget that you promised to pay for that skirt next month, instead of at the checkout. Anecdotally, I've heard of people only remembering they signed up to a BNPL service after their credit score took a dive. The amount they borrowed was so insignificant, it completely slipped their mind and they forgot to pay. You should be sent reminder messages but how often have you seen an email and relegated it to a job for tomorrow? If you move house or go on holiday you could miss letters – it's not the same as one big monthly payment you'd make to a credit card company.

I'm not against some credit. It has its uses in certain circumstances but using it to buy items you don't need doesn't fall under those criteria. You're just bringing an element of risk into your financial plan that doesn't need to be there. You don't need BNPL, you're better than it.

ACTIVITY

Make sure to add an impulse shopping allocation in your budget.
Knowing the average price of luxury items you'll likely want to buy
means you can budget for them. That way, you can shop without
guilt and pay up front with no risk of ruining your credit rating.

SOME STATS TO GET YOU STARTED

Football ticket:
The average price paid for a Premier League ticket is £32.

Night out:
On average Brits spend roughly £65 on a night out.

Festival:
The average cost of going to a music festival is more than
£400.

ASOS basket:
The average amount spent is £71.29.

7 SORTING OUT DEBT

You're here, reading this book, because you want financial wellbeing. You want to live the life of your dreams, stress free and in control. And to do that, you have to take a holistic approach to debt, whether it's a problem in your life or not.

Debt is a necessary evil for the vast majority of us. It's not always a bad thing in itself, in fact it can help improve your life dramatically. However, it is a tricky thing that you need to be very careful about because it can bite you in the arse if you make a mistake.

For a lot of people the problems start when debt becomes unmanageable. The thing you have to understand about debt is that it can spiral out of control very quickly. Small amount after small amount racks up, not only impacting your financial health but your mental and physical health, too.

There isn't a magic number that makes debt a problem – it could be £200 or £200,000. If you are struggling to manage payments and feel stressed, that's problem debt and you should get proper, free and impartial help.

DEBT AND INTEREST BASICS

If you break it down to its simplest form, you're in debt anytime you borrow money from someone, right up until the moment you pay it off, including any interest owed.

So based on that, debt is a mortgage, credit card, overdraft, car payments, personal loans, interest-free payment plans, store cards and Buy Now Pay Later schemes, as well as borrowing £20 from your mum for a takeaway.

Let's be real, lenders aren't loaning you money out of the goodness of their hearts. Whether they're Tony Soprano or the UK's biggest bank, they do it to make money via interest on the loan.

Interest is the additional amount you agree to pay in order to borrow the money and is usually expressed in terms of Annual Percentage Rate (APR). Typically, longer-term loans offer lower interest rates, whereas shorter-term loans can get away with ridiculously high rates.

According to Experian data, the average rate on a personal loan is 9.41 percent, the average credit card is around 22.8 percent and (you might want to sit down for this) it's a whopping 391 percent on a payday loan.

Bear in mind these are only example rates at the time of writing but I want to give you an idea of how interest rates differ depending on the type of loan.

WHAT'S THE DIFFERENCE BETWEEN GOOD AND BAD DEBT?

I grew up thinking that debt was a dirty word. If you want something, you save up, even if it takes years to buy it. I still think that to a degree but I now know there's such a thing as good debt and bad debt.

Good debt can be seen as an investment. As long as it's affordable for you, and it's going to improve your life by helping you buy something that will increase in value and contribute to your longer-term financial wellbeing, which ultimately is a good thing.

An example of good debt is a student loan. Usually a degree and further education will help you get a more well-paid job and open up opportunities. Plus, you don't need to pay your loan back until you're earning past the threshold.

A mortgage is another example as you'll stop 'wasting' your money on rent, and property is an investment that can be profitable in the long term (see chapter 13 for more on home buying). If you need a car for your work then a finance deal might also be considered good debt.

That said, if you can pay for a house in cash and avoid debt that is obviously preferable, but we don't all have Elon Musk as a dad.

Even if you have 'good debt' it's really worth trying to pay it off as quickly as possible. If you're serious about getting out of debt, you will need to set up a budget (check out chapter two for help with this), factoring in your monthly payments.

So that leaves bad debt. This is debt that's purely for the purpose of consumption – clothes, holidays, games or anything that doesn't help your financial situation over the long term. Even if you can afford the debt, you can't afford the items. If you want real financial freedom, you need to make sure these costs are accounted for in your budget and achieved via saving.

The New Grey Middle Ground

Thanks to a myriad of things, but especially the pandemic, a lot of us have been hit hard financially. With wage freezes, increased cost of living and uncertain income, there is now a large group of people who will fall into a grey area in between good and bad debt.

What I mean is that there are many people who are having to use expensive debt to pay for essentials, such as food, housing costs and bills. It's just not that simple these days.

Sometimes people will also get themselves in debt, practically overnight, because of a change in circumstances such as a separation or job loss. One day you're fine and then the next you're struggling to pay your bills through no fault of your own.

If you experience an income shock, the key is to act quickly to ensure that you have a plan to survive financially while you get back on your feet, and protect your mental health.

See chapter 14, which covers financial wellbeing, for a checklist of things you need to do.

HOW CAN YOU TELL IF DEBT IS A PROBLEM?

One of the easiest ways to tell if debt is a problem is if it feels like the situation is out of control and it's impacting your mental health. However, for many people debt might not seem like a problem. Some people might try to not think about debt so don't feel anything, while others have been in debt for so long they are simply used to it.

Here are some signs you should get help with your debt.

You're Hiding Your Spending

Do you watch out for the postman so you can get to him before he rings the doorbell and alerts the household to another package? Or do you hide new purchases from friends and family? If you can't be honest with your loved ones about your debt, chances are you have too much.

You Don't Know How Much You Owe

This is a dead giveaway that things are out of control. You may be consciously or subconsciously ignoring the problem because you don't want to deal with it. You may not know because someone else has taken out loans in your name (which is economic abuse), or perhaps you've forgotten who you owe money to. There are a million reasons why you might not be on top of your debt but it's all very fix-able.

You're Struggling to Sleep at Night

The stress of it all is making it hard to rest properly. You may not have put two and two together but if you have money troubles and struggle to sleep at night, they are likely to be connected.

You Owe More Than You Are Paid Every Month
If this is the case, you won't have enough money to cover your debts, never mind your day-to-day financial needs. Things will get very bad very quickly if you're in this situation without getting help.

You're Dodging Calls, Not Answering the Door and Ignoring Letters From Your Lenders
If you're avoiding the problem it shows you know you are struggling to keep on top of things and your mental health is being negatively impacted.

You're Borrowing Money to Pay Back Your Debts
If you're calling up family and friends, or getting new credit cards or loans to cover pre-existing debt payments, you need to face up to the fact you're in too much debt and get things under control.

You've Drained Your Savings
This means your debt isn't sustainable because what will you do when all your savings have run out?

You're Looking for Ways to Deal With the Stress
You might be drinking too much, using drugs or shopping compulsively. Self-soothing mechanisms to deal with the stress of money problems are likely to make the situation worse.

You're Living in the Red
If you're having to buy essentials like food in your overdraft or on a credit card, it's a sign of a deeper issue.

IF YOUR DEBT IS NOT A PROBLEM

If you have good debt you can comfortably manage, you should still do three things:

1 Make sure you're making your payments, ideally in full, every month. If you can't afford to do that, at least make the minimum payment. After all, one missed payment and you'll knock 100 points off your credit score. A Direct Debit is the easiest way to make sure you don't miss a payment.

2 Regularly check the interest rates you are paying and see if you can switch to a cheaper deal. This will mean you're paying less for what you owe.

3 If you can afford it, try to pay off your debt before it's due. Not only will you get rid of your debt quicker (which means less risk) but it will be cheaper because you're cutting down on the interest you'll have to pay. Just make sure you check the terms of any credit as some may have penalties for early payment.

If you have easy-access cash saving accounts, you'll probably find that interest rates are less than your debt interest rates. It's often better to pay off debt you owe before you start saving (check out chapter four for more information). But remember, you should leave enough savings to cope with any unexpected emergencies, such as a boiler breakdown or car trouble.

THE DEBT HIERARCHY

Not all debt is created equal. Depending on the debt, there are different consequences for not paying it back on time so you need to learn to prioritise.

Priority Debts
These are the debts you pay off first because not paying them can cause you serious problems.

You aren't going to end up in some Oliver Twist-esque workhouse, but in the very (VERY) worst-case scenario you could go to prison.

Priority debts include Council Tax, TV licence, child maintenance, income tax, energy bills, mortgage or rent payments and debts to the Department for Work and Pensions (DWP) or HMRC for unpaid loans or repayment of benefit overpayments.

Non-priority Debts
These debts have creditors (persons or organisations you owe money to) and you'll need to work out a repayment plan for them. If you don't pay, the worst outcome can end with a County Court Judgement (CCJ) and/or bailiffs (sheriffs in Scotland) coming round. These are enforcement agents, sent by your creditor, that will turn up to your home to take any items of yours that your creditor can sell to recoup costs. That will affect your credit score and ability to get credit for a very long time.

These debts include overdrafts, bank loans, Buy Now Pay Later schemes (see chapter six), credit cards, door-stop lenders (where you apply online and a person will come to you to set up the loan), store cards and any money borrowed from family and friends.

A quick note about loan sharks – they are illegal lenders who target people who need money in a hurry and can't access loans in the usual ways. It's not always obvious that someone is a loan shark either as they might be 'friends' or central figures in your community. However, things can turn nasty quickly and you might find yourself in danger if you can't repay the money. If you have already borrowed from a loan shark, please remember that you haven't broken the law and you should report it so you can get help by visiting www.gov.uk/report-loan-shark

WHEN DEBT IS A PROBLEM

You might be thinking that getting debt help is going to be a waste of time, where you're given a stern word and a pamphlet, but it's not like that at all.

You can tackle a debt problem on your own but using a free, confidential and impartial organisation will likely sort the problem out more quickly and efficiently. These organisations have so much experience and can even do things on your behalf that you might find hard to do alone, such as get your lender to temporarily freeze interest (though creditors now have to give you breathing space if you ask them directly yourself).

You can access debt help in a way that feels right for you, whether that be face to face, over the phone or online. Have a look at the below organisations to find one that suits your needs:

- MoneyHelper
- StepChange Debt Charity
- Citizens Advice
- National Debtline
- Payplan
- Christians Against Poverty – you don't need to be a Christian to get help.

Do not pay for debt advice. Ever. Do not get your advice from 'gurus' on social media selling miracle products. You need a qualified debt adviser.

Usually fee-paying debt services take a cut of any of your repayments while free services mean all of your money is going to pay off your debts and you'll get exactly the same service. It's very much not the case that you get what you pay for when it comes to debt help. If you take one thing away from this book, let it be that there is help out there and it's free and waiting for you.

DEBT AND MENTAL HEALTH

When you're in debt, your mental health can suffer so it's important for you to protect yourself. Talking to trusted family or friends can be helpful and is a step in the right direction.

If you are feeling overwhelmed, losing sleep, dealing with anxiety and/or depression then it's always a good idea to visit your GP who can refer you to mental health services in your area.

If you are struggling with your mental health, or any other problems that are making you vulnerable such as an illness or disability, you should always let the people you owe money to know. There are usually special teams that can offer extra support with your debt and repayments. See chapter 14 for more on financial wellbeing.

WHAT TO EXPECT WHEN YOU GET DEBT HELP

So, hands up, I got debt help in my early 20s. I'd love to say I was a grown-up about the situation but I was ignoring the fact I was being chased for £3,000 with no way in the world to pay it back. When I finally admitted the problem to my mum, she marched me down to the bank to demand they stop the charges. One of the employees kindly said, 'Look, I can't do anything but if you were to go to Citizens Advice, they could stop the charges for you and give you some breathing space.'

I didn't really want to go as on one hand going made it seem real, but on the other hand I felt like you only went to Citizens Advice if you were in serious financial trouble with massive debts.

But after just one appointment I can't tell you the relief I felt. They managed to stop the interest on my loan and helped me come up with a plan to pay off the debt.

Importantly, they aren't going to judge how you got into debt, they are solely focused on getting you out of the problem and helping you get back on track. Trust me when I say that they will have seen it all before and worse.

It won't be exactly the same for everyone but you can expect getting debt help to look something like the below:

- If you're being hassled by debt collectors, they'll explain your rights, tell you how to get them to leave you alone and how you can complain about unfair treatment.
- Help decide which debts you should prioritise above others for repayment.
- Assist you in creating a budget and tell you how you can reduce your outstanding debt.
- Negotiate your monthly payments with a debt management plan or find the right debt solution for you. There are lots of options and the one that is best for you may not necessarily be the one you thought would solve your problems.
- Look into agreeing a payment holiday or freeze in interest and charges for a short time. This option is only offered by certain creditors.
- Work out if you can or should get some debts written off – it will depend on the kind of approach you want to take.
- Help you find out exactly how much debt you owe and to whom by checking your credit file.
- Help you print forms, get guidance notes and respond to court claims made against you.

They offer all of this and much more! It's very much not a 'stop buying coffee and get on with it' kind of help.

HELPING YOURSELF BEFORE YOU GET INTO TROUBLE

As with everything, a solution is better than a cure and that's just as true when it comes to debt.

In this post-pandemic world, debt advisers are overrun. Most people don't realise that Citizens Advice, for example, is a charity full of volunteers. For the last couple of years, debt advisers have only been helping if you've missed more than one payment on your debts and there are new commissioning rules coming that suggest that people only get 20 minutes of money guidance. It's not a lot.

So if you feel yourself slipping into debt, it's more important than ever to know the signs and try to get yourself back on track by talking to your creditors, revisiting your budget and maximising your income.

What do I mean by maximising your income? Here are some quick tips but I'll go into more detail about these later in the book.

- Cut the cost of your shopping (see chapter 10)
- Reduce the cost of your bills (see chapter 11)
- Earn some extra money (see chapter eight)
- Claim all the benefits you're entitled to – don't assume you're not entitled to anything or have everything you could possibly receive.

If you have some debt and feel confident dealing with creditors on your own, you can contact them to ask for help with your repayments in the following ways:

- Negotiate payment holidays
- Reduce payments and extend the amount of time you have to pay
- Ask to switch to a better tariff or deal.

Please don't feel embarrassed – get in contact the second you have a problem. The reality is, it can take people months, or even years, to get debt advice by which time things may have spiralled out of control and the problem will take longer to fix.

The minute you start to see warning signs, you need to start taking action.

ACTIVITY

Got manageable debt? See if you can afford to pay off a bit more each month than you are currently. A little increase every month can make a massive difference to your overall repayment amount.

Have unmanageable debt? Bite the bullet and get some free debt help. You don't have to see someone face to face or even speak to anyone in the beginning – some services offer online chats and WhatsApp options. Do some research into the organisations mentioned in this chapter and choose one that suits your needs, then take that first step.

8 SIDE HUSTLES: WHAT YOU NEED TO KNOW

Are you someone who is side hustling, or considering it? Well, you're far from alone because according to research from 118 118 Money, more than half of employed people have a side business to boost their income. The same research showed that the average side hustle makes £411 a month, which is pretty impressive.

They aren't for everyone, because they do eat into your spare time, but in my personal experience my side hustle completely changed my life for the better. Not only did it diversify my income, so I didn't have to rely on one job for my sole revenue, it's my passion, too.

And you never know, you may find that your side hustle income overtakes what you earn in your main job. It's a great way to try out a new business without risking financial stability.

I beat the wage I was earning in my second year of blogging, and as a bonus, it's been so fun!

WHAT IS A SIDE HUSTLE?

They used to be called a second or third job but today a side hustle is a way to make money alongside your full-time job or studies. Sure, some people do it to make extra money doing something they're passionate about but for a lot of people, it's a necessity. It's hard out there.

Typically, you take a skillset and/or passion of yours and make it profitable. A popular side hustle is selling handmade items on Etsy and other selling sites. At least 75 percent of handmade crafts seem to be those non-biodegradable resin pyramids you see all over TikTok (which, if you happen to make them, I'm sure are amazing. Sorry!). But if you are creative and find your market, the sky is the limit.

For me, I was good at writing and deals-hunting. While I worked full time as an editor, I started a blog where I talked about money in the way I wanted to. This got me paid work writing for newspapers, which then got me a better job because I was spotted doing those other things and, well, here I am writing this book alongside my day job (and a new baby!). You've got my very own side hustle in your hands.

Although it's a lot of extra work, having a side gig is a stress reliever for me. I've spent too many months unemployed and I never want to set foot in a Jobcentre again. There's no shame in it but I still feel stressed and upset about my experiences at the beginning of my career. My blog, and the other work it brought, is my insurance policy and potentially part of my retirement plan, too.

HOW TO CHOOSE A SIDE HUSTLE

They can either be skill-based or generic but the best way to start out is by thinking of the below:

- **Evaluate your skills**
  Are you musical? Artistic? Good with words? Good with social media? Photoshop? Physically fit?

- **What's your passion?**
  What do you love doing and can you find a way to make it profitable? You're going to need to really enjoy whatever you do to give up your valuable spare time after a hard day of work.

- **Consider your time**
  How much time do you have to do this? You don't want to get in trouble at your full-time job or studies because you're eating into that time. Can you dedicate a few hours to it in the evenings or at weekends? Be realistic – if you burn yourself out, it's not going to be sustainable.

TYPES OF SIDE HUSTLES

Something to consider is that nothing is likely to be as easy as it seems and you'll need to keep learning and improving your skills. According to the same 118 118 Money survey, 59 percent of side hustles are artistic. So that's people making jewellery, selling art, pottery, embroidery and so on. As much as you need to be good at the craft itself, when it comes to side hustles, you'll need to also develop skills for other aspects of running a business such as marketing, creating and updating a website, photography, copywriting, customer service...

There are an infinite number of ways to make money on the side (I knew a woman who used to sell stinky shoes to blokes on the internet – whatever floats your boat!). But I'll outline some of the most common below.

1 Start a Blog
It can be very cheap to start up and run. Wordpress lets you set up a website for free but you'll need to find a Wordpress host, which will likely have a tiered payment system. The more traffic you get, the more your hosting costs. That said, it's likely to only be a few quid every month. After you get some traffic, you can make money from adverts and sponsorships. In my first year of having a blog, I was able to completely cover my mortgage payments.

2 Selling or Flipping Items Online
Sell any unwanted items you already have first (check the back of the wardrobe or in the attic) on online reselling platforms. There are a few different options, some of which charge a small commission on the sale. You can also think about flipping, which is where you go to charity shops and car boot sales, buy bargains and sell them online for a profit. It takes time to know what to buy and how much items sell for, so start small and don't invest too much money until you know what you're doing.

3 Upcycling

This is one I keep meaning to do, in fact, I even went on an upholstery course with this in mind! Pick up free or cheap furniture from Facebook Marketplace, Gumtree, even the street, and with some skills you can make them beautiful again to sell on.

4 Dog Walking

There is so much money in this – I couldn't believe what a friend of mine pays a dog walker every week!

5 Transcribing

If you're fast at typing, you can transcribe people's videos and audio into text documents. Sign up to websites such as Fiverr, Take Note and UK Transcription to look for work.

6 Fill in Surveys

It's never been my bag but I know people who do really well filling in surveys. Companies do this to see what the general public think and want. Have you ever seen a stat in some marketing campaign that is like '82 percent of people agree that XYZ'? They might have got those numbers from a survey. Prolific and Swagbucks are big ones, but there are tons out there.

7 Cakes, Bakes and Sweets

You'll need to get yourself a hygiene certificate to do this one (though tons on Facebook Marketplace don't seem to bother!). Making cakes, desserts and sweet bags to deliver in your local area, or even nationwide, can be incredibly profitable. I see small brands advertise these on TikTok all the time. It's free advertising and they can become so popular, they can turn it into a full-time business.

8 **Private Tutor**
Whether it be music, art, science or languages, there's always a demand for tutors. Obviously, you'll need to be good at the skill if you want to teach it, and some people might prefer certain qualifications. Look into joining a tutoring agency if you've still got your grade eight piano music memorised!

9 **Paid Instagram Ads**
If you've got a decent following on Instagram, some brands will pay you to promote their products – or at least give you freebies! It's always worth politely reaching out to marketing or press contacts of brands you'd like to work with and ask to collaborate. You could also apply to an affiliate scheme, such as Affiliate Window, Skimlinks or Amazon Affiliates, where you can direct your followers to products via a special link and make a small percentage from items they purchase.

MULTI-LEVEL MARKETING SCHEMES

You might have noticed I've not included any multi-level marketing schemes (MLMs) in the above list. They are companies with a sales structure where members need to recruit other members into their downline to make money, as well as sell products. I'm going to give it to you straight – I think they're a load of old shit and, personally, wouldn't touch them with a 10-foot barge pole.

You might recognise this scenario; you're minding your own business, stalking your ex's new girlfriend's pics on Instagram when suddenly you get a DM from Becky who you were friends with in high school and haven't spoken to in 12 years.

'Hi hun! I know this is random, but I was just looking at your page and thought you would make a great addition to my team. I make tons of £££ working completely from home! Would you be interested in hearing more?'

Making loads of cash from home sounds pretty amazing, right? Nah.

MLM huns – multi-level marketing is never the way to make money, but a pretty good guarantee you'll lose some (along with friends, family and your dignity).

WHAT IS A MULTI-LEVEL MARKETING SCHEME?

Multi-level marketing schemes are companies where distributors do not receive a salary but instead earn money from selling products to people they know. The distributors sign up new recruits who in turn sign people up to the scheme. This continues down multiple levels, hence the name multi-level marketing. Big MLMs you might have heard about include Younique, Herbalife, Avon, The Body Shop, Ann Summers, Usborne, Scentsy. You've likely seen them a lot on Facebook.

As a distributor, the people you recruit to 'your team' are known as your 'downline'. You'll get a commission from the initial investment they had to pay in order to join the MLM. You'll also make money on everything they sell and when they recruit someone, you'll make money on what they sell, too. And so on. The aim is to get as many people in your downline as possible.

You might be thinking, 'Lotty, sounds like a pyramid scheme to me.' And I'd say, 'Sure, the few people at the very top make money while everyone below hires more and more competitors, oversaturating the market in their local area and earning increasingly tiny amounts as each level recruits another, bigger level. Seems to be structured like a giant triangle, right? Maybe even a pyramid? But no, as there are products changing hands, MLMs are not technically pyramid schemes.'

Nine times out of 10, to be a part of an MLM, you'll have to bulk buy products as well as purchasing a training or starter pack. After all, you need something to sell. I have a friend who used to sell Younique products and she told me how she was always encouraged to buy more and more new releases. When she left, she had a ton of expensive stock left over, which she had to sell for a cut price.

Research from the Consumer Awareness Institute, who researched 350 different MLMs, revealed a shocking statistic – 99 percent of people who join the schemes lose money. That means there's not a 1 percent chance of getting rich, there's a 1 percent chance of not losing money. Fuck that.

These businesses often ruin friendships and relationships, cause people to incur a huge amount of debt, and only a tiny amount of 'employees' ever achieve success. To me, that's exploitation.

THE MONEY BIT

Under the government's Trading Allowance, you can earn up to £1,000 from your side hustle (or hustles – it's £1,000 in total across any extra earnings) each tax year without needing to register with HMRC to declare it. You can simply pocket the cash.

If you earn above £1,000 you need to let HMRC know you are earning money as a self-employed person within three months or you could face a £100 fine. You will need to fill in a tax return to declare your earnings. You'll also be required to pay National Insurance on any earnings directly to HMRC. This is important as it will mean you'll be entitled to benefits, such as the State Pension and maternity pay. Check out chapter 12 for more detail on this.

There are three main ways of structuring your own business:

- Sole trader
- Limited company
- Partnership.

There are pros and cons for each option depending on your personal circumstances and business needs. If you're only earning a few hundred quid every month, most people find it best to be a sole trader (commonly called self-employed) but you'll have to do your research and it's always worth speaking to an accountant or lawyer for some advice.

If your side hustle is rocking it and has a taxable turnover of £85,000 or more (go you!), you'll need to register for VAT. This means you'll need to charge VAT on any goods and services you supply but also means you can claim back VAT you pay for goods or services relating to your business. If you get to this point, it's probably worth getting an accountant.

DO YOU NEED AN ACCOUNTANT?

This isn't cut and dried, it all depends on both you and your business. If your situation is relatively simple, you're organised with your records and bookkeeping, confident with numbers and know the rules for doing a tax return (you can get these from the HMRC website), you might want to do your own accounts.

For me, the idea of doing my own accounts is a nightmare. As long as my accountant can save me more than I pay them, I'll use one. My accountant will also give me business advice, which can be useful.

I chose mine because he was a friend of my boyfriend at university so I knew he would look after me. However, if you don't have a personal recommendation, it makes sense to pick one that specialises in your trade and works with smaller clients.

Make sure they are a member of a recognised accountancy body, such as the Institute of Chartered Accountants in England and Wales (ICAEW) or the Association of Chartered Certified Accountants (ACCA). They don't have to be local to your area, as most will just communicate with you online and over the phone, rather than needing to meet you face to face.

BUSINESS INSURANCE

If you're running your own business, it's important to be insured – it doesn't cost much. You may not be raking in millions with your side hustle yet but you still need to protect yourself from the unexpected.

The truth is, you can be sued for just about anything and even if you're in the right, it will cost you time and money. So get protected.

ACTIVITY

If you've got an idea for a side hustle, put together a simple business plan for the next three months. Get a calendar and put in some goals and targets for your business, then write down the steps you need to complete to achieve each goal. There are loads of cheap workbooks and planners you can purchase if that would help motivate and organise your thoughts.

As exciting as it is to start a new business, try to limit your start-up costs to a few quid, or ideally nothing. You don't want to invest loads of money into something in the beginning until you feel confident that it will work out, and that you can stick with it.

9 MAKE YOUR MONEY WORK FOR YOU

Picture it: you're on the phone in The Wolf of Wall Street. You've got $50,000 in shares in a big pharmaceutical company and you need out. You're screaming 'sell, sell, sell!' down a giant 1980s phone while your colleagues are doing tequila shots. Well, I've got news for you, investing is not like that. At all.

Growing up, I thought investing was only for rich blokes in fancy suits but it's really accessible to everyone these days. With a bit of know-how and spare cash, you could potentially make a decent profit.

First things first – there are no guarantees when it comes to investing. Never invest more than you can afford. All investments come with a risk, which means the value of your investments can go down as well as up, so you might get out less than you put in.

WHAT IS INVESTING?

Very simply, investing is when you buy something that you think you'll be able to sell at a higher price later on.

In this chapter I'm going to discuss investing in the stock market, but investing can take many forms, including:

- Gold
- Wine
- Art
- Vintage cars
- Designer bags
- Beanie Babies from the 90s.

One of the above options might float your boat, though more traditional ways to invest would be with funds, bonds, shares, government bonds and getting on the property ladder.

The big reason people invest is because interest rates offered by banks and building societies on your savings are generally pretty low. This means the interest made on your savings is unlikely to beat inflation so your money becomes less valuable as the years tick on. But if you invest the money, and it goes well, you can match or exceed the inflation rate.

If you decide to try investing, the rule of thumb is to do it long term. The longer your money is working for you, five years or more, the more likely it will grow and withstand the ups and downs of the market.

The Eighth Wonder of the World

A big reason to leave money invested for as long as possible is because of a thing called 'compound interest', also known as 'snowballing' (which I discovered is also something VERY different on Urban Dictionary), or the Eighth Wonder of the World, according to Albert Einstein. This is, of course, dependent on the thing you're investing in earning interest as not everything does.

Picture a snowball – that's your money. You roll it down a snow-covered hill and the longer it rolls, the bigger the ball becomes. As the ball gets bigger it has a larger surface area so is able to pick up even more snow, and so on. The longer it rolls, the more your snowball can keep on growing.

So, in theory, the longer you can give an investment to grow, the better – your interest starts earning interest and you have yourself the snowball effect.

And that's some rich people shit right there. Money you're getting 'for free' (the interest), making more money on an exponential scale. That's one of the ways the rich keep getting richer (ignoring the family money bit).

GET-RICH-QUICK SCHEMES

Please, please, please be careful about where you get your advice. In fact, let me break down what 'advice' even is because it means something different when it comes to money.

Unless you have certain qualifications, you are not allowed to use the word *advice* when connected to money unless you want the FCA knocking on the door.

So when a 19-year-old crypto-bro on TikTok is telling you what to invest your money in, you really need to stop and think if it's actually good advice. Most of the time, they are making an affiliate income (they get paid by the company for introducing you to them) by getting you to invest your money in certain places.

One of the newest ways people think they can make money quickly is by investing in cryptocurrencies, which are digital currencies you can buy goods with or trade for profit. Bitcoin is probably the most well-known cryptocurrency but people can create their own currencies, such as Dogecoin. In order to buy cryptocurrency you need actual, real-life money. They're not a get-rich-quick scheme as such, though you can get very rich quickly, but you can also lose everything just as quickly. Investing in crypto is very volatile and you need to be careful.

If you do decide to invest in Bitcoin, or any other cryptocurrency, firstly make sure that you are prepared to lose every penny. It might go well for you, or it might not. Secondly, be careful because there are a lot of crypto-scammers out there. In fact, a lot of high street banks will no longer let you connect your bank account to a crypto platform because of the high risk of fraud. My card was rejected and blocked when I tried to attach my TSB account to Coinbase, a popular cryptocurrency exchange. Make sure you do your research and are buying it from a reputable source. Coinbase allows you to create a wallet (where your money sits until you want to spend it) as well as buy and sell Bitcoin and other cryptocurrencies.

STOCKS AND SHARES ISAS

I bloody love my stocks and shares ISA. It's how I personally invest by putting £100 a month into a fund and watching it grow steadily over the years. I call it my 'last resort' money. It's my money that I refuse to touch until I'm old or something goes very wrong.

If you're thinking about getting into investing, you should consider starting out with a stocks and shares ISA. You get to choose a fund (see page 117), decide on your risk level and potential growth. But because it's all wrapped up in the ISA, which if you remember from chapter three means the money is tax-free, you don't have to pay on any gains. You can put in up to £20,000 every year as part of your tax-free allowance. Though remember that your allowance applies to the total amount you can save across different types of ISA in one year. So if you save £1,000 in a cash ISA, you can only save up to £19,000 in your stocks and shares ISA.

If you invest outside of a stocks and shares ISA, you may have to pay Capital Gains Tax. When you sell (known as 'disposing of') shares, any profit you have made is subject to tax. Everyone has a Capital Gains tax-free allowance, currently £12,300, and anything over this amount will be subject to Capital Gains Tax.

If you're 39 or under, you can also open a variation of a stocks and shares ISA called a Lifetime ISA (LISA) where the government adds a bonus of 25 percent to your account. Check out chapter 13 for a more in-depth explanation of a LISA.

INVESTING IN STOCKS AND SHARES

When most people think about investing, they think about putting their money into the stock market. A good first step for investing is the stocks and shares ISA, as we've discussed, but there are other ways – it depends how you want to manage your portfolio.

What Is a Share?

In its most basic sense, a share is a share of a company. You can potentially buy shares for a certain price, from the stock market. Once you own a share, you become a shareholder meaning you own a portion of the company.

Companies issue shares to raise money for their business and investors buy shares because they believe the company will do well and want to benefit from its success when the share price rises. Think *Dragon's Den*.

There may only be two or three shareholders in a business, or there could be billions of people with shares (like with Apple and Facebook). There's no restriction to how many a company can have. Companies sometimes increase the number of shares by splitting their stock in order to attract more investors.

Once you own a share, you can do whatever you like with it. You can keep hold of it for years, by which point it will hopefully be worth more than what you bought it for, or you can sell it to someone else on the stock market.

The value of your share will change constantly and can be worth more one day, then less the next. The value of shares all depends on how the market and the company are doing. For example, when the pandemic hit, if you had a share in a company that produced face masks, the value of your share would have shot up. When fewer people started to use them, the value will have gone down.

There are two ways to make money from investing – the first one is from selling your share. In the face mask example above, you might have decided to sell your share in the company at the height of the pandemic when the value of each share had risen. Assuming you bought your share for a good price, you would hopefully have made a good profit.

The other way to make money is through dividends. If the company makes a profit, it might decide to give some of the profit back to its shareholders. This could be on a regular basis or as a one-off payment. Everyone has a dividends allowance each year, which means the first £2,000 you receive is tax-free. Above that, you pay dividend tax, which is based on your income and tax band. Be aware that companies are not obliged to pay out dividends and just because they paid one year, they may not the next, or it may be a much smaller or larger amount.

What Is the Stock Market?
The stock market is a place where you can buy and sell shares, along with other things such as stocks and bonds.

A lot of countries have one or more stock markets. The important ones you've probably heard of are the London Stock Exchange (LSE), the New York Stock Exchange and the Tokyo Stock

Exchange. If you're investing in the stock market, you don't actually have to go anywhere to do it. Most people will use a website or app, called a platform, to invest.

People think you need to have a lot of money to invest in the stock market but that is not the case at all. Most fund managers will let you invest from £25 a month. In fact, the general rule of thumb is to not put big chunks of money in, but to drip feed small amounts, which is called 'pound cost averaging'. This way, you protect yourself somewhat from bad months where the market is falling.

What Is a Fund?

A fund is a collection of shares (or stocks and bonds), which is managed by an expert known as a fund manager.

You can, of course, invest in individual shares yourself but you need to be up to the research when it comes to choosing what to buy, have money to potentially lose and feel confident in the processes. If you're not sure, investing in funds is a simpler option.

They work by giving your cash to a fund manager who will pool it together with other investors just like you. They then use the pooled money to buy a larger number of shares in the stock market.

Funds can invest in almost anything. Ethical investing is a popular choice at the moment because not only can you potentially make a profit, you also protect your principles. A lot of people don't know the specifics of the funds they pay into and might be horrified to know that they are supporting companies that don't match up with their morals. Some common areas are arms, fossil fuels, gambling, deforestation and tobacco.

All funds have a theme. If you want, you can specify what sort of funds you are happy to invest in, for example green or ethical funds, places such as the US or emerging markets like China and India. You can also choose a fund that tracks the market for you – more on this opposite.

BUT HOW DO YOU ACTUALLY BUY SHARES?

Let's get to the nitty gritty – you want to buy some shares, how do you go about it? Well, the cheapest and most convenient way to buy a share is to do it via a website or app platform. There are a ton of platforms out there, but some reputable ones include:

- Nutmeg
- Evestor
- Vanguard
- Fidelity
- AJ Bell Youinvest
- Hargreaves Lansdown.

So how do you choose a platform? The big thing to consider is cost but you should also think about customer service and ease of use.

When it comes to costs, things to look out for include set-up charges, an annual account charge, a dealing charge (the cost for when you buy a share) and exit charges (the cost for when you sell a share). Each platform will have different costs and you need to account for all of these when deciding which platform is right for you and your intended investments.

THE TLDR VERSION

Here are three different ways you can invest in shares, from simplest to most complicated:

1   **Index Tracker Fund**
You can buy a fund called an index tracker that essentially follows the market up and down. You don't need to worry about deciding what to buy because in this approach, the fund buys a little bit of everything in proportion to its value on the market. You can buy index tracker funds that follow global markets like the FTSE 100 (Financial Times Stock Exchange). These funds are a good option for those starting out in investing because they are often low cost and the risk is spread out across the market.

2   **Active Funds**
Here, a fund manager (someone who manages your investments on your behalf) will pick and choose individual stocks and shares on your behalf. You can specify what sort of areas you do or don't want to invest in and what risk you are willing to take.

3   **DIY**
You research the companies you want to invest in and buy the shares directly via a stockbroker. If you choose this option, you need to be prepared to keep an eye on the value of your shares and manage them yourself.

Don't Ignore Your Pension

It's not sexy, but if you have spare cash to invest, consider using some of it to take advantage of the ultra-generous tax breaks that come with pension contributions. Check out chapter five for more info.

Don't think you should be investing just for the sake of it though. The whole point of investing is to fund the longer-term goals in your life. How much money do you need to meet your goals and how long do you have to achieve the amount? Remember that investing is always a risk so you shouldn't rely on this money for anything you really need.

ACTIVITY

I've mentioned that compound interest is the Eighth Wonder of the World, so let's test out just how wonderful it can be with a quick bit of maths.

I want you to see how long it would take you to make a million pounds from only putting a small fraction of that in savings. Compound interest is going to do all the heavy lifting here.

A savings calculator works here (I use the MoneyHelper online calculator) so you can play with your goals, age and interest rate. I chose a 5 percent interest rate as I thought that was a fair average spanning decades.

Here's what I worked out:

- If I want to save up a million pounds by saving £150 per month, assuming a 5 percent interest rate, it would take me 68 years and 5 months.

- My actual deposits would only have to be £123,150 – meaning I had earned a whopping £876,850 in interest! £876,850 in free money!

I don't want you to be put off by the £150 figure if you can't afford it right now. This is the average over decades. The most important thing you can do is start saving, even if it's just £20 a month. The odds are that in 10 or 20 years' time, you can save more to get the average up.

Use a savings calculator and play around with amounts and hopefully you'll be inspired to get cracking. I told you compound interest is *chef's kiss*.

10 SHOP LIKE A PRO

My first ever job title was literally bargain hunter at Money Saving Expert (if we're not counting the Maccy D months). I spent my days searching for shopping deals and then when I found one, I'd try to maximise the discount in some way. I loved it, but unfortunately, I usually ended up spending my wage on the things I found. It's fair to say my house was filled with junk at one point.

I then started a blog based around luxury on a budget because I was never tight. In fact, I hate it when people are tight arses – you won't catch me missing a round at the pub because no one likes that person! I like to eat out in the best restaurants, stay in five-star hotels and buy designer bags. I'm just smart about it – very smart.

I could write a whole book about how to save money on shopping but to keep it to just one chapter, I'm going to tell you about some of the easiest ones.

CASHBACK SITES

Cashback sites are my favourite way to make money by a long shot. By shopping as usual, I've made nearly £1,500 with my Quidco account and it requires practically zero effort.

To understand how it works (and how a lot of other money schemes operate), you have to understand affiliate income. It's how I make money with my blog. Let's say that I found a good deal on a pair of shoes. I tell my audience about these shoes and if they buy them through a special tracked link, I'll get a small percentage of the retail value of those shoes as an incentive for telling people about them.

Cashback sites work in a similar way but instead of keeping the money, they'll split it with you. It's not just brands you never shop at though, there are thousands of retailers included, pretty much every major company in the UK. Depending how much you're spending, you can earn a few pennies to over £100 in one transaction.

For example, if you're buying a pair of trousers for £30, you might get 5 percent cashback, so that would be £1.50 in your account. Buying broadband or a phone contract? It's very common to nab over £100 in cashback.

Once your cashback has been tracked and confirmed, which can take between a few weeks to a few months, there are several options to withdraw. The money can be transferred straight into your bank account or you receive gift vouchers for places like Amazon, Tesco, Argos or the Eurotunnel. By choosing a gift card, you'll get a bonus on top.

So, for example, if I had £100 to withdraw from my Quidco account, it would just be £100 if I got the cash, but because Virgin Experience Days are offering a 25 percent bonus, if I withdraw via vouchers with them, they will be worth £125.

Here are a few more examples – at the time of writing Primark offer 6 percent, Footlocker 10 percent, iTunes 6 percent and Just Eat 7 percent, but of course the offers change all the time.

You shouldn't pay to use a cashback site, the best ones are free to use. My top two sites are:

- Quidco (my personal favourite)
- TopCashback.

Some companies also provide additional offers linked to using your card. This means you can get cashback in store, as well as online. If the deals don't come directly from your bank or credit card provider, you'll need to enter your card details so they can see where you shop and when you're eligible for cashback. You usually have to opt in for different brand deals but if you check about once a month you can just forget about it and watch the cashback roll in.

At the time of writing, some of the best card-linked cashback is offered by:

- Airtime Rewards
- Nectar Connect
- Quidco High Street and TopCashback In-Store Offers
- Halifax Cashback Extras
- Amex Offers from American Express

- NatWest MyRewards
- Santander Retailer Offers
- Lloyds Everyday Offers.

You need to think of cashback as a bonus, not a guarantee. So don't buy anything purely because of the potential cashback – think of it as the cherry on top of the cake.

A quick tip when it comes to cashback – don't let the money build up too much in your account because it's not yours until it's sitting in your bank account and it's not protected should the company go bust.

DEALS SITES

I love a deals site. I'm not talking Groupon and the likes, which I don't really rate very highly (for products anyway – experiences, restaurants and spa breaks can have good deals) but websites such as Hot UK Deals (HUKD), Money Saving Expert and LatestDeals. co.uk. I also recommend Facebook groups where these deals sites tend to take their information from, such as Luxury on a Budget, Skint Dad Deals Group and Latest Free Stuff and Competitions UK. I'd also shout out HolidayPirates who are amazing. They specialise in travel deals, including hotel, flight and package holidays.

The community-led sites are the best. The thing about a brand doing it is that inevitably they'll start thinking about the money they can make from affiliate links, rather than if it's actually a good deal.

Random people in the community highlighting something that is a good deal when they have no skin in the game? That's where you'll get the incredible bargains. The king of this is Hot UK Deals, which, incidentally, is run by the same company as Quidco.

I love sites like this for checking if things are a deal especially for tech items. If I'm looking for a new phone, I'll scroll through HUKD to see what 'has heat' (which means it's been voted as a good deal a lot, so it's 'hot') and check out the comments. The people in that forum know what they are talking about.

Facebook groups are a great place to pick up niche items. Whether you're after luxury products, baby clothes or even a car, you'll likely be able to find what you're looking for – there are groups for almost everything.

CAMELCAMELCAMEL

If you shop at Amazon, get acquainted with the brilliant (and free to use), CamelCamelCamel. It's a website that lets you check the historical prices of items that are sold on Amazon.

Amazon pricing is pretty shady at times, with dubious recommended retail prices (RRPs) and discounts that aren't really discounts. CamelCamelCamel lets you see if you're actually getting a bargain.

If you want to check the historical pricing of an item on Amazon, you copy the URL of the item and enter it into the search bar on

CamelCamelCamel. You'll be given the pricing history for that item, which will go back at least 12 months, and longer in some cases. It's displayed in a chart form, so you can see if the item is currently a decent price or if you should wait.

Once you know the cheapest the item has ever been, you can set yourself an alert on Amazon to get an email when it drops to that price again. It's how I used to find deals when I worked at Money Saving Expert.

If you're buying certain stuff for birthdays or Christmas, stick in the items to see what a good deal is then set up an alert so you can buy throughout the year. Need to buy it right now? Try Idealo for price comparison across many different companies.

VOUCHER SITES

I can't buy anything without a discount code. I just can't bring myself to do it. Typically, there's going to be one out there that will knock off 10 percent if you look hard enough. The first place to look is a voucher code site. The biggies include:

- VoucherCodes
- VoucherCloud
- HUKD
- LatestDeals.

They make their money through affiliate marketing (as explained earlier), so when you click a link on a voucher code site and buy something, the voucher site earns a percentage of the money you spend as a thank you for directing your custom.

Let's say I want to buy some shoes from Nike. I literally put 'Nike discount code' into Google and see what comes up – it takes two minutes. There are usually a lot of rubbish sites that pop up on the first page where the links don't work, but stick to the big ones I mentioned and the odds of a discount are more likely.

A newer development is to use voucher code browser extensions. These usually only work through Chrome on a desktop, but once you add them, they'll pop up with a message when you get to the checkout. Click on the pop-up and it will automatically test out the codes it has to see if any work on your basket.

DealFinder by VoucherCodes is the best one I've found for the UK, as some of the American ones have a lot of inactive codes. Pouch, Honey and Karma are some of the other big names on the scene and I expect they'll catch up soon. They do all the work of trawling Google for a valid code for you in just one click.

CLAIM LOYALTY POINTS WHEN YOU SHOP

They say (well, I say many times in this book) that loyalty doesn't pay. But in this one specific case, it kind of does. Sometimes.

If you are going to shop somewhere anyway then signing up to a loyalty programme is a no-brainer. You might as well rack up those points. Loyalty programmes typically use apps or a points card, which exist to encourage you to come back to the store and, well, be loyal.

A loyalty programme might give you:

- Shopping rewards or cashback
- Points that can be redeemed
- Free gifts and early access to products or events
- Free shipping
- Special offers on your birthday.

My favourite loyalty programmes are the Boots Advantage card, Lidl app and Tesco Clubcard. Every loyalty programme is different but if they are free and save you money, you may as well sign up.

You don't have to have a wallet bursting at the seams either. Some offer an app for your phone, or there are specific apps that let you scan a digital version of your loyalty card. Keep hold of the physical card, though, as you'll need it to actually redeem the rewards. Apple Wallet and Google Pay will also let you add loyalty cards to your virtual wallet. I also like the Stocard app, which lets you store all your loyalty cards in one place, including ones from small independent stores.

FREE EVENTS

Sign up to Showfilmfirst – trust me. It's free to sign up and with it, I've been to West End shows, gigs and the cinema, all for free, while the people around me paid full price.

So why would venues give away free tickets? Well, it's not a good look to have a load of empty seats in the audience. Venues will sometimes charge you a couple of quid to secure your tickets because they've found people just wouldn't turn up if they hadn't paid anything. The tickets go quickly though, so don't hesitate for a second if you're interested.

EBAY BRAND OUTLETS

This is such a nice little trick, especially because no one seems to know about it. But did you know that some massive brands have official eBay outlets? Stores include:

- Footasylum
- Dyson
- Trespass
- Joules
- Oliver Bonas
- Jack Wills
- River Island
- Superdry
and a ton more.

Items are up to 70 percent off what you'd pay in store, though the items are typically sale items, old stock and so on. On top of that, eBay have semi-regular discount codes to use in these stores. If I have my eye on something, I'll wait until a 10–20 percent discount code comes along and bag myself a massive bargain.

USING A CREDIT CARD: YOUR RIGHTS

If you're buying something that costs more than £100, it can be a good idea to pay with your credit card (even if it's a partial payment of 50p) because that means you will be protected under Section 75 of the Consumer Credit Act. Sounds boring, but it's really good.

When you pay for anything with a credit card, you're not instantly spending your own money. The credit card company is making the payment and you will pay them back later. What's good about this is that if something were to go wrong, like your payment details get hacked, it's the credit card company's money at risk, not yours.

It's the same if something you buy on your credit card doesn't turn up or breaks sooner than it should. If the brand won't sort it or give you a refund, under Section 75 your credit card provider is legally obligated to act for you.

And I know what you're thinking: 'Sure, but I'm not taking ASOS to court because they won't give me a refund, am I?' Well, you don't have to. I use this protection all the time. Usually there will be a form to fill in on your credit card company's website and, in my experience, nine times out of 10 the company will change its mind and your problem gets sorted.

CHARGEBACK

If you didn't use a credit card to purchase the item you want a refund on and used a debit card instead, you could try chargeback. It isn't as good as Section 75 but it's better than nothing. It's not legal protection but it's a voluntary scheme that American Express, Mastercard, Maestro and Visa have agreed to.

You can claim for a refund if you purchased the goods with a debit, credit or prepaid card. If you did pay for the item with a credit card, Section 75 is likely to be a better option for you.

If the place you've bought from isn't playing ball and won't give you a refund, you can use chargeback in cases where your item(s) hasn't arrived, it's damaged, different from the description or where the merchant has ceased trading.

You'll need to fill out a chargeback form, which will be on your bank's website. However, unlike using Section 75 under a credit card purchase, there are no guarantees as there's no legal obligation.

ACTIVITY

Have a look at the cashback sites and choose one to sign up to now – it's really quick. Then, every time you shop for something online you'll be earning cashback on eligible items.

If you want to go further, try one month of not purchasing anything unless you can find a deal or voucher code to use with the purchase. Once you've started, you won't want to go back to paying full price again!

11 BILLS, BILLS, BILLS

I don't know about you, but I sometimes feel like dealing with my bills is worse than actually having to pay them. It can feel like a lot of work to make sure you've set your Direct Debit up correctly, you're not overpaying or underpaying, that you remember to switch when you come to the end of your contract... the list goes on and on.

I know I have been guilty in the past of ignoring emails telling me to sign into my account to view my bill, or thrown the letters on the kitchen counter to deal with later then watch them pile up with the junk mail.

Bills can be a never-ending battle but they're so much worse if you're not organised. What you don't want is to be paying too much unnecessarily, or find you accidentally miss a payment, which could really hurt your credit score.

BILLS YOU'RE PROBABLY PAYING

There's a seemingly endless list of bills you're likely paying every month or year but there will be some big ones most of us have to deal with. Let's run through them quickly.

Council Tax

This is money that is paid to your local council. It funds local services, such as schools, rubbish collection, road maintenance, parks, libraries, the police and fire services, and so on.

The amount of Council Tax you pay depends on a lot of things, including your Council Tax band (calculated based on the value of your property at a specific point in time. It's a bit of a weird way to do it, in my opinion, but there you go) and the size of your house.

If you're a student, care giver or looking after someone not in the family, you might not have to pay council tax at all. If you live on your own, you should be entitled to a 25 percent reduction.

If you have to live in a larger house because you, or someone you live with, has a disability then you can ask to move to a cheaper band. You can also apply for a Council Tax Reduction from your local council if you are on a low income.

Whatever you pay, be aware that if you miss a bill, the council do not mess about. It's a priority debt, which means they'll throw everything they have at you to get the money back, including legal action, sending bailiffs and, worst-case scenario, prison. For more info on priority bills, refer back to chapter seven.

Utility Bills

When people talk about utility bills, they mean gas, electricity and water.

What's good about these bills is that you have some degree of control over the costs. In this chapter I'm going to sound like a broken record nagging you to switch providers but it's the quickest way you're going to be able to knock £100s off your bill by finding a cheaper deal. There are a few ways to do this:

- Call your current provider and ask for a better deal. It might seem too easy but you'd be surprised how often it works.

- Get on a comparison website, such as MoneySuperMarket, Compare the Market or USwitch. They do all the hard work for you by comparing tariffs. It only takes 10 minutes to see all the best deals out there.

- Join a switching club. These clubs mean you're automatically switched to a cheaper deal when one comes along, without you having to do anything. Money Saving Expert set up the original with its Cheap Energy Club, but of course there are others out there, including Look After My Bills.

Most people will pay for their energy bills directly, but some will have a prepayment meter physically in the home. If you have a meter, that determines how you pay, but it is possible to change these by contacting your landlord and/or energy company.

If your property runs on a prepayment meter, you need to top the money up by taking your gas and electricity card to a shop or topping it up online (you 'pre-pay' to use, hence the name) while with a Direct Debit, you pay after you've used it. Prepayment is typically much more expensive, so if you can switch, do so ASAP. If you rent, speak to your landlord because you might need permission. This has just unlocked a memory of running to the shop with a fiver when all the 'leccy went out as a kid!

If you're on a standard meter your energy provider will estimate the amount of gas and/or electricity you will use over a year and charge you a set amount each month, though you can choose to pay quarterly. The payments are spread out through the year so you're not faced with big bills in winter when you're likely to be using more energy. It's important to send regular meter readings to your supplier so they can adjust the amount you're paying depending on your usage. If you have a couple of months where you use less energy, you can end up with credit on your account, which can be taken off future bills. If you really want to keep track of your usage, ask for a smart meter so you can keep on top of your consumption. That way you will avoid any unexpected bills.

The amount you spend on your utility bills will of course depend on how much you use. Do you like to bask in 30-degree heat in the winter and wash your clothes every other day? That's going to rack up. On the other hand, if you find yourself turning into your dad and turning off lights in unused rooms moaning that 'it's not Blackpool Illuminations in here', then you're cutting your costs.

Unlike gas and electricity, you cannot choose your water provider because, well, there's probably only one reservoir by you. The way water bills are calculated depends on whether you have a meter installed. If you don't have a meter the company will charge based on your home's 'rateable' value. That means you can use as much or as little water as you like and your bill will be the same price. If you have a water meter, you'll be billed for the amount you use. This option means you have some control over how much your bill will be but if you know you use a lot of water, you might be better off unmetered.

Internet, TV and Phone Bills

If you want the internet, you're probably going to have to pay for line rental, which costs £12 to £20 a month on top of your broadband package. This is the cost of maintaining the lines for the broadband network (it used to be so you could make calls from a house phone).

If you're happy to not have a landline phone, you might be able to get a package without this cost if there's the required infrastructure in your area – for example, full fibre, also known as fibre-to-the-premises (FTTP). With this option, you can still have a house phone, but it requires the internet so if your broadband goes down, it won't work. There are sites online that will show if you could get FTTP.

On top of line rental, you pay for a television and/or internet package. The cost of your package will depend on a number of factors such as if you want certain digital or satellite channels, internet speed and data allowance.

Always keep a note in your calendar when your contract ends because your provider will usually swap you to a considerably more expensive rate and you won't get faster internet or more data for your money. As with your utility bills, you can either speak to your current provider and try to get switched to a better deal, or shop around for offers from other providers.

If you have older relatives, or know anyone who might benefit from help with bills, you could help them out with switching. My parents were with Virgin for about 10 years and never switched. It wasn't until I moved back in with them for a while that I realised they were being charged £60 a month for basic TV and slow-ass internet. I've never called customer service quicker!

The same is true when it comes to mobile phone contracts. If you're coming to the end of your contract or it has ended, the first step is to benchmark prices elsewhere. Then call up your provider and say you're leaving if they don't offer something better – don't waste your time with the generic customer service team, you want to be chatting to the retention team (they often call themselves the disconnections department). It's their job to keep you as a customer and they are the ones who can offer better deals.

The thing that's going to radically impact the cost of your contract is whether it comes with a new handset or not. If yours is fine (or you can buy a cheaper new one up front), then ask to move to a SIM-only plan. This will save you a fortune.

Oh, and don't say yes to the first offer – play hardball. They've usually got something else they can pull out of the bag, especially if you are firm about leaving.

When it comes to most service providers, loyalty doesn't pay – in fact, you'll be the one paying!

TV Licence and Streaming Services

You need a TV licence to watch or record live TV on any channel, or to download or watch programmes on the BBC iPlayer. It doesn't matter how you watch it – on a TV, phone or computer – it's the law.

The cost of a TV licence can either be paid in full or spread over the year by paying in monthly or quarterly instalments. If you're a student, you can be covered by the licence at your parents' address as long as the device you're watching on has its own internal batteries, such as a tablet or a mobile phone. Note, this loophole doesn't cover laptops.

If you don't watch any live TV, or use the BBC iPlayer (and by that, I mean any, ever), you don't need to pay for a TV licence and can just watch other streaming services. If you go down this route, you can still access all the usual options, such as:

- Netflix
- YouTube
- Amazon Prime
- Disney+
- NOW
- Non-BBC catch-up services including ITV Player, All4 (anyone else still calling it 4OD?), My5, UKTV Play.

Remember, if you don't pay for a TV licence you can only use catch-up services for on-demand content.

Most streaming services, both for TV and music, can be paid for on a rolling monthly basis, so you can quickly switch between them and save by only paying for them one at a time. It's also good to watch out for any special offers or free trials for new customers. If there's one particular show you're desperate to watch, it might be possible to sign up for a free trial and just binge the whole thing during your trial period!

A lot of the streaming services also let you have multiple users with one paying account. The rules vary but if you can split the cost with housemates that's a way to save.

HOW TO ORGANISE YOUR BILLS

Now that you know what bills you're paying (or will be), here are some little tips and tricks to get them organised.

If You Live in a House Share
If you live in a house with others, you're going to be paying a share of the utility bills. Under no circumstances – and I mean no circumstances, not even a hot housemate asking you – should you get a joint bank account.

You might remember from chapter three that I don't even recommend getting a joint bank account with a life partner, so never mind your housemates. It only takes one person to mess up a payment or go into an unarranged overdraft and your own credit score will be ruined since you're also liable for the mess-up.

The easiest way to deal with shared bills is to use a bill splitting app. This means that everyone knows the total cost of household bills each month and the payment can be taken automatically at a pre-scheduled time.

There are a few out there but good ones include:

- Splitwise
- Tab
- Tricount
- Acasa
- Splid.

Automatic Payments

The easiest way to stay on top of all of your bills is to set up automatic payments as soon as your contract starts. Set up Direct Debits to be paid directly from your bank account every month (or however often your bill is due) so you don't have to worry about remembering when bills have to be paid.

Keep Bills in One Place

You should have a financial centre in your home. It might sound like a fancy term but I don't mean you need to have a whole office, or even a filing cabinet. A simple folder for anything that comes by mail will do and it's useful to also set up a separate folder within your inbox for any email correspondence.

If you're self-employed, or need to keep a record of your bills for accounts or tax purposes, it might be beneficial to scan them in and then either store on a hard drive or upload to a cloud storage system. This will save you from having to keep all the paper copies.

There are also free phone apps that offer this service, or simply take a picture and keep it in a folder on your phone. If you're going to go digital please make sure you have a back up of everything – never keep important documents only on your computer or phone!

Open All Bills

If you're behind on paying bills, or struggling with money, it can be tempting not to open them. You might also just be someone who isn't particularly organised when it comes to paying bills and think you'll get around to it at some point. If you can, open a bill as soon as it comes and put it in your folder to deal with. As mentioned previously, this is when having a Direct Debit set up can be really useful to save you any hassle.

If your mental health is stopping you from dealing with bill payments, ask someone you trust to help you out with bill management, or speak to your bank if you're falling behind.

Help With Paying Bills

If you find you can't afford to pay your bills, there are options out there to help you. First things first, don't assume you're not entitled to any benefits or grants. Check if you are eligible because it can make a massive difference. Some grants include:

- **_Warm Home Discount Scheme_**
  If you're on a low income, you might be entitled to £140 off your electricity bill or a £140 voucher for your prepayment meter. Applications open every autumn and you apply directly to your supplier.

- **_Cold Weather Payments_**
  If you're already receiving income support, income-related employment and support allowance or Universal Credit, you should receive a one-off payment to help you pay for extra heating costs when it's very cold. Each time the temperature drops below a specific point for a set period of time, you'll get

a payment. You don't need to apply for this support – if you're already in receipt of certain benefits it'll be paid automatically. If you meet the criteria and aren't receiving the money, contact the Jobcentre Plus to get the ball rolling.

ACTIVITY

I've got a little challenge for you. Got a bill(s) out of contract? Spend an hour switching and I bet you can save at least £250.

- Pick an out of contract utility to switch.
- Calculate exactly what you're getting or using and how much it costs you a month or over a year.
- Get on the comparison sites, enter your details and see what deals are out there. Money Saving Expert, MoneySuperMarket and ComparetheMarket cover most areas.
- Find the cheapest deal but also consider looking at their customer service reviews. For me, I don't like calling providers to deal with issues so I'll only use providers who will sort out issues through a chat box.
- See what you're going to save and then switch! Picking the deal takes the longest, once you've chosen it's just the click of a button.
- On to the next utility bill!

Consider adding up the total you've saved from switching and set up a direct deposit to a savings account – that way you're earning money from your switch.

12 PAYSLIPS AND TAX CODES

After a tight few weeks, there is nothing sweeter than getting your payslip. You see that nice big number, and bloody hell – how much tax? And what's that payment for, that can't be right? Sound familiar?

The big problem with not understanding how to read your payslip is that there could be a mistake on there that's going to cause you a headache later on. You might even call it a panic a-tax. Thank you very much!

If you're self-employed, the portions of this chapter that cover payslips won't be relevant to you since you don't have an employer. Skip to the tax section and see chapter eight for more information about different ways of structuring your business.

IT'S THE LAW

Unless you've been in a situation where you've needed to provide proof of earnings (and you likely will at some point in your life), you may think that your payslip isn't particularly important. You'd be wrong.

Not only does it have a lot of important information on it, it is also there to protect you. Thanks to the Payment of Wages Act 1991, your employer is legally obligated to make your payslip available to you either on or before the day you're getting paid.

By law, your payslip must contain the following information:

- The total amount you've been paid before compulsory deductions have been made, known as your gross pay
- The amounts of any variable deductions taken from your gross pay and what these deductions are for
- The total amount of any fixed deductions taken from your gross pay – these are deductions that don't change from payday to payday
- The total amount you take home after deductions, known as your net pay
- The method of payment.

Most people now receive a digital payslip rather than a hard copy but it's your employer's right to provide it in any form they wish.

WHAT'S ON YOUR PAYSLIP

1   **Payroll number**
Your payroll, or employee, number, is the number used by your employer to identify you for payroll purposes.

2   **Personal information**
Your name and, usually, home address. If these change, you need to let your HR department know as soon as possible so they can update their records and make sure your payslips are correct.

3   **The date**
The date on your payslip is typically the date that your pay will be transferred to your bank account.

4   **National Insurance (NI) number**
Your National Insurance number is used by HMRC to differentiate you from everyone else in the UK.

You are allocated a National Insurance number when you're 16, or when you move to the UK if you're older than 16. Once you receive it you'll start paying National Insurance contributions on any earnings to build up your entitlement to state benefits, including the State Pension (see chapter five for more information).

5 **Gross pay**
This is the big number. So everything you earn before any taxes or deductions are taken away. Your gross pay will be made up of your Base or Basic pay plus any overtime, bonuses or commissions.

6 **Tax period**
Tax periods are set by HMRC. They always run from the 6th of one month to the 5th of the next month and each tax year always runs from the 6 April to the 5 April the following year.

7 **Tax codes**
Your tax code is set by HMRC and tells your employer how much pay you can receive before they start deducting tax.

If your tax code is wrong, you could end up paying too much or too little tax, so it's really important you check it regularly. The most common time for mistakes to happen is if you've started a new job, especially if you change partway through a tax year.

HMRC should fix the problem but it might be wrong for a month or so. That said, if you've been paying too much, you'll get one of life's little miracles – a tax rebate in the post out of nowhere one day. Or alternatively, if you've been underpaying, you'll get a bill. Ouch!

If you're not sure what tax code you should be on, it's worth visiting the government's website to check your correct tax code.

8 **Tax deductions**
This is the amount of tax that should be deducted based on your tax code and pay level.

9 **National Insurance deductions, also called contributions (NICs)**
National Insurance is deducted from your pay if you are an employee earning more than £184 a week or £797 per month. If you're self-employed you'll pay NI if you're making a profit of £6,515 or above during the tax year.

10 **Pension details**
If you're part of your employer's pension scheme (which is likely thanks to auto-enrolment, see chapter five) the details of this will be shown. Your employer's pension contributions ('ER' = 'employER') will be listed along with your pension contributions ('EE' = 'employEE'), should you pay them.

11 **Pay year to date**
This is how much you've been paid (gross) in the current tax year. It's the biggest number on there and can really make you think 'Damn, where did all that money go?!' It's usually shortened to TD (to date) or YTD (year to date).

12 **Net pay**
The most important figure on your payslip as it tells you the amount that you will take home after all deductions have been made. This is the amount that you'll see in your bank account and what you're going to have to live on until the next payday. It's always worth checking this figure against your bank statement to make sure you've been paid the correct amount.

OTHER DEDUCTIONS FROM YOUR PAYSLIP

Student Loan
After graduating from university and earning a certain amount of money in a job, you'll have to start paying your student loan back, plus interest.

Each month you pay back a percentage of any income over the earning threshold detailed on the repayment plan you are on. So the more you earn, the more you'll pay back.

Other potential deductions:

- **Court orders**
  For things like unpaid fines, debt repayments and child maintenance.

- **Workplace benefits repayments**
  For things like rail season tickets or bike to work schemes.

- **Charity donations**

LET'S CHAT TAX

When you see a salary for a job, sometimes your take-home pay can seem a bit unfair. But every penny you pay in tax and National Insurance contributions goes towards paying for services such as education, healthcare (NHS), policing, culture, the environment and so on. It's what funds the UK – in a way, you're getting that money back in the form of being able to go to hospital and so on.

As I take on freelance work alongside my full-time employment, whenever I do my self-assessment and see my tax bill for the whole year, I seriously consider going to prison for a bit instead of paying up (not that it works like that). Handing over one big lump sum is painful for me but after a few hours of sulking, I remind myself that it's a privilege. The more money I hand over, the better I'm doing and I'm happy to pay towards services that benefit everyone equally.

How You Pay Tax

If you're employed, you'll pay your tax through a system called Pay As You Earn (PAYE). Your employer deducts tax and National Insurance contributions from your wages, along with pension payments, every week or month. You will also have to pay tax on any bonuses or commissions you earn, too.

At the end of the tax year you'll get a form from HMRC called a P60. This details you how much you were paid in total over the year as well as the total amount of tax (and all other deductions such as NI and student loan) you paid.

ON THE MONEY

If you are self-employed, it's a whole other kettle of fish. Rather than paying tax on individual jobs or earnings, you have to do your own taxes via self-assessment. This is something I have to do and I dread it for months because I'm not an organised person.

Since you will have to pay tax in a lump sum, you should set aside money each month to make sure you have enough to cover your tax bill. A good rule of thumb is if you're a standard-rate taxpayer, put 20 percent of your earnings into savings as soon as you're paid. If you're in a higher tax bracket, you'll need to save 40 percent.

If you're organised with your finances and feel confident, you can complete a self-assessment yourself. Or you might want to consider paying an accountant to help with your tax return and accounts in general. You need to make sure the cost of their work is less than the money they'll save you with accountancy magic. See chapter eight for more on whether you need an accountant.

Income Tax Rates and Bands
There are four bands that define how much income tax you need to pay on your earnings. For the 2021/22 financial year, they are:

- **Up to £12,570** — This is the personal allowance level and is tax-free.
- **£12,751 to £50,270** — This is known as the basic rate and is taxed at 20 percent.
- **£50,271 to £150,000** — This is the higher rate and is taxed at 40 percent.
- **Over £150,000** — This is the additional rate and is taxed at 45 percent.

Personal Allowance

When it comes to paying tax, it always amazes me that people don't understand that you don't have to pay tax on everything you earn.

At the time of writing, we're in the 2021/22 tax year so the standard person can earn up to £12,570 without paying a penny in tax – that's your personal allowance. You only start paying tax on anything that you earn over this amount. Note though that you do still pay National Insurance contributions on any earnings under this amount.

Have you ever heard someone say, 'I've been offered a promotion but if I take it I'll be pushed over into the higher tax bracket. Then I'll need to pay 40 percent on all my earnings so I'll actually earn less.' Let me show you how this is a load of rubbish with some quick maths.

Let's say you earn £60,000 a year:

- The first £12,570 is your personal allowance so you don't pay any tax on that amount.
- You'll pay 20 percent tax on £12,571 to £50,270.
  20 percent of £37,700 = **£7,540**
- You'll pay 40 percent tax over £50,270.
  40 percent of £9,730 = **£3,892**
- So your total tax for the year would be **£11,432**.

You don't pay 40 percent of your full salary (which would come to a whopping £24,000!).

These figures are based on the current tax year so are correct at the time of writing. They apply to England, Wales and Northern Ireland, but are different in Scotland as the Scottish government sets its own bands and rates.

SHOULD YOU KEEP YOUR PAYSLIPS?

There's an official answer to this. According to HMRC, you should keep your payslips for as long as 22 months after the end of the relevant tax year. So, for example, if your payslips were issued in the tax year 2020/21, you should keep them until February 2023!

You should also keep your P60s for at least two years, but it's a good idea to keep them for up to six years.

'But why?' you ask. Let me give you some situations in which you'll need them:

- **Mortgage or loan applications**
  The paperwork you'll be asked to provide when applying is next level stressful. They'll want your payslips as proof of income.

- **Tax rebates**
  If you've overpaid throughout the year and need to claim the money back from HMRC.

- **Parental leave**
  You might be asked for payslips to claim for certain benefits, such as Maternity Allowance.

- **Visa applications**
  For some overseas travel and visa applications you may be asked to provide proof of earnings.

- **Queries on past pay**
  It's always easier if you have proof if you ever have questions around tax, student loan payments or pension contributions.

ACTIVITY

Get organised and gather all of your payslips and P60 forms together. It doesn't matter how you keep them – on a hard drive, online, printed out and filed – just make sure you have backups for anything digital.

Try to get as many as you can, with a minimum of 22 months for your payslips and two years for P60s. If you find any are missing, ask your employer or ex-employer(s) to resend them. The sooner you do this, the better, especially if you've moved jobs a few times over the years.

13 BUYING A HOME

Put down your avocado toast because it's time to get on the property ladder!

If only it was that simple. I'm not going to pretend the process is remotely easy or straightforward – it's long, time consuming and you'll need to make a trillion complicated and informed decisions along the way. I've just gone through the process of buying a house myself and I kid you not, I am greyer now than when I started.

Unlike a lot of European countries where it's common to rent your whole life, here in the UK we can be pretty obsessed with homeownership, so it's something a lot of us will try to navigate at some point in our lives.

It's certainly not easy, but if it's something you want to do, there's nothing like the feeling of finally getting those keys to your new home!

A NOTE ON BUYING IN SCOTLAND

Buying in Scotland is different from the rest of the UK. Most homes are sold through a 'blind bidding' system. This means that a seller will ask for offers over or around a minimum price. Homes usually sell for around 5–20 percent over, depending how posh the area is.

A formal offer on a property is put forward by a solicitor, rather than an estate agent. If your offer is accepted, the solicitor will send letters to agree the conditions of sale, known as missives. Once the missives are accepted and terms are agreed, you have a binding contract and if you pull out, can be liable to pay the seller damages.

What a lot of people like about the Scottish system is that you rarely get people 'gazumping' you. This is when a seller accepts your offer for their property but will then let someone with a higher offer come in and 'gazump' you, after the agreement has been made.

WHAT IS A MORTGAGE?

If you want to buy a house, you're going to need a mortgage (unless you win the lottery and are a cash buyer, lucky you!). But what is a mortgage? Very simply, it is a loan you can use to buy a home.

A lender, typically a bank or building society, will check to see if you meet certain eligibility requirements before they will agree to lend you a certain amount of money. There are a whole host of things they will use to determine this but the biggies are a stable and reliable income, a deposit and a decent credit score.

Your lender will also need to know the amount you have offered to pay for the property and will carry out a survey to make sure this is reasonable. This, along with your deposit, will also determine your loan to value (LTV) ratio. The higher the LTV ratio, the more expensive your mortgage's interest rate will be.

When you have a mortgage approved, it is based on the lender giving you a set amount of money that you agree to pay back, with interest, over a period of time. The standard repayment period is usually 25–35 years, although the maximum term is 40 years. It's worth noting that while a longer mortgage term might have lower monthly repayments, it will come at a financial cost thanks to the extra interest accrued. Paying a mortgage over 35 years can add tens of thousands of pounds' interest over the term.

Until you have fully repaid the lender (including all interest), you don't fully own the home. If you stop paying, the lender could potentially take your home, known as repossessing, and sell it to recoup their costs, though this would be the worst-case scenario.

THE MORTGAGE PROCESS

If you are a potential borrower, the first thing you should do is establish how much you are likely going to be able to borrow.

To calculate this, a mortgage lender will carry out an affordability assessment. A multiple of income can be used as a rough guide (usually about four times your salary or combined salaries with a partner) but it's the affordability of the mortgage repayments that will ultimately determine how much a lender will be prepared to loan. This means they will consider other variables including regular spending and outstanding debts.

There are lots of online mortgage calculators that you can use to give you a very rough idea of how much you could borrow, and how much the repayments might cost, such as those found on the MoneyHelper and Which? websites.

Using the Which? mortgage calculator, it suggests that a couple with a combined income of £50,000 could borrow somewhere between £150,000 and £225,000. It also helpfully says that to borrow £225,000 over 25 years with a 3 percent interest rate, they'd have to make monthly repayments of £1066.98.

Once you know what you might be able to borrow and what sort of deposit you will need, you can start to plan ahead. Before you even apply for a mortgage, you'll need to save a deposit and make sure your credit score is good, so let's cover that first.

SAVING FOR A DEPOSIT

This is the aspect that is usually the most difficult for people looking to buy a home, and will likely take the longest to achieve. In an ideal world, you want to save up at least 20 percent of the value of the property you want to buy. The bigger the deposit you can save, the better access you'll have to the best mortgage rates on offer.

Having said that, there are other mortgages available, including a 95 percent mortgage, which means you only need a 5 percent deposit. I'll talk you through different mortgage options later in this chapter but the takeaway here is, the more of a deposit you can save, the more deals will be available to you.

According to the Office of National Statistics (ONS), the average UK house price was a whopping £266,000 in 2021. That would mean you would have to save £53,200 in cash to have a 20 percent deposit. Of course, the average price includes multi-million pound mansions but depending where you live, house prices could even be significantly higher. It's a lot of money to come up with in addition to your usual cost of living.

If you are a first-time buyer, you'll have to save this money from scratch, rather than being able to sell your current property and using the money from that sale to buy a new one. This is where your budgeting and saving skills will have to come into play – refer back to chapters two and four. That said, there are ways to get there as quickly as possible.

Get the Government to Help
I briefly mentioned this in chapter three but this is one I would strongly recommend you look into – you know I love free money! A lifetime ISA (LISA) can be opened by anyone aged 18–39.

You can use a LISA either to help you save for your retirement, or to help save for a deposit on your first home. You can save up to £4,000 each tax year into your LISA and – here's where it gets good – the government will top up your savings by 25 percent each tax year.

This means if you can save £4,000 a year, the government will give you a cash bonus of £1,000! And because it goes by the tax year, if you can deposit £4,000 in March and then £4,000 in April, you'd get a £2,000 bonus in one calendar year.

It gets better. On top of that 25 percent bonus (where else are you going to get that with interest rates as they are!), because it's an ISA, you'll be earning interest on whatever you save, which is tax-free.

There are some rules about the LISA that you need to watch out for. You can only use the LISA to save towards a deposit on a house with a value up to £450,000. As already mentioned, you need to be a first-time buyer, meaning you can't ever have owned a home, or part of a home, however briefly, anywhere in the world.

If you and your partner are both first-time buyers, you can both use a LISA to save but the £450,000 upper limit on property value still applies. There's also a 25 percent penalty applied if you decide to withdraw the money from your LISA for reasons other than buying a home. This more than cancels out the 25 percent government bonus, so you should think carefully before deciding to save this way if you aren't sure you'll meet the criteria.

You need to have a LISA open for a year before you can withdraw your savings without losing the bonus, so put some money in, even if it's just a quid, so it's ready to go when you need it.

Finally, don't forget to tell your solicitor that you're going to use a LISA towards your deposit as they will need to do the paperwork to release the funds in time for your purchase.

If a LISA isn't viable for you, there are other options from the government that could work:

- *Help to Buy Equity Loan*
  This is a loan offered by the government to help people make up the difference in their deposit for a new-build house. With a minimum of a 5 percent deposit based on the property's value, you can borrow up to 20 percent so you can secure a 75 percent mortgage.

- *Help to Buy Shared Ownership*
  This is an option for those who can't afford a big enough deposit, or can't obtain a big enough mortgage, to cover 100 percent of the value of a property. Instead, you can buy a share of the property, usually between 25–75 percent, so you would only need to find a deposit and mortgage to cover that share. However, you then have to pay rent to a landlord on the remaining share, which doesn't go towards paying off the mortgage. See more information on shared ownership later in the chapter.

As with any financial products, you should think carefully about what works best for you. Don't assume that because these are government-backed schemes they will automatically work for you. There are pros and cons with anything and I have heard some horror stories! Consider talking to an impartial expert who can advise you which option works best for your personal circumstances.

Cut Your Rent

Housing is probably going to be your biggest monthly expense, so if you can cut it down, or even better cut it out completely, that's where you will see your biggest savings.

I lived with eight people in a house share in London for about six years while saving up my deposit. It was often incredibly fun but there were also times where I'd come home to a housemate getting it on with a man three times her age on the living room sofa. So you know, swings and roundabouts. It might not be for everyone but it definitely keeps things cheap.

If you have the option, and could bear it, you could consider moving in with your parents for a few years. Being able to live with little to no rent will help you rack up your savings quickly.

Ask Your Family

For many people, the only way they can take that first step is thanks to help from family. It can be an awkward conversation asking for money but your family members may have money put aside for you.

If it's not possible to have a lump sum, you could ask for money instead of gifts for your birthday and Christmas. Take any money you get and stick it in a savings account to accrue interest. Over the months and years you save it will help – you could also consider putting the money into a LISA, as previously discussed.

There are other ways your family can help, for example acting as a guarantor for a mortgage or taking on a family offset mortgage. These options come with some financial risk and even legal obligations so won't be for everyone. If you're interested, always speak to an independent adviser for help.

Of course, asking family for money isn't going to be an option for everyone – don't get dispirited if this is the case. It's certainly not the only way, you just need to have a clear plan to save the money you need.

BUILDING UP YOUR CREDIT SCORE

We talked about the importance of your credit score in chapter seven where we covered debt.

A lender will use your credit score as an indicator of your financial health. If you've missed a payment for your phone bill, it will be on your file. Got store cards? Yep, it's been noted. Paid off your credit card on time every month for two years? They know about it.

Your credit score is compiled by credit reference agencies who, in a quite scary way, know far too much about us, but what can you do? The big three in the UK are Equifax, Experian and TransUnion.

You will need a good credit score to increase your chances of being accepted for a mortgage and to get a lower interest rate. The process by which a lender determines your score is all a bit murky and mysterious because there is no such thing as a universal credit score. Each lender has its own eligibility criteria in place to decide whether they'll give you a loan or not and no one knows the systems, or differences between them. One lender might accept you while another might turn you down.

To give you an indication of how a lender might see you and your finances, the credit reference agencies produce their own version of a credit score. The higher the number, the better you look but it's certainly no guarantee you'll be successful.

You can check your credit score for free, without negatively impacting it. If your score is low you'll need to try and improve it to better your chances of getting a mortgage offer. This won't happen overnight – it can be a bit of a slog. It's all about showing the lenders that you are good with credit so pay your bills and accounts on time, over as long a period of time as possible to build a strong credit history.

A warning to you: a simple missed payment of any kind will negatively impact your score, so get organised. You'll kick yourself for knocking 100 points off just because you were careless about paying a bill.

If you have already missed payments, don't worry. Defaults and County Court Judgements (CCJs) on your report will hang around for six years but the negative impact of them should reduce as the record ages, as long as you've paid them off.

There are a few things you can do to help build your credit score and make sure you're moving in the right direction.

Register to Vote
This is an easy one. Make sure you're on the electoral register at your current address as lenders will use this to check your name, address and where you've lived before. If you're not on it, they could turn your application down.

Prove You're Good With Managing Debt

It seems counterproductive because not needing debt seems
to show you're good with money. But if you haven't borrowed
before, it's difficult for a bank to judge how likely you are to meet
repayments, which impacts your credit score.

Taking a small amount of credit out can help you borrow larger
amounts in the future, as long as you manage it well.

You could consider getting a credit builder card, which can help
you build up or rebuild your credit score. They typically have low
spending limits (just a couple of hundred quid) but very high interest
rates. Ideally you want to pay off the full outstanding balance each
month so you're not getting into unnecessary debt.

Pay on Time and Stay Within Your Limits

This is non-negotiable – you have to be able to show a lender
that you always make regular repayments. A missed payment will
negatively impact your credit score. Your behaviour over the last
12 months is the most important to lenders so if you've messed up
in the past, it's not the end of the world.

Avoid Multiple Applications Within a Short Period of Time

You don't want to look desperate. Too many applications for credit
tell a lender that you're struggling for money.

Check for Mistakes

Check your credit report to make sure there are no mistakes.
You can get a copy of your credit report from one of the previously
mentioned credit agencies – it's free if you sign up for a free trial.
Or try CheckMyFile, which gives you a 30-day trial to see your

Equifax, Experian and TransUnion reports in one place. Don't forget to cancel the trial after you've looked or it will cost you.

Even small mistakes, such as a mistyped address, can affect your score and could be enough for a lender to refuse you credit.

Keep Old Accounts Open
Like I've said, the key is to show lenders that you can manage credit well, over a long period of time. Keeping old accounts open shows a longer credit history and can look good on your report.

WHAT'S THE DIFFERENCE BETWEEN MORTGAGES?

You've got your deposit and a decent credit score, now it's time for you to choose your mortgage. There are so many options on offer, and what is available can change, so there's no one-size-fits-all situation here. So trust me when I say this: talk to a mortgage adviser.

A mortgage adviser is a qualified professional who looks at your very specific circumstances and finds the right mortgage deal for you. London & Country are a mortgage broker that is recommended by a lot of experts. They don't charge as they take a fee from the lender but take the time to find an option that works for you. If you know anyone who has recently gone through the process, a personal recommendation can also be helpful. If you're self-employed or run your own business, it might be worth looking for an adviser with experience in this area. There will likely be different requirements when applying for a mortgage, such as your lender requesting previous tax bills.

You can use a broker to help you look for a good mortgage deal on a new property, or to help you get the best deal when remortgaging (which is when you switch to a new mortgage on your existing property).

The Loan to Value (LTV) Ratio

As briefly mentioned, the LTV is an important factor used to determine the cost of your mortgage. It is the ratio of the value of the loan to the value of the property, and is expressed as a percentage. So, for example:

- You want to buy a £100,000 property and you have a £10,000 deposit.
- You would need a loan (mortgage) of £90,000 to cover the cost of the property, minus your deposit.
- Your loan to value ratio would be **90 percent**.

The higher your LTV, the greater the risk to the lender. This means they will charge a higher interest rate to cover themselves, making your mortgage more expensive. You should aim for a mortgage with the lowest LTV you can, although of course first-time buyers will normally have a high LTV mortgage unless they have a large deposit. Over the years, as your mortgage is paid off, you can switch to a lower LTV and comparatively better interest rate.

Interest Rates

Interest rates are one of the most important things to consider when choosing a loan. They are determined by two things:

- The current market
- The level of risk the lender takes on to lend you money.

The bigger your deposit and the better your credit score, the cheaper your mortgage is likely to be. You have cash and have proved that you're good with credit, which makes you less of a risk.

TYPES OF MORTGAGES

I'm going to briefly talk you through different types of mortgages so you get an overview of what is on offer. The below isn't all of the information you'll need when deciding on a mortgage but it's a good jumping-off point.

REPAYMENT VS INTEREST-ONLY MORTGAGE

You'll have to choose either a repayment or an interest-only mortgage. Here's how they work.

Repayment
Over the term of your mortgage, every single month, you'll pay back a set amount of the money you've borrowed, plus the interest. At the end of the mortgage term, you'll have paid off the entire loan so 100 percent of the house is owned by you.

Interest-only
This option means that, each month, you are only paying the interest you have accrued on your loan. You don't actually pay

off any of the balance on your mortgage. Hence the name, interest-only.

Over the term of your mortgage, the amount you pay every month will be lower so in that sense it's more affordable. However, at the end of your term you'll have to pay the total amount in full, which, depending on how much you borrowed, could be a hefty sum. New rules around interest-only mortgages mean you have to show a suitable repayment plan to pay off the original loan when you take out the mortgage.

FIXED-RATE VS VARIABLE RATE MORTGAGE

The interest rate plays a big part in how expensive your mortgage is and how long it will take you to pay it off. They have been reasonably static for a while, and are still at historic lows, but can and will change.

Tracker Mortgages

Tracker mortgages have a variable interest rate, which can go up as well as down. This means your monthly payments can vary month to month.

In the UK, tracker mortgages work by following the Bank of England base rate. This is the rate at which the Bank of England pays interest to commercial banks on money they hold with them. This in turn influences the rates at which those banks pay or charge interest on savings and loans with their customers.

The rate you pay will be calculated on the base rate, plus an agreed percentage on top. If the base rate changes, so does the rate you will pay on your mortgage.

Fixed-Rate Mortgages

When a lender says 'rate', they mean interest rate. So, with a fixed-rate mortgage, your lender guarantees your interest rate will stay the same for an agreed-upon fixed term.

A fixed-rate mortgage will specify the period – usually two, three or five years – after which the interest rate can change. Once it has expired, you would look to remortgage and find a new deal.

Short-term deals are cheaper than a longer-term fix, but the advantage of them is that you know exactly how much you need to pay further into the future, so it's easier to plan for. A fixed rate will protect you against interest rate rises in the economy in general, but if the interest rates drop then you will be stuck paying a comparatively more expensive mortgage.

95 Percent Mortgage

A 95 percent mortgage allows you to borrow 95 percent of the value of the property with just a 5 percent deposit. Your loan to value ratio (LTV), as discussed, will be 95 percent, hence the name.

This option means you might be able to get on the property ladder if you don't have a big deposit. But, and it's a big but, because there's a bigger risk of falling into negative equity with a smaller deposit, lenders will charge a much higher interest rate to cover any potential losses. Equity is simply the value of the property that you own outright, and negative equity is when your property is worth less than the outstanding mortgage balance.

For example, say you bought your house for £100,000 with a £10,000 deposit and took out a £90,000 mortgage. Over two years, you paid off £5,000, leaving an outstanding mortgage balance of £85,000.

If the value of your property increased by £20,000 in that time, it would now be worth £120,000 and you would have equity of £35,000 (£120,000 - £85,000 = £35,000). However, if the value of your property decreased by £20,000 in that time, it would now be worth £80,000 and you would have negative equity of £5,000 (£80,000 - £85,000 = -£5,000).

Another drawback is that because these mortgages have a higher interest rate, more of your repayments go towards paying the interest and less on paying off the outstanding balance. This makes it more difficult to build up equity in your home and you might not be able to remortgage and secure a better deal on a lower LTV ratio when your current one ends.

Joint Mortgage
A joint mortgage means you've taken out the loan with another person. This is often the option couples choose but you can take out a joint mortgage with anyone. The benefit of a joint mortgage is that you can combine your incomes to increase the amount a lender is likely to offer. This means you can afford a more expensive property than you could on your own and, for some people, this is the only way to get on the housing ladder at all.

There are a couple of options for a joint mortgage that you will need to make a decision about when you apply. Under a joint tenancy, both partners jointly own the whole property, while tenants-in-common means each person owns a specified share, which doesn't need to be equal.

Standard Variable Rate (SVR) Mortgage

A standard variable rate mortgage is your lender's default interest rate. It's probably not a particularly good rate and won't have any offers attached.

After the initial mortgage deal has expired, a lot of people find themselves automatically put on their lender's SVR mortgage, which might not be the best rate. At this point, you should look into remortgaging or speak to a broker to explore your options.

SHARED OWNERSHIP

If you ask people about shared ownership, you'll get some strong opinions. Some people really like it as an option because it helped them get on the property ladder, while others feel that entering into a shared ownership scheme has ruined their lives. The scheme itself isn't necessarily good or bad but you need to make sure you thoroughly research the pros and cons before entering into one.

Shared ownership is a halfway house between renting and buying and is usually only open to first-time buyers. Very simply, they work by letting you take out a mortgage on a portion of your home, ranging from 25–75 percent, and then you pay rent on the remainder of the value.

One of the biggest draws for first-time buyers is that shared ownership helps to reduce the biggest obstacle – the need to raise a large deposit. A typical shared ownership deposit is 5–10 percent of the share you are purchasing.

Over time, you can increase your owned share of the property through a process called 'staircasing'. This means you buy a further percentage, or share, of your home, with the aim of eventually owning it outright.

However, this can be very expensive. Each time you want to buy a share, the housing association will carry out a property valuation of your home, meaning you must purchase at the current market value, not the price at the time you first bought. If you live in an area where house prices are rising, this can be thousands of pounds at a time. When you buy a share, you will also need to remortgage, meaning you could pay fees or lose a good deal, as well as having to pay solicitor fees for yourself and the housing association.

SO, WHAT ARE THE DOWNSIDES?

You're Still a Tenant
Even though you own a share, you are still effectively a tenant until you own 100 percent of the property. If, for example, you couldn't keep up with payments you could possibly be evicted and lose the portion of the home that you have already paid for.

Service Charges
Since you live in a shared building, you have to pay a service charge to cover the cost of maintaining the communal areas.

Usually you have a limited say in costs, which can go up with little warning. I heard one example of someone whose charges went up £295 over two years and there's really nothing you can do about it.

The Lease

Shared ownership properties are run by housing associations so are leasehold. I'll discuss leaseholds further later, but let's just say they are tricky things. Plenty of people live in and sell leasehold properties with no problems but there are many who are stuck in their homes because of loopholes and extortionate charges from the landlord to extend the lease. This should be less of an issue with housing association properties, but it is something to consider.

Restrictions

Under your lease there are likely to be various restrictions, ranging from if you are allowed pets in the building to permission for structural changes. If there is anything you are required to ask the housing provider's permission for, you will have to pay a fee. The fee is just to ask – and they can say no!

If you think shared ownership might be your only option to purchase your own home, carefully consider the pros and cons of this versus private renting. If you can rent somewhere that isn't too expensive and save up for a larger deposit, it might give you more freedom in the long run.

CHOOSING A PROPERTY

I'm going to be honest with you: when it comes to choosing a place to call your own, it can be a bit of a nightmare. It isn't quite like TV favourite *Location, Location, Location* when you don't have much money to play with and you have visions of a beautifully designed home like the ones you see on Instagram. You won't believe the state of some of the flats we saw when buying our first home but they were the only properties within our budget.

That said, knowing what I know now, here are a few things that I would always consider when buying a property.

Aim for a Property You Can Stay in for a Long Time

One thing I can promise you is that buying a house is very expensive and can be borderline traumatic. In an ideal world, try and buy a property that you see yourself being happy in for the long term.

Of course, this won't be possible for everyone as budget restrictions often play a factor, but try to future-proof where you can. If, for example, you think you might have children in the near future, consider schools and bedroom space. This will help you to avoid having to go through the whole process again after a couple of years.

Chain Free Is the Dream

When buying a property, it's the 'chain' that is going to cause you the sleepless nights. If the current owner of your chosen property is also buying somewhere, that's already a chain of three.

Everyone is linked because everything needs to run smoothly for all involved in order to complete the buying process. If someone pulls out of a sale or something goes wrong with a mortgage application (which happens a lot), then the chain breaks and you're back to square one. The longer the chain, the more likely it is that something will go wrong, which can be very time consuming and expensive.

'No onward chain' are the three magic words every buyer wants to see when purchasing a property. This means the property you want to buy is not reliant on the successful purchase or sale of other properties up the chain. There's often no onward chain for properties owned by older people who have either moved into care or passed away.

If you are a first-time buyer, you are chain free since you are moving out of rented accommodation or similar. This can be used to your advantage – you'd be surprised how much it's worth to a seller and gives you a lot of bargaining power to get prices knocked down.

Carefully Consider Freehold vs Leasehold Properties

As briefly mentioned, a leasehold property means that you have a lease from the leaseholder (aka a landlord) to use the home for a specified number of years. Leaseholders will have to pay ground rent, maintenance fees, annual charges and a portion of the buildings insurance. It's more common for flats to be leasehold properties.

In contrast, a freehold means you own the building and the land it sits on. There is no landlord, you own the 'title' absolute. If possible, most people prefer this option as it's all theirs and they are not at the mercy of a landlord.

I was told numerous times to buy a freehold rather than leasehold property but I ignored this advice because I could only afford a flat and the vast majority of flats are leasehold. If I could go back in time, I would listen and spend more time saving or searching for a flat that had a joint freehold.

Listen: a leasehold property isn't of itself a bad thing and it could be right for you. For some people, especially in London or big cities, a leasehold is pretty much your only option. But in my experience, selling one has meant nearly a year of stress, many tears and thousands of pounds wasted on fees and solicitors. If you are thinking of buying leasehold, it would be worth checking out the Facebook group National Leasehold Campaign (NLC) and reading some of the stories there, as well as speaking to an adviser.

That said, if you're buying a leasehold property you need to check two things:

Length Left on the Lease
Once the lease on a property falls below 80 years, the value of your property can decrease. It makes it incredibly hard to sell since most lenders won't give you a mortgage on a lease that short. On top of that, if you need the lease extended in order to sell, landlords can literally charge whatever they want to extend the term.

The flat I sold had 97 years left on the lease and buyers were still asking us to pay for an extension, with our landlord quoting £20,000 for a 16-year increase. Of course that's only one example, but it shows the costs that can be associated with lease extensions.

The shorter the time left on the lease, the more expensive the fee to extend. For people who can't afford to pay, they can become stuck in the property, unable to sell.

Rising Ground Rent Clause
A tricky thing you need to be aware of is if your lease includes a rising ground rent clause.

Ground rent is paid to the freeholder annually. If your lease has this clause written into the contract, your ground rent can increase over time, which can have serious financial repercussions later down the line.

We also had this problem with our flat. The clause specified that ground rent doubled every 30 years, and as it was £200 a year we thought it wasn't going to be an issue. It was very affordable, even in 25 years when it would double to £400.

However, because it would eventually get to large sums that are unsustainable, some lenders will not give you a mortgage even though the problem is decades away. And, of course, the landlord can charge as much as they like to provide you with 'peppercorn rent', which practically stops the doubling, by making the ground rent cost nominal. We were quoted £12,000 to amend our lease, with lawyer's fees on top.

HOME BUYING COSTS YOU MIGHT NOT HAVE CONSIDERED

Okay, you've got a mortgage and have a property in mind. You're almost there! But buying a home isn't easy so you need to account for several additional costs beyond the purchase price. Often forgotten, these costs can add more than 10 percent to the total bill. I've listed some of the most common below but speak to your mortgage adviser and solicitor to check what will apply to you.

Stamp Duty

Stamp Duty Land Tax (SDLT) is a tax that is charged by the treasury on property purchases and will vary depending on the cost of the home. Stamp duty must be paid by the buyer, not the seller.

Stamp duty applies in England and Northern Ireland. In Scotland a similar tax but with different rates and bands called the Land and Buildings Transaction Tax applies, and in Wales there is a tax called Land Transaction Tax. The following information relates only to SDLT, but you can find more information about the taxes in Scotland and Wales on the Scottish and Welsh government websites.

SDLT works in rates and bands (a bit like income tax) and at the time of writing they are:

- Property value up to £125,000: zero stamp duty
- Property value £125,001 to £250,000: 2 percent
- Property value £250,001 to £925,000: 5 percent
- Property value £925,001 to £1.5 million: 10 percent
- Property value above £1.5 million: 12 percent

For example, on a £400,000 home, the SDLT owed would be:
£125,000 x 0 percent
+ £125,000 x 2 percent
+ (£400,000 - £250,000) x 5 percent
= £0 + £2,500 + £7,500 = £10,000

There are calculators on the government website to help you work out how much stamp duty you would have to pay. Your solicitor will calculate the actual rate and let you know how much you need to pay.

The good news here is that, at the moment, there is a discount for first-time buyers. Note, all people buying must be first-time buyers to qualify. There is currently no SDLT due up to £300,000 and a 5 percent rate applies on the portion from £300,001 to £500,000. If the purchase is for a property over £500,000, you can't claim the discount.

Conveyancing Fees

Conveyancing is the legal process involved in buying a property. You'll need a qualified lawyer for this and it's the part where it feels like nothing is happening and everything takes forever, but is costing you a lot of money (I'm sure they are working as quickly as possible!). These fees can be split into two parts:

- **The legal fees**
  The cost of the lawyers doing the work.

- **The disbursements**
  The searches the lawyers do that flag up any issues you should be aware of. They also register the change of ownership with the Land Registry.

If you have a leasehold property, you might need a lawyer to fix any problems and/or try to extend the lease for sale. This can cost a fortune – personally, my lawyer quoted me £250 an hour to do this (not including the practice's general fees for doing the work and VAT), and I was told that's a pretty decent price.

Survey Costs

It's well worth getting a professional survey carried out to determine the state of your building's construction and condition before you buy it. Surveys can be very expensive, depending on the type of report you choose to have done.

There are three types of report:

- **Condition Report**
  This tells you what condition your property is in and what risks, legal issues and defects there are. Costs range from around £400 to £950.

- **Homebuyer Report**
  This includes everything on the condition report but also gives advice on potential repairs and maintenance. This costs around £450 to £1,000.

- **Building Survey**
  This is an in-depth look at the property's condition that also gives advice on repairs and maintenance. A building survey is often advised for larger and/or older homes. They cost about £600 to £1,500.

When you receive your report, you might be horrified by the list of things that need fixing. On my last one, I was told there was a radioactivity risk!

What's more annoying is that if something comes up in the survey that is potentially serious, you have to get a specific professional in to do an advanced survey, which costs even more. It can all add up to a lot of money but I suppose it's better than the place falling down after you buy it.

Mortgage Valuation Fees
Some mortgage lenders will want to conduct a valuation survey, which is typically around £200 to £300.

Mortgage Arrangement Fees
A mortgage lender might also charge you mortgage arrangement fees, which can cost from around £200 to £1,000+. This covers their administration costs.

Mortgage Broker Fees
We discussed mortgage brokers earlier – some will charge a fee, usually up to £400, while others do it for free and then take a fee from the lender when your application is accepted.

Life Insurance
You don't have to get life insurance, but your lender will (or should!) strongly suggest you get some, because if you, or someone you own the home with, were to die or become unable to work, then the insurance can cover the missing mortgage payments. This ultimately means you, or your family, won't lose the home if payments became unaffordable.

Buildings Insurance
Your mortgage lender will usually require you to get buildings insurance. It covers repair and rebuild costs if your home is damaged or destroyed. According to MoneySuperMarket, the average cost is £111 a year. .

Removal Costs

If you're a first-time buyer, you're unlikely to have accumulated lots of furniture you'll need to move but you might need to hire a van at the very least. If I was you I'd start buttering up some strong mates who could help you carry things for free!

If you do have a lot of stuff, you might need to get in a professional firm, which can cost thousands of pounds depending on the size of your house and how far you're moving.

Furniture and Redecorating

Now you have a home, you have to fill it! I'd say take your time, wait for deals (see chapter 10 for my deal-hunting tips) and get on resale websites such as Gumtree or Facebook Marketplace. I am obsessed!

And if you've got a do-er upper, always bear in mind it's going to cost more than you think it will to do any work. Sometimes you'll end up with a money-pit, which is a home that always seems to need repairs.

You may have to completely replace kitchens, bathrooms, carpets or maybe even knock down walls to get the dream layout. This can all run in the tens of thousands of pounds.

Some advice I was given is to live in it first. Don't buy and make big, expensive changes straight away as you may end up regretting them. Settle in, see what works and what doesn't and slowly make changes over the years.

ACTIVITY

Whether you've saved the money for your deposit and are ready to apply for a mortgage, or you're at the start of the process, it's always a good idea to check your credit score.

You need to know what you're working with, face up to any problems and ultimately improve it so you're in the best position to get a mortgage offer.

So, use one of the free online credit reference agencies to check your score.

Once you know what you're dealing with, use the tips in the Building Up Your Credit Score section starting on page 164 to improve it and get on your way to homeownership!

14 FINANCIAL WELLBEING

They say 'health is wealth', and that is true but I think the phrase also works the other way around.

How comfortable you are in your current financial situation is intrinsically linked to your mental health. They impact each other, so when one aspect isn't doing well, you can find yourself stuck in a downward spiral.

Money problems stress you out so much it impacts your mental health. It could leave you with stress, anxiety or depression.

Your stress, anxiety or depression (or a combination of all three) makes it hard for you to manage your money. You might not have the energy to deal with bills, or be able to concentrate on your budget, for example.

You develop money problems, or existing ones start to get worse.

Your mental health declines further, maybe even impacting your physical health. You might have to take time off work.

Because of this, your money problems get more severe.

And so on.

I want to talk to you about spotting the signs that financial stress is starting to impact you, as well as give you the tools to deal with it in a practical way. I'll also touch on some prevention techniques.

Everyone gets stressed out about money now and then, but if it is constant over long periods of time and starts impacting your life negatively, you need to do something about it.

And don't worry, there are ways to get through tough economic times, ease your stress and anxiety and regain control of your finances. You're not alone.

IF YOU'VE HAD AN INCOME SHOCK

There is nothing much more stressful than experiencing an unexpected income shock. An income shock is when something happens in your life that causes your income to suddenly drop.

This could be through:

- Losing your job
- Becoming too sick to work
- Having a relationship break down
- Changes to your benefits.

Hopefully you'll have an emergency fund available to get you through the next three months (see chapter four for more on this) but if not, you're going to have to work extra hard to get back on your feet financially and protect your mental health.

Get Down to the Jobcentre Straight Away

Get every single benefit you're entitled to. Don't wait weeks to go because there is usually a lengthy delay from you 'signing on' to actually getting the cash. Check online to see what you're entitled to.

Speak to Your Creditors

If you have outstanding debts and don't think you'll be able to make the repayments, make sure you speak to the people you owe money to ASAP. They'll help you work out an affordable payment plan or give you a repayment break. The same goes for all of your bills. Don't wait until you can't pay them and miss a payment as this will negatively affect your credit score.

The sooner you do these two things, the better. It will mean that you're getting some income and people won't be stressing you out by chasing you for money.

Now that you've taken the first steps, you need to start thinking ahead.

Maximise Your Income

This might mean sorting out your CV and applying for new jobs, starting up a side hustle (see chapter eight), cutting back on bills (see chapter 11), or anything that either increases your income or decreases your outgoings.

Relook at Your Budget

You need to put a new strategy in place that takes into account your current financial situation. Look back at chapter two for budgeting tips.

Get Very Organised

Even more so than usual. This will help with your mental wellbeing, as well as financially. Create a checklist of things you want to achieve and break everything down into small, manageable steps. This will give you some control and let you take charge of the situation.

You Have No Time for Shame

You are likely to be experiencing a lot of emotions that need to be addressed and are very valid, but shame shouldn't be one of them. You've had a major setback but you're dealing with it, doing your best and you have the right to ask for help. Financial shocks happen to all of us at some point so don't feel ashamed of your situation.

I've been made redundant twice and both times I felt like my world was imploding. I remember sobbing, SOBBING, outside the office with my things, while everyone looked at me as they passed (it was London so obviously no one gave a shit and asked if I was okay!).

Both times I allowed myself 24 hours to mope. I could cry, bitch, get pass-out drunk, whatever. But after that it was action stations time.

Giving myself a set period of time to acknowledge my feelings and then move on really worked for me and could be a useful strategy for you, too.

IF YOU'RE STRESSED ABOUT MONEY ALL THE TIME

If the feelings of stress and anxiety are non-stop and you're feeling miserable because of your financial situation, the worst thing you can do is ignore them and let them spiral out of control.

Financial stress can lead to:

- Sleep difficulties
- Depression
- Anxiety
- Relationship difficulties
- Social withdrawal
- Physical ailments
- Unhealthy coping methods.

Get Professional Debt Help and Advice

If you have problems with debt, there are a lot of things you can do to ease the pressure. Read chapter seven for more detailed information on dealing with debt, but one of the easiest things you can do is speak to your creditors, as previously mentioned. If you tell them you can't make your payments and your mental health is suffering, they have to help you.

Open Up About Your Feelings

Keeping your problems and feelings inside doesn't make them go away. If you feel comfortable, and it's safe to do so, talk to your friends or family about your situation. They say a problem shared is a problem halved and sometimes just sharing how you are feeling can help to take the pressure off.

There might also be occasions where they are unwittingly making your situation more stressful by asking you to participate in expensive nights out, gift giving and so on. If they know what you are dealing with, they can support you through it.

If you don't feel able to talk to friends or family, consider speaking to a professional. You can speak to your GP, who might be able to refer you to services, or certain charities and organisations offer free counselling services, such as Mind, Rethink Mental Illness or local Turning Point branches. If you are a student, your university or college should offer you access to free cognitive behavioural therapy (CBT).

If things become too much and you are thinking about harming yourself, the Samaritans is a free 24-hour helpline. It's free to call on 116 123.

Do a Financial Inventory

If you have a constant feeling that life isn't as good as you want it to be and a lack of money means you can't enjoy yourself, then you need to start your money intentions again. Go back to the first chapter, where you visualise exactly what would make you happy. Once you have an idea, work out the chain of events that would lead to you achieving that goal, adjust your budget and put a plan in place to make it happen.

And when it comes to your budget, it's not good enough to do it once and assume it will continue to work for you for months or years. Your budget should adapt with your life, whether that's through income changes, savings goals, investments or more.

To fix a problem, you need to understand the problem. It might not always be pleasant to face, but it is a vital step in gaining back control of your finances.

Manage Your Overall Stress
You might find that stress from another area of your life can also impact on your financial wellbeing.

UNHEALTHY COPING MECHANISMS

The worst thing you can do if you're dealing with stress, mental health issues and financial problems is turn to unhealthy coping mechanisms. This will not only make your financial situation worse but it brings with it a whole new host of issues to contend with. The most common coping mechanisms I see through my work are:

- Over-drinking
- Gambling
- Compulsive spending.

When it comes to drinking or gambling addictions, I'm not qualified to give you advice. If you feel you're struggling with drinking, there are lots of options to get support. Speak to your GP, look for an

Alcoholics Anonymous (AA) meeting in your local area or contact Drinkline, the national alcohol helpline. You can call Drinkline for free, and in complete confidence, on 0200 123 1110.

If you are struggling with gambling, speak to your GP or contact GamCare who offer a free, confidential helpline, open 24 hours a day for information, advice and support. You can contact them at 0808 8020 133.

Compulsive Spending

This one is personal for me as it's a problem I've had in the past and I still need to control myself to this day. I was lucky – I didn't have a full-blown addiction where it was all I could think about so I racked up huge debts. But, if I'm feeling sad or angry, I still turn to shopping to make myself feel better.

The thing is, for a lot of us, buying something new feels so good. That little rush of dopamine when you press the buy button is, frankly, delicious. The problem is that rush doesn't last long so you have to buy something else before those feelings you don't want to properly address reappear. Shopping is a great distraction but only masks the real, underlying problem.

Just being aware that you shop to deal with stress or negative emotions is useful. It at least means that you understand what you are doing so can make better, more informed decisions in the heat of the 'buy now' moment.

Some signs that you have a spending problem include:

• You hide purchases from yourself or others.

- You go shopping in secret.
- You avoid looking at letters or financial statements that show your spending.
- Stress or negative emotions cause you to shop.
- You feel a high after shopping then low shortly afterwards.
- You own a lot of items with the tags still attached.
- You're losing sleep thinking about shopping.
- You're in debt from all of your purchases.

Depending on the cause, and how bad the problem is, there are different ways to cope with compulsive shopping. I've outlined some tips below, but if you are in debt, get yourself some free money advice – see chapter seven.

- *Recognise what you're doing*
  Are you shopping because you're upset, stressed or angry? Acknowledge your feelings and what has led you to shop.

- *Use your basket*
  For me, spending hours scrolling through my favourite websites and putting things in my basket, but never going to the checkout, scratches the itch.

- *Buy and return*
  When buying something I know is a bit of an impulsive buy, I make sure at the very least returns are free. This means if I change my mind or realise I bought the item for the feeling, I can send it back.

- **Block websites**
  Most of us will have specific places we like to shop from. If you're trying to stop or cut back on your shopping, download a free website blocker for your browsers. At the very least it will make you stop and think when you consider spending money.

- **Ask for help**
  If you think you have a shopping addiction that is seriously impacting your life and mental health, get some professional help. Speak to your GP.

TIPS FOR MAINTAINING FINANCIAL WELLBEING

The goal of financial wellbeing, and maybe one of the reasons you've bought this book, is to avoid a downward money spiral. You can't control everything, and life can be cruel sometimes, but you now have the tools to protect yourself and know how to dust yourself off and start again.

As a recap, here are the biggies when it comes to maintaining financial wellbeing:

- Budget, budget, budget
- Avoid income comparisons
- Have an emergency fund
- Consider a side hustle as backup income
- Build your savings
- Reduce your debt
- Have a retirement strategy.

WHOOMP, THERE IT IS! These are the things I've been telling you to do in my book. They protect your mental and financial health – because, once you're stuck in that spiral, it's hard to get out.

ACTIVITY

What's Your Financial Personality?
In order to achieve financial wellbeing, it helps to know your financial personality. Read the descriptions below and choose which sounds most like you.

- **The Bargain Hunter**
  You love the buzz of finding an item at a discount. No one can navigate a sale like you!

  Do you get a bit carried away and regret spending too much money? Think about joining a shopping forum (such as HUKD) where you can search for bargains but use that skill to help other people.

- **The Avoider**
  You put off making money decisions. It all seems a bit overwhelming and 'I'll do it later' has become a mantra for you.

  Try a monthly money date. Ask someone you like and trust (I find bribing them with food/beer works) and get them to either keep you company or help you with financial organising. It could be setting up Direct Debits, working out a budget, or getting debt help. You'll probably find things don't take a huge amount of time and can be fun with good company. It's getting started that's hardest.

- **The Collector**
  You have the things you want and enjoy saving. You keep on top of your finances but would like to diversify your money.

  If you don't already, research stocks, shares or bonds (see chapter nine) and consider investing some money. You could even get into slightly more exotic investment, such as wine or whiskey. The sky is the limit. Though remember investing is a risk so don't use any money you aren't willing to lose.

- **The Thinker**
  You feel guilty about spending or having more money than others. You overthink decisions and worry about money or the future.

  Consider going back to the beginning and visualising what it is you want to achieve. Once you have done that, put together a plan to save the amount you need. If you've budgeted for it, you shouldn't feel remotely bad about spending.

Once you've chosen your financial personality, write three personal finance tips to help you with your finances going forward. You've got this!

CONCLUSION

You've made it! I really hope you found the book entertaining (at least for a book about money!) and have learned a thing or two. I genuinely think personal finance can be incredibly interesting, and learning to master it is completely life-changing.

A lot of people expect some kind of miracle answer when it comes to being good with money. Some flashy, Tony Robbins-esque 'advice' that no one else knows about, all wrapped up in inspirational quotes. But there isn't a secret cure, it's just finding strategies and tips that actually work. No get rich-quick-schemes and no gimmicks.

You now have the tools to start planning and living whatever kind of life you want – there's nothing stopping you.

IT'S NOT GOING TO BE LINEAR

Don't expect it's going to always be easy. You'll have good months and bad months when it comes to money. Hell, you'll have good years and really shitty years.

But it doesn't matter. You have to understand that success is built over years making small, sound financial decisions – it's not going to come instantly.

You could start saving £1 a week now and be stashing away £100 a week in five years. You have to look at the bigger picture and not beat yourself up for something you can't do right now.

It's not too late, either. There's a Chinese proverb, 'The best time to plant a tree was 20 years ago, the second best time is now.' Act now, get a plan together and do what you can.

I asked my social media followers what they wish they could tell their 20-year-old selves about money. Sure, there were plenty of 'invest in Apple' and 'marry rich' type answers, but responses pretty much fell into four categories:

- Start a pension ASAP and make the most of your workplace scheme (not doing this was the biggest regret by a mile).
- Start saving and spend less on things you don't need.
- Don't get into debt – if you can't afford it, you can't have it.
- You can't buy happiness, love or acceptance from other people.

For me personally, I would add to give myself a break. I felt like I had to achieve a lot, quickly, and failure of any kind wasn't an option. I blame it on peaking in primary school! I was an overachieving child and put an incredible amount of pressure on myself to keep it up. It became harder and harder as I got further into the real world. Hello, anxiety!

But what I know now is that everything I was doing (including the stupid mistakes I made) got me to where I am. Be kind to yourself because you can only control so much.

And I can't emphasise enough that *doing something* from this book, and building on it, is more than most people will ever do.

Good luck!

INDEX

REFERENCES

8: Money and Pensions Service, 'UK Strategy for Financial Wellbeing sets out ten-year vision to improve millions of lives' [https://moneyandpensionsservice.org.uk/2020/01/21/uk-strategy-for-financial-wellbeing-sets-out-ten-year-vision-to-improve-millions-of-lives/]

56 & 57: Financial Capability, 'How can we encourage people to save, and to save more?' [https://www.fincap.org.uk/en/thematic_reviews/encourage-people-to-save]

58: Compare the Market, 'How much should you save?' [https://www.comparethemarket.com/savings-accounts/content/how-much-should-you-save-calculator/#/]

61: Shelter, 'Almost half of working renters only one paycheque away from losing their home' [https://england.shelter.org.uk/media/press_release/almost_half_of_working_renters_only_one_paycheque_away_from_losing_their_home]

66: Carehome, 'Care home fees and costs: How much do you pay?' [https://www.carehome.co.uk/advice/care-home-fees-and-costs-how-much-do-you-pay]

67: ONS, 'National life tables – life expectancy in the UK: 2018 to 2020' [https://www.ons.gov.uk/peoplepopulationandcommunity/birthsdeathsandmarriages/lifeexpectancies/bulletins/nationallifetablesunitedkingdom/2018to2020#:~:text=The%20modal%20age%20at%20death,years%20in%202015%20to%202017]

77: *The Times*, 'What is the best pension for self-employed workers?' [https://www.thetimes.co.uk/money-mentor/article/best-pension-self-employed/]

78: MoneyHelper, 'Pension calculator' [https://www.moneyhelper.
org.uk/en/pensions-and-retirement/pensions-basics/pension-
calculator]

81: Compare the Market, 'Serious concerns over "Buy Now Pay
Later" credit during lockdown' [https://www.comparethemarket.
com/news-and-views/concerns-over-buy-now-pay-later-during-
lockdown/]

84: Premier League, 'Premier League 2019/20 ticket price research
details' [https://www.premierleague.com/news/1536734]; Statista,
'Expected average spend on late night leisure activity in the United
Kingdom (UK) as of June 2021, by type of spend' [https://www.
statista.com/statistics/1088573/spending-on-nights-out-in-the-
uk/]; Money, 'How much do festivals cost and what should you
take?' [https://www.money.co.uk/guides/how-much-do-festivals-
cost-and-what-should-you-take.htm]; ASOS, '2020 Annual
Report' [https://www.asosplc.com/~/media/Files/A/Asos-V2/reports-
and-presentations/2020-annual-report.pdf]

86: Experian, 'What's a Good Personal Loan Interest Rate?'
[https://www.experian.com/blogs/ask-experian/whats-a-good-
interest-rate-for-a-personal-loan/]

99: *Express*, 'Britons are earning £411 extra per month via side
businesses – with some making over £900' [https://www.express.
co.uk/finance/personalfinance/1463201/side-business-extra-
money-savings-tips-entrepreneur]

101: HR News, 'Brits are making almost £5k extra a year from "side
businesses"' [http://hrnews.co.uk/brits-are-making-almost-5k-
extra-a-year-from-side-businesses/]

107: Consumer Awareness Institute, 'The Case (for and) against
Multi-level Marketing' [https://www.ftc.gov/sites/default/
files/documents/public_comments/trade-regulation-rule-
disclosure-requirements-and-prohibitions-concerning-business-
opportunities-ftc.r511993-00008%C2%A0/00008-57281.pdf]

120: MoneyHelper, 'Savings calculator' [https://www.moneyhelper.org.uk/en/savings/how-to-save/savings-calculator]

159: Which?, 'Mortgage calculators' [https://www.which.co.uk/money/mortgages-and-property/mortgage-calculators]

160: ONS, 'UK House Price Index: June 2021' [https://www.ons.gov.uk/economy/inflationandpriceindices/bulletins/housepriceindex/june2021#:~:text=The%20average%20UK%20house%20price,same%20period%20a%20year%20ago]

183: MoneySuperMarket, 'Home insurance UK price index' [https://www.moneysupermarket.com/home-insurance/price-comparison-index/]